Lincoln's Ethics

Unlike many important leaders and historical figures, Abraham Lincoln is generally regarded as a singularly good and morally virtuous human being. *Lincoln's Ethics* assesses Lincoln's moral character and his many morally fraught decisions regarding slavery and the rights of African Americans, as well as his actions and policies as commander in chief during the Civil War. Some of these decisions and policies have been the subject of considerable criticism. Lincoln undoubtedly possessed many important moral virtues, such as kindness and magnanimity, to a very high degree. Despite this, there are also grounds to question the goodness of his character. Many fault him as a husband, father, and son, and many claim that he was a racist. Thomas L. Carson explains Lincoln's virtues and assesses these criticisms.

Thomas L. Carson is Professor of Philosophy at Loyola University Chicago. He is the author of three other books – *The Status of Morality* (1984), *Value and the Good Life* (2000), and *Lying and Deception: Theory and Practice* (2010). He is also the co-editor (with Paul Moser), of two anthologies: *Morality and the Good Life* (1997) and *Moral Relativism* (2001). Carson was previously a member of the editorial boards of *American Philosophical Quarterly*, *Public Affairs Quarterly*, *Journal of Happiness Studies*, and *Business Ethics Quarterly*.

Lincoln's Ethics

THOMAS L. CARSON

CAMBRIDGE
UNIVERSITY PRESS

CAMBRIDGE
UNIVERSITY PRESS

32 Avenue of the Americas, New York, NY 10013-2473, USA

Cambridge University Press is part of the University of Cambridge.

It furthers the University's mission by disseminating knowledge in the pursuit of
education, learning, and research at the highest international levels of excellence.

www.cambridge.org
Information on this title: www.cambridge.org/9781107030145

© Thomas L. Carson 2015

First published 2015

Printed in the United States of America

A catalog record for this publication is available from the British Library.

Library of Congress Cataloging in Publication Data
Carson, Thomas L., 1950–
Lincoln's ethics / Thomas L. Carson.
pages cm
Includes bibliographical references and index.
ISBN 978-1-107-03014-5 (hardback)
1. Lincoln, Abraham, 1809–1865 – Ethics.   2. Lincoln, Abraham, 1809–1865 –
Philosophy.   3. United States – History – Civil War, 1861–1865 – Moral and
ethical aspects.   I. Title.
E457.2.C34   2015
172–dc23   2014046179

ISBN 978-1-107-03014-5 Hardback

For Judy, with love and gratitude

"It may seem strange that any men should dare to ask a just God's assistance in wringing their bread from the sweat of other men's faces; but let us judge not that we not be judged."
Abraham Lincoln, Second Inaugural Address

Contents

Plates follow page 228.

Detailed Contents

List of Maps and Figures

Acknowledgments

I have received a great deal of help from many people. It is a pleasure to acknowledge these debts here.

My greatest debt is to Joe Mendola. He has patiently read numerous drafts of the book: four or five drafts of all of it and more than ten drafts of much of it. He discussed and debated the book with me during many caffeine-fueled mornings at Royal Coffee. Few people have ever given anyone as much help with a book manuscript. He suffered through a huge amount of very rough material. His influence and ideas are everywhere in the book and have enabled me to improve the book in many ways.

My editor at Cambridge, Robert Dreesen, has been extremely helpful and accommodating in every way. He also read the manuscript and made many excellent suggestions about how to improve the book and make it more readable. Two anonymous reviewers for the Press provided me with extremely helpful and detailed advice on the manuscript and pointed out many errors of substance and style. Thanks to my very able copy editor, Gail Naron Chalew, and to Minaketan Dash for their help in correcting and preparing the manuscript. Thanks also to Elizabeth Janetschek of

Cambridge for her help with permissions, photos, and the preparation of the manuscript.

In 2011, I presented the Belgum Lectures at Saint Olaf College. My topic was "Lincoln's Ethics: A Philosophical Assessment." I want to thank the Saint Olaf Philosophy Department and the college for their hospitality. I am particularly grateful to Charles Taliaferro, Vicki Harper, and Corliss Swain. The audience gave me wonderful comments and criticisms. Special thanks to Ian Maitland, Mike Fitzpatrick, Rachel Kitze, Danny Muñoz-Hutchinson, and Michael Fuerstein.

Michael Burlingame gave me very helpful comments on a draft of the book. I also thank him for illuminating discussions and emails. He has saved me from many errors. A glance at the footnotes for this book will reveal the extent of my debt to his work.

My wife Judy and my children, Nora and Dan, have cheerfully endured my preoccupation with this project during the past six years. I have spent a great deal of time talking about Lincoln with them, particularly with Judy. Their questions, ideas, and criticisms have been extremely helpful.

Since the beginning of this project, I have worked closely with my Loyola History Department colleague, Ted Karamanski. His wise advice has been invaluable to me, and he has been extremely generous with his time.

My former colleague at Virginia Tech, Harlan Miller, read several drafts of the entire manuscript and offered many helpful criticisms of substance and style.

Chapters 4 and 5, which deal with the justice of the Union cause during the Civil War, proved to be the most difficult parts of the book for me to write. My discussions and correspondence with Jeff McMahan helped me greatly. He gave me very detailed and helpful comments on an earlier version of these chapters. I was not able to act on all of his advice, but this part of the book is much better for his help. I also thank my Loyola colleagues Ted Karamanski and James Murphy for help with this part of the book.

Thanks to James McPherson for very helpful answers to my email questions and for taking time to meet me while he was in Chicago in 2012. I also owe a great debt to his work.

Thanks to Douglas Wilson for helpful discussions and email correspondence. I have learned much from him and his work.

Jane Currie, Loyola's reference librarian for Philosophy and History, helped me with my research on the U.S. Census and demographics used in Chapter 4. She also helped me locate other materials that I needed for this project.

Ken Winkle offered very apt and helpful advice about the things I needed to read for this project; his advice came early enough in my work that I was able to act on most of it.

J. L. A. Garcia, Jon Nielson, and Jackie Scott gave me very helpful comments on Chapter 10. Garcia's work on racism figures importantly in this chapter.

John Hoffman read large parts of this manuscript and offered helpful criticisms.

Bob Bucholz of the Loyola history department took considerable pains to help me with my questions about democracy in Britain, which are relevant to the justification that Lincoln gave in favor of fighting the American Civil War.

I have benefited greatly from e-mail correspondence with a number of historians and scholars who answered my questions and helped me find needed sources and information. In addition to those mentioned earlier, I thank John Fabian Witt, Bruce Levine, Brian Jordan, Michael Vorenberg, James Oakes, Richard Carwardine, Jeff Tulis, Sanford Levinson, Roger Ekirch, Charlie Reed, Onesimo Almeida, Roquinaldo Ferreira, and Jessie Carney-Smith. Historians and other scholars who write about history are a very collegial and helpful lot. Sometimes a quick answer to a simple historical question can be a very big help.

My Loyola TAs – David Atenasio, Christina Drogalis, Marcella Russo, Amelia Rhys, and Sean Petranovich – helped me correct and edit the manuscript. Marcella and Amelia also did research related to this project. David's extremely careful reading of the final version of the manuscript (which caught many errors of substance and style) helped me greatly. He also helped me create the index for the book. I thank all of them for their fine work.

Parts of this book were presented in a paper at the Rocky Mountain Ethics Congress in 2012. Russ Jacobs asked me a very good question that is addressed at length in Chapter 4.II.4.

Part of Chapter 2 was presented to the American Philosophical Association in 2014. I thank Todd Franklin for his helpful comments and for pushing me to say more about Lincoln's letter to Horace Greeley. Thanks also to Elizabeth Anderson for helpful comments during and after my talk.

Anita Superson gave me very helpful comments on Chapter 9.

Other parts of this book were presented to my friends and colleagues at the Illinois Philosophical Association in 2010, 2012, and 2013. I am grateful to Bob Sterling, Grant Sterling, Jim Swindler, Jason Waller, Joanne Lau, Eric Krag, Todd Stewart, Jason Hanna, and Mylan Engel.

Thanks also to David Braun, Chris Meyers, David Schrader, Julia Driver, Arnold Cusmariu, Doug Cannon, and Lay Phonexayphova.

Others who helped me with this book in important ways are Leslie Rice, Kevin O'Neil, Al Gini, Michelle Kuipers, Mikiah Nuutinen, Aaron Kinskey, JD Trout, Guy Hammond, Victoria Wike, David Schweickart, Jason Rheins, Blake Dutton, Bob Sporel, Martha Holstein, Julie Philips Roth, Arya Zandi, Dominic De Marco, Sam Rasche, and Art Lurigio.

My work on this book was supported by a paid leave of absence from Loyola University Chicago and a research support grant from Loyola that enabled the publisher to include photo plates. Thanks also to Loyola for a small grant to help prepare the index.

There are no doubt others who helped me, but whom I have overlooked and not mentioned here. I beg their forgiveness for not calling them to mind.

How This Book Came to Be

Because some might wonder how a philosopher came to write a book about Lincoln, I offer the following account.

Since grade school, I have had a very strong interest in history. During junior high and high school, I read many history books, often to the exclusion of working on my homework. In college, I fell in love with philosophy and, for a time, stopped reading much history. Then, in 1974, during the middle of my time in graduate school, I purchased a battered edition of Carl Sandburg's six-volume biography of Lincoln in a used bookstore in Providence, Rhode Island. I loved this book. Reading it was a pleasure I cherished every evening for a long time. I was then in the thrall of a rather facile dismissal of Lincoln as a racist who did not care nearly enough about slavery, this despite the cogent arguments of my friend David Braun to the contrary. After reading Sandburg's biography I found Lincoln to be a much more impressive and compelling person than I had imagined. Jeff Tulis suggested that I next read Lord Charnwood's beautiful and appreciative biography of Lincoln. After that, I continued to read a number of other books about Lincoln.

In the late 1970s, David Braun and I went to the Lincoln Memorial. I read the words of Lincoln's Second Inaugural

Address carefully for the first time and was deeply moved. It is by far the most beautiful and compelling political speech I have ever read. I noticed that other people reading it were also moved (some were in tears). My wife Judy was also moved by the words of this speech when we went to the memorial several years later.

Once I started teaching, I continued to read history regularly most evenings for recreation and escape. This became my most serious hobby. I made use of historical cases in my classes about war and morality and in some of my writing about ethics.

By the time I reached the age of fifty, I was spending as much time reading history as philosophy. I enjoyed this very much, but this indulgence seemed somewhat detrimental to my career. My 2010 book on lying and deception includes several chapters that discuss historical examples and issues in detail. This required me to do a great deal of historical reading and research. I greatly enjoyed this work, though it proved to be difficult.

Starting in the late 1980s, a very large number of excellent books about Lincoln and the Civil War began to appear. I read many of these, beginning with James McPherson's *Battle Cry of Freedom* and David Herbert Donald's *Lincoln*, and my interest in Lincoln and the Civil War deepened considerably. I noticed the following in the preface to Donald's *Lincoln*:

My interpretation of Lincoln's political philosophy and religious views has been much influenced by the ideas of John Rawls, who collaborated with me in teaching the first seminar ever offered on Abraham Lincoln at Harvard University. (p. 17)

I would have given anything to be in that class and I thought that it would be wonderful to be able to teach such a course. Some years later, William Lee Miller's book *Lincoln's Virtues* appeared. It occurred to me that I could use this book as a main text for a course on Lincoln. At this point, it seemed possible for me to teach such a class by myself, but the press of other commitments postponed that project.

As the bicentennial of Lincoln's birth drew near in 2007–8, I decided that I should teach a class on Lincoln's ethics. Ted Karamanski and I organized a symposium on Lincoln's character at Loyola University Chicago in fall 2008. Douglas Wilson and Kent Graham gave wonderfully stimulating talks. Eric Foner, Doris Kearns Goodwin, and Joshua Wolf-Shenk also presented splendid talks about Lincoln at Loyola during that period.

In fall 2008 and 2010 I taught my class on Lincoln's ethics. I had wonderful discussions with some outstanding students, several of whom are named in the Acknowledgments. In late 2009, I received an invitation from my alma mater, Saint Olaf College, to give the 2010–11 Belgum Lectures. We discussed three possible topics for my lectures. The last one that I mentioned was Lincoln's ethics. They indicated a strong preference for that topic, even though it was the topic I was least prepared to speak on and I had to stretch myself to prepare the lectures in time. They formed a detailed outline for much of the present book.

Introduction

Unlike most other important leaders and historical figures, Abraham Lincoln is generally regarded as a singularly good and virtuous human being. The mythical Lincoln many Americans learn about as schoolchildren is "Honest Abe," who walked many miles from his store to return a few pennies to someone who had been overcharged and, at great difficulty to himself, faithfully paid off his debts from his failed store. He was a self-made man who was almost completely self-educated. His family was shockingly poor and lived one winter in a three-sided cabin, with the fourth side open and exposed to the elements.[1] He was a "rail splitter" who did hard manual labor and was a man of the people with a great sense of humor – everyone loved to hear his stories and jokes. He was a kind and patient husband to a difficult and troubled woman. He was an exceptionally kind and compassionate person who was deeply distressed by his first encounter with slavery in New Orleans as a young man. Later, he was moved by his deep compassion and strong sense of justice to become the Great Emancipator. He was a resolute and

---

[1] Burlingame, *Abraham Lincoln: A Life*, I, pp. 20–1.

determined commander in chief despite his great compassion for the immense suffering caused by the Civil War.

This narrative of Lincoln's life is a wonderful national myth that exalts genuinely good and admirable qualities. The mythical Lincoln is a thoroughly marvelous and lovable human being and an excellent model for people to admire and emulate.

But we must ask, is this myth *true*? In particular, how much of the myth about Lincoln's moral goodness is true? It is the aim of this book to show that the myth is accurate for the most part: cynics would be surprised and confounded by how much truth there is in the myth. And, in some important ways, it even *understates* his goodness and virtue.

This book addresses central ethical issues regarding Lincoln's actions and character. I believe that philosophers can shed considerable light on these issues.[2] Part I discusses his policies concerning slavery and the rights of African Americans and his actions and policies as commander in chief during the Civil War. Part II discusses his character.

Part I

The first part of the book addresses moral questions raised by some of Lincoln's most controversial actions and policies. Some consider Lincoln to have been immoral because he was not an abolitionist until 1864, late in his presidency. When he ran for the Senate in 1858 and for president in 1860, he

---

[2] Many books about Lincoln discuss ethical questions, but none of these books was written by a philosopher. The only other book about Lincoln written by a philosopher, Elton Trueblood's *Abraham Lincoln: Theologian of America's Anguish*, discusses Lincoln's religious views, not ethical questions. William Lee Miller's *Lincoln's Virtues: An Ethical Biography* and *President Lincoln: The Duty of a Statesman* are among the very best books written on Lincoln's ethics. Although Miller was an important historian, he received his doctorate in religious ethics.

opposed any further extension of slavery, but did not advocate its immediate abolition. In his First Inaugural Address, he made many concessions to slaveholding interests to try to placate the South and avert a civil war: he promised to enforce the Fugitive Slave Law (which provided for the capture and return of escaped slaves), not to interfere with the institution of slavery where it existed, and not to oppose a proposed "irrevocable" constitutional amendment that would have prohibited the federal government from interfering with slavery in the states. Many say that his initial war aims were misplaced; he put preserving the Union ahead of abolishing slavery. He rescinded General Fremont's order for partial emancipation for the state of Missouri in September 1861; he also revoked a broader order for emancipation by General Hunter for the states of South Carolina, Georgia, and Florida in May 1862. When the Emancipation Proclamation was issued in 1863, it was half-hearted: it did not free slaves in the border states, Tennessee, or in most of the Confederate territory occupied by the Union Army when it went into effect. It also gave the Confederate states the option to keep slavery if they rejoined the Union within one hundred days. Some critics indeed said that the Emancipation Proclamation freed no one: "It applied where the Union had no power and did not apply where it did."[3]

President Lincoln suspended habeas corpus during the Civil War and imprisoned thousands of people without due process of law. Many contend that these actions were unconstitutional and that he greatly abused and exceeded the powers of his office. He supported the colonization of African Americans outside of the United States and was a member of the American Colonization Society. Many take this to be evidence of his racism and his desire to "cleanse" America of black people. During his long political career in Illinois

[3] Miller, *President Lincoln: The Duty of a Statesman*, p. 269.

before becoming president, he never publicly opposed the state's black exclusion laws, which were designed to prevent blacks from settling in the state. He publicly endorsed other unjust laws that were part of Illinois's "black codes," including laws forbidding blacks to vote, serve on juries, or marry white people. He never supported granting full political and civil rights to all African Americans: even at the end of his life, he supported giving voting rights to just some black men.

Some contend that, largely because of his lack of concern for the rights and interests of African Americans, the situation of black people after the Civil War was not significantly better than it had been under slavery. If this is true, his justification for fighting the war was much weaker than is generally thought. His actions and policies as commander in chief can be questioned because their moral status depends on the justice of the Union cause in the American Civil War, which itself is open to question. Given that the abolition of slavery was not a Union war aim in April 1861, there are reasons to question whether the Union was morally justified in fighting the Civil War at its beginning. Even if the Union had just cause for fighting the war, it is debatable whether it fought the war justly. Lincoln bears considerable personal responsibility for the conduct of the war and the Union Army's treatment of Confederate civilians.

This is a long list of possible moral criticisms of Lincoln. Given the tremendous evil and injustice of slavery, there is a strong case for thinking that he should have been an abolitionist earlier and that he acted wrongly in pursuing the policies set forth in his First Inaugural Address, in pursuing his initial war aims, and in his actions regarding Fremont and the Emancipation Proclamation. Nonetheless, I defend him against all these criticisms. My arguments are broadly utilitarian. Roughly, utilitarianism holds that the rightness or wrongness of an action is determined solely by its consequences and that a person's action is morally right, provided that it has better consequences than any alternative course of action that he or she could have taken instead. I argue that his policies and compromises concerning slavery while he was president were morally justified because they were necessary for him to have enough public support to fight and win the Civil War. I therefore claim that he opposed and limited slavery as much as possible. Even at the beginning of the war, he was fighting slavery – not to completely abolish it, but to prevent it from spreading.

The criticisms about his war aims and the Emancipation Proclamation are also mistaken for another reason: they rest largely on historical misunderstandings. The claim that he cared only about preserving the Union and not about fighting slavery ignores the *many* strong measures that he took against slavery before he issued the Emancipation Proclamation. The criticism that the Emancipation Proclamation was half-hearted overlooks the fact that many of the slaves in areas exempted by the proclamation had already been made free or effectively free by other actions taken by the president and his administration.

In connection with these issues, I also offer an interpretation of Lincoln's moral views. *In practice*, he was a utilitarian, and he would have defended his actions in these five cases (his policies on slavery prior to 1861, his policies in his First Inaugural Address, his initial war aims, and his actions regarding Fremont and the Emancipation Proclamation) on utilitarian grounds. So not only were his actions justified on utilitarian grounds but he himself would also have given a utilitarian defense of these actions. But utilitarianism is a very controversial view. So I also try to show that his actions can be defended independently of the truth of utilitarianism.

The utilitarian tradition has developed since Lincoln's lifetime. Since the early twentieth century, philosophers have commonly distinguished between two versions of utilitarianism: one holds that the moral rightness of actions depends on

their actual consequences; the other holds that moral rightness depends on the antecedently probable consequences of
actions. This distinction sheds light on moral issues, but it
also complicates our analysis considerably. The actual consequences of Lincoln's actions were not what he expected them
to be: they were both much better and much worse than he
anticipated. He did not believe that the war would be so terrible, nor did he think that it would end slavery. Not only
did he and others fail to foresee many of the consequences of
his actions but also those consequences could not have been
reasonably predicted. Thus, the antecedently probable consequences of his actions were quite different from the actual
consequences.

I argue that Lincoln's policies about habeas corpus and colonization were largely, if not entirely, justified. The criticisms
of these two matters are often overstated in ways that distort the historical record. But his support for or silence about
many provisions of Illinois's extremely unjust black codes is
much more difficult to justify. Still, it is doubtful that he could
have been a viable politician in central Illinois had he spoken
out against these laws. Another criticism is that, even at the
end of his life, he did not publicly support giving full political and civil rights to all African Americans. He supported
giving voting rights to some, but not all, black men. On its
face, this was very unjust, but his support for extending voting rights to many black men was also a radical change for
the better and something that enraged John Wilkes Booth
just three days before he assassinated the president. In this
book I argue that, during his lifetime, Lincoln was justified
in moving slowly and cautiously about such matters and in
focusing on winning the Civil War and ending slavery. However, had he lived out his second term of office, he should
have pushed hard for equal rights for African Americans. For
the purposes of assessing his morality, it is important to ask
whether he would have done this, but the answer is that we

do not know. Everything we say about his policies concerning the rights and status of African Americans in post–Civil War America needs to be hedged in light of this uncertainty.

President Lincoln's actions as commander in chief of the U.S. military during the Civil War and the justice of the Union cause in the war are central to any moral assessment of his life. They are particularly important because he played a decisive role in determining that the North would fight a civil war rather than allow the Confederate states to secede peacefully. Many people in the North, including many abolitionists, preferred to "let the South go in peace." Lincoln chose to fight a civil war rather than allow the country to fall apart without waging war, and he knowingly risked provoking the Confederates into beginning the war when he resupplied Fort Sumter. Lincoln's actions during the Fort Sumter crisis were taken against the advice of almost all his close military and civilian advisors. Yet the Confederate attack on Fort Sumter united the North to fight the war. He clearly bore great personal responsibility for the outbreak of the American Civil War. He also bore great responsibility for the conduct of the U.S. military during the war. He approved of the "Lieber Code," rules of war for the Union military, which permitted much harsher treatment of civilians than the rules they replaced. It also permitted much harsher treatment of civilians than the rules of war initially endorsed by the leaders of the Confederacy.

There *appears to be* a strong case for the view that the Union did not have adequate moral justification for fighting the Civil War at its beginning. Arguably, it was not then a war to protect important human rights, such as the right to liberty. The good consequences of keeping the nation together were arguably not nearly enough to justify the immense evil of the death and suffering caused by the war. Further, the justification for fighting the war that President Lincoln stressed in his public statements – that disunion would create a precedent for the further splintering of the United States and other democratic nations that would greatly harm the cause of democracy all over the world – is speculative and open to question.

But despite these considerations, in the chapters that follow I attempt to show that the Union *did* have just cause for fighting the war from the very beginning, because of the extremely bad consequences that would have resulted from Confederate independence. Slavery would probably have continued much longer in the American South, and it is very likely that the Confederate States of America (CSA) would have annexed parts of Latin America and prolonged slavery there. Further, the rights that blacks would have possessed in the CSA after such time as the CSA abolished slavery would probably have been considerably less adequate than those they actually possessed in the United States between 1865–1990. The actual consequences version of utilitarianism, the probable consequences version of utilitarianism, and standard versions of just war theory (which are decidedly non-utilitarian theories) all imply that the Union was justified in fighting the war from the very beginning. But that this is so is clear only in the case of the actual consequences version of utilitarianism. Because the Union's war aims changed significantly between the beginning of the war and the time of the Emancipation Proclamation, and again after Lincoln ran for reelection as a supporter of an amendment to abolish slavery, the case for the justice of the Union cause was much stronger at the end of the war than at the beginning. All three of these moral theories *clearly* imply that the Union had just cause for fighting at the end of the war.

President Lincoln's policies concerning the treatment of civilians during the war were largely, but not entirely, justified. It is widely thought that the Civil War was a "total war" that involved very harsh and ruthless treatment of Southern civilians on a very large scale. Some infamous statements by various Union generals and certain provisions of the Lieber Code lend credence to this claim. But recent historical work on this topic thoroughly discredits this view. The number of civilians who died as a result of the war was quite small compared with other wars that are not generally regarded as total wars.

The actions of the Union army did not justify the extreme bitterness (a bitterness that lingers to this day) in the South after the war. This bitterness was fueled by distorted and dishonest accounts of the conduct of the Union Army. This dishonesty began near the beginning of the war in a speech by Confederate president Jefferson Davis. In July 1861, *before* the Union began its invasion of the Confederacy, Davis told the Confederate Congress that the United States was "waging an indiscriminate war on them all, with a savage ferocity unknown to modern civilization."[4]

In connection with these issues, we need to discuss what philosophers call "moral luck." Roughly, a person has good or bad moral luck provided that the moral rightness or wrongness of what she does (or the goodness or badness of her character) depends on things beyond her control that happen as a matter of chance. I argue that moral luck is a very widespread phenomenon, that Lincoln enjoyed very good moral luck in that the Civil War, and was lucky that his earlier policies and compromises about slavery turned out very well when they easily might not have. But he also had bad moral luck in that he lived in a time and place where strong racial prejudices were almost universal.

Part II

The second part of the book discusses Lincoln the person and his moral character, as opposed to his actions and policies.

[4] Neely, "Was the Civil War a Total War?," pp. 455–6.

He possessed many important moral virtues, some to a very high degree. Some of his virtues – his kindness, compassion, benevolence, mercy, courage, strong sense of justice and great concern with moral questions (without being self-righteous), honesty, magnanimity, and willingness to ignore personal slights for the sake of the greater good – are well known. He made his great personal ambition virtuous by acting in accordance with his oft-stated desire to gain the esteem of his fellows by making himself *worthy* of their esteem. Some less well-known virtues that he also possessed were his skepticism, nonconformity, independence of mind, and openness to criticism. He was, in many important respects, an extraordinarily good person.

Despite his great virtues, many people deny that he was an unusually good human being. There are at least seven reasons to question the goodness of his character. The most damning criticism is the charge that he was a racist. This issue looms very large in recent discussions of Lincoln. The second reason for questioning his goodness is surprising. Despite his reputation as "Honest Abe," there are reasons to question his honesty. The third criticism is that he was ungrateful and cold-hearted. The fourth criticism is that, as a young man in his twenties and thirties, he was a very partisan politician who frequently attacked and ridiculed his political opponents. He often did this in ways that were unfair, underhanded, and even cruel. The fifth criticism concerns his decision to marry Mary Todd. Some contend that he entered into a loveless marriage because he wanted to marry a woman from a prominent family to help gain increased access to polite society. The sixth criticism is that because of his career and political ambitions he spent a great deal of time away from home and therefore neglected his family and did not do enough to protect his sons from Mary's bad temper and harsh discipline. The seventh criticism stems from his very cold and strained relationship with his father, Thomas Lincoln.

He never introduced his father to his family during the eight years that Thomas Lincoln lived after his son's marriage.

The second part of the book presents evidence for thinking that Lincoln did indeed possess the moral virtues mentioned earlier, and it also assesses the seven criticisms. I argue that some of the criticisms are unfounded, but that several have at least some merit.

He was extremely honest and upright in his business dealings and his work as a lawyer. But in politics, he was sometimes slippery and evasive in his public statements, especially when his actual views were unpopular with the public. He also frequently pandered to the racial prejudices of Illinois voters. In his personal life, those who knew him best described him as "secretive," "shut-mouthed," and lacking in candor. But I argue that it was not wrong for him to sometimes pander to the voters to be an electable politician. Lincoln was not honest in the "positive sense" of being candid, open, and willing to reveal information. However, he was honest in the more familiar "negative sense" of the term: he had a strong principled disposition not to lie, deceive, steal, or engage in fraud. On balance, he deserved his nickname "Honest Abe," and his honesty was a very significant moral virtue.

Despite the claims of some people to the contrary, he was not ungrateful or cold-hearted. I present grounds for questioning the reliability of these criticisms and considerable evidence to the contrary.

As a young man, Lincoln was a very partisan politician who often mocked and ridiculed his political opponents. He wrote some very coarse and insulting anonymous articles and letters ridiculing prominent local Democrats for a local Whig newspaper. Once, on the political stump, he reduced a local Democratic politician to tears; on another occasion, a satirical letter he published under a pseudonym provoked the Democratic auditor of the State of Illinois into challenging him to a duel. He did not give up his penchant for denigrating his political opponents until he reached middle age. Only after this time can we say that he was a kind person without qualification.

He married badly to a very troubled and ill-tempered woman. Some say that he entered into a loveless marriage because of his ambition and his desire to marry a woman from a prominent family to help him gain access to polite society. This is possible, but we do not know enough about his reasons for marrying his wife to pronounce a clear judgment about this.

His marriage reveals some of his moral virtues and strongly confirms the image of him as kind, magnanimous, and forgiving. But more than anything else, his marriage shows the great strength and force of will he needed to do the things he did as president under extremely difficult circumstances. Mary Lincoln fell apart psychologically after their son Willie's tragic death in February 1862. Later her mental state deteriorated further because of a serious head injury she suffered after being thrown from a carriage in an accident and hitting her head on the ground – this injury caused her to suffer violent headaches afterward. She became a very difficult, jealous, and temperamental wife and frequently caused her husband great distress and embarrassment. Lincoln's achievements as president are all the more impressive when one contemplates the extreme difficulty of his marriage and personal life.

He had little love or regard for his father, Thomas Lincoln, but because he had many reasons to dislike his father, we cannot fault him very much on account of this. His failure to introduce his family to his stepmother, who by all accounts, was a wonderful person to whom he was greatly indebted, is much stronger grounds for criticism. But the blame for this failure rests largely with Mary Lincoln.

The final chapter of the book addressees the important question of whether Lincoln was a racist. The short answer is that it depends on what we mean by racism and on what times in his life we are talking about. There are many different definitions of racism, and the word "racism" is used in different ways and different senses. To date, discussions of his alleged racism by historians have largely overlooked the many different possible definitions of racism. Further, historians have not made use of the important work by philosophers on the concept of racism.

One particularly salient definition is that racism is the belief that certain races of people are inferior to others and that it is permissible for members of superior races to exploit and enslave members of inferior races. Two other important definitions are the following: "racism is racially motivated ill will toward members of a certain race of people" and "racism is racially motivated indifference to the welfare of members of a certain race of people." Being a racist according to any of these three definitions is a serious moral failing. But clearly, Lincoln was never a racist according to any of these definitions. He never thought that any race of people was justified in exploiting or enslaving members of other races, and he was never hostile to or indifferent to the welfare or interests of black people or other races. There is abundant evidence to the contrary.

Racism is often defined as the belief that certain races are morally or intellectually superior to other races. Being a racist in this sense is a matter of having certain beliefs and is not necessarily a trait of character or a moral vice. It is unclear whether or not Lincoln was a racist in this sense.

For the purposes of assessing his character, we need to pay particular attention to the following two definitions of racism:

To be a racist is to be *inadequately concerned with the welfare* of a certain race of people, on account of their race.

To be a racist is to be *disrespectful* of a certain race of people, on account of their race.

There is considerable prima facie evidence that he was a racist in both of these senses during most of his political career. But we need to make an important qualification. In certain respects, he had a very great concern for the welfare of blacks. He was very concerned for their happiness, their freedom, and their right to enjoy the fruits of their labor. This concern was morally virtuous. His racial attitudes changed during his presidency, and by the end of his life, it was no longer clear that he was a racist according to either of these definitions.

I contend that, even on the least charitable interpretation of Lincoln's racism that is at all defensible, this vice was too mixed with extremely virtuous benevolence for the same people who were the objects of his racist attitudes to detract *greatly* from the goodness of his other virtues. He was, on balance, a very good and morally virtuous person, even if he had racist vices.

The mythical Lincoln presented to many American schoolchildren is without flaw, or at least the myth never mentions his flaws. He did have flaws, but, in many ways, the Lincoln myth *understates* his goodness, because it does not adequately describe the extreme stress and difficulty of his life, especially the crushing pressures and stresses of his time as president, his marriage to a very troubled and difficult woman, and his very bad moral luck in being raised in, and running for elective office in, an atmosphere of *extreme* racial prejudice and intolerance. Some historians even think that racial prejudice was stronger in Illinois and Indiana, especially central and southern Illinois and Indiana where he lived for most of his life, than anywhere else in the United States.

As a young man, Lincoln had many rough edges and faults to overcome. An important part of the story of his life is his capacity for self-improvement by learning from his mistakes and the criticisms of others. He worked hard at becoming a better person throughout his life, and he succeeded in this goal. He evolved from being a partisan politician who mocked and personally attacked his political opponents in speeches and anonymous writings to become a great statesman who was fair and respectful to his opponents. He also became an abolitionist and adopted much more enlightened views and policies regarding African Americans and their place in American society.

Three Important Notes to My Readers

Before I begin, it is necessary to clarify and defend several methodological assumptions and limitations that have informed this book.

1. The historical record is incomplete. In some respects central to moral questions – in particular the motivations and inner lives of historical figures – it is radically incomplete.

The available historical evidence leaves open many important questions about Lincoln. We do not know all of the important facts about his outward behavior, much less all of the important facts about his motivations for his actions and his inner life and emotions. Many of the moral judgments we make about him need to be hedged in light of this uncertainty. I make clear when I think that the paucity of historical evidence leaves open important moral questions. Here is one example. Some say that he entered into a loveless marriage with Mary Todd because of his ambition; he wanted to marry a woman from a prominent family to gain access to polite society. This is possible, but we do not know enough about his reasons for marrying his wife to pronounce a clear verdict on this matter.

2. Some historians question the legitimacy of "counterfactual history." They claim that the proper work of historians is to describe what actually happened, rather than
   speculate about what would have happened or might
   have happened had the past been different.[5]

At best, counterfactual historical claims are uncertain and
highly fallible. In addition, there are very serious philosophical problems and puzzles about counterfactual statements.
Some philosophers argue that many counterfactual statements about what would have happened if the past had been
different or if certain individuals had acted other than they
did have no determinate truth value. (They deny not only that
it is possible for us to have knowledge about those counterfactuals but also that there are any determinate truths about
them for us *to know*[6].)Nonetheless, we need to make counterfactual claims if we are to make *any* moral judgments
about historical events and actions. For example, if we say
that it was morally right or wrong for the Union to fight the
Civil War, we are presupposing the truth of certain judgments
about what would have happened if it had not fought the war.
The good and bad consequences of the Union fighting the
Civil War are surely relevant to determining whether the war
was justified. We cannot assess the morality of fighting a war
if we know nothing about its consequences; we need to know
the extent of the death and suffering it caused. We also need
to know about other important consequences that it brought
about. If we say that Lincoln's decision to fight the Civil War
made the world better or worse, on balance, we are unavoidably comparing what actually happened with what *would
have happened* if the Union had not fought the war. Indeed,

[5] For a critique of counterfactual history see Evans, *Altered Past: Counterfactuals in History*.
[6] Mendola, *Human Interests*, Chapter 2, "The Indeterminacy of Options." See Mendola for references to the relevant literature.

we cannot make moral judgments about *any* actions or decisions without indulging in this kind of speculation.

The consequences of *any* action are at least *among* the things (if not the only things) that are relevant to its rightness or wrongness. Therefore, making any moral judgment to the effect that an action is right or wrong requires that we be able to say roughly what would have happened if the action had not been performed and compare the consequences of *what actually happened* with the consequences of *what would have happened* if the act had not been performed. At the very least, we need to know whether or not the action led to or prevented very bad consequences and whether or not it brought about or prevented very good outcomes. So to say *anything* about the morality of any of Lincoln's actions, I need to tread where some historians scorn or fear to go.

In addition, when we give historical explanations or make claims about historical causation, we commit ourselves to the truth of certain counterfactual statements. For example, if one claims that Jefferson Davis's decision to replace Johnston with Hood as commander of the Confederate army defending Atlanta in 1864 caused Lincoln to win the 1864 presidential election, one is committed to saying that Lincoln would have lost the election had Davis left Johnston in command.[7]

3. Finally, there is a great deal of disagreement about morality and moral theories. This book applies moral philosophy to a historical figure; it is not a work in ethical theory.

---

[7] When we make moral judgments about what we ought to do in the future, we must act on the basis of conditional judgments that are very similar to the kinds of counterfactual statements in question. For example, suppose that I judge that I ought to do act X, rather than A, B, C, or D. At a minimum, I need to rely on conditional judgments such as the following: "if I do X I will not cause a terrible disaster (with no remotely comparable countervailing benefits) that I can avoid causing if I do A, B, C, or D instead."

In this book I do not attempt to settle any controversial questions in moral theory; rather, I try to appeal to relatively uncontroversial assumptions about morality that I am confident most philosophers and most readers will accept. Chapter 2 defends some of Lincoln's most controversial polices concerning slavery. My strategy is to argue that all reasonable moral theories support my conclusions. These policies were clearly justified according to utilitarianism, but they can also be justified according to many reasonable non-utilitarian theories. Only extreme anti-utilitarian views bordering on moral absolutism will disagree, and I argue that those views are untenable.

I use the same general strategy in the two chapters that discuss the Civil War, but disagreements about questions of ethical theory make more of a difference there. In Chapter 4, I argue that the Union had just cause for fighting the Civil War from the beginning of the war, even before abolishing slavery became a Union war aim. The view that the Union was justified in fighting the war at the beginning is clearly true, given the truth of at least one reasonable moral theory (the actual consequences version of utilitarianism), but that this is so is much less clear given the truth of several other reasonable moral theories. In Chapter 5, I contend that all reasonable views about the morality of war imply that all of the means actually employed by the Union that were necessary to win the war were morally justified. But some important questions of *jus in bello* (justice in war) must be left open, because ostensibly reasonable moral theories disagree about them. For example, it is possible that Sherman's march through Georgia and the Carolinas was not necessary to win the Civil War, but that it caused the war to end more quickly and thereby saved many lives and greatly minimized suffering, on balance. Given this, it is likely that proponents of utilitarianism and just war theory will disagree about the morality of Sherman's march. Short of writing a treatise on

ethical theory and giving arguments for accepting or rejecting utilitarianism (or arguments for accepting or rejecting just
war theory), I am unable to resolve this disagreement.

I am *not* claiming that there are no answers to controversial questions in ethical theory, nor am I endorsing a version
of moral relativism that says that no comprehensive moral
theory, utilitarian or anti-utilitarian, is objectively true. I am
only claiming that the extent of disagreement about issues
in moral theory among ostensibly reasonable people (and
among outstanding philosophers) makes it very difficult to
know the truth about such matters, and that these controver-
sies cannot be resolved in a book of this sort.[8]

A Note to Philosophers and Scholars of Ethics

This is a work of applied philosophy that does not attempt
to answer any questions in ethical theory. Instead I try to
show how ethical theory can shed light on ethical questions
about Lincoln and the Civil War. However, this book still
has some important lessons for philosophers and teachers of
philosophy.

Topics such as the morality of war and the nature of virtues
and vices are illuminated by illustrating and discussing them
in light of the great complexity of the Civil War and the
rich and complicated details of Lincoln's life, rather than
the abstract and piecemeal examples that populate most
philosophical writing and classrooms. The Civil War with
its changing aims and objectives and mounting casualties
raises extremely interesting and important questions of *jus
ad bellum* and *jus in bello*. Lincoln's many compromises with

---

[8] For the record, I have written extensively on the issues of moral objectivity
and moral relativism, and I am by no means a relativist who denies that moral
judgments are objectively true or false. See my books *Value and the Good
Life* and *Lying and Deception: Theory and Practice*, and my paper "Divine
Will/Divine Command Moral Theories and the Problem of Arbitrariness."

slavery are wonderful examples (by far the best that I know of) to consider in connection with moral questions about compromise, principle versus expediency, and utilitarianism, more generally.

When discussing moral character and virtues and vices, it is essential to discuss concrete examples. For that purpose, to be able to talk about an individual's entire life and make judgments in light of that person's entire life and character is greatly preferable to talking about piecemeal aspects of a person's character and imputing virtues and vices to her on the basis of a very limited knowledge of her life history. (It is even less satisfactory to use very brief and sketchy hypothetical cases as the primary examples when making such judgments.) Given his historical importance, his very considerable moral development and moral progress, his many moral virtues, his claim to being a moral exemplar, and the complexity and intrinsic interest of his character, Lincoln is an ideal subject for such an exercise.

So whatever the merits (or lack of merit) of the arguments and analysis of this book, the examples that I focus on are much better and more interesting fodder for philosophical reflection than the hypothetical examples and sometimes wildly improbable thought experiments that dominate philosophical writing about ethics.

History and the details of history matter a great deal from the moral point of view. Moral philosophers should do their work as if history mattered. Lincoln and the Civil War are not the only interesting and important historical examples to consider, but they are surely among the best and most available for American audiences. This is especially the case because the consequences of the Civil War and Lincoln's actions are still playing themselves out.

PART ONE

LINCOLN THE POLITICIAN AND COMMANDER IN CHIEF

2

Lincoln's Evolving Policies Regarding Slavery

Compromise and Utilitarianism

Lincoln thought that slavery was morally wrong and famously said, "If slavery is not wrong, nothing is wrong."[1] He called slavery a "monstrous injustice"[2] and said that no people were ever wronged as greatly as African slaves in America.[3] Yet before 1864, he made many political compromises with slavery, including the following:

1. He was not an abolitionist until 1864, late in his presidency. When he ran for the Senate in 1858 and for president in 1860, he opposed any further extension of slavery but did not advocate its immediate abolition.

2. In his First Inaugural Address, delivered in March 1861, Lincoln made many concessions to slaveholding interests to try to placate the South and avert a civil war. For instance, he promised to enforce the Fugitive Slave Law. On other occasions around this time, he even promised

---

[1] Letter to Albert Hodges, April 4, 1864, in Abraham Lincoln, *Speeches and Writings*, II, p. 585.

[2] Speech on the Kansas-Nebraska Act, in Peoria, October 16, 1854, in Abraham Lincoln, *Speeches and Writings*, I, p. 315.

[3] During a meeting with African American leaders in 1862, Lincoln told them, "Your people are suffering, in my judgment, the greatest wrong inflicted on any people" (Abraham Lincoln, *Speeches and Writings*, II, p. 353).

to enforce it better than had previous presidents.[4] He promised not to interfere with the institution of slavery where it existed and also not to oppose a constitutional amendment to prohibit the federal government from interfering with slavery where it existed.

3. His initial war aims put the preservation of the Union ahead of the abolition of slavery.

4. He rescinded General Fremont's order of partial emancipation in Missouri in 1861 and in 1862 he rescinded General Hunter's order of emancipation for the entire states of Florida, Georgia, and South Carolina.

5. The Emancipation Proclamation was seemingly half-hearted; it failed to free slaves in the border states, Tennessee, or most of the Confederate territory occupied by the Union Army when it went into effect. Some critics indeed said that the Emancipation Proclamation freed no one: "it applied where the Union had no power and did not apply where it did [have power]."[5]

There is much to question here. Given the tremendous evil and injustice of slavery, all of these actions were prima facie very wrong. However, they were all morally justified because they were necessary for the Union to win the Civil War and because they limited slavery as much as possible. Lincoln himself would have justified his actions on similar grounds: in practice, he was a utilitarian. The actions that critics contend that he should have taken to defend the rights of African American slaves would have been futile and counterproductive with respect to protecting the very rights in question. The criticism that he cared only about preserving the Union and not about fighting slavery ignores the *many* strong measures

---

[4] Burlingame, *Abraham Lincoln: A Life*, II, p. 119.
[5] Miller, *President Lincoln: The Duty of a Statesman*, p. 269.

that he took against slavery before issuing the Emancipation Proclamation on January 1, 1863.

I. Lincoln's Compromises with Slavery: A Utilitarian Defense

1. Lincoln was not an abolitionist before 1864.

When he ran for president in 1860, Lincoln's platform did not call for the abolition of slavery in states where slavery already existed. Instead it called only for slavery to be prohibited in federal territories in the hopes that this would make it unlikely that any new slave states would be admitted to the Union. But he also said that if "a Territory from which slavery had been excluded should present herself with a State Constitution sanctioning slavery – a most unlikely thing and wholly unlikely ever to happen – I do not see how I could avoid voting for her admission."[6]

Lincoln believed that stopping the growth of slavery would be the first step in setting slavery "in the course of ultimate extinction."[7] This is a formulation he repeated on many occasions. This policy was unacceptable to voters in the Deep South who insisted that slavery be allowed to expand into new states and territories: the states of the Deep South seceded from the Union for that reason. The other states that left the Union (Arkansas, Tennessee, North Carolina, and Virginia) did so only after the Civil War began at Fort Sumter. Many Southerners were emboldened by the Dred Scott decision, which permitted Scott's master to continue owning him despite having brought Scott into a free state,

---

[6] Abraham Lincoln, *Speeches and Writings*, I, p. 576.

[7] He talked about the need to "arrest the further spread of [slavery] and place it where the public mind shall rest in the belief that it is in the course of ultimate extinction;" "House Divided Speech," June 16, 1858, in ibid., p. 426. Also see his October 1854 speech in Peoria, in ibid., 307–48.

and they claimed the right to practice slavery in every part of the United States.

Lincoln always loathed slavery and desired its end. In July 1858 he said, "I have always hated slavery, I think as much as any Abolitionist."[8] Yet, although he passionately denounced the immorality of slavery and expressed the hope to speed its end, he was not willing to call for laws to abolish it immediately. His opposition to slavery might seem all too moderate and tepid, but his policies were largely motivated by his pessimism about the prospects for ending it in the foreseeable future. He did not think that slavery could be abolished quickly, but that its abolition would be a very long process that might take one hundred years.[9]

There were reasons for his pessimism. During his debates with Stephen Douglas, he said that the Dred Scott decision had the effect of establishing slavery in all the states and territories of the United States[10]: he repeatedly charged that there was a "conspiracy" to spread slavery throughout the entire United States involving members of the Supreme Court and Douglas[11] (for more details, see Chapter 4.II.4). Given the climate of opinion in the country, abolitionists were not politically viable presidential candidates in 1860. At this time, much less than half of the population of the United States supported the immediate abolition of slavery. Non-Republicans who did not vote for Lincoln in the 1860 presidential election constituted slightly more than 60 percent of the electorate and almost none were abolitionists; even most Republicans were not abolitionists. Of the relatively small number of abolitionists, an even smaller number would have been willing to fight

---

[8] Ibid., p. 447.
[9] Foner, *The Fiery Trial*, pp. 89–90.
[10] Abraham Lincoln, *Speeches and Writings*, I, p. 735.
[11] Ibid., pp. 488, 519, 544, and 772.

and die in a bloody civil war to free the slaves. Being an abolitionist was even less of a viable option for a politician from central Illinois. I give evidence for this in Chapters 3 and 10, but briefly, there is reason to think that central and southern Illinois and Indiana were the regions of the country in which white racial prejudice and aversion to the presence of blacks were the strongest.

Lincoln knew that slavery and the interests of slave owners were protected by the U.S. Constitution and that the abolition of slavery could come about only through a constitutional amendment or the very unlikely event that each slave state chose to abolish slavery on its own (within its borders).[12] Further, he knew that the passage of a constitutional amendment to abolish slavery was extremely unlikely because the slave states could easily block it. Article 5 of the U.S. Constitution requires that, to be adopted, amendments must be "proposed" to the states by either (1) a two-thirds vote in each House of Congress or (2) the state legislatures in two-thirds of the states asking Congress to call a national convention to propose an amendment (this method has never been used). After amendments have been "proposed" to the states, the states must ratify them. For an amendment to be ratified and go into effect, one of the following must happen: (1) the state legislatures in three-quarters of the states approve it, or (2) with the approval of Congress, the states hold conventions to consider ratification, and the ratifying conventions in three-quarters of the states approve it (this method has been used only once – to ratify the Twenty-First Amendment).

---

[12] Foner, *The Fiery Trial*, p. 292. In February 1864, Senator Lyman Trumbull presented the Thirteenth Amendment to the U.S. Senate. Preferring that the abolition of slavery come about through the actions of individual states to abolish slavery within their borders, initially Lincoln was reluctant to support it (p. 292). His first public statement in support of its passage came in a letter accepting his nomination for president in June 1864 (p. 299).

To make the ratification process even more difficult, the U.S. Supreme Court has ruled that ratification must come within "some reasonable time after the proposal."[13] In 1860, there were nineteen free states and fifteen slave states. These fifteen states could easily block the ratification of any constitutional amendment to abolish slavery. As James Oakes notes, "By 1860 an anti-slavery amendment would have required the unanimous votes of forty-five free states to secure ratification over the opposition of the fifteen slave states then in the Union. That would be impossible, even today"[14] (because there are only fifty states). The eleven states that later formed the CSA could have blocked the ratification of an amendment to end slavery any time before the total number of states reached forty-four (there were only thirty-four states in 1860).

Only the very unusual circumstances created by the Civil War permitted the ratification of the Thirteenth Amendment, which abolished slavery in the United States. Between February and December 1865, several former Confederate states – Virginia, Louisiana, Tennessee, Arkansas, South Carolina, Alabama, North Carolina, and Georgia – voted to ratify it. These states had pro-Union governments – those who participated in such governments and elections for them included only people who opposed secession – and their votes did *not* reflect popular opinion among white voters in those states. To take just one example, in Tennessee the Unionist government that ratified the Thirteenth Amendment was appointed, not elected. Later, in February 1865, Tennessee voters endorsed the amendment, but the only people permitted to vote were those who took a loyalty oath and swore that they "ardently" desired the defeat of the Confederacy and the end of slavery.[15]

---

[13] Longley, "How to Amend the US Constitution."
[14] Oakes, *Freedom National*, p. 137.
[15] Foner, *The Fiery Trial*, p. 280.

Southern voters would have prevented the ratification of a constitutional amendment abolishing slavery under ordinary circumstances.

Before the Civil War, Lincoln fervently desired the end of slavery, but he knew that American slavery could be abolished only with the general support of voters in the Southern states, something that he *correctly* believed was extremely unlikely to happen in the foreseeable future. The abolition of slavery seemed to him to be an unreachable utopian goal. Only the very unusual circumstances of the Civil War made abolition possible; and, once the war made it possible, he seized the opportunity and pushed very hard to help pass the 13th Amendment.

After the 1860 election, numerous proposals were offered to try to keep the Union together. The most notable was a package of six "irrevocable" constitutional amendments and four supplementary resolutions proposed by Kentucky senator John Crittenden. It included a proposal that the Missouri Compromise line (which continued the southern border of Missouri westward and divided free territory from slave territory in the parts of the Louisiana Purchase west of Missouri) be extended west all the way to California. In existing territories and any that might be added later, slavery would be protected south of that line (this area included the New Mexico Territory).[16] Lincoln was emphatically opposed to Crittenden's proposals even though they offered some hope of keeping the country together.[17]

But this needs to be qualified. Apparently, shortly before his 1861 inauguration, Lincoln told several people that he would consider permitting slavery in parts of the New Mexico Territory if that would help keep the country together. Here are some of the details. William Seward supported a plan

[16] Burlingame, *Abraham Lincoln: A Life*, I, p. 697.
[17] Ibid., p. 715.

to try to keep the states of the Upper South in the Union by creating two large states in the west, one slave and one free.[18] He lobbied Lincoln very hard to accept this proposal, but Lincoln initially rejected it out of hand. On February 1, 1861, he wrote Seward a letter that first stated his opposition to it:

On the territorial question – that is, the question of extending slavery under national auspices, – I am inflexible. I am for no compromise which *assists* or *permits* the extension of slavery on soil owned by the nation. And any trick by which the nation is to acquire territory, and then allow some local authority to spread slavery over it, is as obnoxious as any other. I take it that to effect some such result as this, and to again put us on the road to slave empire is the object of all these compromises. I am against it.[19]

But then Lincoln added the following:

As to fugitive slaves, the District of Columbia, slave trade among the states, and whatever springs of necessity from the fact that the institution is amongst us, I care but little, so that what is done must be comely, and not altogether outrageous. Nor do I care much about New-Mexico, if further extension were hedged against.[20]

Around this time, he also told several visitors that he would be willing to divide the western territories into free and slave zones along the Missouri Compromise line if it would save the Union and restore harmony.[21] Burlingame regards Lincoln's new position on New Mexico as a "momentous policy shift" and thinks that he might have changed his position because he thought that slavery would never take root there; indeed the 1860 census indicated that there were no slaves

[18] Ibid., p. 747.
[19] Abraham Lincoln, *Speeches and Writings*, II, p. 197.
[20] Ibid., pp. 197–8.
[21] Burlingame, *Abraham Lincoln: A Life*, I, p. 749.

in New Mexico.[22] In this connection, it is worth mentioning that, shortly before Lincoln wrote his letter to Seward, Charles Francis Adams and several other House Republicans supported a measure that would immediately grant statehood to New Mexico, with or without slavery as decided by its citizens, as a means to placate the South.[23] Before submitting this proposal, Adams had been assured by several officials who had lived in New Mexico that it was unlikely that slavery would ever take hold there.[24]

Clearly Lincoln wavered in his policies about the spread of slavery, but it would be too strong to say that he changed them. Earlier, he had flatly rejected any compromises on the question of the extension of slavery. He never made his new flexibility on this matter well known to the general public nor did he announce it in any of his public statements. And nothing ever came of the concessions he proposed in his February 1, 1861, letter to Seward. At most, he wavered only for a brief time, and he offered no concessions about the further extension of slavery into New Mexico or anywhere else in his First Inaugural Address on March 2, 1861.

2. Lincoln has been criticized for his many concessions to slaveholding interests (including a promise to enforce provisions of the Constitution calling for the return of fugitive slaves) in his First Inaugural Address and other public statements around the time he became president.

These concessions (at least most of them) were justified because they were necessary for him to retain enough public

---

[22] Ibid., pp. 749–50. In contrast to the census findings, there were a very small number of black slaves, less than twenty, living in New Mexico in 1860; "they were all the house servants of army officers or federal officials posted to New Mexico;" Stegmaier, "The Imaginary Negro in an Impossible Place? The Issue of New Mexico Statehood in the Secession Crisis, 1860–1861," p. 265.

[23] Stegmaier, "The Imaginary Negro in an Impossible Place?," pp. 266–76.

[24] Ibid., pp. 271 and 273.

support to fight and win the Civil War. At the time of the secession crisis, it was not clear that the North would be willing to fight a civil war to maintain the Union. Many abolitionists in the North had no desire to keep the Confederate states in the Union and thought that the North should "let the erring brethren go" (see the later discussion).

Shortly after the war began in the summer of 1861, Congress passed the Crittenden resolution by an overwhelming majority (the vote was 117 to 2 in the House and 30 to 5 in the Senate). The resolution stated that the war was being waged to "maintain the supremacy of the Constitution, and to preserve the Union" and not for the "purpose of overthrowing or interfering with the rights or established institutions [namely slavery]" of the states that seceded.[25] Yet there was stronger support in Congress for antislavery measures than this vote suggests. According to James Oakes, Republican support for this resolution was largely symbolic, and many Republicans were willing to endorse emancipation as a means to preserving the Union.[26] Around the same time, a resolution saying that the military "had no business abolishing slavery or interfering with it in any of the States" was voted down 30 to 9 in the Senate.[27] Very notably, on December 4, 1861, the House voted against reaffirming the Crittenden resolution.[28] By the end of 1861, many Republicans were willing to support emancipation as a means to winning the war. But it was still too soon for Lincoln to try to declare the end of slavery because abolition was still strongly opposed by most Northern Democrats and by most voters in the border states – and the president needed their support to win the war.

---

[25] Burlingame, *Abraham Lincoln: A Life*, II, p. 174.
[26] Oakes, *Freedom National*, pp. 128–30.
[27] Ibid., pp. 113 and 118.
[28] McPherson, *The Battle Cry of Freedom*, p. 358.

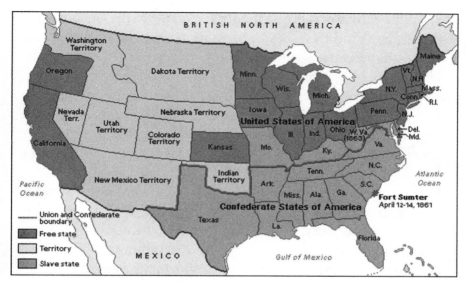

MAP 1: Map of the United States and the Confederate States of America in 1861

When the Civil War began, Lincoln was not willing to demand the abolition of slavery. He feared that if he moved strongly against slavery the border states would secede and tip the balance of power against the Union. The border states were the five slave states that did not join the Confederacy: Missouri, Kentucky, Maryland, Delaware, and West Virginia (which was then in the process of seceding from Virginia). He thought that keeping these states in the Union was essential for winning the war.

The Confederacy also included large parts of Appalachia, eastern Tennessee, western North Carolina, northern Georgia, and northern Alabama that were pro-Union but that would not have supported the Union cause if the war had been a war for emancipation (see Map 1).

At the beginning of his presidency, Lincoln did not have the political support needed to make the war a war for abolition. Had he declared the complete abolition of slavery in all the states of the Union, including the border states, the

Supreme Court would probably have ruled this unconstitutional. It would have been an empty gesture that very likely would have caused some of the border states to secede. It would also have greatly weakened support for the war among Northern Democrats and moderate Republicans, who were a large majority in the North and the Union Army. It is also possible that he would have been impeached and removed from office. In that case, Lincoln's successor, Hannibal Hamlin, would have led a deeply divided North against a very large, united, and powerful Confederacy. The North would have had very little prospect of winning a civil war under those circumstances. Only the extremely conciliatory policies that Lincoln actually pursued could have united people in the North and gained significant support in the border states, which were necessary to fight and win a civil war. He was politically, constitutionally, and militarily constrained. Making abolition an explicit war aim was a nonstarter in 1861, and Lincoln should not be criticized for failing to pursue more radical policies.

It is arguable that he was too willing to appease the South with his promises to enforce the Fugitive Slave Law, though we need to recognize his need to *appear to be* conciliatory to the South in order to gain support from Northern Democrats and the border states to fight the Civil War. However, we should not overestimate the importance of these promises. In 1860, only 803 American slaves succeeded in escaping from slavery.[29] At the time of his election, the Underground Railroad was only minimally successful in securing the liberty of American slaves.

Given that he wanted to oppose slavery within the limits of the law and the U.S. Constitution, Lincoln could not defy the Fugitive Slave Law. The Constitution explicitly provided

---

[29] U.S. Census, 1860, Introduction, pp. xv–xvi, cited in Burlingame, *Abraham Lincoln: A Life*, I, p. 693.

for the capture and return of fugitive slaves (see Chapter 2.II.5). One might object that slavery is so unjust that it was not morally permissible for Lincoln to oppose slavery only through legal means. But I disagree: it is unlikely that Lincoln could have effectively opposed and ended American slavery in any other way. His adherence to the rule of law allowed him to eventually bring the full power of the U.S. government to bear against slavery.[30]

He promised not to oppose Crittendon's proposed "irrevocable" constitutional amendment forbidding the federal government from interfering with slavery where it already existed. It was a good thing that this amendment was never adopted. Had it been adopted, American slavery might have continued much longer. Nonetheless, it probably was politically expedient for him to offer gestures like this to gain support for the war in the North, especially because they were very unlikely to be accepted.

Lincoln's Role in the Fort Sumter Crisis and the Beginning of the Civil War. It is important to digress to note Lincoln's central role in handling the Fort Sumter crisis. Were it not for the part he played, it is quite possible that the Civil War would not have been fought at all and that the North would

---

[30] Lincoln greatly disliked the Fugitive Slave Law. He said that he hated to see slaves hunted down and returned to slavery, "but I bite my lip and keep quiet." He also said that the great body of Northern people had to "crucify their feelings, in order to maintain their loyalty to the constitution and the Union," Abraham Lincoln, *Speeches and Writings*, I, pp. 360–1. He is reported to have said, "I own, if I were called upon by a Marshal, to assist in catching a fugitive, I would suggest to him that others could run a great deal faster than I could" and that "the legal obligation to catch and return . . . runaway slaves" was "degrading" to people in the free states; Miller, *Lincoln's Virtues*, p. 235. (The Fugitive Slave Law of 1850 included a provision that required U.S. marshals and deputies to help slave owners capture fugitives, and it gave marshals the power to deputize citizens on the spot to aid in capturing fugitive slaves; McPherson, *Battle Cry of Freedom*, p. 80.) This provision of the law greatly angered many opponents of slavery. Also see Abraham Lincoln, *Speeches and Writings*, I, p. 620.

not have been sufficiently united to win the war if it had been fought. In his First Inaugural Address and other public statements at this time, he promised not to attack the Confederates first, but he also promised to "hold, occupy and possess" federal property and to use force necessary for that objective.[31] Very shortly after becoming president, he was informed that the garrison at Fort Sumter would run out of food and water by April 15, 1861.[32] After much agonized vacillation, he informed the governor of South Carolina that he would send a naval squadron to provision the fort with food and water. The commander of the army, Winfield Scott, and *all but two members of Lincoln's cabinet*[33] recommended against this course of action, which they thought would be too provocative; Scott argued instead for the evacuation of Fort Sumter.[34] The president thought it likely that resupplying the garrison at Fort Sumter would provoke the hotheaded "fire eaters" of South Carolina to attack the fort.[35] McPherson goes even further, claiming that Lincoln probably expected that his order to resupply Fort Sumter would cause the Confederates to attack and fire the first shots.[36] Lincoln believed that it was vital that the Confederates should fire the first shot if there was to be a war,[37] and so he announced his intention to resupply Fort Sumter on April 6, 1861. On April 9, Confederate president Jefferson Davis ordered the Confederates to attack Fort Sumter before the Union supply ships arrived at Charleston. The Confederate commander

---

[31] Abraham Lincoln, *Speeches and Writings*, II, p. 218.

[32] Burlingame, *Abraham Lincoln: A Life*, II, p. 105.

[33] Ibid., p. 102. Chase supported Lincoln's plan with reservations; Blair was the only member of the cabinet who fully supported the president's plan to provision Fort Sumter.

[34] Ibid., p. 100.

[35] Donald, *Lincoln*, pp. 292–3.

[36] McPherson, *The Battle Cry of Freedom*, p. 272.

[37] Donald, *Lincoln*, p. 293.

Beauregard attacked Fort Sumter on April 12, and the fort surrendered on April 14.

Historians debate whether Lincoln deliberately tried to provoke the Confederates into starting a war.[38] Even if it is too strong to say that Lincoln intended or hoped that his order to resupply Fort Sumter would provoke an attack, he knew that a Confederate attack would likely be the result of his actions, and he thought that this would be a good result. He welcomed the news of the attack on Fort Sumter, telling his friend Orville Browning, "The plan [to resupply Fort Sumter] succeeded. They attacked Fort Sumter. It fell and did more good than it otherwise could."[39] Similarly, he wrote to the commander of the Union naval unit that was sent to resupply the fort, Gustavus Fox,

You and I both anticipated that the cause of the country would be advanced by making the attempt to provision Fort Sumter, even if it should fail; and it is no small consolation now to feel that our anticipation is justified by the result.[40]

Lincoln was under greater stress during this period than at any other time during his presidency. Mary Lincoln reported that, at one point during the Fort Sumter crisis, her husband keeled over from stress and had to take to bed.[41] On this matter, we simply have to marvel at his boldness, prescience, and force of will. We also have to shudder at how far out on a limb he was. In his determination to fight and win a civil war rather than permit the Confederate states to leave the Union, he was more firm and militant than almost any Northern leader, abolitionists included. His leadership made

[38] See, McPherson, *The Battle Cry of Freedom*, p. 272, for a discussion of this debate.
[39] Fehrenbacker and Fehrenbacher, *Recollected Words of Abraham Lincoln*, p. 62; cited in Donald *Lincoln*, p. 294.
[40] Abraham Lincoln, *Speeches and Writings*, II, p. 238.
[41] Burlingame, *Abraham Lincoln: A Life*, II, p. 69.

a huge difference in this respect – it was not inevitable that secession would lead to a civil war. The attack on Fort Sumter was a pivotal event that deeply angered and united the North. Stephen Douglas called on the president and offered him his full support for the war.

As mentioned earlier, many opponents of slavery in the North had no desire to keep the Confederate states in the Union and thought that the North and the president should "let the erring brethren go." Salmon Chase, who is generally credited with being much more of an abolitionist than Lincoln, said, "Let the South go; it is not worth fighting for."[42] Many prominent abolitionists, including William Garrison, Wendell Philips, and Frederick Douglass, preferred permitting the secession of the Southern states to compromising with the South. Philips thought that disunion would bring the country closer to abolition.[43] Douglass said, "If the Union can only be maintained by new concessions to slaveholders, let the Union perish."[44] Garrison said that it was time for "a separation from the South.... Is it not evident that we are, and must be ... two nations?"[45] Garrison and Wendell Philips had long advocated that the North separate from the South to free itself from any connection with slavery.[46]

On this point, these abolitionists were dead wrong, and Lincoln was absolutely right. The independence of the Confederacy would have been a catastrophe for the antislavery cause: it would have greatly expanded and perpetuated American slavery (for a detailed defense of this claim, see Chapter 4.I.1 and 4.I.3).

---

[42] Ibid., p. 102.
[43] Foner, *The Fiery Trial*, p. 146.
[44] Ibid.
[45] Ibid.
[46] Ibid., p. 164. Both Garrison and Philips were pacifists before the Civil War. Given the militancy of the South and its willingness to fight to preserve slavery, it is unclear how they expected slavery to be abolished without a resort to violence.

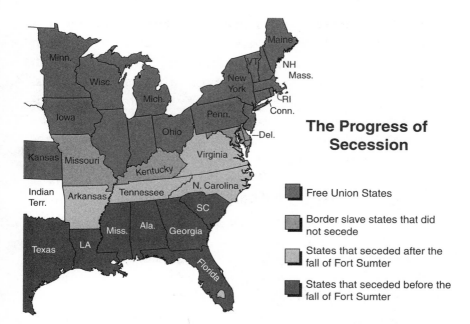

The Progress of
Secession

■ Free Union States

■ Border slave states that did
not secede

□ States that seceded after the
fall of Fort Sumter

■ States that seceded before the
fall of Fort Sumter

MAP 2: Map Showing the Progress of Secession

Yet, the following points should be noted as well. First, after Fort Sumter, four states of the Upper South – Arkansas, Tennessee, Virginia, and North Carolina – which had decided against secession earlier, left the Union;[47] once the Civil War began, they wanted to join their fellow Southerners (see Map 2).

The secession of these four states surprised the president. In this and other ways, he overestimated the extent of pro-Union sentiment in the South.[48] But I conjecture that it was for the best that those states left the Union. Had they remained in the United States, they probably would not have supported a war against their fellow Southerners. Like Kentucky, they probably would have wanted to remain neutral in the war, and it is difficult to see how the North could have invaded the South without advancing through those states. Further, if

[47] Burlingame, *Abraham Lincoln: A Life*, II, p. 139.
[48] Ibid.

those states had remained in the Union, then the Union would have included eight slave states, and it is unclear that Lincoln could have pushed through the Emancipation Proclamation and the Thirteenth Amendment under those circumstances. For a time in April 1861, Lincoln was willing to surrender Fort Sumter on the condition that Virginia stay in the Union.[49] It was probably for the best that Virginia did not take him up on this offer.

3. Lincoln is frequently criticized for his initial war aims, which put preserving the Union ahead of abolishing slavery. But the idea that he put preserving the Union ahead of *opposing slavery* implies a false dichotomy.

At the beginning of the secession crisis, he opposed slavery as much as he could have. He needed the support of the border states and Democrats in the North, and early in the war, any proposals for the immediate abolition of slavery would have been unacceptable to them. He did not have the power to abolish slavery in 1861, and therefore it is a mistake to say that it was wrong for him not to abolish slavery then. To say that he ought to have done this implies that it was within his power to do so – "ought" implies "can." He could have *declared* the abolition of slavery in 1861, but he could not have enforced this order then. Indeed, his declaring the complete end of slavery in 1861 would have virtually guaranteed the independence of the Confederacy and probably would have caused some of the border states to secede. It would have been an empty and counterproductive gesture. The criticism that he cared *only* about preserving the Union and not about ending slavery is completely mistaken and overlooks several strong measures that he took against slavery early in

---

[49] Ibid., p. 121.

the Civil War. Before issuing the Emancipation Proclamation, he pushed three measures to induce states to *voluntarily* emancipate their slaves.

i. In November 1861, Lincoln supported a bill in the Delaware state legislature that provided that all slaves in Delaware would be freed by 1893; slave children born after passage of the bill and slaves older than thirty-five years of age would be freed immediately (this bill was modeled after a bill that was almost passed by the Delaware Whigs in 1847). He promised his support to get the federal government to pay the state $500 for each slave to be used by the state to compensate slave owners. He defended this plan on the grounds that it would be cheaper than fighting the war; he viewed it as an experiment that might induce other border states to follow suit. The plan also provided that the freed slaves would be given the option to form colonies outside of the United States "at some place or places in a climate congenial to them."[50] This plan was voted down by a very narrow margin in the Delaware legislature, just as it was in 1847.[51]

ii. In March 1862, he submitted a resolution to Congress stating that "the United States ought to cooperate with any state which may adopt a gradual abolitionment of slavery, giving to such states pecuniary aid, which may be used to compensate slave owners." Congress passed this resolution by a wide margin. The president hoped that the border states would sign on to it and hinted darkly to border state politicians that they had better accept this offer because later he might have to abolish slavery without compensating slave owners.[52]

[50] Ibid., pp. 229–30.
[51] Ibid., p. 231.
[52] Ibid., pp. 333–43.

iii. In his Annual Message to Congress in December 1862 Lincoln proposed a constitutional amendment giving federal funds to any state that abolished slavery before 1900. The proposed amendment authorized, but did not require, Congress to aid in colonizing freed people "with their consent."[53]

Had they succeeded in enticing the border states to abolish slavery, these three proposals would have greatly changed the balance between free and slave states and moved things closer to a situation in which the free states would have had the supermajority (three-fourths of the states) needed to ratify a constitutional amendment to abolish slavery.

Three other federal laws supported by the president and enacted during the first half of the war did succeed in freeing thousands of slaves. In April 1862, Congress passed and the president signed a bill to abolish slavery in Washington, D.C. This bill gave financial compensation to "loyal" slave owners and also made it a felony for slave owners to attempt to remove emancipated slaves from Washington, sell, or reenslave them. The law also permitted former slaves to testify as to the loyalty (to the Union) of their former owners and appropriated funds to support the voluntary colonization "of such free persons of African descent . . . as may desire to emigrate."[54] In June 1862, Congress passed and Lincoln signed a bill prohibiting slavery in all U.S. territories (areas owned by the United States that were not parts of states).

In 1861, the western counties of Virginia voted overwhelmingly against secession from the United States. When those counties constituted themselves as West Virginia and applied for statehood, Republicans required that the state

---

[53] Oakes, *Freedom National*, pp. 273–4; also see Burlingame, *Abraham Lincoln: A Life*, II, p. 439 and Abraham Lincoln, *Speeches and Writings*, II, p. 412.

[54] Burlingame, *Abraham Lincoln: A Life*, II, p. 344.

abolish slavery as a condition of admission to the Union.[55] On December 31, 1862, the president signed a bill admitting West Virginia to the Union against the objections of his conservative attorney general Edward Bates. Less than six months later, Lincoln "imposed a similar condition on Louisiana, requiring the state to endorse the Emancipation Proclamation as a condition for readmission to the Union. Eventually the federal government would impose the same requirement on every one of the defeated Confederate states."[56]

In addition, from nearly the beginning of the war, the Union military began to free thousands of slaves in the Confederacy without giving financial compensation to their owners. The Union Army also harbored fugitive slaves and, in the Confederate states, made it a policy not to return any slaves who came to their lines.

a. In May 1861, Union General Ben Butler refused to return runaway slaves to their owners in Virginia. He called these slaves "contraband of war" and justified his actions on the ground that, because Virginia had seceded from the Union, Virginians had forfeited their constitutional right to the return of fugitive slaves. Butler also claimed that the laws of war permitted that "all the property of the enemy may be seized" and that "property of whatever nature, used or capable of being used for warlike purposes, and especially when being so used, may be captured on sea or on shore as property

---

[55] Congress had considerable difficulty specifying the terms of the emancipation requirement, but a compromise was reached. The law that was passed immediately freed the great majority of West Virginia's slaves (90% according to Congressman John Bingham) and called for the complete end of slavery in West Virginia in twenty-one years. Charles Sumner opposed this compromise, but most of his fellow radical Republicans supported it (Oakes, *Freedom National*, pp. 293–9).

[56] Ibid., p. 299.

contraband of war."[57] The president and his cabinet approved Butler's policies on May 30, 1861, just six weeks after the war began at Fort Sumter.[58] On the same day, the War Department issued instructions to Union solders in the field. They were not permitted to interfere with the ordinary operation of slavery, even in seceded states; however, they were also to "refrain from surrendering" slaves who had fled to Union lines to their alleged masters.[59] At this time, the Union military also made it a policy to consider all slaves left on the land after their owners fled from the Union Army to be free.[60]

b. In August 1861, Congress passed and the president signed the First Confiscation Act. This law immediately freed all slaves who were "used for insurrectionary purposes" (i.e., slaves used in the service of the Confederate military).[61] This law freed thousands of slaves and gave no compensation to their owners.[62]

c. In March 1862, Congress passed and Lincoln signed a law prohibiting the military from enforcing the Fugitive Slave Law.[63]

d. The Militia Act of July 1862 freed any slave who enlisted in the Union Army and also freed his mother, wife, and children. Democrats and border state congressmen claimed that the "federal government had no constitutional authority to free any slaves of any loyal masters in a loyal slave state."[64] Lincoln shared these scruples

[57] Ibid., pp. 96–7.
[58] Ibid., p. 99.
[59] Ibid., pp. 99–100.
[60] Ibid., p. 225.
[61] Ibid., pp. 137–9.
[62] Ibid., p. 144.
[63] Ibid., p. 189.
[64] Ibid., pp. 386 and 433.

about freeing the slaves of loyal masters in the border states, but beginning in October, 1863 Union recruiters in the border states enlisted "all able-bodied black men, regardless of the loyalties of their owners."[65]

e. On July 17, 1862, Congress passed the Second Confiscation Act. This act gave the president the authority to proclaim the freedom of the slaves of disloyal slave owners in all states and territories rebelling against the authority of the United States (this area included most or all of the CSA), if those slave owners did not cease aiding and abetting the rebellion within sixty days of being given a public warning and of the proclamation by the president. Because most of the CSA was disloyal to the United States and because a great majority of slave owners in the CSA supported the Confederacy, this act applied to the great majority of the slaves in the CSA. If carried out by presidential proclamation, it would clearly destroy slavery in seceded states and grant freedom to most of the slaves in the United States.[66] The Second Confiscation Act also authorized the president to use black soldiers for the purpose of suppressing the rebellion and authorized him to make provisions for the voluntary colonization of blacks in tropical lands outside of the United States, provided that governments of the lands in which they settled consented to this and gave the new settlers "all of the rights and privileges of freemen."[67]

On July 22, 1862, Lincoln told his cabinet that he intended to issue a proclamation of the sort described in the act. (He had informed Navy Secretary Gideon Welles and Secretary of State Seward of his intention to issue the proclamation on

[65] Ibid., p. 464.
[66] Ibid., pp. 239–43 and Grimsley, *The Hard Hand of War*, p. 132.
[67] Second Confiscation Act.

July 13, 1862.[68]) He issued such a proclamation two months later, and it became known as the Emancipation Proclamation.

After the Union captured New Orleans and large parts of southern Louisiana in 1862, General Ben Butler became the military governor of the area. Butler seized the plantations of disloyal slave owners and paid the newly freed slaves wages to continue working. He went beyond the provisions of the Second Confiscation Act and required even slave owners loyal to the Union to adopt the same labor practices that were used on government-run plantations: they were required to pay their workers wages and were forbidden to impose corporal punishment on them. "In this way, de facto free labor was being established by loyal whites in Southern Louisiana."[69] Lincoln corresponded with Butler about this and approved of his policies.[70]

Thus Lincoln and his administration freed many slaves and tried to free even more from almost the very beginning of the Civil War, long before the Emancipation Proclamation.

Lincoln's Public Letter to Horace Greeley. But what about Lincoln's letter to Horace Greeley of August 22, 1862? This letter was a public response to Greeley's "The Prayer of Twenty Millions," an open letter to the president that urged him to call for the abolition of slavery.[71] The president's letter included the following very well-known statement:

If there be those who would not save the Union, unless they could at the same time *save* slavery, I do not agree with them. If there be those who would not save the Union unless they could at the same time *destroy* slavery, I do not agree with them. My paramount object in this struggle is to save the Union, and is not either to save or to destroy slavery. If I could save the Union without freeing any

---

[68] Grimsley, *The Hard Hand of War*, p. 132.
[69] Oakes, *Freedom National*, pp. 252–3.
[70] Ibid., pp. 253–5.
[71] In Holzer, ed., *The Lincoln Anthology*, pp. 40–6.

slave I would do it, and if I could save it by freeing all of the slaves I would do it, and if I could save the Union by freeing some and leaving others alone I would also do that. What I do about slavery, and the colored race, I do because it helps to save the Union; and what I forebear, I forebear because I do not believe it would help save the Union... I shall try to correct errors when shown to be errors; I shall adopt new views so fast as they appear to be true views.

I have here stated my purpose according to my view of my *official* duty; and I intend no modification of my oft-expressed *personal* wish that all men every where could be free.[72]

Many people cite this letter as evidence that Lincoln cared only about preserving the Union and not about ending slavery – but it is not good evidence for that position. When he wrote this letter, he had already signed the Second Confiscation Act into law; he had already drafted the Emancipation Proclamation and was waiting for a military victory before he issued it. In part, this letter was a public relations tactic to soften opposition to the Emancipation Proclamation, and as we see shortly, his fears about opposition to the Emancipation Proclamation were entirely justified. Finally, it must be stressed that he did not value the Union solely as an end in itself. He valued preserving the Union partly as a means to limit the extension and perpetuation of slavery (see 2.I.2 and Chapter 4.II.4).

Despite the rhetoric of his letter to Greeley, Lincoln and the Union army had already freed thousands and thousands of slaves. Thus, preserving the Union without freeing any slaves was no longer an option. Freeing all the slaves (including those in the border states) was also not an option for Lincoln: he had no legal/constitutional basis for doing that short of a constitutional amendment to end slavery. When he wrote this letter, he had already decided on the option of saving the

---

[72] Abraham Lincoln, *Speeches and Writings*, II, p. 358.

Union by freeing *most* of the slaves after a significant military victory.

In 1862 many soldiers in the Union Army and many people in the North were willing to fight for the Union but not to end slavery. There is evidence that only 30 percent of Union soldiers supported emancipation as a war aim at the time the Emancipation Proclamation was issued.[73] The letter to Greeley was calculated to avoid offending people who were not strongly antislavery. Because he needed to keep their support for the war and needed to have a constitutionally sound basis for the proclamation he then planned to issue, Lincoln needed to say that he was freeing the slaves as a means to preserving the Union.

The end of slavery was something Lincoln fervently desired. He told his friend Joshua Speed that in freeing the slaves his fondest hopes (to gain honor by doing something that greatly benefited others) had been realized (see Chapter 7.I.7). When he signed the Emancipation Proclamation, he told Seward and Seward's son that "I never, in my life, felt more certain that I was doing right, than I do in signing this paper."[74] Even though in his letter to Greeley he stated that his primary purpose *in fighting the war* was not to end slavery, he had already aimed to end slavery *by other means*, such as using federal money to induce individual states to abolish slavery (see Chapter 10.V.2 for more on the Greeley letter). In his actions as president, he did as much as possible to *oppose* and limit the evil of slavery.

> 4. Another criticism concerns Lincoln's revocation of General Fremont's order for partial emancipation in Missouri and of General Hunter's later order for the

---

[73] McPherson bases this estimate on a study of letters written by Union soldiers during the war. He adds that *later* many more Union soldiers supported the Emancipation Proclamation (*What They Fought For, 1961–1865*, p. 56.)

[74] Burlingame, *Abraham Lincoln: A Life*, II, p. 469.

FIGURE 1: Lincoln Attacked by Abolitionists for his Actions in the Case of Fremont

emancipation of all the slaves in South Carolina, Georgia, and Florida.

To address this criticism, I need to digress and discuss the situation in Kentucky at this time. When the Civil War began, Kentucky remained in the Union, but it rejected Lincoln's call to send troops to put down the rebellion. Beriah Magoffin, the governor of Kentucky, said, "Kentucky will furnish no troops for the wicked purpose of subduing her sister southern states."[75] The state voted for "armed neutrality" and to prohibit non-Kentucky armies (both Union and Confederate) from entering the state. By looking at a map of the United States (Map 1), one can see that this prohibition posed a

[75] Miller, *President Lincoln: The Duty of a Statesman*, p. 122.

very big problem for the Union. The Union could not control the Ohio and Mississippi rivers without the support of Kentucky, and attacking the states of Tennessee, Mississippi, and Alabama was not feasible without first moving through Kentucky. On September 3, 1861, Confederate general Leonidas Polk brought his army into Kentucky on the pretext that there were Union troops across the river in Missouri. Although the Kentucky legislature demanded that the Confederates leave the state,[76] Polk stayed in Kentucky and was not recalled by Confederate president Jefferson Davis. Lincoln prudently left Kentucky alone.[77] This wise policy allowed pro-Union people to gain control of the Kentucky government. In elections held around this time, nine of the ten Kentuckians elected to the U.S. House of Representatives supported the Union cause.[78] Additionally, Polk's invasion gave the Union a pretext to send troops into Kentucky.

On August 30, 1861, Union general John C. Fremont, who had been a very incompetent and corrupt commander in Missouri,[79] issued an order that the slaves of "all persons in the state of Missouri who shall take up arms against the United States" were free (whether or not those slaves had been used in support of the Confederate cause).[80] Fremont also ordered the execution of all who fought for the Confederates.[81] This order went beyond the provisions of the First Confiscation Act, which only called for the emancipation of slaves used to support the Confederate War effort and did not mandate the execution of any prisoners of war. Four days later, on September 3, Lincoln wrote Fremont a note urging him to "modify" his order to bring it in line

---

[76] Ibid., p. 124.
[77] Miller, *President Lincoln: The Duty of a Statesman*, p. 125.
[78] Ibid., pp. 126–7.
[79] Burlingame, *Abraham Lincoln: A Life*, II, p. 201.
[80] Oakes, *Freedom National*, p. 157.
[81] Ibid., pp. 156–7.

with the First Confiscation Act. Fremont refused to do this unless the president ordered him to do so. On September 11, 1861, Lincoln did just that, expressing the worry that executions would lead to retaliation by the Confederates and forbidding Fremont from ordering any executions without his (Lincoln's) prior approval.[82] Yet he did not relieve Fremont from command in Missouri at this time. "Lincoln waited to give Fremont one more chance to redeem himself by beating back the Confederate military invasion, but when he failed at that, the president finally relieved the Pathfinder [Fremont] of his command."[83]

Lincoln's close friend and Kentuckian Joshua Speed warned the president that Fremont's actions in Missouri would greatly harm the Union cause in Kentucky.[84] Fort Sumter commander, Kentuckian Robert Anderson, wrote to the president that after learning about Fremont's order an entire company of Kentuckians who had volunteered to fight for the Union "threw down their arms and disbanded."[85]

Lincoln wrote his friend Orville Browning, "I was assured [by Anderson], as to think it probable, that the very arms we had furnished Kentucky would be used against us."[86] During this time, the Kentucky legislature was considering a proposal to abandon neutrality and fight for the Union, but said it would only pass it if Fremont's order was reversed. After the president overruled Fremont's order, the legislature voted to abandon neutrality and passed a measure calling for the state to raise forty thousand volunteers for the Union Army.[87]

---

[82] Ibid., pp. 157–8.
[83] Ibid., p. 166; Fremont was relieved of command in November 1861, Thomas, *Abraham Lincoln: A Biography*, pp. 278–9.
[84] Burlingame, *Abraham Lincoln: A Life*, II, p 202.
[85] Miller, *President Lincoln: The Duty of a Statesman*, p. 129.
[86] Ibid.
[87] Ibid., pp. 129–30.

Lincoln was clearly right to revoke Fremont's order to execute all who fought for the Confederates. Not only was it extremely questionable morally but had this order stood, it would have been met by retaliation in kind by the Confederates and caused the war to become even more bloody and bitter.

Yet was he justified in revoking that part of Fremont's order calling for partial emancipation in Missouri? He was very harshly criticized for his actions in this matter (see Figure 1). Ohio Senator Ben Wade blasted Lincoln and said that his attitudes about slavery "could only have come from someone born of 'poor white trash.'"[88]

Lincoln's actions in this case were prima facie very wrong and prevented Fremont from freeing a number of people from slavery.[89] Nonetheless, he was morally justified in revoking Fremont's order. If he had not done so, it is quite possible that the Civil War would have been lost then and there, because allowing Fremont's order to stand would have greatly undermined support for the Union cause in the border states and among Northern Democrats. The people that Fremont's order might have freed could not have retained their freedom unless the Union won the war. Therefore, by overruling Fremont, he probably did not harm *most of those particular individuals*; they benefited as a result of his actions. The great majority of them were eventually freed and would not have been able to maintain their freedom if the Union had lost the war in 1861 or 1862. The number of individuals affected was less than might be supposed because the First Confiscation Act of 1861 was already in

---

[88] Burlingame, *Abraham Lincoln: A Life*, II, p. 203.

[89] It is unlikely that Lincoln's actions caused many people who had been freed by Fremont's order to be returned to slavery because it was only in effect for twelve days. Very likely the only people it could have freed were those who came to Union lines during those twelve days, and at least some of them would have been freed independently by the First Confiscation Act.

force at the time of Fremont's actions. This act gave the federal government the authority to seize slaves used to help the Confederate Army.[90] In addition, it is very probable that the U.S. Supreme Court would have overturned Fremont's order, even if Lincoln had not done so. Therefore, it is unlikely that he could have prevented Fremont's order from being overturned, even if he had wanted to.

James Oakes thinks that the Fremont order actually caused less furor in Kentucky than Lincoln supposed.[91] Still, many people in Kentucky were greatly angered by it, and President Lincoln's decisions were reasonable in light of the circumstances and the information available to him at the time. Fremont's order had a very significant chance of causing a disaster, and the significant, but relatively small, amount of good it might have done was not worth the risk it ran.

A similar situation arose on May 9, 1862, when Union general David Hunter declared the emancipation of all the slaves in the states of Georgia, Florida, and South Carolina. Lincoln immediately rescinded this order because of concern for its effect on the border states and on his own plans for gradual compensated emancipation. However, in this case he stated that, although Hunter did not have the authority to issue this order of emancipation, he, Lincoln, did.[92] In his order revoking Hunter's proclamation, he pointedly urged the border states to accept his proposal for gradual compensated emancipation and told them not to be "blind to the signs of the times."[93] He told border state congressmen that they had better accept his offer for compensated emancipation, because if they did not he might have to issue an

---

[90] Donald, *Lincoln*, p. 314.
[91] Oakes, *Freedom National*, p. 163.
[92] "Proclamation Revoking General Hunter's Emancipation Order," Abraham Lincoln, *Speeches and Writings*, II, pp. 318–19.
[93] Ibid.

order similar to Hunter's. His appeals to the border state congressmen were unsuccessful. On July 12, 1862, Lincoln met
again with the congressmen and again pushed his proposals
for compensated emancipation. They refused again. He was
deeply disappointed and gave up on this idea. *The very next
day* he told two members of his Cabinet that he had decided
to issue the Emancipation Proclamation.[94] Lincoln's actions
in the Hunter case were justified for exactly the same reasons
that they were justified in the case of Fremont.

5. The final criticism of the morality of Lincoln's actions
   concerning slavery is that the Emancipation Proclamation did not go nearly far enough.

Lincoln issued the preliminary version of the proclamation on
September 22, 1862. It stated that, on January 1, 1863, all
persons held as slaves in those territories judged to be in rebellion against the United States "shall be, then, thenceforward,
and forever free." The September version of the proclamation was a *threat* – a threat to end slavery in those parts of
the country that were rebelling against the Union unless the
Confederate states agreed to submit to federal authority and
rejoin the Union within one hundred days. He invoked his
constitutional authority as commander in chief of the military "in time of actual armed rebellion against the authority
and government of the United States." This was his only legal
ground for overriding the very strong legal and constitutional

---

[94] "On July 12 [1862] . . . Lincoln met with twenty-seven border state Congressmen and Senators and urged them again to support a program of compensated
emancipation." "Their failure to do so profoundly disappointed him." The
very next day, July 13, 1862, he decided to issue the Emancipation Proclamation. "Hard on the heels of his unsuccessful interview with the border state
congressmen, Lincoln made his fateful decision to emancipate the slaves by
executive order. In a private conversation with Navy Secretary Gideon Welles
and Secretary of State Seward on July 13, he told them of his intention"
(Grimsley, *The Hard Hand of War*, p. 132).

protections that were otherwise enjoyed by American slave owners. Near the end of the final version, issued on January 1, 1863, Lincoln said, "And upon this act, sincerely believed to be an act of justice, warranted by the Constitution, upon military necessity, I invoke the considerate judgment of mankind, and the gracious favor of Almighty God."[95]

The proclamation did not apply to slaves held in the border states. It exempted the entire state of Tennessee, as well as most of the Confederate territory occupied by the Union Army as of January 1, 1863. Only fifty thousand slaves in parts of Arkansas, Mississippi, North Carolina, South Carolina, Georgia, and Florida were freed immediately on that day[96] – only a little more than 1 percent of American slaves. Map 3 shows where slaves were and were not freed on January 1, 1863.

The January 1, 1863, version states that it applies to the following areas:

Arkansas, Texas, Louisiana, (except the Parishes of St. Bernard, Plaquemines, Jefferson, St. John, St. Charles, St. James Ascension, Assumption, Terrebonne, Lafourche, St. Mary, St. Martin, and Orleans, including the City of New Orleans), Mississippi, Alabama, Florida, Georgia, South Carolina, North Carolina, and Virginia, (except the forty-eight counties designated as West Virginia, and also the counties of Berkley, Accomac, Northampton, Elizabeth City, York, Princess Ann, and Norfolk, including the cities of Norfolk & Portsmouth); and which excepted parts, are for the present, left precisely as if this proclamation were not issued.[97]

This is not an inspiring piece of writing. It is written like an insurance contract with all sorts of exceptions. Karl Marx likened it to "the trite summonses that one lawyer sends to

---

[95] Abraham Lincoln, *Speeches and Writings*, II, p. 425.
[96] Foner, *The Fiery Trial*, p. 243.
[97] Abraham Lincoln, *Speeches and Writings*, II, p. 425.

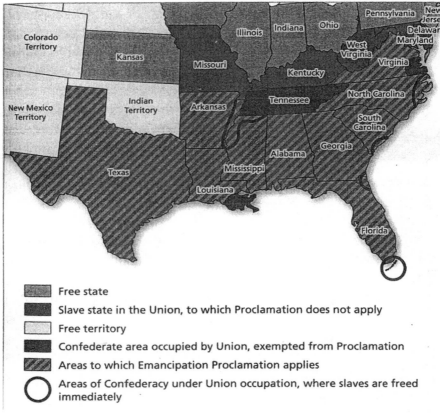

MAP 3: Map for the Emancipation Proclamation

an opposing lawyer, the legal chicaneries and pettyfogger-
ing stipulations of an *actiones juris*."[98] Richard Hofstadter
wrote that the Emancipation Proclamation "had all the moral
grandeur of a bill of lading."[99] An editorial in the London
Magazine *Spectator* said, "The [moral] principle is not that a
human being cannot justly own another, but that he cannot
own him unless loyal to the United States."[100]

---

[98] Karl Marx, "On Events in North America," in Holzer, ed., *The Lincoln
Anthology*, pp. 47–50.

[99] Cited in Guelzo, *Lincoln's Emancipation Proclamation*, p. 2; a bill of lading
is a list of cargo.

[100] Stout, *Upon the Altar of the Nation*, p. 178.

As mentioned earlier, the Emancipation Proclamation is the proclamation that the Second Confiscation Act authorized the president to make. The Second Confiscation Act stipulates that the president's proclamation should give slave owners in the Confederate states sixty days notice (i.e., sixty days in which they could cease aiding and abetting the rebellion and still retain their slaves). So that the Emancipation Proclamation could conform to this provision of the Second Confiscation Act, Lincoln needed to make freeing the slaves contingent on the rebellion continuing for some specified period of time. The Emancipation Proclamation gave the Confederate *states* (as opposed to individual slave owners within the Confederacy) one hundred days to return to the Union without giving up the institution of slavery. Yet, in some ways, the Emancipation Proclamation went far beyond the Second Confiscation Act by freeing all slaves in rebel territory, not just those owned by disloyal masters.

The Emancipation Proclamation was a legalistic document because Lincoln needed to make sure that the Supreme Court would not overturn it. He needed to write it in such a way to ensure that it would be constitutional (the U.S. Constitution then strongly protected the rights of slave owners and all of the property rights of individuals[101]) and to retain the support of the border states. Roger Taney, the author of the infamous Dred Scott decision, was then the Chief Justice of the Supreme Court.

Given that American slavery was such an unjust institution that so grossly violated the rights and dignity of millions of human beings, it seems reasonable to claim that Lincoln should have declared a complete and unqualified emancipation of all American slaves at the beginning of the Civil War. He should not have waited nearly two years to issue a limited emancipation order, he should not have exempted so much

---

[101] The Fifth Amendment to the Constitution prescribes that no person shall be deprived of property "without due process of law."

territory from his order, and he should not have given the Confederacy the option to rejoin the Union with the institution of slavery intact. Julius Lester, for example, claims that Lincoln should have issued the Emancipation Proclamation much earlier, at the beginning of his presidency:

Blacks have no reason to be grateful to Abraham Lincoln. Rather, they should be angry at him. How come it took him two whole years to free the slaves? His pen was sitting in his desk the whole time. All he had to do was get up one morning and say, "Doggonnit! I think that I'm gon' free the slaves today. It just ain't right for folks to own other folks." It was that simple.[102]

Lester is criticizing Lincoln for not freeing the slaves much earlier and claiming that he could have done so at any time he was President, since the pen was in his desk – "it was that simple."

But it *was not* "that simple." Lester and other critics to the contrary, it was not within Lincoln's power to do more to end slavery much earlier than he did. He did not have the power or legal authority to completely abolish slavery at the beginning of the Civil War. He had to act within the limits of the U.S. Constitution, which strongly protected the institution of slavery and the interests of slave owners. A much earlier proclamation of emancipation would have been strongly opposed by Congress and the U.S. Supreme Court – it is likely the Court would have overruled him and possible that Congress would have impeached him and removed him from office. Further, Lester seems to be unaware of the *many* strong measures that Lincoln took against slavery before the time he issued the Emancipation Proclamation. These measures began just six weeks after he became president (see the earlier discussion in 2.1.3).

---

[102] Lester, *Look out Whitey!: Black Power's Gon' Get Your Mama!*, p. 58.

President Lincoln had the power to take his pen and *declare* the slaves free in 1861, but he did not have the power to *actually* free them in 1861. Because being able to do something is a necessary condition of one's having a moral obligation to do it, it does not make sense to criticize him for failing to free the slaves in 1861: he did not have the power to do this. But perhaps Lester and others would say that Lincoln should still have *declared* abolition in 1861, even if he knew that doing so would not have freed anyone. But this would not only have been futile; it would also have been extremely counterproductive and harmful to the interests of the slaves. It would have made slavery much worse by fatally weakening support for the Union cause and ensuring the victory of a powerful Confederate States of America, a nation dedicated to slavery and the proposition that all people are not created equal. The independence of the CSA would have been a catastrophe.

Simply *declaring* the end of slavery would have been an empty gesture unless the Union won the war. Lincoln had to move slowly and cautiously in order to retain enough public support to fight and win the Civil War. He could not afford to do anything that would cause the border states to leave the Union. As it was, there was a tremendous amount of opposition to the Emancipation Proclamation within the Union Army; it was bitterly opposed by General McClellan, the commander of the Army of the Potomac.[103] There is reason to think that only 30 percent of Union soldiers supported emancipation as a war aim at the time the Emancipation Proclamation was issued (see note 73). The state legislatures in Illinois and Indiana denounced the Emancipation Proclamation. The Illinois legislature also voted to block the immigration of free blacks into Illinois. In response, the Republican governor of Illinois requested that Lincoln be prepared to send Union

---

[103] Burlingame, *Abraham Lincoln: A Life*, II, p. 436.

troops to disperse the state legislature if necessary; the president immediately endorsed this proposal.[104] The Republican governors of Illinois and Indiana delayed calling their legislatures into session, and the governor of Indiana (Morton) ran the state for two years without legislative authorization. When Morton ran out of money, Lincoln's administration sent him funds from the War Department.[105]

Lincoln did *not* have the power to emancipate the slaves in the border states because that would have been unconstitutional. The legal bases for the Emancipation Proclamation were his powers as commander in chief of the U.S. military and his need to subdue the rebellion. Because the border states were not rebelling against federal authority, this rationale for emancipation clearly did not apply to the border states. For this same reason, he did not have the constitutional authority to free slaves in those parts of the Confederacy controlled by the Union Army as of January 1, 1863. Those areas were not then in rebellion against the government of the United States.

Lincoln regarded Tennessee as a loyal state that was still part of the Union because its governor, Andrew Johnson, led a Unionist government.[106] That is why the final version of the Emancipation Proclamation exempted Tennessee. President Lincoln and Governor Johnson were able to abolish slavery in Tennessee before the end of the Civil War.

A large percentage of the slaves exempted by the provisions of the Emancipation Proclamation (including most of the slaves or former slaves in West Virginia, the Union-occupied areas of Louisiana, and the costal areas of Virginia) were free or effectively free prior to January 1, 1863. Of the six states completely exempted from the provisions of the Emancipation Proclamation – Missouri, Kentucky, Tennessee,

---

[104] Donald, *Lincoln*, pp. 418–19.
[105] Ibid. and McPherson, *The Battle Cry of Freedom*, pp. 595–6.
[106] Oakes, *Freedom National*, p. 387.

Maryland, West Virginia, and Delaware – all but Kentucky abolished slavery before the end of the Civil War,[107] and Lincoln strongly supported the movements to end slavery in all of these states. The states he exempted from the Emancipation Proclamation "were the *most* likely to abolish slavery before the Civil War ended."[108] Exempting them thus did not mean that he was not concerned with the freedom of their slaves.

Lincoln made freeing the slaves contingent on the rebellion not ceasing within some specified period of time so that the Emancipation Proclamation would conform to the Second Confiscation Act. He also needed to appear to be conciliatory to the South to ensure he would have enough popular support to win the war and maintain control of Congress in the 1862 elections. Further, he knew that the Confederate states would not return to the Union in the hundred days he specified.

Chief Justice of the Supreme Court Roger Taney held that, although the Emancipation Proclamation was constitutional as a war measure, it would become null and void at the end of the war and that those who were freed by the proclamation were only freed temporarily for the duration of the war.[109] In a letter to Orville Browning dated September 22, 1861,

---

[107] Ibid., p. 367.

[108] Ibid.

[109] Guelzo, *Abraham Lincoln: Redeemer President*, p. 344. In this connection, it is noteworthy that Lincoln changed the wording of the final version of the Emancipation Proclamation to drop the words "forever free." The September 22 version reads: "all persons held as slaves within any State or designated part of a State, the people whereof shall then be in rebellion against the United States, shall be then, thenceforward, and forever free." In contrast, the January 1 version reads: "all persons held as slaves within said designated States, and parts of States, are, and henceforward shall be free."

Guelzo writes, "He [Lincoln] had never believed that a military proclamation could guarantee freedom *forever*, beyond the time of the war emergency that called for it. Rather than give the judges even one more spike to hang the Proclamation on, at the last minute Lincoln withdrew what he knew he could not actually promise" (Guelzo, *Lincoln's Emancipation Proclamation*, pp. 180–1).

Lincoln seemed to endorse a very similar view. Speaking with respect to Fremont's order of emancipation, he said that the Constitution does not permit either a general or a president to "make permanent rules of property by a proclamation."[110] There was considerable uncertainty about how the Supreme Court would rule about the constitutionality of the Emancipation Proclamation after the war ended (particularly as long as Chief Justice Roger Taney lived (he died in October 1864)) and whether it would make the people freed during the war "forever free." This fact (together with the fact that the proclamation did not apply in all the areas of the United States that practiced slavery) meant that it was important for the opponents of slavery to push for a constitutional amendment to end slavery in the United States.

This brings me to my last point. The Emancipation Proclamation was not Lincoln's final word on slavery. His compromises with slavery ended in 1864 when he ran for reelection as a full-blown abolitionist and supported a constitutional amendment calling for the immediate and complete abolition of slavery. The president lobbied very aggressively to make sure that the Thirteenth Amendment, which ended slavery in the United States, received the necessary two-thirds vote in each House of Congress. It did receive the needed votes in the Senate, but on the first two votes, it fell short of the needed majority in the House of Representatives. He then authorized his political operatives to make patronage offers to induce congressmen to change their votes.[111] He told Congressman John Alley of Massachusetts to procure votes for the Thirteenth Amendment *any way he could*.[112] One border state congressman who voted for the amendment was subsequently appointed ambassador to Denmark.[113]

---

[110] Abraham Lincoln, *Speeches and Writings*, II, pp. 268–9.
[111] Burlingame, *Abraham Lincoln: A Life*, II, pp. 745–50.
[112] Foner, *The Fiery Trial*, p. 312.
[113] Ibid., p. 313.

Earlier, I stressed how little political support there was for the abolition of slavery when Lincoln became president in 1861. How did things change so quickly? The war was responsible for the huge change in public opinion in the North. Slavery came to be seen as the cause of the war and the immense suffering that it brought about, and people in the North wanted to do away with it. Many Northerners wanted to punish the slave owners; some people went so far as to call for the extermination of all 300,000 American slaveholders.[114] The public came to understand and appreciate the bravery and sacrifices of black soldiers that Lincoln went out of his way to emphasize. In addition, the war greatly undermined the institution of slavery. Hundreds of thousands of slaves freed themselves by running away during the war, and by the end of the war the institution was disintegrating, particularly in the border states. Delaware, Maryland, Missouri, Arkansas, Louisiana, and Tennessee all voted to abolish slavery before the end of the Civil War.[115] At the end of the war, Jefferson Davis offered to abolish slavery in the Confederate States of America in exchange for European diplomatic recognition. He also authorized the recruitment of slaves to be soldiers in the Confederate Army; those who served were promised their freedom.

Because of the tremendous evil and injustice of slavery, Lincoln's actions in all five of these cases might appear to be very wrong. However, his actions were morally justified in all of them.

II. Lincoln's Moral Philosophy: Senses in which He Was and Was Not a Utilitarian

In Part I, I argued that Lincoln's actions and policies in these five cases were justified because they had very good

---

[114] Burlingame, *Abraham Lincoln: A Life*, II, p. 365.
[115] McPherson, *Drawn with the Sword*, p. 207.

consequences, on balance. There are reasons to think that he would have justified his actions on similar grounds. He endorsed explicitly utilitarian moral principles on a number of occasions, but he also endorsed other moral principles. So to determine whether the utilitarian justification for his five actions/policies would have been acceptable to him, we must try to determine more clearly what were his moral views.

It is doubtful that Lincoln was a utilitarian, strictly speaking. It is more likely that he endorsed a qualified version of utilitarianism: utilitarianism subject to "side constraints" or a divine will moral theory. Further, there is reason to think that his views changed over time. In some respects – in particular, in his views about the obligation to keep promises – he moved closer to utilitarianism, but in other ways (e.g., his deepening belief in God and the duty to follow God's will), he seemed to move away from utilitarianism. However, in any case, by the end of his life, there was *no practical difference* between his moral views and those of utilitarians: the actions that his moral principles required him to perform were exactly the same as those that utilitarianism would require him to perform. For all practical purposes, he was a utilitarian by the end of his life and probably during the entire time he was president. So I conclude that he would have accepted the utilitarian justification of his five policies discussed in Part I. Now for the details of my argument.

    1. Utilitarianism is a moral theory about what makes actions right or wrong. It holds that the rightness or wrongness of an action is determined solely by the goodness or badness of its consequences and that an action is morally right provided that its consequences are at least as good, on balance, as those of any alternative action the agent could have performed instead.

This makes for a simple test of right and wrong: an action is morally right provided that there is no other alternative course of action that would have better consequences. If the agent could have done something else with better consequences, then her act is wrong. Utilitarians hold that a government policy is morally right or just provided that its overall consequences are at least as good as those of any alternative policy the government could have adopted instead. Standard versions of utilitarianism hold that the good to be maximized is human well-being or happiness and that we should act so as to maximize net human well-being or happiness, where each person's well-being or happiness counts equally. Bentham expressed this by saying that we should aim at "the greatest good of the greatest number,"[116] a formulation that Lincoln himself used.

2. There is considerable prima facie evidence that Lincoln was a utilitarian. He said that we should judge actions by their "fruits" (by which he meant consequences).[117] He also said,

I hold that while a man exists, it is his duty to improve not only his own condition, but to assist in ameliorating mankind; and, therefore, without entering into the details of the question, I will simply say, that I am for those means which will give the greatest good to the greatest number.[118]

The true rule, in determining to embrace, or reject any thing, is not whether it have any evil in it; but whether it have more of evil than of good. There are few things wholly evil, or wholly good. Almost everything, especially governmental policy, is an inescapable compound of the two; so that our

---

[116] Bentham's well-known catchphrase can be seriously misleading because it suggests that we should always do what benefits the majority of people. But utilitarianism does not say that. Sometimes a large benefit to a small number of people can outweigh a small benefit to a larger number of people.

[117] Miller, *Lincoln's Virtues*, p. 195 and Abraham Lincoln, *Speeches and Writings*, I, pp. 111–12.

[118] Abraham Lincoln, *Speeches and Writings*, II, p. 203 and Burlingame, *Abraham Lincoln: A Life*, II, p. 9.

best judgment of the preponderance between them is continually demanded.[119]

I would consent to any GREAT evil, to avoid a GREATER one.[120]

In a very early speech to the Washington Temperance Society of Springfield, he talked about the great good that the temperance movement had done without causing very much, if any, harm:

If the relative grandeur of revolutions shall be estimated by the great amount of human misery they alleviate, and the small amount of harm they inflict, then, indeed, will this be the grandest the world shall ever have seen.[121]

From the context of the speech, it is clear that he *is* saying that we should estimate the goodness of social movements by how much human misery they alleviate and inflict. In his "Eulogy on Henry Clay," he praised Clay for not wanting to *immediately* eradicate slavery because doing so would produce "a greater evil, even to the cause of human liberty itself."[122]

In an 1848 speech in Worcester, Massachusetts, Lincoln said that "when divine or human law does not clearly point out what *is* our duty" we must discern what our duty is "by using our most intelligent judgment of the consequences."[123]

---

[119] "Speech in the U.S. House of Representatives on Internal Improvements," Abraham Lincoln, *Speeches and Writings*, I, p. 192.

[120] "Speech on the Kansas-Nebraska Act," in ibid., p. 333.

[121] Ibid., p. 89.

[122] Ibid., p. 269.

[123] This speech criticized the "Free Soil" party and its presidential candidate Martin Van Buren. Lincoln claimed that the Whigs and their candidate Zachary Taylor were just as much opposed to the extension of slavery as the Free Soil party. Lincoln argued that supporting Van Buren would promote the election of the Democratic candidate, Cass, who supported the extension of slavery into new states and territories. Here is a larger portion of Lincoln's speech that contains this quoted passage:

Yet, despite this evidence for thinking that Lincoln was a utilitarian, there is also evidence to the contrary.

3. Utilitarianism requires that one violate the law whenever doing so will produce better consequences than obeying the law. But this feature of utilitarian is at odds with Lincoln's reverence for the law.

In a very early speech from 1838, Lincoln said, "Let every American... swear by the blood of the Revolution, never to violate in the least particular, the laws of the country; and never to tolerate their violation by others."[124] Still, his reverence for the law seemed to have a utilitarian rationale: his fear that general lawlessness and mob rule would result were people able to break the law with impunity.[125] And he clearly did not think that all people at all times and places

The "Free Soil" men in claiming that name indirectly attempted a deception, by implying the Whigs were *not* Free Soil men. In declaring that they would "do their duty and leave the consequences to God," merely gave an excuse for taking a course that they were not able to maintain by a fair and full argument. To make this declaration did not show what their duty was. If it did we should have no use for judgment, we might as well be made without intellect, and when divine or human law does not clearly point out what *is* our duty, we have no means of finding out what it is by using our most intelligent judgment of the consequences. If there were divine law, or human law for voting for Martin Van Buren, or if a fair examination of the consequences and the first reasoning would show that voting for him would have the best consequences and first reasoning would show that voting for him would bring about the ends they pretended to wish – then he [Lincoln] would give up the argument. But since there was no fixed law on the subject, and since the whole probable result of their action would be an assistance in electing Gen. Cass, he [Lincoln] must say that they were behind the Whigs in their advocacy of the freedom of the soil (Basler et al., ed., *The Collected Works of Abraham Lincoln*, Vol. 2, pp. 3–4).

This passage is from a summary transcription of Lincoln's speech in a Boston paper, the *Daily Advertiser*, September 14, 1848. That accounts for the fact that this is not written in the first-person voice and it talks about what "he" [Lincoln] said.

[124] Abraham Lincoln, *Speeches and Writings*, I, p. 32.
[125] "Address to Young Men's Lyceum of Springfield," in ibid., pp. 28–36.

have an unconditional duty to obey the law, because he held
that people oppressed by unjust governments have the right to
revolution and he approved of the American Revolution.[126]

His 1848 speech in Worcester seems to give priority to
following the law over doing what will have the best consequences in case of conflict. But, as president, he was willing
to defy the law for utilitarian reasons. He ignored and defied
Judge Taney's order overruling his suspension of habeas corpus in the Merryman case (see Chapter 3.I). In that case,
he was concerned with minimizing violations of the law as
opposed to maximizing welfare. He asked, "Are all the laws,
but one, to go unexecuted, and the government itself go to
pieces, lest that one be violated?"[127] In effect, he said that
he violated one law so that many other laws would not be
violated ("go unexecuted"). In that case, he put utilitarian
considerations ahead of obeying the law. Arguably, by the
end of his life he gave priority to doing what has the best
consequences over obeying the law.

4. Another reason to think that Lincoln was not a utilitarian is that he had a strong commitment to keeping
   promises. Sometimes following utilitarianism by doing
   what will have the best consequences requires one to
   break promises.

But as a young man, he had a very strong commitment to
keeping his promises, come what may. In an early letter,
from 1838, discussed in Chapter 9.I.4, he wrote, "I made
a point of honor and conscience in all things to stick to
my word, especially if others had been induced to act on
it."[128] In his personal life, he felt honor bound to keep his

---

[126] Ibid., pp. 167 and 32.
[127] "Address to Congress July 4, 1861," in Abraham Lincoln, *Speeches and Writings*, II, p. 253.
[128] Abraham Lincoln, *Speeches and Writings*, I, p. 38.

promises to marry Mary Owens and Mary Todd, even though he had grave doubts about the wisdom of getting married in both cases (see Chapter 9.I). He seemed to think that morality/honor required him to keep those promises, even at the cost of his personal happiness. In this connection, he quoted and endorsed his father's saying: "If you make a bad bargain, *hug* it the tighter."[129] He seemed to accept a very strong prohibition against breaking promises, a prohibition that sometimes superseded utilitarian considerations, making it right or obligatory to keep a promise in cases in which breaking it would result in much better consequences.

But his views about the duty to keep promises changed quite radically by the end of his life. In his last public speech on April 11, 1865, just three days before his assassination, he discussed his December 1863 Annual Message to Congress, which included a plan for the reconstruction of the United States after the end of the Civil War. He said that his earlier speech had made a promise to states that had seceded from the Union and added,

But as bad promises are better broken than kept, I shall treat this as a bad promise, and break it, whenever I shall be convinced that keeping it is adverse to the public interest. But I have not yet been so convinced.[130]

His final view that bad promises should be broken rather than kept was a sharp departure from his earlier position that bad bargains should be kept ("held all the tighter"). His criteria for bad promises in his April 11 speech were explicitly utilitarian; he said that bad promises should be broken, provided that keeping them would be adverse to the public interest. But Lincoln apparently made a sharp distinction between

---

[129] Ibid., p. 91.
[130] Ibid., p. 698.

ordinary promises and oaths, which we might describe as
solemn promises.

> 5. He took very seriously his oath of office to "faithfully
> execute the Office of President of the United States,
> and... preserve, protect, and defend the Constitution
> of the United States," calling it "an oath registered in
> Heaven."[131] He made a distinction between his official
> duty as president, which required him to follow the U.S.
> Constitution and execute the laws of the United States,
> and his personal moral beliefs.

He thought that slavery was morally wrong, but that his
public duty required him to follow and execute laws that
protected the institution of slavery.[132] In his third debate
with Douglas, he said that although he believed that slavery
is wrong, it would be his duty as a member of Congress to
vote for a fugitive slave law.[133] His argument was that members of Congress take an oath to support the Constitution of
the United States and the Constitution includes this explicit
provision: "No person held to service or labor in one State
under the laws thereof, escaping into another, shall in consequence of any law or regulation therein be discharged from
such labor, but shall be delivered up on claim of the party
to whom such labor or service may be due." He quoted this
passage and then said,

[T]here is a Constitutional right which needs legislation to enforce
it. And although it is distasteful to me, I have sworn to support
the Constitution, and having so sworn cannot conceive that I do

---

[131] First Inaugural Address, in Abraham Lincoln, *Speeches and Writings*, II,
p. 224. One might take "an oath registered in heaven" to mean "an
oath/promise to God." But a more likely and literal reading of this is "oaths
noted by heaven/God." Oaths *noted* by (registered by) God are not necessary
oaths *to* God.
[132] "Letter to Horace Greeley," in ibid., p. 358.
[133] Abraham Lincoln, *Speeches and Writings*, I, p. 620.

support it if I withheld from that right any necessary legislation to make it practical.[134]

In his January 1863 public letter to the workingmen of Manchester, England, which was read during a rally in support of the Union, Lincoln said that he was bound by his oath of office "to maintain and preserve at once the Constitution and the integrity of the federal republic."[135] In a public letter from April 1864, he wrote,

I am naturally antislavery. If slavery is not wrong, nothing is wrong. I can not remember when I did not so think, and feel. And yet I have never understood that the Presidency conferred upon me an unrestricted right to act officially upon this judgment and feeling. It was in the oath I took that I would, to the best of my ability, preserve, protect, and defend the Constitution of the United States. I could not take the office without taking the oath. Nor was it my view that I might take an oath to get power, and break the oath in using the power. I understood, too, that in ordinary civil administration this oath even forbade me to practically indulge my primary abstract judgment on the moral question of slavery. I had publicly declared this many times, and in many ways. And I aver that, to this day, I have done no official act in mere deference to my abstract judgment and feeling on slavery. I did understand however, that my oath to preserve the constitution to the best of my ability, imposed upon me the duty of preserving, by every indispensable means, that government – that nation – of which that constitution was the organic law.[136]

In that letter he seemed to take his duty to abide by his oath of office to be an absolute or unconditional obligation.

6. Lincoln's frequent statements to the effect that we should follow God's will are another objection to the view that he was a utilitarian.

---

[134] Ibid.
[135] Abraham Lincoln, *Speeches and Writings*, II, pp. 431–2.
[136] Ibid., p. 585.

In his 1848 speech in Worcester and other statements discussed later, he gave priority to following God's will over
following utilitarianism. He seemed to say that the obligation to follow God's will, *when one can discern it*, is an
absolute unconditional obligation. In a public response to
a group pressing him to free the slaves in September 1862,
just nine days before he issued the preliminary version of the
Emancipation Proclamation, he said,

I hope it will not be irreverent for me to say that if it is probable
that God would reveal his will to others, on a point so connected
with my duty, it might be supposed he would reveal it directly to
me . . . it is my earnest desire to know the will of Providence in this
matter. *And if I can learn what it is I will do it!* These are not,
however, the days of miracles, and I suppose it will be granted that
I am not to expect a direct revelation. I must study the plain facts
of the case, ascertain what is possible and learn what appears to
be right.[137]

Here, as in his 1848 speech in Worcester he gave priority to following God's will over utilitarian considerations. In
his reflection "On Pro-Slavery Theology," from 1858, he discussed the views of Frederick Ross, who defended slavery and
claimed that American slavery was in accordance with God's
will. He endorsed the idea that we should follow God's will,
but said that there is difficulty in ascertaining it: "Certainly
there is no contending against the will of God; but still there is
some difficulty in ascertaining, and applying it, to particular
cases."[138]

He was clearly committed to the view that if God exists
and we can discern God's will, then we should follow it.
But from these passages alone, we cannot conclude that he
believed that God exists or that we can, in fact, ever discern
God's will. (An atheist could hold that *if* God existed and

---

[137] Ibid., p. 361.
[138] Abraham Lincoln, *Speeches and Writings*, I, p. 685.

revealed his will to us, we should follow God's will.) But there is considerable evidence that, while he was president, he believed in God and earnestly prayed and sought to learn and do God's will (see Chapter 8.6). On at least one occasion he claimed to have discerned and followed God's will. In 1862, during Lee's first invasion of the North, he made a solemn vow to God to issue the Emancipation Proclamation if the Union defeated Lee's invasion. He reported this vow to his cabinet and told them that, because of the Union victory at the Battle of Antietam on September 17, 1862, "God had decided this question in favor of the slaves."[139] In an 1859 speech he came close to saying that he had discerned God's will concerning slavery:

I hold that if there is any one thing that can be proved to be the will of God by external nature around us, without reference to revelation, it is the proposition that whatever any one man earns with his hands and by the sweat of his brow, he shall enjoy in peace. I say that whereas God Almighty has given every man one mouth to be fed, and one pair of hands adapted to furnish food for that mouth, if anything be proved to be the will of Heaven, it is proved by this fact, that the mouth is to be fed with those hands, without being interfered with by any other man who has hands to labor with. I hold that if the Almighty had ever made a set of men that should do all the eating and none of the work, he would have made them with mouths only and not hands, and if he had ever made another class that he had intended should do all the work and none of the eating, he would have made them with all hands.[140]

7. Utilitarianism can, in principle, conflict with these other principles that Lincoln endorsed. It is doubtful that he had a fully worked out and consistent moral philosophy.

---

[139] This was reported by Secretary of the Navy Gideon Welles; see Fehrenbacher and Fehrenbacher, *Recollected Words of Abraham Lincoln*, p. 474.

[140] Abraham Lincoln, *Speeches and Writings*, II, p. 85. Also see Lincoln's Speech at Hartford, March 5, 1860, in Basler, ed., *The Collected Works of Abraham Lincoln*, IV, p. 9.

Because he apparently thought that, in practice, there were few, if any, serious conflicts between utilitarianism and these other moral principles (I justify this claim in 2.II.9), he might not have been interested in determining which principles were most fundamental or which took precedence in case of conflict. So one interpretation of his moral views is that he endorsed a number of different moral principles and had no opinion about which were most fundamental.[141]

But there are several other possible interpretations of Lincoln's moral philosophy. Perhaps he was a full-fledged utilitarian without qualification, and perhaps he endorsed utilitarianism subject to side constraints (i.e., he held that people should act so as to produce the best consequences within certain constraints, such as obeying the law and keeping one's promises). Two other possible interpretations are these: (1) he believed that following God's will or obeying God is the ultimate moral standard, but that it is seldom possible to discern God's will and that we should follow utilitarianism when we cannot discern God's will, or (2) he believed that following God's will or obeying God is the ultimate moral standard, but also believed that it is seldom possible to discern God's will and that we should follow a version of utilitarianism with side constraints (e.g., keeping solemn promises) when we cannot discern God's will.

8. There is evidence that Lincoln's moral views at the end of his life were considerably different from his earlier moral views.

Some of Lincoln's early writings show both utilitarian leanings and reverence for the law, so the view that he endorsed utilitarianism with side constraints might be the most accurate interpretation of his views in the 1830s when he was

---

[141] However, even if this is the case, there still might be facts about what he would have thought and done if he had thought about possible conflicts between these different principles.

a strong critic of conventional Christianity (see Chapter 8.6). But it is doubtful that he was ever an atheist, and another possible interpretation of his early moral views is that he endorsed a divine will moral theory and held we should follow a version of utilitarianism with side constraints (e.g., keeping solemn promises), when, as is generally the case, we cannot discern God's will. This latter interpretation makes the most sense of his 1848 speech in Worcester in which he said "when divine or human law does not clearly point out what *is* our duty" we must discern what our duty is "by using our most intelligent judgment of the consequences."

At the end of his life, Lincoln did not endorse the duty to keep ordinary promises as a side constraint on utilitarianism. He may have also not endorsed obeying the law as a side constraint. So it is possible that he was a full-blown utilitarian at the end of his life. But this interpretation requires us to say that his frequent statements to the effect that we should follow God's will when we can discern it and about his duty to abide by his oath of office were insincere. But this is unlikely, and it is also unlikely that he lied to his cabinet about his reasons for issuing the Emancipation Proclamation.

In private notes that were written to himself and clearly not intended to mislead the public about his piety, he clearly endorsed the view that we must follow God's will when we can discern it. (See his reflection "On Pro-Slavery Theology" from 1858 that I quoted earlier.) His "Meditation on the Divine Will," written in early September 1862 shortly before he issued the preliminary Emancipation Proclamation,[142] also provides strong evidence that he sought to discern and follow God's will:

In the present civil war it is quite possible that God's purpose is something different from the purpose of either party – and yet human instrumentalities, working just as they do, are of the best adaptation to effect His purpose. I am almost ready to say this is

---

[142] Abraham Lincoln, *Speeches and Writings*, II, p. 359.

probably true – that God wills this contest, and that it not end
yet. . . . He could have either *saved* or *destroyed* the Union without
a human contest. . . . Yet the contest proceeds.[143]

This note supports the view that Lincoln was sincere when
he told his cabinet that he sought to discern God's will when
he issued the Emancipation Proclamation several weeks later.
I think that his final moral view is roughly this: he thought
that we should follow God's will when we can discern it,
and when we cannot discern God's will we should follow
utilitarianism subject to the side constraint that we should
abide by our solemn oaths.

9. Although Lincoln was not a utilitarian in the strict sense,
   by late in his life, the actions that he thought it was
   morally right for him to perform were the same as those
   that he thought would have the best consequences.

Further, because he very seldom thought that he could discern
God's will and because he usually made choices about issues
to which his oath of office did not apply, his actions were
usually consciously guided by utilitarian considerations. His
views about the obligation to keep promises were explicitly
utilitarian. His views about the duty to obey the law may have
also been utilitarian. And even if his views about obeying the
law were not fully utilitarian, they differed very little in practice from what utilitarians would say about the obligations of
leaders in his position, because he had very limited ability to
defy the law. He knew that the powers of the Supreme Court
and Congress were such that he was unlikely to succeed in
any course of action that was clearly contrary to the U.S.
Constitution and his oath of office. He never took himself to
be in a position in which utilitarian principles required him to
violate the duties created by his oath of office. (It is important

[143] Ibid., p. 339.

to stress that in the Merryman case when he defied the order of Taney's Court and thus broke the law, he still took himself to be acting in accordance with his oath of office to "execute" the laws of the United States [see Chapter 3.I]).

Even near the end of his life, Lincoln apparently endorsed two absolute or nearly absolute moral obligations: the duty to obey God and the duty to keep solemn oaths. In principle, these two obligations could conflict with utilitarianism. However, because he did not think that humans could reasonably discern God's will very often, he very seldom guided his actions by the duty to obey God. His decision to issue the Emancipation Proclamation was an exception. He also claimed (or came close to claiming) to know that slavery was contrary to God's will. But these are surely cases in which he took following God's will to be consistent with the utilitarian goal of maximizing human welfare. So, *in practice*, there was *no difference* between his moral views and those of a utilitarian. There is *not a single case* during his time as president in which he took himself to be in a position in which by bringing about the best results (following utilitarianism) he would be violating his oath of office or the will of God.

In conclusion, it is not simply the case that utilitarianism justifies his actions and policies in the five cases in question. He himself would have justified them on utilitarian grounds even though, strictly speaking, he probably was not a utilitarian.

III. Complications: Two Versions of Utilitarianism and a New Criticism

The utilitarian tradition has developed considerably since Lincoln's lifetime. Since the early twentieth century, philosophers have commonly distinguished between two versions of utilitarianism. This distinction not only sheds light on moral issues regarding Lincoln but also complicates our analysis considerably. What I call the "actual consequences version" of utilitarianism holds that an action is morally right if, and only if, it results in the best consequences overall of all the courses of action open to the agent. This is the traditional version of utilitarianism and the version that Lincoln understood and frequently invoked. It says that we should always do whatever will have the best consequences and that the rightness or wrongness of actions depends on their *actual* consequences. More precisely, this version of utilitarianism holds that:

An act is morally right if and only if there is no other possible alternative act open to the agent that would result in a better balance of good consequences relative to bad consequences. (This is equivalent to saying that utilitarianism is the view that an action is morally right if, and only if, no alternative course of action would result in better consequences overall.)

An alternative version of utilitarianism first formulated (but not endorsed) by G. E. Moore[144] can be stated as follows:

An act is morally right if, and only if, of all the courses of action open to the agent, that action's antecedently probable or likely consequences are the best overall.

I call this the "probable consequences version" of utilitarianism.

The actual consequences of Lincoln's actions were not what he or anyone else expected them to be. They were both *much better* and *much worse* than he or almost anyone else expected. He stated this very memorably in his Second Inaugural Address. Hardly anyone expected that the Civil War

---

[144] G. E. Moore considers this option in the following passage:

For these reasons many people are strongly inclined to hold that they [right and wrong] do *not* depend upon the *actual* consequences, but only upon those which were antecedently *probable*, or which it was *possible* for him to *foresee* (Moore, *Ethics*, p. 99).

de and duration" that it had or that
iding result" of ending slavery.

This raises the question of whether Lincoln's actions were
justified according to the probable consequences version of
utilitarianism. My answer is "yes." There are several prob-
abilities we need to consider. The probable consequences of
the independence of the Confederate States of America were
much as he believed them to be. He correctly and justifiably
believed that if he did not make the five compromises out-
lined earlier, the South would win the Civil War and gain
its independence. In addition, he correctly and justifiably
believed that an independent CSA would strengthen, enlarge,
and perpetuate the institution of slavery in the South. Had it
gained its independence, the Confederacy would also likely
have reinvigorated and prolonged slavery in Latin America.
I defend these claims at length in Chapter 4.I.

We also need to determine the probable consequences of
his decision to fight the Civil War in 1861 (and his decisions at later times to continue fighting the war). The war
was extremely bloody and protracted and caused immense
suffering. It is controversial whether the actual extent and
gravity of the war were antecedently probable at the beginning of the war. But, later when the extent and horror of the
war were clear to all, these very bad consequences were overwhelmingly probable consequences of his repeated decision
to continue fighting the war. I discuss these issues at length
in Chapter 4.II and argue that both the actual and probable
consequences versions of utilitarianism imply that the Union
was justified in fighting the Civil War. An important part
of my argument there is that, as the war continued and the
extent of the death and suffering it caused became clear to
all, the Union's war aims also changed: the war became a war
to end slavery, and thus the probable good that would come
from fighting and winning the war greatly increased.

One might respond to my defense of Lincoln's actions earlier in this chapter by saying that, even if we accept all of this, he was just *very lucky* that things turned out for the best. Even if what he did was right, that was largely a matter of luck. The actual consequences of his actions might have been for the best, but he did not know and could not have known their actual consequences. My arguments in the first part of this chapter appeal to the actual consequences version of utilitarianism. Just as one can do or fail to do the action that actually has the best consequences due to good or bad moral luck, so one can perform or fail to perform the action whose antecedently probable consequences are best due to good or bad moral luck. The probable consequences version of utilitarianism also allows for the possibility of moral luck. So, for the purposes of assessing his moral luck, it is not sufficient to determine the antecedently probable consequences of his actions. We also need to consider what he expected (and reasonably expected) would be the consequences of his actions.

Lincoln was an extraordinarily farsighted politician who understood the likely outcomes of his policies better than any of his contemporaries (see Chapter 6.II). He clearly did not have the kind of blind moral luck that is involved when a person's actions have good consequences and turn out to be morally right contrary to all reasonable expectations. But the issue of his moral luck is very complicated and needs to be discussed in much more detail. I address these questions in Chapter 4.II.4 and Chapter 6 where I argue that he enjoyed considerable good moral luck in that many of his most important actions and policies turned out very well, when they easily might not have. However, I also argue that he was *justified* in thinking that those actions and policies would turn out for the best, even though almost no one, including Lincoln, accurately predicted the outcome of the Civil War.

IV. A Non-Utilitarian Defense of Lincoln

Given either version of utilitarianism, his actions and policies concerning slavery can be readily defended. For my own part, I am sympathetic to the idea that these kinds of questions should be answered on utilitarian grounds, but it is very controversial whether utilitarianism is true. I do not want my defense of him to depend on the truth of utilitarianism, even if he was a utilitarian or close to being one. I now propose an alternative argument that appeals to non-utilitarian moral principles that are much less controversial than utilitarianism.

American slavery was such a great evil and violation of human rights that the need to minimize that evil overrode all other considerations. In saying this, I am not assuming the truth of the utilitarian view that any means are justified to achieve ends that are slightly better, on balance, than any other ends one might bring about. I am only assuming that sometimes certain evils are so great that the need to minimize them outweighs all relevant countervailing moral considerations.

Lincoln's actions can be justified on these reasonable non-utilitarian grounds. The objection to utilitarianism that is most salient for thinking about the five cases discussed earlier is that it holds that one can be justified in violating fundamental rights such as the right to liberty in order to maximize human happiness or welfare. Many anti-utilitarians would argue that, by not moving earlier and more forcefully against slavery, he violated the rights of American slaves – in particular, the rights of those people who were not freed from slavery because he countermanded Fremont's and Hunter's orders for emancipation.

The gist of my non-utilitarian defense of his actions in these five cases is that public officials are not obligated to violate unjust laws that deprive people of their moral rights in order to try to protect the rights in question, if doing so would be self-defeating and make things much worse with respect to the very rights in question. More specifically, he was not obligated to defy the extremely unjust laws constitutive of the institution of slavery that deprived people of their right to liberty because (1) doing so would not have done much good (it would have been futile), (2) doing so would have led to much greater violations of people's right to liberty (it would have been counterproductive), (3) relatively few of the slaves who would have been freed if he had upheld Fremont's and Hunter's orders for emancipation or if he had declared emancipation in 1861 would have been able to retain their freedom for very long, and (4) his willingness to enforce these unjust laws was necessary for him to succeed in eventually eliminating those very same laws and thereby securing every American's right to liberty. (Again, the great majority of the people he might have freed if he had upheld Fremont's and Hunter's orders or if he had declared the emancipation of all the slaves in 1861 were not harmed by his actions – they were better off and enjoyed much greater liberty during their lives because of his actions.)

The following non-utilitarian moral principle[145] justifies all of Lincoln's actions in question:

P. It is morally permissible for a public official to comply with and enforce an unjust law that permits violations of people's right to X and publicly agree to do this, provided that (1) refusing to enforce the law would be *futile*: it would not succeed in preventing the unjust law from being enforced and violating people's right to X; (2) refusing to enforce the law would be *counterproductive*: it would result in a much greater number of violations of the right to

---

[145] P is a non-utilitarian principle in that accepting it is consistent with rejecting utilitarianism, but P is also consistent with utilitarianism. It is a principle that both utilitarians and non-utilitarians can and should accept.

X and make things much worse with respect to violations of right X; (3) only a small percentage of those whose right to X would be protected if the official defied the unjust law in question would have their right to X protected for more than a brief period of time; and (4) the official eventually eliminates the unjust law in question and thereby secures everyone's right to X and his or her following and enforcing the unjust law in question is *necessary* in order to bring this about.

P is quite defensible: indeed it cannot be reasonably rejected, because it is unreasonable for those who care about human rights to insist that public officials try to protect people's rights by defying unjust laws when doing so would be both futile and counterproductive with respect to the very rights in question. More generally, it is unreasonable to insist that people pursue morally desirable ends by means that are both futile and counterproductive.

Lincoln's compromises with slavery at the beginning of his presidency (in particular, his willingness to enforce the very unjust laws concerning slavery mandated by the U.S. Constitution and his rescinding of Fremont's and Hunter's orders for emancipation) satisfy all four conditions of P. If he had not made these compromises, the Confederacy would have gained its independence, and the evils of American slavery (and the violations of human rights inherent in it) would have been greatly enlarged. If he had done otherwise, very few of those he might have freed (and very few of those Fremont and Hunter might have freed) would have been able to maintain their freedom for very long, because those actions would probably have caused the Union to lose the Civil War. In addition, it is likely that he would have been overruled by the Supreme Court or Congress. He and his supporters abolished slavery; they could not have done this unless the Union won the Civil War, and winning the war required him to make the compromises he made early in the war.[146] Only by acting in accordance with the law could he have eventually brought the full power of the U.S. government to bear against slavery.

P should not be confused with the following view, which is sometimes called "utilitarianism of rights":

P2. One should act so as to minimize violations of people's moral rights.

My defense of Lincoln does not require me to endorse P2 or any other principle as similar to traditional utilitarianism as P2. However, I do endorse the following principle:

P3. Other things equal, it is morally permissible to do something that violates certain people's moral rights, provided that doing so is *necessary* to prevent an *enormously greater* violation of moral rights.

Some of my arguments in Chapters 3–5 appeal to P3.

---

[146] *A Digression for Philosophers and Economists.* Consider what I call the "Pareto optimal version" of P, which involves replacing condition 3 of P with the following:

3'. *None* of the people whose right to X would be protected if the official defied the unjust law in question would have their right to X protected for more than a brief period of time, and *all* of them would be better off and better off with respect to right X if the official does not defy the law.

There are very compelling reasons to accept the Pareto optimal version of P – it would be extremely unreasonable to reject it, but it is doubtful that all of Lincoln's actions satisfied condition 3'. At least some of the people in Missouri who would have been freed if he had not rescinded Fremont's order (and at least some of the people who would have become free if he had declared a general emancipation in 1861) might have escaped to Canada. Those individuals might have benefited from such actions, even if I am correct in thinking that those actions would have led to Confederate victory and, on balance, would have had very bad consequences for the great majority of people held in slavery. My defense of Lincoln only requires me to defend something like my original version of P.

Conclusion

Lincoln's many compromises with slavery during his first three and a quarter years as president were morally justified because they were necessary for him to fight and win the Civil War. The independence of the CSA would have been a catastrophe for the antislavery cause. In Chapter 4, I explain why and argue that Lincoln and the Union were morally justified in fighting the war.

Some readers might think that my arguments still smack far too much of utilitarianism. But I can show that most of these criticisms of Lincoln are unjustified (as opposed to giving a positive argument to show that his actions in these cases were morally right) without appealing to any utilitarian or quasi-utilitarian principles. If one accepts my account of the facts, then one must reject the criticism that he did not try to abolish slavery at the beginning of his presidency, as well as the criticisms about Fremont and the Emancipation Proclamation. These criticisms violate obvious and noncontroversial constraints on moral judgments – they violate the principle that "ought implies can" (Lincoln did not have the power do the things that the critics contend that he ought to have done) and the principle that it makes no sense to demand that someone try to achieve goals by means that are *self-defeating*. It is absurd to demand that one pursue ends by means that are self-defeating.

3

Habeas Corpus, Colonization, and the Status and Rights of Free African Americans

This chapter addresses five of Lincoln's most controversial and morally questionable actions and policies.

I. Lincoln's Suspension of Habeas Corpus

The principle of habeas corpus stated in the U.S. Constitution requires that people who are held in jail be charged with a crime or else released. It forbids the government from imprisoning people indefinitely without charging them with a crime. Article One, Section 9 of the Constitution says that "[t]he privilege of the writ of habeas corpus shall not be suspended, unless when in cases of rebellion or invasion the public safety may require it." Lincoln suspended the writ of habeas corpus during the Civil War, causing thousands of people to be imprisoned without due process of law. Some argue that this suspension was unconstitutional and that Lincoln acted wrongly and greatly abused and exceeded the powers of his office.

1. What Lincoln Did

Very early in the Civil War, in April 1861, he suspended the writ of habeas corpus between Philadelphia and Washington,

D.C.[1] He did this in response to the actions of Confederate sympathizers in Maryland who attacked Union troops passing through Baltimore, tore down telegraph wires, and burned railroad bridges linking the capital with the North.[2] Several months later, in September 1861, a special session of the Maryland legislature was called to consider voting for secession. James McPherson describes Lincoln's response:

Lincoln decided to take drastic action. Union troops sealed off Frederick (where the legislature was meeting) and arrested thirty-one secessionist members along with numerous other suspected accessories to the plot, including Mayor George Brown of Baltimore. All were imprisoned for at least two months, until after the election of a new legislature in November.[3]

On October 14, 1861, Lincoln extended the suspension of habeas corpus to the entire Eastern Seaboard from Washington, D.C., to Bangor, Maine.[4]

The following year, on August 8, 1862, the government published an order authorizing U.S. marshals and police to arrest "any persons who may be engaged, by act, speech, or writing, in discouraging volunteer enlistments, or in any way giving aid or comfort to the enemy, or in any other disloyal practice against the United States."[5] Lincoln suspended habeas corpus throughout the entire United States on September 24, 1862; in doing so, he also authorized martial law and trials by military courts of "all Rebels and Insurgents, their aiders and abettors within the United States, and

---

[1] Neely, *The Fate of Liberty*, p. 8.
[2] McPherson, *This Mighty Scourge*, p. 213.
[3] McPherson, *Battle Cry of Freedom*, p. 289. Generals Scott and Butler wanted to arrest members of the Maryland legislature who supported secession earlier in April 1861, but Lincoln did not permit this then; Neely, *The Fate of Liberty*, pp. 6–7. The new legislature elected in September refused to vote on an ordinance of secession; ibid., p. 7.
[4] Neely, *The Fate of Liberty*, p. 14.
[5] Ibid., p. 53.

all persons discouraging volunteer enlistment, resisting military drafts, or guilty of any disloyal practice, affording aid and comfort to Rebels against the authority of the United States."[6] In March 1863 Congress passed a law giving Lincoln the authority to suspend habeas corpus.[7] Lincoln issued a revised order for the suspension of habeas corpus throughout the entire United States for the duration of the war on September 15, 1863. At least 14000 people were jailed as a result of Lincoln's actions.[8] Most were only held for a few weeks or months and then released after taking an oath of loyalty.[9]

One exception was the case of former Ohio congressman Clement Vallandigham. In May 1863, he was arrested and tried by a military tribunal, which sentenced him to prison for the rest of the war.[10] He was charged with uttering "disloyal sentiments and opinions, with the object and purpose of weakening the power of the Government [to suppress] an unlawful rebellion." Lincoln was surprised and embarrassed by the tribunal's action, but decided not to overturn Vallandigham's conviction.[11] Instead he commuted Vallandigham's sentence to banishment to the Confederacy. Vallandigham left the Confederacy for Canada and was then nominated by the Democrats to be governor of Ohio (he lost the election).

In a public statement about this case, Lincoln denied that Vallandigham had been arrested simply because of his political statements. Vallandigham and other opponents of the war sought to undermine the military draft. Noting that the

---

[6] McPherson, *This Mighty Scourge*, p. 213; McPherson quotes a passage from Abraham Lincoln, *Speeches and Writings*, II, p. 371.

[7] McPherson, *This Mighty Scourge*, p. 215.

[8] Neely, *The Fate of Liberty*, pp. 231 and 130.

[9] McPherson, *This Mighty Scourge*, pp. 213 and 215.

[10] Ibid., p. 215.

[11] Ibid.

penalty for desertion from the army was death, Lincoln said, "Must I shoot a simple-minded soldier boy who deserts, while I must not touch the hair of a wily agitator who induces him to desert?"[12]

However, Lincoln's denial to the contrary, imprisoning Vallandigham *was* tantamount to punishing political expression. The president's wartime policies (which called for the arrest of "aiders and abettors" of the rebel cause and those who discouraged enlistments in the Union Army) clearly permitted the punishment of people for expressing certain political views. The policy authorizing the arrest of anyone who discouraged people from enlisting in the military and of anyone who gave aid or comfort to the enemy during the Civil War constituted a significant abridgement of freedom of expression in the United States.

2. Constitutional Issues

Was it constitutional for Lincoln to suspend habeas corpus? He claimed that it was, because the U.S. Constitution states that habeas corpus can be suspended in time of rebellion or invasion when public safety may require it.[13] However, it does not explicitly state who has the authority to suspend habeas corpus. Chief Justice Roger Taney, acting in his dual capacity as a judge in a lower federal court, said that only Congress had the authority to do this. The fact that permission to suspend habeas corpus is stated in a part of the Constitution that deals with the powers of Congress supports Taney's interpretation.[14]

---

[12] Ibid., p. 216.

[13] Address to Congress July 4, 1861, in Abraham Lincoln, *Speeches and Writings*, II, p. 253.

[14] McPherson, *This Mighty Scourge*, pp. 213–14. One might argue that because Congress was not in session during April 1861, it fell to Lincoln to suspend habeas corpus. But this consideration does not get Lincoln off the hook for defying the Constitution. Congress returned to session after April 1861, but

But this consideration alone is not decisive. Lincoln claimed that he had a higher constitutional duty to preserve the Union. According to McPherson, Lincoln claimed that his oath to

"preserve, protect, and defend the Constitution of the United States" ... overrode his obligation to heed a less specific provision in the Constitution – or, as a modern constitutional scholar expressed it, "*a part cannot be supreme over the whole, to the injury or destruction of the whole.*"[15]

Another way of expressing Lincoln's claim is that he thought that he best preserved and protected the Constitution as a whole by violating one of its particular provisions. In an address to Congress he said,

The whole of the laws which were to be faithfully executed, were being resisted, and failing of execution in nearly one-third of the States. Must they be allowed to finally fail of execution ... [because] some single law ... should, to a very limited extent, be violated? To state the question more directly, are all the laws, *but one*, to go unexecuted, and the government itself go to pieces, lest that one be violated?[16]

Lincoln frequently appealed to his oath of office, which he called "an oath registered in heaven" (see Chapter 2.II.5), to defend his actions. This oath required him "to faithfully execute the office of President of the United States" and to "preserve, protect, and defend the Constitution of the United States." His office, as head of the executive branch of the federal government, required him to ensure the execution of federal laws. Given Judge Taney's order, Lincoln had to defy one law (one court order) in order to protect the entire system of law. His argument seemed to be that in suspending habeas

did not vote to give Lincoln the authority to suspend habeas corpus until March 1863 – almost two years after Lincoln's initial action.

[15] Ibid., p. 213.

[16] Address to Congress July 4, 1861, in Abraham Lincoln, *Speeches and Writings*, II, p. 253.

corpus he much more fully fulfilled his duty to execute the laws of the United States than he would have otherwise.

The presidential oath of office requires the president both to execute the laws of the United States and to uphold and defend the Constitution. If it was unconstitutional for Lincoln to suspend habeas corpus, then he had a conflict of duties: he could not fully execute the laws of the United States without suppressing the rebellion, and he could not do that without at least partly suspending habeas corpus, which, by hypothesis, was unconstitutional. If he faced this kind of conflict of duties, then it is arguable that his obligation to execute the laws in one third of the country was greater than his duty to follow one particular provision of the Constitution.

So it is something of an open question whether Lincoln's actions were constitutional. But, constitutional or not, his first suspension of habeas corpus between Philadelphia and Washington at the beginning of the Civil War was morally justified. There was a grave danger that the capital and government would be cut off from the rest of the country at the beginning of the Civil War. That would have made it impossible for the federal government to function properly and made it very difficult for the U.S. government to prevent the CSA from gaining its independence.

3. Moral Questions

Was he justified in later extending the order to the entire country and keeping it in effect until the end of the war? Was he justified in imposing the limitations on freedom of expression and political speech involved in this action? I hold that roughly those measures that were necessary for winning the war were justified, and those measures not necessary for winning the war were not justified. It is unclear what we should say about those measures, if any, that were not necessary to win the war but that still helped to win it more quickly and thus saved lives.

Lincoln's suspension of habeas corpus and the limitations on freedom of expression that he ordered were justified if they were necessary to win the Civil War. However, saying this does not commit me to the view that the leaders of a nation are justified in suspending habeas corpus and limiting freedom of expression whenever doing so is necessary for winning a war. For example, that a nation needed to suspend habeas corpus and severely limit the rights of its citizens in order to win an unjust war of conquest would not justify it in taking such actions. (It should be noted that the U.S. Constitution does not permit the suspension of habeas corpus for foreign wars, but only in case of "rebellion or invasion when public safety may require it.") To the extent that they were necessary to win the war and prevent the *enormous* evils that would have resulted from Confederate independence (see Chapter 4.I), Lincoln's actions were morally justified. His suspension of habeas corpus resulted in an *enormously smaller* violation of human rights than those that would have occurred as a result of the independence of the Confederate States of America. So, his actions that were necessary to win the war were clearly justified according to principle P3 from Chapter 2.IV:

P3. Other things equal, it is morally permissible to do something that violates certain people's moral rights, provided that doing so is *necessary* to prevent an *enormously greater* violation of moral rights.

The relevant historical facts that bear on these principles are considerably less clear. Were suspending habeas corpus throughout the entire country and suppressing the expression of antiwar views that gave "aid and comfort to the enemy" necessary to win the Civil War? Even if they were not necessary for victory, did some of these measures help the Union win the war or win more quickly (thereby saving lives)? These are very difficult questions that I do not venture to answer.

But even if the answer to these questions is "no" (which I think would imply that these policies were wrong), Lincoln's actions were not unreasonable. The country was in mortal peril. In the summer of 1863 there were huge draft riots in New York City that killed more than a hundred people.[17] He erred on the side of protecting the country and avoiding much worse violations of human rights that would have followed from a Confederate victory.

A further issue: how greatly did Lincoln suppress free political discourse during the Civil War? Some earlier historians argued that he oversaw a very large-scale suppression of political speech and political freedom during the war, but that he was justified in his actions because they were in response to large-scale opposition to the war in the North. However, Mark Neely rejects those earlier justifications of Lincoln's actions and claims that careful research by Frank Klement "has proved, beyond any reasonable doubt, that no systematic, organized disloyal opposition to the war existed in the North."[18] This prompts the question of whether Lincoln or his subordinates succumbed to the temptation to eliminate political opposition by the use of military arrests.[19] To answer this question, Neely did a careful analysis of the records of those imprisoned by the U.S. military during the war and reached the following conclusions:

Precise figures are not available [because the records of those arrested are scattered and incomplete], but historians can nevertheless be precise about what the available figures mean. They indicate that there were few arrests above the border states. They show that after 1862 a majority of the citizens arrested were citizens of the Confederacy. They suggest a variety of causes for arrest of Northerners, among which, speaking, writing, and gathering

---

[17] McPherson calls it the worst riot in U.S. history, McPherson, *Battle Cry of Freedom*, p. 610.

[18] Neely, *The Fate of Liberty*, p. xii; also see p. 229.

[19] Ibid., p. xii.

in political groups were rare. They show that more citizens were arrested than . . . any historian writing since the turn of the century had thought. There were more arrests, but they had less significance for traditional civil liberty than anyone has realized.[20]

Thus, according to these findings, a large percentage of those arrested were blockade runners, Confederate deserters, and people trading with the Confederates.[21] For the most part, their political views were irrelevant to their being arrested, and a majority of the arrests would have occurred without Lincoln's suspension of habeas corpus.[22]

But Neely is still very critical of Lincoln's August 8, 1862, order authorizing U.S. marshals and police to arrest "any persons who may be engaged, by act, speech, or writing, in discouraging volunteer enlistments, or in any way giving aid or comfort to the enemy, or in any other disloyal practice against the United States" (Lincoln reaffirmed these provisions of the August 8 order in his September 24, 1862, suspension of habeas corpus throughout the entire United States).[23] This was a very bad precept, but it did not seem to have been enforced zealously.

Lincoln's actions were much less radical and a much less serious violation of people's rights than those taken by President Wilson in World War I and President Roosevelt in World War II, despite the fact that the nation was in much greater peril during the American Civil War than it was during either of the world wars. Wilson interned 6,300 enemy aliens under the Alien Sedition Act of 1798.[24] His administration also permitted the arrest of 40,000 Americans who were suspected of resisting conscription by the American Protective League

[20] Ibid, pp. 137–8.
[21] Ibid., pp. 147 and 233.
[22] Ibid, p. 233.
[23] Ibid, pp. 53, 131, and 234.
[24] Ibid, p. 181.

in its quasi-vigilante "Slacker Raids."[25] Franklin Roosevelt interned 120,000 Japanese Americans on the West Coast during World War II.[26]

II. The Colonization of Free Blacks

Lincoln is frequently criticized for his long-standing support for the colonization of African Americans outside of the United States. For many years before becoming president, he followed his political hero, Henry Clay, in supporting colonization, and he was a member and officer of the American Colonization Society. Two of his proposals that were intended to induce individual states to end slavery included provisions for colonizing the newly freed slaves abroad (see Chapter 2.I.3). This seems very problematic, but, with some qualifications, I argue that his actions and policies about colonization were morally defensible and that many of his critics distort or misrepresent those actions and policies. The critics also ignore the fact that Lincoln's administration actually did *very little* to implement colonization.

1. *The Issue.* Many whites supported the colonization of freed African American slaves because of their aversion to the very presence of black people. Similarly, many people opposed the extension of slavery because they wanted to exclude blacks from the states and territories in which they lived.

---

[25] Ibid.

[26] Ibid., p. 183. Despite this evidence, Thomas DiLorenzo claims that the "consensus among historians is that more than 13,000 political prisoners were held in American prisons" during the Civil War; DiLorenzo, *The Real Lincoln*, p. 140. However, the most accurate evidence indicates that there were not nearly this many political prisoners held in Union military prisons. Although he cites Neely's book, DiLorenzo makes no mention of Neely's careful research and arguments that show that relatively few of those jailed by the military during the war were imprisoned for their political views or activities.

In some of his speeches from the 1850s, Lincoln appealed
to this sentiment and the deep racial prejudices of Illinois
voters.[27] Illinois voters reaffirmed their state's existing black
exclusion laws in 1862.[28] During the 1862 elections, Ohio
Democrats appealed to "voters' dread that freed slaves would
swim across the Ohio River and adopted as their slogan: 'The
Constitution as it is, the Union as it was, and the Negroes
where they are.'"[29] Former Ohio governor William Allen
said that "[e]very white laboring man in the North who does
not want to be swapped off for a free nigger should vote
the Democratic ticket."[30] He predicted that if the slaves were
freed, hundreds of thousands of them, "with their hands reek-
ing in the blood of murdered women and children," would
"cross over into our state" seeking work.[31] Ohio congressman Samuel Cox appealed to what he called the "Eleventh
Commandment": "Thou shall not degrade the white race by
such intermixtures as emancipation will bring."[32] After the
Emancipation Proclamation, many people in the North continued to want to prevent the newly freed blacks from coming
to the North.

2. A Qualified Defense of Lincoln's Colonization Policies

Unlike the politicians just quoted, Lincoln's support for colonization was not motivated by the desire to rid the country
of black people. He likened emancipation and colonization
to the biblical exodus of the Jewish people from slavery in
Egypt to their promised land and said that it would restore
"a captive people to their long-lost fatherland."[33] Lincoln

[27] Abraham Lincoln, *Speeches and Writings*, I, pp. 309, 331, 379, 401, and 455.
[28] McPherson, *Battle Cry of Freedom*, p. 507.
[29] Burlingame, *Abraham Lincoln: A Life*, II, p. 420.
[30] Ibid.
[31] Ibid.
[32] Ibid.
[33] Frederickson, *Big Enough to Be Inconsistent*, pp. 57–8, and Lincoln, "Eulogy on Henry Clay," in Abraham Lincoln, *Speeches and Writings*, I, p. 271.

endorsed Henry Clay's view that "[t]here is a moral fitness in the idea of returning to Africa her children, whose ancestors have been torn from her by the ruthless hand of fraud and violence."[34] He apparently thought that blacks would be better off in a tropical climate suitable to them.[35] He also believed that, because of white prejudice, blacks would never enjoy full rights in the United States and that, therefore, they would have a better chance of improving their situation in Africa.

What was most objectionable about the views of many of the supporters of colonization is that they wanted to impose it *involuntarily*, without the consent of those who were to be colonized: they advocated ethnic/racial cleansing. In contrast, Lincoln only supported *voluntary* colonization and did not endorse the involuntary deportation of freed slaves. In a cabinet meeting that discussed colonization on September 24, 1862, Attorney General Bates wanted to make colonization non-voluntary. The president strongly rejected this option, saying, "Their emigration must be voluntary and without expense to themselves."[36] All of his major proposals for ending slavery that called for colonization specified *voluntary* colonization. His November 1861 plan to abolish slavery in Delaware provided that freed slaves would be voluntarily colonized "at some place or places in a climate congenial to them"[37] (see Chapter 2.I.3). The preliminary version of the Emancipation Proclamation from September 1862 stated

---

[34] "Eulogy on Henry Clay," in ibid.

[35] It was widely held that God had created different peoples for different climates: Wisconsin senator James Doolittle said that there were "natural laws of climate, in accordance with difference of constitution existing between the two races." Burlingame, *Abraham Lincoln: A Life,* II, p. 385. This is an odd, arguably crackpot, belief, but it is not racist in the sense of implying that some races are superior to others.

[36] As reported by Navy Secretary Gideon Welles in Fehrenbacher and Fehrenbacher, *Recollected Words of Abraham Lincoln,* pp. 474–5.

[37] Burlingame, *Abraham Lincoln: A Life,* II, pp. 229–30.

that efforts to "colonize persons of African descent, *with their consent* [my emphasis] . . . will be continued."[38] In his Annual Message to Congress in December 1862, Lincoln proposed a constitutional amendment to give federal funds to any state that abolished slavery before 1900. The proposed amendment authorized but did not require that Congress aid in colonizing freed people "with their consent."[39] He commented on this feature of the proposed constitutional amendment in his same message to Congress:

This ought not be regarded as objectionable, on the one hand, or on the other, in so much as it comes to nothing, unless by the mutual consent of the people to be deported, and the American voters.[40]

He went on to say that he regarded the popular sentiment against allowing free blacks to remain in the country as largely unjustified:

I cannot make it better known than it already is, that I favor colonization. And yet I wish to say that there is an objection urged against freed colored persons remaining in the country, which is largely imaginary, if not sometimes malicious.[41]

Yet Lerone Bennett repeatedly claims that Lincoln wanted to get rid of blacks and goes so far as to say that Lincoln advocated an "ethnic cleansing" of America. Chapter 10 of Bennett's book *Forced into Glory* is titled "Toward the Ethnic Cleansing of America," and he writes that "racial cleansing became, 72 years before the Third Reich, 133 years before Bosnia, the cornerstone of Lincoln's policy."[42] This seems quite unfair, because voluntary emigration can

---

[38] Abraham Lincoln, *Speeches and Writings*, II, p. 368.
[39] Burlingame, *Abraham Lincoln: A Life*, II, p. 439, and Abraham Lincoln, *Speeches and Writings*, II, pp. 406–14.
[40] Abraham Lincoln, *Speeches and Writings*, II, p. 412.
[41] Ibid.
[42] Bennett, *Forced into Glory*, p. 382.

hardly be equated with forcible ethnic cleansing or forcible expulsion.

Bennett acknowledges that some of Lincoln's public statements about colonization specify voluntary colonization,[43] but he questions Lincoln's sincerity and tries to justify his claim that Lincoln endorsed ethnic/racial cleansing with the following argument:

Lincoln said that his proposed amendment . . . would come to nothing "unless by the mutual consent of the people to be deported, and the American voters, through their representatives in Congress." He thus pretended to believe, as most of his defenders pretend to believe, that there was no moral difference between a person making an individual decision to emigrate and a country making a collective decision to deport a whole group for racial reasons. And he had to know, as his commissioner of Black emigration had told him, that if American voters made a national decision to deport a group for racial reasons, it would have been easy – in 1862 or 2007 – to get consent by private and public violence and indirect government pressure.[44]

Bennett's argument badly misconstrues the third article of Lincoln's proposed constitutional amendment. It clearly does *not* call for a decision (or an expression of preference) from voters as to whether black people should be permitted to remain in the United States. Here is the third article in its entirety:

Congress may appropriate money, and otherwise provide, for colonizing free colored persons, with their consent, at any place or places without the United States.[45]

Nowhere in his message to Congress did Lincoln say that the voters should decide the question of whether blacks should be permitted to remain in the United States. The

---

43 Ibid., pp. 401 and 511.
44 Ibid., p. 516.
45 Abraham Lincoln, *Speeches and Writings*, II, p. 407.

mutual consent that he referred to is the consent of the voters to fund emigration and the consent of individual people
to emigrate; he also noted that some voters would object to
paying for this measure.[46] Bennett's argument rests on a clear
misinterpretation of Lincoln's speech, and his characterization of Lincoln's policy as one of "ethnic cleansing" is clearly
mistaken. That he likens "the cornerstone of Lincoln's policy
[colonization]" to the ethnic/racial cleansing practiced by the
Third Reich is extremely unfair. Nor does Bennett offer good
evidence to question the sincerity of Lincoln's statements that
he wanted colonization to be voluntary. Especially because
these statements are confirmed by the diary of Naval Secretary Gideon Welles (see note 36), it is clear that they were
sincere and represented Lincoln's firm convictions.

Further, Bennett's arguments about colonization appeal to
things that Lincoln said or did before 1863. Bennett never
acknowledges the very clear evidence that Lincoln did not
push strongly for large-scale colonization after the end of
1862 and did very little to implement colonization (see the
later discussion). He also fails to acknowledge John Hay's
well-known diary entry from 1864 that reports that Lincoln
had "sloughed off the idea of colonization" (see later).[47]

---

[46] Ibid., p. 408.

[47] In his December 1862 Messages to Congress Lincoln talked about *deporting*
blacks *with their consent* – which is an odd use of the word "deporting."
Bennett plays on Lincoln's use of the word, and we need to take a closer look
at Lincoln's use of it.

  In his Cooper Union address before he became president, Lincoln quoted
with approval a statement by Jefferson that endorsed the idea of emancipating
and deporting slaves so that the country would be "filled up by free white
laborers":

  In the language of Mr. Jefferson, uttered many years ago, "It is still in our
  power to direct the process of emancipation, and deportation, peaceably, and
  in such slow degrees, as that the evil will wear off insensibly; and their places
  be, pari passu, filled up by free white laborers. If, on the contrary, it is left to
  force itself on, human nature must shudder at the prospect held up."

Lincoln greatly overestimated support for colonization among African Americans. On August 14, 1862, he met with five black leaders from Washington, D.C.[48] They discussed a congressional plan to colonize freed slaves in Panama and

to make provision for the transportation, colonization, and settlement in some tropical country beyond the limits of the United States, such persons of the African race, made free by the provisions of this act, as may be willing to emigrate, having first obtained the consent of the Government of said country to their protection and settlement within the same, with all the rights and privileges of freeman.[49]

The president told this group that he wanted to consult with them about how to carry out this plan. He said that both the black and white races suffered from living in the presence of each other. He explained that these ill effects on whites grew out of the institution of slavery,[50] and in this context it was clear that he was talking about the moral harms to white slave owners caused by having great power to mistreat their slaves. Lincoln spoke to this issue elsewhere, famously saying that "no man is good enough to rule another man without

Mr. Jefferson did not mean to say, nor do I, that the power of emancipation is in the federal government. He spoke of Virginia; and, as to the power of emancipation, I speak of the slaveholding States only. The Federal Government, however, as we insist, has the power of restraining the extension of the institution – the power to insure that a slave insurrection shall never occur on any American soil which is now free from slavery (Abraham Lincoln, *Speeches and Writings*, pp. 124–5).

Because it is clear that Lincoln did not use the word "deportation" to refer only to involuntary emigration, his favorable mention of the statement from Jefferson does not show that he supported the involuntary deportation of slaves at the time he gave the Cooper Union address. In any case, it is clear that, *during his time as president*, he never endorsed the involuntary deportation of freed slaves.

[48] Guelzo, Lincoln's Emancipation Proclamation, p. 142.
[49] Burlingame, *Abraham Lincoln: A Life*, II, pp. 385–6.
[50] Ibid., p. 386.

that man's consent."[51] Despite this, his comment to the black leaders was objectionable because the harmful effects of slavery on whites were something that American whites could have eliminated by ending slavery. African Americans were not responsible for the moral harm that slavery caused whites. He said that many blacks suffered "very greatly" from living among whites and "your race are suffering, in my opinion, the greatest wrong inflicted on any people."[52] He reminded them that, because of the prejudices of whites, nowhere in America were blacks treated as equals and said that blacks would be better off in another place where they would be so treated. He did not say that this treatment was justified, but that it was a fact that could not be ignored. Notoriously, he also said, "Were your race not among us there would not be a war." (Because bitter controversy over the legitimacy of the enslavement of Africans in America was the major cause of the war, this statement is *true*, but responsibility for the war rested almost entirely with whites.) Lincoln concluded that it "is better for us both, therefore, to be separated."[53] He assured them that he would "endeavor" to make sure that blacks would be treated as equals where they were colonized [in Panama].[54]

Some important black leaders such as Martin Delany, Henry Highland Garnet, and Lewis Woodson did support colonization.[55] Frederick Douglass had been a supporter of colonization as late as 1861.[56] But generally the response from blacks to his proposals at this meeting was quite negative. In a public letter, Robert Purvis wrote, "In the matter of rights, there is but one race, and that is the *human* race. God has made one blood of all nations to dwell on the face of the

---

[51] Abraham Lincoln, *Speeches and Writings*, I, p. 328.
[52] Burlingame, *Abraham Lincoln: A Life*, II, p. 386.
[53] Ibid.
[54] Ibid., p. 388.
[55] Ibid., p. 389.
[56] Ibid., p. 235.

earth. . . . Sir this is our country as well as yours, and we will not leave it."[57] Frederick Douglass called Lincoln "a genuine representative of American prejudice and negro hatred and far more concerned with the preservation of slavery and the favor of the Border States, than for any sentiment of magnanimity or principle of justice and humanity."[58] According to Douglass, Lincoln was telling blacks, "I don't like you, you must clear out of the country."[59] William Lloyd Garrison was equally harsh in his response to this meeting. He said that Lincoln's "education (!) with and among 'the white trash' of Kentucky was most unfortunate for his moral development," and he also said, "Such driveling folly! Such brazen impudence! Such glaring selfishness!"[60]

Historians debate about how long Lincoln seriously pushed the idea of colonization. James McPherson says that Lincoln's actions regarding colonization in August 1862 were part of his effort to prepare the public for emancipation.[61] According to Michael Vorenberg, he proposed colonization to

sweeten the pill of emancipation for conservatives from the North and the border states . . . [A] clear picture emerges of Lincoln using the prospect of colonization to make emancipation more acceptable to conservatives and then abandoning all efforts at colonization once he made the determined step toward emancipation in the final Emancipation Proclamation.[62]

Miller quotes this passage and endorses Vorenberg's view.[63] Burlingame claims that in mid-1862 "Lincoln urged colonization not primarily because he still believed in it, but rather because he wanted to make emancipation more palatable

[57] Ibid., p. 390.
[58] Ibid.
[59] Ibid.
[60] Ibid.
[61] McPherson, *Battle Cry of Freedom*, p. 509.
[62] Vorenberg, "Abraham Lincoln and the Politics of Black Colonization," pp. 25 and 24.
[63] Miller, *President Lincoln*, p. 299.

to the Border States, to Unionists in the Confederacy, and to Northern conservatives."[64] According to Eric Foner, by 1864 Lincoln no longer tried to bring about large-scale colonization, although he "still saw voluntary emigration as a kind of safety valve for individual blacks dissatisfied with their condition in the United States."[65] Foner cites as evidence for this view the following entry in the diary of Lincoln's secretary and close friend John Hay (July 1, 1864): "I am glad that the President has sloughed off the idea of colonization."[66] If the McPherson/Vorenberg/ Burlingame/Foner interpretation is correct, then we cannot criticize Lincoln for his views and policies about colonization as president, except for his inept and offensive comments in his meeting with the five black leaders described earlier. In contrast, however, Lerone Bennett contends that Lincoln never gave up his plans for colonization and that he preferred an America without blacks.[67] Michael Lind says that it is unclear whether Lincoln ever abandoned his belief in colonization.[68]

The truth about Lincoln's final views about colonization probably lies somewhere between these competing interpretations, but is *much closer* to the views of McPherson, Vorenberg, and Burlingame than those of Bennett and Lind. One very important piece of evidence of his waning enthusiasm for colonization is that, although the preliminary version of the Emancipation Proclamation states that "the effort to colonize persons of African descent, with their consent... will be continued,"[69] the final version of the proclamation makes no mention of any such plans. Foner is correct to note that

---

[64] Burlingame, *Abraham Lincoln: A Life*, II, p. 384.
[65] Foner, *The Fiery Trial*, p. 260.
[66] Burlingame and Ettlinger, *Inside Lincoln's White House: The Complete Civil War Diary of John Hay*, p. 217 and Foner, *The Fiery Trial*, p. 260.
[67] Bennett, *Forced into Glory*, p. 230 and see Chapter 10.
[68] Lind, *What Lincoln Believed*, p. 224.
[69] Abraham Lincoln, *Speeches and Writings*, II, p. 368.

Lincoln wanted limited colonization as an *option* for people dissatisfied with their position in the United States. Even after the Emancipation Proclamation went into effect, Lincoln toyed with the idea of colonization and wanted it as an option. It is reported that he met with the British ambassador in January 1863 to discuss plans to resettle American blacks in British colonies.[70] In April 1863, he pursued colonization on a limited scale on an island off the coast of Haiti where he planned to settle five thousand people. The colony was a dismal failure; only five hundred people resettled there, and those who went suffered from disease and hunger. He sent an American ship to evacuate them in February 1864 and was distressed by their suffering.[71] Had he simply wanted to get rid of American blacks, he would not have taken the trouble and expense to rescue the colonists and bring them back to the United States.

Other proposals of this sort were in the air and discussed at the time. There were plans to designate certain parts of the United States as areas for free black citizens. Senator James Lane of Kansas wanted to create a state for free blacks in southern Texas.[72] Union General Jacob wanted to create a black state where blacks would enjoy full political rights in coastal areas of South Carolina, Georgia, and Florida.[73] General Sherman also supported this idea and said that blacks should be given the vote and admitted to Congress only if they agreed to be colonized in Florida.[74] Later, in the 1960s, Malcolm X advanced similar proposals. He proposed that part of the territory of the United States be used to create a separate black nation.[75] One measure of white reluctance to

[70] Guyatt, review of Foner, p. 30.
[71] Foner, *The Fiery Trial*, p. 259.
[72] Guyatt, review of Foner, p. 30.
[73] Ibid.
[74] Ibid.
[75] Malcolm X, *The Last Speeches*, pp. 69, 72, and 74.

allow large numbers of blacks to remain in the United States
is that, as late as 1868, "the *New York Times* told its readers
that the US should annex Cuba and deport the entire black
population to the island."[76]

After 1862, Lincoln did not push the idea of colonization
very hard or talk about it much in his public statements.
Therefore the claim that he strongly pushed for *large-scale*
colonization after 1862 is very far off the mark. After his proposed constitutional amendment in December 1862, he never
again publicly proposed any measures calling for large-scale
colonization. Bennett and other critics of Lincoln's views on
colonization also fail to mention that, as president, Lincoln
did *almost nothing* to implement colonization apart from
establishing the colony on the island off the coast of Haiti
and that he soon abandoned this venture. Late in his life, Lincoln made preliminary statements about the place of blacks
in the postwar United States, which *clearly* indicated that he
assumed that blacks would remain in the country after the
war. (These statements, which include his last speech on April
11, 1865, are discussed in 3.V.)[77]

3. A Further Objection and Reply: Ben Butler's Reports about Lincoln's Views on Colonization in 1865

In 1885, General Ben Butler reported that he had had conversations about colonization with Lincoln in early 1865.
Butler said that Lincoln was worried then about the possibility that former black soldiers would commit violence when
they returned to the South after the war. According to Butler, Lincoln feared "a race war" or a "guerrilla war" between

---

[76] Guyatt, review of Foner, p. 31.

[77] On this point, Frederick Douglass correctly stated that, as president, "Lincoln
soon outgrew his colonization ideas and schemes and came to look upon the
Black man as an American citizen" (Burlingame, *Abraham Lincoln: A Life*, II,
p. 829).

black veterans and their former masters.[78] He claimed that Lincoln was not then worried about what former white (Confederate) soldiers would do after the war.[79] Butler said that he would look into the matter and that he met Lincoln a few days later with a proposal that fifty thousand black veterans be sent to dig a canal across Panama. According to Butler, the president thought that this was a good idea and said, "There is meat in that, General Butler."[80]

Most historians give little credence to Butler's account of these alleged meetings with Lincoln.[81] Butler had a reputation for being a corrupt and dishonest administrator. That his account was written twenty years after the alleged event occurred also raises doubts about it. Mark Neely makes a very strong case for discounting Butler's claims.[82] First, he argues that the meetings Butler reports could not possibly have taken place at the time and location he specified. According to Butler, the meetings took place in Washington, D.C., shortly before Lincoln's death. Although Butler did not give dates for these meetings, what he did say about their time and place is inconsistent with the known facts. Butler said that the meetings took place very shortly before Lincoln left Washington, DC, for City Point, Virginia, near Richmond. On March 20, 1865, Lincoln accepted Grant's invitation to visit City Point. He left for City Point at 1 P.M. on March 23, 1865, and stayed there until April 5.[83] Butler also said that "some days afterward" (after his meetings with Lincoln) he made an arrangement to see Seward for dinner, but Seward suffered a serious carriage accident on April 5 and the

---

[78] Butler, *Butler's Book*, p. 903.
[79] Ibid., p. 903.
[80] Ibid., p. 907.
[81] Foner, *The Fiery Trial*, p. 402 n.52 and Guyatt, review of Foner, p. 27.
[82] Neely, "Abraham Lincoln and Black Colonization: Benjamin Butler's Spurious Testimony."
[83] Ibid., pp. 79–80.

planned meeting never took place. Thus, the interviews had
to have taken place between March 20 and April 5. Because
Butler said that the meetings took place in Washington, they
could only have taken place between March 20 and 1 P.M.
on March 23 (the president was not in the capital between 1
P.M. on March 23 and April 5). But we also know that Butler
was not in Washington, D.C., during that time;. he was in
Lowell, Massachusetts, on March 20 and left for New York
City that day. He stayed in New York until noon on March
23, at which time he boarded a train to Washington. So, he
could not have been in Washington until after Lincoln left for
City Point.[84] According to Butler, these meetings took place
in Washington between the time Lincoln decided to go to
City Point and the time of Seward's accident. But Neely has
shown that these meetings could not have taken place then,
because Lincoln and Butler were never both in Washington
during that time.

Second, Butler's account is self-serving in that it claims
that Butler had Lincoln's "full confidence" and that Lincoln
greatly valued his advice and expertise in moving troops by
water. According to Butler, the president praised him for his
"magnificent" movement of troops by river and his amphibi-
ous landing near Richmond in May 1864. This praise is
most improbable because this landing was a military disaster. Butler's army of thirty thousand soldiers was initially
opposed by only five thousand Confederates, and he had a
good chance of capturing Richmond and cutting the rail line
to the south that supplied the Confederate capital. If he had
succeeded, this might have ended the war. But Butler failed to
advance on Richmond quickly and his troops were bottled up
by a much smaller Confederate force.[85] Afterward, Butler's
superior officers, Grant and Halleck, thought him unfit for

---

[84] Ibid. p. 79.
[85] McPherson, *The Battle Cry of Freedom*, pp. 723–4.

command in the field. It is very improbable that Lincoln would have praised Butler for this operation.[86] But the main self-serving purpose of Butler's story was to "obscure the *real* reason for Butler's trip to Washington: he was under fire from the Treasury Department for alleged irregularities in his accounts."[87]

Neely's third point is that Butler's anecdote is at odds with Lincoln's known views on two important matters. First, according to Neely, "Lincoln thought of black soldiers as a group especially deserving of privilege, not exile,"[88] and he wanted to give them the right to vote. "Second, Butler's assertion that Lincoln expressed confidence in the peaceful nature of white Confederate soldiers to be discharged at war's end is at odds with Lincoln's view on that subject as well."[89] In fact, Lincoln feared that forces in the disbanded Confederate Army would turn into robber bands and guerillas.[90]

Even if Butler's story were largely true, its significance has been greatly overstated by many scholars. It was not unreasonable for Lincoln to fear that there would be racial violence in the South between former Union and Confederate soldiers, and he should not be criticized if he did fear this, as Butler claims. In retrospect, Southern blacks were remarkably peaceful toward whites in the aftermath of the war and emancipation, but Lincoln could not have known this at the time. It is unfair to criticize him for entertaining ideas in a brainstorming session and making polite responses to the ideas of subordinates. But what is most important is this: Butler did not say that Lincoln endorsed the wholesale deportation of blacks or the involuntary permanent deportation of *anyone*. Instead the proposal that Butler claimed Lincoln endorsed

---

[86] Neely, "Abraham Lincoln and Black Colonization," pp. 81–2.
[87] Ibid., p. 82.
[88] Ibid.
[89] Ibid.
[90] Ibid., p. 83.

only involved fifty thousand people during the term of their
enlistment in the military.[91]

4. *Conclusion.* Whatever the merits of the colonization
   plan, it was wise and politically expedient for Lincoln
   to have it on the agenda to soften opposition to the
   Emancipation Proclamation.

There was a serious possibility that opposition to the Emancipation Proclamation would cost him control of Congress
in the 1862 elections and also undermine the willingness of
many Union soldiers to fight (see Chapter 2.I.5). Lincoln's
earlier policies about colonization might have been mistaken,
but they were prompted by real and legitimate concerns and
they were not unreasonable. Illinois's "black codes" might
have colored his judgment about the extent of white racial
intolerance, but his fear that blacks would not be treated as
equals in the United States was vindicated for a very long
time.

III. Lincoln's Silence about Illinois's Black Exclusion Laws

Lincoln's silence about Illinois's blatantly unjust black exclusion laws, which were designed to prevent blacks from settling in the state, raises serious ethical questions. But his failure to publicly oppose these laws during his political career in
Illinois was probably morally justified for reasons of political
expediency.

At least until the end of the Civil War, a considerable
majority of whites in Illinois had a strong aversion to the
very presence of blacks. Some historians think that this aversion was stronger in Illinois than almost anywhere else in the
United States.[92] In 1813 the territorial legislature of Illinois

---

[91] Butler, *Butler's Book*, p. 904.
[92] Frederickson, *Big Enough to Be Inconsistent*, p. 35.

prohibited the immigration of free blacks into the state.[93] At that time, there were a small number of slaves in Illinois; they had lived in the Illinois Territory and continued to live in bondage until their deaths long after Illinois became a "free state" in 1818: the 1830 U.S. Census reports that there were 747 slaves in Illinois.[94] A move to make Illinois a slave state was voted down in 1824 in large measure because many people wanted to keep Illinois nearly all white.[95] "In 1829, the regulations impeding the entry of free blacks into the state were strengthened when the state legislature passed a comprehensive 'black code' that discriminated against blacks in every aspect of public life."[96] In 1848 a new state constitution put before the electorate in Illinois included a "Negro exclusion" clause that was voted on separately: it was approved by 70 percent of the voters in the state. In Sangamon County, where Lincoln lived, an overwhelming 90 percent of the voters approved of the clause.[97] He was a member of Congress serving in Washington, D.C., at the time and was neither part of the discussion about the new constitution nor did he vote on it. To my knowledge, there is no record of his views on this matter. However, most of the leaders of the Springfield colonization society to which Lincoln belonged opposed this clause.[98]

In 1853 Illinois passed what the historian Eugene Berwanger characterizes as "undoubtedly the most severe

[93] Ibid., p. 37.

[94] U.S. Census, 1830, Abstract, p. 46; Illinois had 917 slaves in 1820, 331 in 1840, and none in 1850; United States Census, 1850, Compendium, p. 82. In addition, many Illinois blacks were indentured servants whose freedom was severely limited. Illinois laws established a system of indentured servitude for blacks that was in effect until February 1865; see Hart, "Springfield's African-Americans as a Part of the Lincoln Community," p. 43.

[95] Frederickson, *Big Enough to Be Inconsistent*, p. 37.

[96] Ibid.

[97] Ibid., p. 38.

[98] Winkle, *The Young Eagle*, p. 262.

anti-Negro measure passed by a free state."[99] It called for heavy fines and prison sentences for people who brought blacks into the state (except for slave owners and their slaves in transit) and heavy fines (often paid in the form of forced labor) for blacks who independently crossed the border and stayed for longer than ten days.[100] Lincoln was out of politics at the time and took no public stance on this law.[101] Illinois voters reaffirmed their state's black exclusion laws in 1862; 40 percent of Republicans and most Democrats supported them.[102]

In his Annual Message to Congress in December 1862, Lincoln said that states worried about the influx of blacks freed by the Emancipation Proclamation could pass laws to exclude them, just as Illinois and other states had done before the Civil War.[103] Michael Lind takes this statement to be "the moral low point of Lincoln's career."[104] But Lind is too harsh; Lincoln was trying to save the Emancipation Proclamation and quell the firestorm of opposition to it in the Union (see Chapter 2.I.5): he erred on the side of pandering to the prejudices of the voters rather than endangering the Emancipation Proclamation.

Illinois's black exclusion laws were extremely unjust and wrong – shockingly so. They reflected deep animus toward blacks on the part of Illinois whites. But what can we conclude from Lincoln's public silence about these laws? It is reasonable to conclude that he did not strongly support these laws; if he had strongly favored them, he presumably would have said so, because during most (if not all) of his

[99] Frederickson, *Big Enough to Be Inconsistent*, p. 38.
[100] Ibid., pp. 38–9.
[101] Ibid., p. 39.
[102] McPherson, *The Battle Cry of Freedom*, p. 507.
[103] Abraham Lincoln, *Speeches and Writings*, II, p. 413; see Frederickson, *Big Enough to Be Inconsistent*, p. 26.
[104] Lind, *What Lincoln Believed*, p. 208.

political career in Illinois, there was little political downside in doing so.

Still, one might argue as follows. Either, Lincoln did not think that these laws were morally wrong, which reflects badly on him. Or he thought that those laws were morally wrong and did not speak out about them, because his lack of moral courage prevented him from raising these doubts or objections.

But this criticism fails to appreciate the political reality of his situation. It would have been futile and fatal to his hopes of winning elective office in Illinois in 1858 or earlier for him to have opposed these laws, given that they had such strong support, particularly in central and southern Illinois. Politicians need to choose their battles. It is not wrong for them to keep silent about great wrongs that enjoy great popular support (and which cannot be altered for the foreseeable future) and, instead, try to gain office and attempt to promote justice in other ways.

IV. Lincoln's Support for Illinois Laws that Discriminated against Blacks

Lincoln publicly endorsed other unjust laws that were part of Illinois's black codes – laws forbidding blacks to vote, serve on juries, or marry whites. During his debates with Douglas in 1858, Lincoln repeatedly said that he opposed giving blacks the right to vote, the right to serve on juries, the right to hold office, or the right to marry whites. He began his opening speech at the Charleston debate by saying that he was asked by a man at his hotel whether he "was really in favor of producing a perfect equality between Negroes and white people."[105] "Great laughter" followed. Here is part of his opening statement:

[105] Abraham Lincoln, *Speeches and Writings*, I, p. 636.

I will say then that I am not, nor ever have been in favor of bringing about in any way the social and political equality of the white and black races, [applause] – that I am not nor ever have been in favor of making voters or jurors of negroes, nor of qualifying them to hold office, nor to intermarry with white people; and I will say in addition to this that there is a physical difference between the white and black races which I believe will ever forbid the two races living together on terms of social and political equality. And inasmuch as they cannot so live, while they do remain together there must be the position of the superior and inferior, and I as much as any other man am in favor of having the superior position assigned to the white race. I say upon this occasion I do not perceive that because the white man is to have the superior position the negro should be denied everything. I do not understand that because I do not want a negro woman for a slave I must necessarily want her for a wife [Cheers and laughter.]. . . . I will add to this that I have *never* [my emphasis] seen to my knowledge a man, woman, or child who was in favor of producing perfect equality, social and political between negroes and white men.[106]

These are undoubtedly very unjust laws. It would be helpful to know whether Lincoln believed that these laws were just and, if he did, whether he had serious doubts about their justice. (For evidence that he might not have really been opposed to interracial marriage, see Chapter 10.V.1.)

Granted that these laws were very unjust, was it wrong for him to publicly endorse them at this time? The overwhelming majority of Illinois voters supported these laws, and given that, he could not do much to change public opinion at the time. It would have been tantamount to political suicide for him to have endorsed full civil and political rights for blacks

---

[106] Ibid., I, pp. 636–7. In his rejoinder to Douglas at the end of the Charleston debate, Lincoln reiterated that he was against citizenship for Negroes:

Now my opinion is that the different states have the power to make a negro a citizen under the constitution of the United States if they choose. The Dred Scott decision decides that they have not that power. If the state of Illinois had that power I should be opposed to the exercise of it (ibid., p. 675).

in 1858 (or in 1860, or arguably even in 1864). A defender of the actual consequences version of utilitarianism would say that it was morally right for Lincoln to support these unjust laws because it helped his political career and enabled him to do the great things that he later did. But, even if we accept this view, we should also add that the rightness of what he did was largely a matter of moral luck: endorsing, and acting, on false and mistaken moral views is rarely morally right. Especially early in his political career,[107] long before he became an important national leader of the antislavery movement, it was quite improbable and unforeseeable that any great good would result from his active support for these extremely unjust laws. (A person has good or bad moral luck if the rightness or wrongness of what she does depends at least partly on things beyond her control, such as the truth or falsity of the factual beliefs on which she acts and the future consequences of her actions. See Chapter 6.II for a discussion of Lincoln's moral luck.)

---

[107] Lincoln supported these laws from the very beginning of his political career at least until the time of his 1858 debates with Stephen Douglas. In 1836, Lincoln said that he supported giving voting rights to all *whites* [emphasis added] "who pay taxes or bear arms, (by no means excluding females)," Ibid., p. 5. In 1836 he wrote several anonymous letters to the *Sangamo Journal*. One of these letters supported the idea that "the elective franchise should be kept free from contamination by the admission of colored voters," Burlingame, *Abraham Lincoln: A Life*, I, pp. 109–10. Burlingame also quotes from a letter that appeared in the *Sangamo Journal* in 1836 ostensibly written by a black man named "Sees-her" that he thinks "in all likelihood was composed by Lincoln." This letter that, among other things, states that "Wanjuren [Van Buren] says de nigger all shall vote," is extremely crude and offensive. The context of these letters is that Lincoln and other Whigs had denounced the Democratic presidential candidate, Martin Van Buren, for his earlier support for laws permitting free blacks to vote in New York State.

During the 1840 presidential campaign, Lincoln made several speeches in which he denounced President Van Buren for supporting voting rights for free blacks in New York State; Donald, *Lincoln*, p. 80; also see "Speech in Tremont, Illinois, May 2, 1840," in Basler, ed., *Collected Works of Abraham Lincoln*, I, p. 210.

V. Lincoln on the Status and Rights of African Americans after the Civil War

Lincoln's policies with respect to the postwar status and rights of African Americans have generated considerable criticism. He did not want to make giving blacks the right to vote and sit on juries a condition of readmitting Confederate states to the Union, and he refused to support a bill that would have given blacks the right to vote and sit on juries in the provisional state governments that were created in the former Confederate states after the war. In the last speech he ever gave, on April 11, 1865, he said that he "preferred that for now" blacks who had fought in the war and those who were "very intelligent" be permitted to vote. These are questionable actions, but I argue that it was right for him to be cautious, move slowly, and not *immediately* push for the radical change of giving full rights to all blacks. Had he done so, he would have risked undermining the ratification of the Thirteenth Amendment and sparking a guerilla war in the South. Granting this, many people still ask whether he would have done enough to protect the rights and interests of black people if he had lived longer and overseen reconstruction. But the answer is that we simply do not know the answer to this question. Everything we say about his policies regarding the rights and status of African Americans in post–Civil War America needs to be hedged in light of this uncertainty.

1. *What Lincoln Did Near the End of His Life*

In 1864, Congressman James Ashley introduced a bill that would have permitted blacks to vote and serve on juries in the temporary governments established in the former Confederate states before they were readmitted to the Union. Lincoln opposed this part of the bill, which was later dropped by acts of Congress.[108] So revised, Ashley's bill was incorporated into legislation introducing the Thirteenth Amendment into Congress.[109]

Lincoln's friend Ward Lamon reports that Lincoln said the following apropos to the Ashley bill:

> While I am in favor of freedom to all of God's creatures, with equal political rights under prudential restrictions, I am not in favor of unlimited social equality. There are questions arising out of our complications which trouble me greatly. The question of universal suffrage for freedman in his unprepared state is one of doubtful propriety. I do not oppose the justice of the measure; but I do think it is of doubtful political policy and may rebound like a boomerang not only on the Republican party, but upon the freedman himself and our common country.[110]

This alleged statement needs to be treated with great caution. Note that Lincoln did not question the justice of giving blacks full voting rights; rather, he questioned whether doing that was wise politically and he feared that it might be counter-productive for the well-being of the freedman. He did not explain what he meant by "social equality" nor the "prudential restrictions" on black voting rights that he endorsed. The statement also leaves open the question of Lincoln's views about voting rights for blacks who had been free before the war. Additionally, there are grave doubts about Lamon's reliability as a historical witness; this particular quotation was not recorded contemporaneously.[111]

In his last public speech delivered three days before his assassination, Lincoln addressed the issue of voting rights for blacks. He said that he "would prefer that it were for now

---

[108] Frederickson, *Big Enough to Be Inconsistent*, p. 119.

[109] Ibid., pp. 121–2.

[110] Feherenbacher and Feherenbacher, *Recollected Words of Abraham Lincoln*, p. 291; also cited in Frederickson, *Big Enough to Be Inconsistent*, p. 122.

[111] Feherenbacher and Feherenbacher, *Recollected Words of Abraham Lincoln*, pp. 281 and 291.

conferred on the very intelligent and those who serve our cause as soldiers."[112] Many think that by "very intelligent" he meant "literate."[113] He thought that the U.S. Constitution left questions about voting rights and citizenship to be answered by individual states.[114]

It was prudent for Lincoln to want to drop Ashley's proposal about black suffrage from the bill to introduce the Thirteenth Amendment to Congress. There was not enough support for this measure to gain the two-thirds vote required in both the House and the Senate, and Lincoln needed to focus on abolishing slavery first. He was well justified in worrying that fighting for equal rights for blacks would imperil attempts to pass the amendment.[115] Even without Ashley's proposal, the Thirteenth Amendment barely received the needed two-thirds vote in the House.

But what are we to think about his speech of April 11, 1865? At the very end of his life, he seems to have thought that many black men should be denied the right to vote. However, he did think that educated (intelligent?) blacks who were prepared for the franchise should be allowed to vote. He also thought that blacks should be educated.[116] Therefore, his position in this speech is compatible with the view that most

---

[112] "Speech on Reconstruction, April 11, 1865," in Abraham Lincoln, *Speeches and Writings*, I, p. 637.

[113] See Gates, "Abraham Lincoln on Race and Slavery," in Gates and Yacovone, *Lincoln on Race and Slavery*, p. xxvi. What Lincoln meant by "intelligent" in this context needs more attention from historians. A more literal reading of this statement is that, except for veterans, Lincoln wanted only unusually intelligent black people to be permitted to vote, although he wanted whites of average or below-average intelligence to continue to possess the right to vote.

[114] Abraham Lincoln, *Speeches and Writings*, I, p. 637 and Frederickson, *Big Enough to be Inconsistent*, pp. 122–3. Also see Guelzo, *Abraham Lincoln: Redeemer President*, p. 433; on this point also see note 106.

[115] Guelzo, *Abraham Lincoln: Redeemer President*, p. 427.

[116] Burlingame, *Abraham Lincoln: A Life*, II, p. 588 and McPherson, *The Battle Cry of Freedom*, p. 709.

black men should eventually be given the vote (assuming that by "intelligent" he meant "educated").

Still, Lincoln's April 11, 1865, speech sanctions unjust racial discrimination against blacks. He never proposed prohibiting unintelligent (uneducated) whites who had not served in the military from voting.[117] But his important qualification "for now" strongly implies that he proposed this only as a temporary measure. Given that the war was still going on when he died, the uncertainty about the political situation, Lincoln's very real worries about a protracted guerrilla war in the Confederate states after the end of the Civil War, and the preeminent need to get three-quarters of the states to ratify the Thirteenth Amendment, he was justified in not pushing for full equality and justice *at this time* – "for now." Sometimes aiming at bringing about the ideal immediately is counterproductive: the ideal can be the enemy of the good or "the better."

We should not underestimate what a huge change for the better his last speech represented. Several months later, Frederick Douglass said that although Lincoln's statement about black suffrage "seemed to mean but little" at the time, it actually meant a great deal:

It was just like Abraham Lincoln. He never shocked prejudices unnecessarily. Having learned statesmanship while splitting rails, he always used the thin edge of the wedge first – and the fact that he used it at all meant that he would if need be, use the thick as well as the thin.[118]

Burlingame adds the following:

Owen Lovejoy used this same image to describe Lincoln's approach to emancipation. In dealing with slavery, he had inserted the thin edge of the wedge in March 1862 (with the recommendation to

---

[117] See Lind, *What Lincoln Believed*, pp. 223–4.
[118] Ibid., pp. 802–3.

help compensate those Border States adopting gradual emancipation), drove it deeper in 1863 (with the Emancipation Proclamation), and fully drove home the thick part in 1865 (with the
Thirteenth Amendment).

Tragically, one member of Lincoln's audience did not underestimate the importance of Lincoln's call for limited black suffrage. On hearing the president's words, John Wilkes Booth
turned to a friend and declared, "That means nigger citizenship. Now, by God, I'll put him through." He added, "That
is the last speech he will ever make."[119]
Lincoln's actions were reasonable, and they were compatible with his attaching equal intrinsic weight to the rights and
interests of blacks and whites. We cannot fault him very much
for what he did during his lifetime. We should not wish that
he had proposed or supported anything like the Fourteenth
and Fifteenth Amendments before the time of this death. He
was prudent not to take any big risks that would have imper-
iled the ratification of the Thirteenth Amendment.

2. *What Would Lincoln Have Done Had He Lived*
   Longer? The following counterfactual question is
   extremely important for our purposes: "What would
   Lincoln have done had he lived out his term of office?"

In particular, would he have supported the Fourteenth and
Fifteenth Amendments, which were the basis for good things
that happened much later? (The Fourteenth Amendment
states that "all persons born or naturalized in the United
States...are citizens of the United States and of the State
wherein they reside" and that states must not "make or
enforce any law which shall abridge the privileges or immu-
nities of citizens of the United States." The Fifteenth Amendment says that "the right of citizens of the United States to
vote shall not be denied or abridged by the United States or

---

[119] Burlingame, *Abraham Lincoln: A Life*, II, p. 803.

by any State on account of race, color, or previous condition of servitude.") Surely, Lincoln *should have* eventually supported these or similar amendments if he had lived until the end of his term.

Strong prima facie arguments can be given both for and against the proposition that Lincoln would have supported something like the Fourteenth and Fifteenth Amendments. His innate caution and conservatism; his desire to show mercy to the South; his interpretation of the U.S. Constitution that led him to think that laws concerning voting rights and other civil rights of citizens were within the purview of the states, but not the federal government; and his fear of violence and guerilla war would have all inclined him against endorsing anything like these amendments: they were a very sharp departure from his past policies. On the other hand, Lincoln *was* capable of radically altering his views. He became an unequivocal abolitionist after a little more than three years as president. He closed his April 11, 1865, speech by saying that "it may be my duty to make some new announcement to the people of the South. I am considering and shall not fail to act, when satisfied that action will be proper."[120] His last cabinet meeting was held on April 14, 1865, the day he was assassinated. The pro-radical attorney general James Speed commented to Chase about that meeting saying that Lincoln "never seemed so near our views."[121]

Lincoln had a great deal of power and prestige at the end of his life. The war was almost won, and he no longer had to worry about being reelected. Had he lived, he could have used his position to push hard for the rights of blacks. We simply do not know whether he would have done this nor how he would have reacted to the massive resistance of

---

[120] Abraham Lincoln, *Speeches and Writings*, II, p. 701, cited in Burlingame, *Abraham Lincoln: A Life*, II, p. 804.
[121] Burlingame, *Abraham Lincoln: A Life*, II, p. 804.

every former Confederate state to the abolition of slavery (see Chapter 4.I.2). His plans for reconstruction were never written down, and as far as we know, he never confided them to anyone. Indeed, it is doubtful that he had any such detailed plans when he died. Perhaps there are no determinate facts of the matter. The postwar status of blacks was becoming a salient issue only at the end of his life, and given his crushing workload as commander in chief he was only beginning to devote his full attention to this issue at the time of his death.

Lind, Bennett, and others who think that Lincoln never would have supported full equality for African Americans if he had lived out his term of office might be correct. If they are right about this, his historical reputation and place in the American memory probably benefited from his assassination at the end of the war.

Many people connect these issues with the questions about racism and Lincoln's character. But this is a dubious connection. Even in an uncharitable reading, his flawed but steadily improving views and policies about the postwar rights and status of blacks bespeak excessive caution and concern for popular opinion, justifiable fears about a guerrilla war, a commitment to a reading of the Constitution that makes the political and civil rights of citizens the prerogative of individual states rather than the federal government, a desire to be merciful to the South, and perhaps also poor judgment – but not deep flaws of character. I address this issue of racism in much greater detail in Chapter 10.

4

Did the Union Have Just Cause for Fighting the American Civil War?

Earlier, in Chapter 2, I defended some of Lincoln's most controversial actions and policies on the grounds that they were necessary for him to fight and win the Civil War. These arguments presuppose the justice of the Union cause in the war, but this assumption is open to question and needs to be defended.

The question of the justice of the Union cause in the war is particularly important for assessing Lincoln's ethics because, as we have seen, he played a decisive role in determining that the North would fight a civil war rather than allow the Confederate states to secede peacefully, as the Confederacy strongly preferred. Many people in the North, including many abolitionists, also wanted to "let the South go in peace." But Lincoln deliberately risked provoking the South into beginning the war when he resupplied Fort Sumter against the advice of most of his close military and civilian advisors (see Chapter 2.1.2). In so doing, he succeeded in uniting public opinion in the North to fight the war, and so he clearly bore great personal responsibility for its outbreak.

The question of whether the Union had just cause for fighting the war needs to be divided into distinct questions that address the justice of fighting (or continuing to fight) the war at different times.

There appears to be a case for saying that, when the Civil War began, the Union did not have adequate moral grounds for fighting it. It is debatable whether the good of keeping the Union together and not creating a precedent for further instances of secession in the United States and other democratic nations were enough to justify the immense evil of all the death and suffering caused by the war. Yet there were other considerations that justified the Union in fighting the war. It would have been a catastrophe if the Confederate States of American (CSA) had gained its independence. Had it been able to do so, it is very probable that slavery would have continued much longer in the American South, and it is also likely that it would have persisted longer in Latin America. Even if it is true that the CSA would have eventually abolished slavery, the legal rights that blacks would have possessed in the CSA after such time as it abolished slavery would probably not have been nearly comparable to those they actually possessed in the United States from 1865 until the present.

I argue that (1) the actual consequences version of utilitarianism (the theory that holds that a person acts rightly provided that he brings about the best consequences that it is possible for him to produce in the circumstances), (2) the probable consequences version of utilitarianism (a theory that holds that the rightness of an action is determined by its antecently probable consequences, rather than its actual consequences), and (3) standard versions of just war theory all imply that the Union was justified in fighting the war from the very beginning. But that this is so is *clear* only in the case of the actual consequences version of utilitarianism. The case for the justice of the Union cause at the beginning of the war is much more debatable given the truth of either of the other two theories. Because the Union's war aims changed significantly between the very beginning of the war and the time of the Emancipation Proclamation, and again after Lincoln ran for reelection as a supporter of a constitutional amendment to abolish slavery, the case for the justice of the Union cause was stronger at the end of the war than at the beginning. All three of these moral theories *clearly* imply that the Union had just cause for fighting at the end of the war.

My general strategy for addressing questions of *jus ad bellum* is to argue that Confederate independence would have very predictably led to the perpetuation and expansion of the massive injustices and violations of human rights involved in American slavery. This argument, which also demonstrates the egregious injustice of the Confederate cause, does most of the argumentative work in this chapter. I do not try to defend any particular theory of just war. Rather, I argue that the Confederate cause was so unjust that this war counts as an *extreme case* and that all reasonable views about the morality of war will agree that the Union had just cause for fighting the war.

I. It Would Have Been Catastrophic if the Confederacy Had Gained Its Independence

Because my arguments in this chapter rest largely on my claim that the independence of the CSA would have had extremely bad consequences, I begin by defending this claim at considerable length. As Lincoln knew and feared, the existence of a powerful and independent CSA would have strengthened, enlarged, and perpetuated the institution of slavery. It is also likely that it would have helped reinvigorate and prolong slavery in Latin America. But there are many details to consider, and a great deal depends on the answers to the following questions: (1) How long would slavery have continued in the CSA if the Confederacy had gained its independence? (2) Assuming that the CSA would have eventually abolished slavery, what kinds of rights and freedoms would African Americans have enjoyed in the CSA? Would those rights have been comparable to the extremely inadequate rights and freedoms they enjoyed in the post–Civil War United States? (3) Would an independent CSA have prolonged or enlarged slavery in Latin America? And (4) Would an independent CSA have renewed the African slave trade? Let us consider these questions in turn.

1. How Long Would Slavery Have Continued in an Independent CSA?

The CSA was quite militant, and its leaders were deeply committed to its pro-slavery ideology. Part of the evidence for this is that the Confederacy was very determined and willing to make huge sacrifices in its war effort. In *Battle Cry of Freedom*, McPherson estimates that one of every four white men of military age in the Confederacy died in the war.[1] In light of David Hacker's recent evidence that Confederate dead were greatly undercounted (see note 61), this estimate might be too low. McPherson reports that he agrees with Hacker's findings that the Confederate death toll was considerably higher than was thought earlier and now thinks that three in ten is a better estimate of the percentage of white men of military age in the Confederacy who died in the war.[2] Despite these terrible losses, the Confederate nation continued to fight long after the Union aimed at ending slavery. If there had been no war and the CSA had seceded peacefully, slavery would have probably continued in the CSA for at least two more generations. There was very little popular support for ending slavery among voters in the states of the CSA, and it would have taken a long time for an antislavery movement to develop and gain the support of most voters. The

[1] McPherson, *Battle Cry of Freedom*, p. 818.
[2] Emails to Thomas Carson, April 28 and 29, 2014.

development of such a movement would have been greatly impeded by severe restrictions on the publication and dissemination of abolitionist sentiments on the grounds that they were incitements to slave uprisings. Before the Civil War, local authorities routinely seized abolitionist literature sent to the South via the post office.[3] The development of abolitionism in the Confederacy would also have been greatly impeded by violence against abolitionists and the widespread view that such violence was entirely justified.[4] A large-scale movement to end slavery probably could not have arisen and succeeded in the Confederacy in less than fifty years. Admittedly, this claim about how long slavery would have lasted in the CSA is speculative, but large-scale social movements that oppose deeply entrenched institutions and interests generally take a long time to develop. This would have been particularly true in the present case because of Southern fears of slave rebellions and because of regional antagonisms: abolitionism was associated with the much hated Yankees of the North and New England.

Yet, to the contrary, some neo-Confederate apologists have contended that the leaders of the CSA were planning to end slavery before too long. In the late nineteenth and early twentieth centuries, the United Confederate Veterans and the United Daughters of the Confederacy went to very great lengths to argue that the CSA fought for states' rights and constitutional liberties, not to defend slavery,[5] as at this meeting:

"Think of it, soldiers of Lee!" declared a speaker at a reunion of the United Confederate Veterans in 1904. "You were fighting,

---

[3] In 1836, Congress passed a law forbidding local postmasters to prevent the delivery of publications, but the Southern states defied this law and continued to suppress the delivery of antislavery literature and Northern newspapers to the South; Miller, *Arguing about Slavery*, pp. 103–5.

[4] Ibid., p. 76.

[5] McPherson, *This Mighty Scourge*, p. 93.

they say, for the privilege of holding your fellow man in bondage! Will you for a moment acknowledge the truth of that indictment? Oh no!...You could not have followed a banner that was not a banner of liberty."[6]

In another example, the "historian general" of the United Daughters of the Confederacy, Mildred Rutherford, claimed that "Southern men were anxious for the slaves to be free. They were studying earnestly the problems of freedom, when Northern fanatical Abolitionists took matters into their own hands."[7]

But this view is *wildly* mistaken. The Confederacy was not planning to abolish slavery; rather, it was planning to *expand* and *perpetuate* it. The Confederate states seceded because of Lincoln's avowed desire to stop the spread of slavery and his frequently expressed hope that stopping the spread of slavery would be the first step in setting slavery "in the course of ultimate extinction." Despite their states' rights rhetoric, many Southern politicians demanded that new states and territories *not* have the right to prohibit slavery. In this demand, they were emboldened by the Dred Scott decision that overruled congressional prohibitions of slavery in federal territories. Rutherford to the contrary, Lee's army did *not* fight for liberty; during the invasion of Pennsylvania before the Battle of Gettysburg, his army kidnapped scores of former slaves and free blacks and brought them back to slavery in the CSA.[8] Further, the Confederate Army continued to fight, long after Lincoln made the complete abolition of slavery an aim of the Union cause.[9]

---

[6] Ibid., p. 94.

[7] Ibid., p. 102.

[8] McPherson, *The Battle Cry of Freedom*, p. 649.

[9] Here, I am talking about the aims and intentions of the Confederate government and its leaders, not the motives and intentions of individual Confederate soldiers. Many of them did not fight primarily to defend the institution of slavery and many of them were not supporters of slavery at all. On the motivations

The states of the Upper South – Arkansas, Tennessee, North Carolina, and Virginia – did not secede before Fort Sumter despite Lincoln's clear aim of limiting the spread of slavery. But, when the war began, they sided with the states of the Deep South, which had left the Union because they insisted on their sacred right to expand slavery. The states of the Upper South chose to fight with their sister Southern states for those aims, rather than fight with the Union or remain neutral.

Many border state politicians, including Lincoln's political hero, Henry Clay, were formulating plans to end slavery. In 1847, Whigs in Delaware formulated a plan to free all of the slaves in the state; it was defeated by a single vote in the state legislature.[10] In 1849, Clay urged the constitutional convention in Kentucky to adopt proposals for the gradual emancipation and colonization of Kentucky's slaves.[11] In 1858, Francis Blair led a movement for the gradual emancipation and colonization of Missouri's slaves.[12] But these opponents of slavery did not support the secession of the Confederate states from the Union.

Despite the claims of Rutherford and many other apologists for the CSA, the Confederacy *was* fighting for the institution of slavery. It is true enough that, at the beginning of the war, the CSA was not fighting to oppose Union efforts to immediately end slavery because there were no such

---

of Confederate and Union soldiers, see McPherson's *For Cause and Comrades*. No doubt, the following helps explain the motivations of many Confederate soldiers. "Yanks were given to asking Rebs why they were fighting. One Reb, captured in Virginia early on, answered 'Because you are here.' It was, and remains, as good an answer as any" (Keegan, *The American Civil War*, p. 20). Most Confederate soldiers took themselves to be defending their country and their homes and families against attack, and no doubt many were motivated by fears that the "abolitionist hosts" of the Union army would incite a violent slave rebellion that would endanger them and their families.

[10] Burlingame, *Abraham Lincoln: A Life*, II, pp. 229–31.
[11] Heidler and Heidler, *Henry Clay: The Essential American*, p. 450.
[12] Stevens, *Centennial History of Missouri*, 2, p. 138.

efforts then, but it was still fighting to protect its legal right to
expand and *perpetuate* slavery. As Lincoln later aptly said in
his Second Inaugural Address, the institution of slavery "constituted a peculiar and powerful interest. All knew that this
interest was somehow the cause of the war. To strengthen,
perpetuate, and extend this interest was the object for which
the insurgents would rend the Union even by war; while the
government claimed no right to do more than to restrict the
territorial enlargement of it."[13]

One of the strongest pieces of evidence for the proposition
that the Confederacy was fighting for the institution of slavery and was determined to continue it for a very long time
is the speech given by Confederate vice president Alexander
Stephens in Savannah, Georgia, on March 21, 1861. This
speech has subsequently come to be known as the "Cornerstone Address." In it Stephens claimed that Jefferson and
most of the other founders of the United States thought that
the enslavement of Africans was morally wrong, but that the
institution of slavery in the United States would pass away
before too long. Stephens sharply rejected both beliefs:

Those ideas, however, were fundamentally wrong. They rested on
the assumption of the equality of the races. This was an error. It
was a sandy foundation, and our government built upon it fell
when the "storm came and the wind blew."

Stephens then said that the CSA was founded on the opposite
idea: the idea that slavery is the natural condition of the
Negro and that the enslavement of Negroes is morally right:

Our new government is founded on the opposite idea; its founda-
tions are laid, its corner-stone rests, upon the great truth that the
negro is not the equal of the white man; that slavery, subordina-
tion to the superior race, is his natural and normal condition. This,

[13]   Abraham Lincoln, *Speeches and Writings*, II, p. 686.

our new government, is the first, in the history of the world, based upon this great physical, philosophical, and moral truth.[14]

It is noteworthy that Stephens was among the most *moderate* of the Confederate leaders. He was a personal friend of Lincoln's (going back to their time together in Congress in the late 1840s), and he publicly opposed secession at the time when his home state of Georgia voted to leave the Union.

But one might still object that, regardless of the aims of the Confederate leaders at the beginning of the war, slavery would have died out soon for economic reasons. One of the most prominent defenders of this view is Thomas DiLorenzo. DiLorenzo claims that the border states would have ended slavery before too long and that, because slavery was already becoming economically inefficient, slavery would have ended in the Confederacy long before the end of the nineteenth century.[15] But this argument is very dubious. The economic self-interests of slave owners would not have given them reasons to voluntarily end slavery for a very long time. The purchase of slaves was, and would have continued to be, a very profitable investment. Between 1820 and 1860 slave owners received an annual net return of about 10 percent on the market value of slaves, and there was no downward trend in the rate of return during this time.[16] There is no compelling reason to think that slavery was incompatible with industrialization or that it would have automatically disappeared after the South industrialized. Slaves were used successfully as workers in the iron and textile industries,[17] and many slaves worked as skilled tradesmen, craftsmen, and managers on plantations.[18] Slave owners also found ways to give their

---

[14] Stephens, "The Cornerstone Address."
[15] DiLorenzo, *The Real Lincoln*, pp. 276–7.
[16] Fogel and Engerman, *Time on the Cross*, pp. 4 and 70.
[17] McPherson, *Battle Cry of Freedom*, p. 97.
[18] Berlin, *Many Thousands Gone*, pp. 135–6, 168–9, and 311.

slaves incentives to do good work and be productive. These incentives included the opportunities to earn money, obtain better housing, and engage in skilled and managerial work.[19]

Many claim that the institution of slavery was doomed by the poor quality and low productivity of slave labor; this view was widely held by opponents of slavery at the time. But Fogel and Engerman give extensive evidence to the contrary, and they demonstrate serious flaws in standard versions of this argument. They argue that the quality and productivity of slave labor were as high as, and in some important respects higher than, that of free white labor in the South.[20] The claim that slavery was doomed for economic reasons is further contradicted by the fact that per capita income in the slave states grew rapidly between 1840 and 1860 – 30 percent more rapidly than the rest of the nation. In 1860 only three other nations in the world had a higher per capita income than the slave states of the United States.[21] Further, because many of the states of the CSA were deeply committed to the institution of slavery and "the Southern way of life," they likely would have continued slavery until well after it became economically inefficient.

For all these reasons, it is very unlikely that the CSA would have ended slavery "long before" the end of the nineteenth century. As DiLorenzo himself admits, slavery was a very viable system for growing cotton. Even if we accept his argument that "slavery would have become uneconomical altogether with the invention and widespread use of modernized cotton picking machinery,"[22] the viability of slavery for producing cotton counts strongly against his claim that the CSA would have ended slavery "long before" the end of the

---

[19] Ibid., pp. 136, 169, 270, and 313.
[20] Fogel and Engerman, *Time on the Cross*, pp. 170–232.
[21] Ibid., pp. 4–6 and 250–1.
[22] DiLorenzo, *The Real Lincoln*, p. 297.

19th Century. Mechanized cotton-picking machines were not generally used until the 1950s. Prior to that time, a very large labor force was needed to hand-pick cotton.[23] The need for laborers on cotton plantations continued to grow long after

[23] The first mechanical cotton harvesters were patented in the mid-nineteenth century, but the early models had many problems. The Great Depression of the 1930s depressed wages and delayed the mechanization of cotton farms (Holley, *The Second Great Emancipation*, pp. 35–53 and 75). Cotton production in California and the Far West was mechanized earlier than in the rest of the country. Even so, 1951 was the first year in which more than 50% of the cotton produced in California was harvested by machines. In 1951 almost all the cotton harvested in Arkansas was hand-picked and, as late as 1957, more than 80% of the cotton produced in Arkansas was hand-picked (ibid., pp. 130–1).

Another measure of the very long persistence of labor-intensive methods of cotton production in the United States is the amount of labor involved in the production of cotton. Here are some figures for the average number of hours of labor per acre of cotton in the United States:

Year	Hours of Labor Per Acre
1840	135
1935–44	99
1955–9	66
1960–4	47
1965–9	30
1970	24

Here are figures for the amount of labor required to produce a bale of cotton:

Year	Hours of Labor Per Bale
1840	438
1880	303
1915–19	299
1935–9	209
1955–9	74
1965–9	30
1970	26

Note that the yield of cotton per acre grew from less than one-third of a bale per acre to roughly one bale per acre by 1965–9 (ibid., p. 14).

1860. The land area devoted to cotton doubled between 1860 and 1890 and doubled again between 1890–1925.[24] Given that slavery was an economically viable means of producing cotton prior to mechanization, American slavery would have remained economically viable as long as the production of cotton required a very large labor force.

This, of course, is not to say that cotton could *only* have been produced with slave labor. The continued and increased production of cotton after the end of slavery clearly refutes that proposition. My point is that, because cotton production remained very labor intensive into the 1950s and the production of cotton greatly increased for many years after the Civil War, slavery would have long continued to be an economically viable institution for that reason alone had the CSA retained its independence.

My general conclusion that slavery would have probably continued for a considerable period of time in the CSA is supported by David Brion Davis, who writes,

Given the economic growth and vitality of Southern slavery in 1860, it is difficult to imagine any other historical scenario [any scenario that didn't involve a civil war between the North and the South] that would have led to full and universal slave emancipation in the nineteenth or even the early twentieth century.[25]

Not only did the CSA intend to continue slavery where it already existed but it also clearly intended to expand slavery into new territories. The Confederate constitution *required* that slavery be permitted and protected in new territory acquired by the CSA. Article IV, Section 3, subsection 3 of the constitution of the Confederate States of America states,

---

[24] Fogel and Engerman, *Time on the Cross*, p. 96.
[25] Davis, *Inhuman Bondage: The Rise and Fall of Slavery in the New World*, p. 299. Davis adds, "This conclusion lends support to the argument that the Civil War was a necessary and 'good' war."

The Confederate States may acquire new territory; and Congress . . . may permit them . . . to form States to be admitted into the Confederacy. In all such territory the institution of Negro slavery, as it now exists in the Confederate States, shall be recognized and protected by Congress and by the territorial government.[26]

2. How would African Americans have fared in the CSA after such time as the CSA ended slavery?

African Americans were treated very badly in the United States after the Civil War, but the situation of free blacks would probably have been much worse in the CSA. Even if the CSA would have eventually abolished slavery, it is likely that blacks would have been subjected to something like serfdom, lifelong apprenticeships under the close supervision of whites, or debt bondage – a status much worse than the second-class citizenship they actually endured in the United States. It is very unlikely that anything similar to the Fourteenth and Fifteenth Amendments to the U.S. Constitution would have been passed in the CSA. (The Fourteenth Amendment made African Americans, and all other persons born or naturalized in the United States, citizens and guaranteed them "equal protection" under the law. The Fifteenth Amendment gave blacks and former slaves the right to vote in any state.) These amendments were the basis for many good things that happened later in the United States, including the 1954 Supreme Court decision on school segregation, the 1964 Civil Rights Act, and the 1965 Voting Rights Act. In addition, it is unlikely that very many free blacks from the CSA would have been able to move to the United States, both because of Confederate laws and of Negro-phobia and racially discriminatory immigration laws (see 4.II.1) in the United States. It is also questionable whether Negro colleges such as Tuskegee, Spellman, and Morehouse,

---

[26] Ransom, *The Confederate States of America*, p. 282.

founded mostly by Northern white philanthropists, including the Rockefellers, would have sprung up in the CSA for
a long time; as a result, there probably would have been no
indigenous class of highly educated Confederate blacks such
as George Washington Carver and Martin Luther King Jr.
during the first part of the twentieth century. An independent
CSA would have been much like South Africa before 1994.
But the Confederate system of racial inequality would likely
have been much stronger and longer lived because whites
were a majority in the CSA but only a small minority in
South Africa.

Some apologists for the Confederacy reject this argument
and claim that race relations and the treatment of blacks
would have been better in the CSA than they actually were
in the United States. They blame the Yankees for poisoning
race relations by turning blacks against their former masters during Reconstruction.[27] They also attribute Southern
mistreatment of blacks to bitterness over the war and their
mistreatment by Northern whites during Reconstruction. But
this claim is very dubious. It assumes that the freedmen, their
former masters, and Southern whites who did not own slaves
would have had similar interests were it not for the malign
influence of Yankees.

This argument badly misconstrues the history of Reconstruction. In the immediate aftermath of the war, *all* of
the former states of the CSA attempted to defy the Emancipation Proclamation and the Thirteenth Amendment and
restore something close to slavery. In 1865 and 1866 these
states adopted "black codes" – "a set of vagrancy laws, legal
apprenticeships, and broad local police powers that forced
ex-slaves to enter into labor contracts against their will."[28]

[27] DiLorenzo claims that "if the Republican Party had not used ex-slaves as
political pawns in the South and turned them against whites, acts of violence
against the ex-slaves and the institution of Jim Crow laws might never have
happened (*The Real Lincoln*, p. 277).
[28] Vorenberg, *Final Freedom*, p. 230.

In Mississippi and South Carolina, these codes were particularly harsh:

They defined vagrancy in such a broad fashion as to allow magistrates to arrest almost any black man whom they defined as unemployed, fine him for vagrancy, and hire him out to a planter to pay off the fine. Both states required blacks to obtain special licenses for any occupation other than agriculture.[29]

These black codes were adopted *before* the implementation of the radical Reconstruction that so embittered many Southerners. The army and the Freedman's Bureau prevented the enforcement of these laws, but those laws were a clear indication of the intentions of Southern whites.[30] Later, some Southern states had prison labor policies for blacks and some whites that were tantamount to "slavery by another name," although they were not instituted on anything like the scale of the black laws passed in 1865–6.[31] This neo-Confederate argument also ignores the power of bad ideas. The doctrine of white supremacy was the foundation of America's racially based slavery, and it was crucial to keeping poor Southern whites aligned with the aristocratic planter class. This doctrine was deeply entrenched in the South and most of the United States before the Civil War and Reconstruction.

The best evidence of how white Confederates would have treated blacks after slavery when left to their own devices, free from interference by the U.S. federal government, was the attempt by *every* former Confederate state in 1865 and 1866 to impose severe limitations on the labor mobility of blacks and the rights of blacks to negotiate favorable labor

---

[29] McPherson, *Ordeal by Fire*, p. 512; also see Oakes, *Freedom National*, pp. 489–92.

[30] McPherson, *Ordeal by Fire*, p. 512.

[31] See Blackmon, *Slavery by Another Name*. The Thirteenth Amendment includes an exception that helped make these prison labor policies possible. The amendment prohibits slavery and involuntary servitude "except as a punishment for a crime whereof the party shall have been duly convicted."

agreements (noted earlier). Additional strong evidence can be found in the very bad treatment of blacks in the American South during the period when the federal government exerted very little control over the South to protect the rights of blacks: roughly between 1880 and 1960. Before the civil rights revolution of the 1960s, local whites *never* willingly granted all blacks full civil, legal, and political rights in any of the former Confederate states. Some would say that whites in these states have *never* willingly granted blacks full equality.

It is absurd for neo-Confederates to blame Northern whites for what the Southern whites did to blacks. The Yankees did not compel Southern whites to oppress black people. Apologists for the Confederacy overlook the fact that Southern bitterness about the war was largely the result of systematic misunderstandings, distortions, and lies about the history of the war (for some of the evidence, see 4.I.1). The lies and deliberate distortions began in a speech by Jefferson Davis near the beginning of the war (see Chapter 5.II).

3. Would the independence of the CSA have prolonged slavery in Latin America?

My answer is "probably yes, but it is not clear for how long." There was a long-standing desire on the part of many people in the South to annex Cuba as a slave state. Many Southerners and some Northern Democrats such as Stephen Douglas supported the annexation of Cuba as a slave state.[32] In 1848 President Polk said that he wanted the United States to acquire Cuba and authorized his minister to Spain to offer Spain $100 million for the island.[33] In 1854 President Franklin

---

[32] Burlingame, *Abraham Lincoln: A Life*, I, pp. 714–15. Douglas said this during the third Lincoln Douglas debate, in *Lincoln's Speeches and Writings*, I, p. 601.

[33] McPherson, *The Battle Cry of Freedom*, p. 104.

Pierce authorized his minister to Spain to offer Spain as much as $130 million for Cuba.[34] In 1858 Douglas said that he wanted the United States to acquire the entire continent of North America.[35] During the secession crisis in the winter of 1860–1 following Lincoln's election, President Buchanan urged that the United States acquire Cuba as a slave state to placate the South.[36]

Several small-scale invasions of Cuba by private groups that aimed at making Cuba a slave state in the United States were launched from the South in the early 1850s.[37] These invasions were easily stopped by the Spanish authorities in Cuba, but they demonstrated the determination of some Southerners to unite and make common cause with Latin American slave owners. In 1856, an American, William Walker, established himself as president of Nicaragua. During his time in power, Nicaragua legalized slavery and reopened the African slave trade.[38] Walker appealed to Southern slave owners to join him in Nicaragua. Some did, but his disease-ridden army was defeated by a Central American alliance in 1857.[39] An independent Confederate States of America would likely have supported similar ventures into Latin America and, very likely, would have tried to annex parts of it. It is possible that the United States or Britain would have intervened and prevented these actions, but they could not have prevented the CSA from lending powerful moral and material support to slave-owning interests in Latin America. It is possible that an independent CSA would have created a very large confederation consisting of the CSA and parts of

---

[34] Ibid., p. 110.
[35] Also in the third Lincoln-Douglas debate, in Abraham Lincoln, *Lincoln's Speeches and Writings*, I, p. 601.
[36] McPherson, *The Battle Cry of Freedom*, p. 251.
[37] Ibid., pp. 105–6.
[38] Foner, *The Fiery Trial*, p. 125.
[39] McPherson, *The Battle Cry of Freedom*, pp. 113–14.

Latin America that practiced slavery. Had this happened, it would have been a powerful confederation.

Perhaps most importantly, it is very possible that Brazilian slavery would have continued much longer had the CSA become independent. Many people in the American South desired an alliance with Brazil as a hedge against abolitionist pressure. A large influential Southern organization with one hundred thousand members, the Knights of the Golden Circle, planned to create a great slave empire including Brazil in the Western Hemisphere.[40] John C. Calhoun, the most important defender of slavery in the antebellum United States, wanted the United States to ally itself with Brazil and Cuba and said that they had a mutual interest in resisting interference with slavery.[41] Many other Southerners urged the South to ally itself with Brazil to protect their common interest in slavery and resist pressure to end it.[42]

The outcome of the American Civil War and the end of slavery in the United States had a profound effect on slavery in Brazil and other places in the Americas: it greatly demoralized slave-owning interests in Brazil and made it clear to them that the tide of history had turned.[43] The emperor of

---

[40] Horne, *The Deepest South*, pp. 4 and 127.

[41] Ibid., p. 55.

[42] Ibid., pp. 117, 134, and 158. Some people in the Confederacy discussed the idea of keeping the French-installed Mexican emperor, Maximilian, in power and reintroducing slavery into Mexico (ibid., p. 208). Confederate envoys contacted Maximilian and "offered to recognize him if he would help obtain French recognition of the South. Maximilian was willing, but by January 1864," the French government had lost interest in this plan (McPherson, *The Battle Cry of Freedom*, p. 683). "In addition to his brief take-over of Nicaragua, William Walker led a small scale invasion of two Mexican Provinces in 1853. He and his pro-slavery followers briefly captured the Capitol of Baja California. This invasion was roundly defeated by Mexico. Walker retreated across the US border in May 1854. Many people in California hailed him as a hero. He was put on trial for violating US neutrality laws, but the jury in San Francisco acquitted him after deliberating for eight minutes" (ibid., p. 111–12).

[43] Horne, *The Deepest South*, p. 229.

Brazil said that the outcome of the American war compelled his government to reconsider the institution of slavery.[44] That outcome also convinced Brazilian slaves that they would soon be free.[45] Brazil completely abolished slavery in 1888, and all children born to slave mothers as of 1871 were to be free.[46] The Spanish abolition cause became a nationwide movement immediately after Spain learned of the Emancipation Proclamation, and it invoked Lincoln's example. Spain ended slavery in Puerto Rico in 1873, and in 1886 it ended slavery in Cuba.[47] The Dutch abolished slavery in Surinam during the Civil War in 1863.[48]

Some think that Britain would have pressured the CSA and Latin America to end slavery, but Britain did *nothing* to pressure the United States to abolish slavery before the Civil War and it happily purchased huge quantities of slave-produced American cotton. Further, Britain did not support the Union war effort, and indeed the United States and Britain nearly went to war as a result of the Trent incident in 1861.[49] Britain and France recognized the Confederates as legitimate belligerents and sold them armaments.[50] For all these reasons, it is very possible that slavery would have continued a

---

[44] Ibid., p. 229.

[45] Ibid., p. 230.

[46] Thomas, *The Slave Trade*, p. 788.

[47] Howe, "Lincoln's Worldwide Audience."

[48] *Encyclopedia Britannica*, 10th edition, "Guiana."

[49] The U.S. Navy forcibly stopped the British ship, *The Trent*, on the high seas and arrested two Confederate ministers, James Mason and John Slidell who were on board the ship. There were calls for war in Britain, and the British government issued an ultimatum demanding an apology and the release of Mason and Slidell. Lincoln was forced to yield to this humiliating demand, but added some face-saving provisions; McPherson, *The Battle Cry of Freedom*, pp. 389–91.

[50] For this and other evidence of considerable support for the Confederate cause among the upper classes in Britain, see McPherson, *Battle Cry of Freedom*, pp. 546–51. "In July 1862 the supply of raw cotton in Britain stood at one-third of the normal level. Three-quarters of the cotton-mill workers were unemployed or on short time" (p. 548). The Chancellor of the Exchequer "favored British

generation or two longer in parts of Latin America if the CSA
had established its independence.

4. Would the CSA have continued the Atlantic slave trade?

I think that the answer is "probably not on a large scale."
Article I, Section 9, subsection 1 of the Confederate constitution prohibits "the importation of African negroes from
any foreign country other than the slave-holding states of
the United States."[51] Despite the legal prohibition of the
African slave trade and the attempt of the British and American navies to enforce this ban, the Atlantic slave trade from
Africa to the Americas continued on a large scale until the
beginning of the Civil War. Brazil acquired one million slaves
from Africa during the first half of the nineteenth century –
500,000 arrived between 1835 and 1855 – and some think
that the Atlantic slave trade reached its peak during the
1840s.[52] Robert Hall estimates that 250,000 African slaves
were brought to the United States after the 1808 prohibition on the African slave trade.[53] Hugh Thomas and Philip
Curtin give a much lower estimate of fifty thousand.[54] Very
high profits for slave traders, who sold slaves in the Americas
for much higher prices than they paid for them in Africa,[55]
and ineffectual punishments for slave traders accounted for
this trade. The United States refused to grant permission to
the British Navy to search suspected slave ships flying the
U.S. flag; this encouraged pirates and slavers of many nation-
alities to fly the American flag.[56] A very large percentage of

intervention to stop the war and start the flow of cotton across the Atlantic"
(p. 548).
[51] Ransom, *The Confederate States of America*, p. 272.
[52] Horne, *The Deepest South*, p. 2.
[53] Ibid., p. 14.
[54] Thomas, *The Slave Trade*, p. 616.
[55] Horne, *The Deepest South*, p. 129.
[56] Ibid., pp. 7–8.

the Atlantic slave trade in the nineteenth century was carried on by ships displaying the American flag.[57]

The South itself was divided over the issue of the African slave trade. Shortly before the beginning of the Civil War, a South Carolina court declared that the importation of slaves who had been slaves in Africa was not in violation of U.S. laws.[58] Generally the resumption of the Atlantic slave trade was opposed in the Upper South, but widely supported in the Deep South. These views reflected the very different economic interests of slave owners in those two regions. The prohibition on the importation of slaves raised the price of slaves in the United States, which benefited slave owners in the Upper South who sold slaves to the Deep South; for this same reason, it harmed the economic interests of those slave owners in the Deep South.

The Civil War brought about a very steep decline in the African slave trade. It was deterred in 1862 by the very first execution of a U.S. citizen, Nathaniel Gordon, for his participation in the slave trade. Lincoln had the power to commute Gordon's sentence, but declined to do so. Also that year, the U.S. government signed a treaty with Britain "for the suppression of the African Slave Trade." This treaty permitted the navies of each nation to search the ships of the other nation and also stipulated that if ships were found to have items such as shackles or large quantities of rice, then that would be considered "prima facie evidence that the ship was involved in the African Slave Trade."[59]

It is likely that some of the states of the Deep South would have tried to continue the African slave trade despite the strictures of the Confederate constitution. These states could have

[57] Ibid., pp. 3, 7–8, and 37.
[58] Ibid., p. 132. As a legal ruling, this was absurd, because Congress outlawed the importation of African slaves into the United States after 1808.
[59] Ibid., p. 185.

defied Confederate laws, just as they had defied U.S. laws. The blockade of the CSA during the Civil War and Lincoln's 1862 treaty with Britain greatly reduced and suppressed the African slave trade.[60] In fact his role in suppressing the African slave trade is one of Lincoln's greatest achievements. But because he could have signed and enforced this treaty with Britain even if he had allowed the CSA to secede peacefully, it is doubtful that the ending of the Atlantic slave trade can be counted as a good consequence of the war. (However, whatever role the Union naval blockade of the Confederacy played in ending the Atlantic slave trade can be counted as a good consequence of the war.)

II. Two Utilitarian Arguments for the View that the Union Had Just Cause for Fighting the American Civil War

1. *The Implications of the Actual Consequences Version of Utilitarianism.* The actual consequences version of utilitarianism (which claims that a person acts rightly provided that she brings about the best consequences that it is possible for her to produce in the circumstances – see Chapter 2.III) implies that the Union had just cause for fighting the Civil War from its very beginning, because the actual good achieved by fighting the war outweighed the bad that it caused.

Roughly, we need to weigh the badness of the deaths of 750,000 soldiers,[61] 750,000 other casualties (soldiers who

---

[60] For evidence of the very sharp decline and end of the Atlantic slave trade during the 1860s, see Oakes, *Freedom National*, pp. 261–3. According to Oakes, "The number of African slaves sold to Cuba dropped from fourteen thousand in 1861 to ten thousand in 1862 to under four thousand in 1863. Within another few years, four centuries of Atlantic slave trading came to an end" (p. 263).

[61] For a very long time, the generally accepted figure was 620,000 military deaths, but in an important and widely cited recent study, "A Census Based Count of the Civil War Dead," J. David Hacker gives a considerably higher estimate of

were missing, wounded, or made seriously ill by the war),[62] the war-related deaths of 50,000 civilians,[63] and a great deal of damage to property and the economy in the Confederate states against the goodness of the liberty of ten to twenty-five million people and greatly improved rights for thirty two million other people.

How do I arrive at these figures for the good consequences (benefits) of the war? There were roughly 3.5 million slaves in the CSA at the beginning of the Civil War.[64] I assume that slavery would not have ended in the CSA for at least two more generations, not until roughly 1910–13 (see the earlier discussion). If we assume that the slave population would have continued to double every twenty-six years as it had prior to that time,[65] then the slave population of the CSA would have been fourteen million in 1913. But this number is probably too high. In 1910, the total black population of the United States was 9,836,000, and that number included the descendants of slaves from the border states, the descendants of people who were free in 1860, and some later immigrants and their descendants.[66] (But we can discount the effect of immigration on the total black population, because the number of black immigrants to the United States was very small

Civil War deaths. Hacker claims that the Confederate war dead were greatly undercounted due to poor record keeping by the Confederates and that the best estimate is 752,000 deaths (possibly as high as 851,000 deaths).

[62] Hacker does not give an estimate of the total number of nonlethal casualties in the war. For the purposes of my estimate, I assume that the number is 750,000, even thought it is likely that this number is much too high. The Wikipedia article on the Civil War gives a much higher figure for total deaths than nonlethal casualties (it estimates that there were 670,000 deaths and 1,030,000 total casualties). If, as this article suggests, I am being cautious in greatly overestimating the number of nonlethal casualties, then that *strengthens* the case for the view that the good consequences of the war outweighed the bad.

[63] McPherson, *The Battle Cry of Freedom*, p. 619.

[64] Catton, *The American Heritage Picture History of the Civil War*, p. 96; also see U.S. Census, 1860, "Introduction," pp. xii–xxiii.

[65] McPherson, *The Battle Cry of Freedom*, p. 37.

[66] Morton, *Historical Statistics of the United States: Bicentennial Edition*, Part I, p. 14.

before 1910. In 1900 the total number of black immigrants living in the United States was only 41,000.[67]) If the slave population of the Confederate states in 1910 had remained the same in terms of its proportion of the total black and mulatto population of the United States as in 1860 (79.5% or 3.5 million of 4.4 million),[68] then there would have been more than 7.8 million slaves in the CSA in 1910. At least half of the 3.5 million people who were slaves in Confederate states in 1861 would have died of natural causes during the next fifty years, and we can add that number (1.75 million) to the 7.8 million people counted earlier. Because the life expectancy of slaves in 1860 was a little less than forty years[69] this is a safe number. We can also add at least 450,000 Confederate slaves who would have been born and died between 1860 and 1910. (This is also a safe number given the life expectancy of slaves in 1860.) On the assumption that the CSA would have ended slavery in 1910 or 1913, the total number of people who enjoyed freedom because of the war is at least ten million. (I am counting both people who were never slaves because of the war and people who were slaves and then later became

---

[67] Myrdal, *An American Dilemma*, p. 165.

[68] The total slave population of the United States in 1860 was 3,950,000; 1860 U.S. Census, "Introduction," p. vii.

[69] I calculate this on the following basis. In 1860, the life expectancy of the total U.S. population was 41.8 years; Sutch and Carter, *Historical Statistics of the United States*, I, p. 440. I assume that the life expectancy of slaves would have continued to be more than two years less than this, as it was ten years earlier. In 1850 the life expectancy of American slaves was 36 years (Fogel and Engerman, *Time on the Cross*, p. 125); the life expectancy of the total U.S. population in 1850 was 38.3 years (Sutch and Carter, *Historical Statistics of the United States*, I, p. 440. It is safe to assume that the life expectancy at birth of blacks would have continued to be lower than that of whites. The available data (in ibid., pp. 440–1), which give actual figures comparing the life expectancies of blacks and whites for the years 1900, 1910, and 1970–98, strongly confirm this racial gap. Whites had a greater life expectancy than blacks during all those years. The gap in life expectancy greatly *widened* between 1850 and 1910 – in 1900 the figures are 49.6 years for whites and 41.8 years for blacks versus 54.6 years for whites and 46.2 years for blacks in 1910.

free because of the war.) Given this figure, the ratio of the number of people who enjoyed freedom as a consequence of the war to the number of people killed by the war is about twelve (12.5) to one.

My estimate of the number of people who enjoyed freedom because of the war is very conservative because the rate of population growth among slaves before the Civil War was more than twice as great as that of free blacks during the same time period and was much higher than the rate of growth among free blacks after the war.[70] It is also conservative because the slave population of the Confederate states grew at a considerably faster rate between 1830 and 1860 than the slave population of the border states (Missouri, Kentucky, Maryland, and Delaware).[71] These facts give us reasons to think that the slave population of the CSA would have grown at a faster rate between 1860 and 1910 than the rate at which the black population of the United States actually grew during that period. Furthermore, my estimate neither includes the 450,000 slaves in the border states who were freed as a result of the war nor the descendants of those 450,000 who might have lived in bondage were it not for the war. Finally, my estimate is also conservative because it does not include any of the slaves in Latin America whose freedom would have been delayed – perhaps long delayed – by the independence of the CSA.

---

[70] 1860 U.S. Census, "Introduction," p. ix. According to the Census, between 1840 and 1860 the slave population of the United States grew at more than twice the rate of the free black population. The total free black population of the United States after the war did not grow nearly as fast as the slave population had grown before the war. Before the war, the slave population was doubling every 26 years. It took nearly 50 years for the total black population in 1860 (4,441,830) to double (p. xii).

[71] There were 2,009,000 slaves in the United States in 1830 (1830 Census, "Abstract," p. 46). Of these, 296,000 slaves (14.7% of the total slave population) lived in the four border states (p. 46). In 1860 there were 3,950,000 slaves of whom 450,000 slaves (11.3%) lived in the border states.

My figure of ten million people is not so much an estimate of the actual number of people who enjoyed freedom because of the war, but rather it is *a number such that no lower estimate is plausible*. It is likely that the actual number is considerably higher than 10 million, but if so, that would only strengthen the case for thinking that the good consequences of the Civil War outweighed the bad.[72]

The higher estimate of the number of people who would have been slaves were it not for the war, twenty-five million, is based on the possibilities that slavery in the CSA might have continued well past 1913 and that the independence of the CSA would have greatly prolonged slavery in Latin America. Given this higher estimate, the ratio between the number of people who would have been slaves were it not for the war and the number of people who were killed by the war is more than 30 to 1.[73]

---

[72] I am not even claiming that ten million is the "lower bound" – the lowest plausible estimate. The lower bound may be higher than that. Very simply, my claim is that *at least* ten million people enjoyed freedom because Lincoln chose to fight the Civil War. If the lower bound is higher, that would strengthen my argument.

[73] *Digressive Footnote for Philosophers*. Strictly speaking, I cannot say that there were ten million people who were free (and who *themselves* otherwise would have been slaves) because of the Civil War. Many of those I am counting in this number would not have been born if the Civil War had not been fought; rather, they never would have been conceived and never existed at all.

The American Civil War was a huge event in human history. It had many repercussions that radically altered the lives of most Americans. To the extent that anyone's existence is dependent on one's parents having met and having had sexual relations at *exactly* the same time and in *exactly* the same way they actually did, anyone's existence is likely to depend on many contingencies (e.g., someone's sneezing or not sneezing at a particular instant). For example, my existence is almost certainly dependent on the fact that World War II was fought. My mother and father met after the war because they were both trained in the weather service of the U.S. military. Given that they grew up in different parts of the country, it is extremely unlikely they would have ever met otherwise.

The lives of all American slaves living at the time were radically altered by the Civil War. So it is very unlikely that all of the former slaves who created children would have created children with *exactly* the same partners at *exactly* the same time and in *exactly* the same way if the Civil War had

The entire black population of an independent CSA would probably have suffered a severe diminishment in civil rights for at least 130 years. South Africa did not grant blacks full legal rights as citizens until the 1990s, and there is reason to think that Confederate-style racial oppression would have lasted at least until then (see 4.I.2). Whites in the CSA were a majority, and they were in a much stronger position to dominate blacks than were South African whites.

The total number of "free" black people in the Confederacy who would have suffered severely diminished rights had the CSA become an independent nation was more than thirty-two million. How do I arrive at this estimate? The total black population of the United States in 1990 was roughly thirty million.[74] Of these at least 23,850,000 blacks would have been living in the CSA (this is 79.5% of thirty million).[75] To that number, we can add at least 8.15 million people who

---

not been fought in 1861. Therefore, it is very likely that many/most/almost all of the descendants of slaves who were conceived during or after the war would not have been conceived (or existed at all) had the war not been fought and fought then. The 10 million former slaves and their descendants who were free between 1865–1910 were not the *same individuals* as the 10 million people and their descendants who would have been slaves in the United States between 1865–1910 had Lincoln and the Union allowed the CSA to become independent.

So I cannot say that there were ten million individuals who were free (who *themselves* would have been slaves) if the Civil War had not been fought. Rather, I have to say that, as a consequence of the Civil War, ten million fewer people suffered from being slaves. This does not affect the aggregate totals in my cost-benefit estimate. It is just that the roughly ten million more people who would themselves have been slaves if the CSA had been allowed to secede are not the same individuals as the *actual* 10 million former slaves and their descendants who enjoyed freedom between 1865–1910. Standard versions of utilitarianism do not regard this difference as morally relevant, and I can still say that for every one person killed and one wounded during the war, there were twelve people who would have been slaves had the war not been fought. For discussions of this issue, see Parfit, *Reasons and Persons* and Roberts, "The Non-Identity Problem."

74 Sutch and Carter, *Historical Statistics of the United States*, I, pp. 61 and 63. This figure is very slightly rounded up from the actual figure of 29,985,000.

75 Given the higher rate of population growth among slaves than free blacks, this number is very likely too low.

would have lived as "free people" in the CSA and died before 1990. (This is a safe number because the life expectancy of American blacks in 1910 was only 46.2 years.[76]) It is unlikely that very many free blacks in the CSA would have emigrated to the United States because of strong racial prejudice there throughout most of the twentieth century; before 1965, U.S. immigration laws severely restricted the immigration of non-Europeans. Thus, at least thirty-two million people enjoyed vastly better rights and status because Lincoln fought the Civil War and did not allow the CSA to become an independent nation. Given all of this, more than forty people enjoyed considerably greater rights because the Civil War was fought and won for each person killed in the war (32,000,000 divided by 800,000 equals 40).[77]

I do not have any precise way of weighing the relative badness of being killed, wounded, or made ill against the badness of being a slave or having one's rights severely diminished. Some people would say that it is obscene or repugnant to attach numbers to these things. Others would contend that these goods and bads are incommensurable and that their relative proportion cannot be quantified. But leaders such as

---

[76] Sutch and Carter, *Historical Statistics of the United States*, I, p. 440.

[77] *Another Digressive Footnote for Philosophers.* For the same reasons explained in note 73, I cannot say that 32 million people enjoyed greater freedom because of the war than they *themselves* would have enjoyed otherwise. The 32 million actual African Americans I am talking about are not the same *individuals* as the people who would have lived had there been no war and the CSA became independent. The war caused different individual people to be conceived and not conceived. But I can still say the following. Because Lincoln and the Union chose to fight the war rather than permit the CSA to become independent, there were 32 million African Americans who enjoyed much greater rights and liberties than the roughly 32 million black people who would have existed as free people in the CSA between 1910–90. And, most crucially, I can say that for every one person killed and one wounded in the war, there were more than forty African Americans who enjoyed much greater rights and freedoms during their lifetimes than the "free Afro-Confederates" (comparable in number) would have had in the CSA between 1910–90.

Lincoln are sometimes forced to decide between such competing goods and bads, and it is most unreasonable to hold that there are *never* compelling reasons to choose certain alternatives over others in such cases.

The great disproportion between the number of people whose freedom was assured by the war and the number of people whose rights were greatly enhanced as a result of the war, as compared with the number of people who were killed or wounded in the war, shows that the good achieved by the Union war effort outweighed the badness of the deaths and suffering caused by the war. Surely one person dying and one person being wounded or made ill are less bad than twelve people being slaves in circumstances similar to those of typical slaves in the United States and forty more people suffering a severe diminishment of their civil rights. My rough numbers provide a way to see that the war was not as great an evil as the continuation of American slavery and the other evils that would have resulted from the independence of the CSA. Suppose that a typical slave in the antebellum South could gain her freedom (and ensure greatly improved rights for three (3.2) of her descendants) through a course of action that had a one in twelve chance of causing her to be killed and a one in twelve chance of causing her to be wounded or become very ill. A rationally self-interested person would take that risk and attempt to secure her freedom and the rights of her descendants, and that is strong evidence that the good achieved by ensuring the freedom of ten million people and greatly enhancing the rights of thirty-two million other people outweighed the evil of the war and for the claim that, on balance, the war enhanced human welfare. If we make a higher estimate of the number of people who would have been slaves were it not for the Civil War, the argument is stronger.

An Objection and Further Complication. My cost-benefit analysis of the Civil War counts the freedom of the slaves who lived in Arkansas, Tennessee, Virginia, and North Carolina and many of their descendants as benefits or good consequences of the war. But it is debatable whether they should count as benefits, because those four states had decided against secession before Fort Sumter and joined the Confederacy only after Lincoln's decision to fight a war and his call for volunteers to suppress the rebellion (see Map 2 in Chapter 2). So it is arguable that I have considerably overestimated the benefits of the Union fighting the Civil War.

The relevant time line is this. Fort Sumter was attacked on April 12, 1861, and it fell two days later on April 14.[78] On April 15, 1861, Lincoln called for 75,000 troops to suppress the rebellion.[79] In response Governor Magoffin of Kentucky said that his state would "furnish no troops for the wicked purpose of subduing her sister Southern States."[80] The secessionist governor of Missouri said, "Not one man will the State of Missouri furnish to carry on any such unholy crusade."[81] On April 17, an ad hoc convention in Virginia voted for secession; this vote was ratified by the voters of Virginia on May 23.[82] Arkansas, Tennessee, and North Carolina left the Union in May 1861.[83]

Reply. The relevant comparison to consider is that between what actually happened and what would have happened if Lincoln and the U.S. government had allowed the original seven Confederate states to secede. Arguably, I then need to redo the cost-benefit calculation presented earlier. Let me first do this on the basis of assumptions that are the least favorable to my case. In 1860, the seven original states of the CSA held 65.5 percent of the total slave population of the

[78] McPherson, *The Battle Cry of Freedom*, p. 273.
[79] Ibid., p. 274.
[80] Ibid.
[81] Ibid., p. 276.
[82] Ibid., pp. 279–80.
[83] Ibid., p. 282.

eleven states of the Confederacy, roughly two-thirds of the slaves.[84] If we revise the earlier calculations in light of that number, we get the following figures: at least eight people (perhaps as many as twenty) lived as free people because of the war for every one person who died in the war and for every one person who was wounded in the war, and roughly twenty-six people enjoyed much better legal rights and life prospects because the war was fought for every one person who died and every one person who was wounded during the war. This, I believe, is still enough to justify the war. In addition, these are *extremely* conservative estimates. The slave population of the seven original Confederate states was growing *much faster* than the slave population of the other four states. In 1830 slaves in the four states of the Upper South were 50.6% of the total slave population of the eleven states that later formed the Confederacy, compared to only 34.5 percent in 1860.[85]

If the seven original Confederate states had been allowed to secede peacefully in 1861, then the United States would have had eight remaining slave states. It is very likely that several of those eight states would have later joined the CSA; they would have been strongly tempted to do so had strong antislavery measures been seriously considered or enacted in

---

[84] According to the 1860 U.S. Census, there were 1,208,825 slaves in the four states of the Upper South – 34.5% of the 3.5 million slaves in the eleven states of the Confederacy.

[85] According to the 1830 U.S. Census, there were 861,537 slaves in the four states of the Upper South – 50.6% of the 1,702,386 slaves in the eleven states that later formed the Confederacy. According to the Census, there were 2,009,050 slaves in the United States in 1830, of whom 296,580 lived in the four border states (Missouri, Kentucky, Maryland and Delaware), 3,975 lived in the North, and 6,119 lived in Washington, D.C. (Arkansas was not a state at the time, but it had 4,576 slaves and I count those slaves toward the total of the four states). Texas was not a state in 1830. But because Mexico had outlawed slavery before 1830, the overwhelming majority of the slaves in Texas at the time that it became part of the United States were people who had been brought to Texas from the United States or their descendants.

the United States. Slave owners in those eight states would likely have sold many of their slaves to the seven Confederate states – this commerce was going on before the war, and it would have likely increased in response to antislavery movements in the North. Therefore, very probably, either the U.S. federal government would have left slavery alone in those eight slave states for a very long time, or had it tried to end slavery in any of those eight states, some or all of them would have left the Union and/or sold their slaves to the CSA.

Still, each of these eight states would have had the option of ending slavery within its own borders. But it is unlikely that all (or even most of them) would have chosen to do so for a long time. In 1860, most of these eight states were strongly committed to retaining the institution of slavery. Here is my evidence for that claim. Before Lincoln issued the Emancipation Proclamation, the border states all refused to adopt Lincoln's proposals for compensated emancipation, even though at that time they knew that they risked losing their slaves without receiving any financial compensation. The four states of the Upper South were even more strongly committed to defending slavery than the border states. Unlike in Missouri, Kentucky, and Delaware, there was no recent history of large-scale movements to end slavery in the states of the Upper South.

So the basis for assessing the good and bad consequences of Lincoln's decision to fight a civil war in the spring of 1861 is difficult and uncertain. But *in any case*, after May 1861 and then for the rest of the war, the proper cost-benefit estimate of Lincoln's decision to continue fighting the war and not permitting the eleven Confederate states to become independent includes the freedom of all the slaves in the eleven Confederate states and many of their descendants. My earlier cost-benefit estimate holds for that entire period and for the decision repeatedly made by Lincoln and the U.S. government to continue fighting the war.

Another Objection. Some contend that the situation of freed blacks after the Civil War was not much better than it had been under slavery. Given this view, my claim that the end of slavery was an enormous benefit of the Civil War is mistaken. If correct, this criticism also seriously undermines my arguments for the justice of the Union cause in the war. James McPherson gives a very good statement of this objection, although he himself strongly rejects it:

By such devices as the crop lien system, debt peonage, sharecropping, and a host of legal restrictions on black labor mobility, the planters kept their labor force subservient and poor in a manner little different from slavery.... the war and reconstruction produced no "fundamental changes" in the "antebellum forms of economic and social organization in the South." No "social revolution" took place because the abolition of slavery produced no "specific changes either in the status of the former slaves or in the conditions under which they labored."[86]

It is undoubtedly true that most Southern blacks were kept in poverty and subservience and (after Reconstruction) effectively denied the right to vote for a very long time. Further, a large number of blacks (and some whites) were subjected to forced labor in prisons for "crimes" such as vagrancy – something that deserves the name "slavery by another name."[87] Nonetheless, the social, economic, and educational status of Southern blacks improved dramatically after the war. McPherson documents this improvement:

The slaves in the seven cotton states of the lower South had received in the form of food, clothing, and shelter only 22 percent of the income produced by the plantations and farms on which they worked. With the coming of freedom, the proportion jumped to 56 percent.... Blacks were getting a bigger share of the pie, but it was a smaller pie. Nevertheless... between 1857 and 1879 the

[86] McPherson, *Abraham Lincoln and the Second American Revolution*, p. 14.
[87] See Blackmon, *Slavery by Another Name.*

per capita income for blacks in southern agriculture increased by 46 percent, when the per capita income of whites declined by 35 percent. Put another way, black per capita income in these seven states jumped from a level of only 23 percent of white income under slavery to 52 percent of the white level by 1880.[88]

On the basis of this evidence, McPherson reaches the following conclusion:

Thus, while blacks still had a standard of living only half as high as whites in the poorest region of the country ... this relative redistribution in the South was by far the greatest in American history.[89]

There were also dramatic improvements in literacy rates and educational opportunities for Southern blacks after the war. At the time of the Civil War, the literacy rate for blacks was 10 percent. This increased to 29 percent in 1880, 43 percent in 1890, 55 percent in 1900, 70 percent in 1910, 73 percent in 1920, and 84 percent in 1930.[90] Although it was considerably less than justice required, this was a dramatic improvement.

But despite the continuing improvement in literacy rates, the socioeconomic position of Southern blacks worsened considerably after Reconstruction, particularly after 1900. As W. E. B. Du Bois wrote, "The slave went free; stood a brief moment in the sun; then moved back toward slavery."[91] One very important indication of the way in which the situation of Southern blacks deteriorated after 1900 is the following. In 1900, per student spending on the education of white students was 50 percent greater than spending on black students in the South, but by 1930, this figure had dramatically increased to 350 percent (i.e., in 1930, per student spending

---

[88] McPherson, *Abraham Lincoln and the Second American Revolution*, p. 18.
[89] Ibid.
[90] Smith and Horton, *Historical Statistics of Black America*, I, p. 670; also see McPherson, *Abraham Lincoln and the Second American Revolution*, p. 16.
[91] Foner, *Reconstruction*, p. 602.

in Southern public schools was 3.5 times greater for white students than black students).[92] After a federal court ruling in 1940 that different salary scales for black and white schools were unconstitutional, the situation began to improve slowly, although the court ruling applied in only one county.[93]

Black income levels have always been well below the national average. Although precise aggregate figures on black incomes and how they compare with white incomes for times before 1967 are very difficult to obtain.[94] But available data on black incomes strongly support a picture similar to the one just sketched of the educational opportunities for blacks. In 1940 the median annual income of black males was less than 41 percent of that of white males, and the median annual income of black females was less than 36 percent of that of white females.[95] Over the next fifty-five years, the

---

[92] Franklin, *From Slavery to Freedom*, p. 547.

[93] Ibid., pp. 548–9. Several counties in Virginia, Maryland, and South Carolina equalized the salaries of black and white teachers after court action was initiated or threatened. In 1944 North Carolina implemented a statewide program to reduce differences in funding for education. Despite the "separate but equal interpretation" of the Fourteenth Amendment in the case of *Plessy* v. *Ferguson*, that amendment did considerable good in these cases, even before the U.S. Supreme Court overturned *Plessy* v. *Ferguson*.

[94] The U.S. Census did not compile such records until recently. *The Historical Atlas of Black America* gives figures comparing the incomes of whites and nonwhites but doesn't include aggregate figures comparing black and white incomes before 1969, although it includes incomplete data for this going back to 1959 (Smith and Horton, I, pp. 998–1000). The 1975 edition of the *Historical Statistics of the United States* gives statistics on median income in the United States between 1947–70. It compares the median incomes of whites and nonwhites, but does not include any figures on black incomes and how they compare with the incomes of other groups (Morton, I, p. 297). The 2006 edition of the *Historical Statistics of the United States* gives statistics comparing the median and mean income of blacks with those of other racial groups but these do not begin before 1967 (Sutch and Carter, II, p. 660).

[95] Thernstrom and Thernstrom, *America in Black and White*, p. 195. This figure is based on census data. In 1940 the census did not compile data on black versus white incomes, but only compared the incomes of whites and nonwhites. In 1940 the income of nonwhite males was 41% of the income of white males, and the figure for females was 36%. These figures include a small number of

economic situation of blacks improved dramatically. In 1970, the median annual income of black males was 59 percent of that of white males, and the median annual income of black females was 73 percent of that of white females. In 1995, the figures for black males and females, respectively, were 67 percent and 89 percent.[96]

That the situation of blacks badly deteriorated for a long time after Reconstruction is not an objection to my thesis that blacks in the United States were much better off than they would have been in the CSA. Rather it is strong prima facie evidence of the much worse fate that would have likely befallen them in an independent CSA. The dramatic improvements during Reconstruction and after 1940 were largely the result of the actions of the U.S. federal government taken against the wishes of whites in the Confederate states: these actions included various court rulings that addressed inequality in education; President Roosevelt's executive order of June 25, 1941, prohibiting discrimination in employment in the defense industries and in the government;[97] the integration of the armed forces; and the civil rights laws of the 1950s and 1960s. The opportunities to move to the North and work in industry, vote in elections, and obtain a better education also greatly benefited blacks. These opportunities would probably not have been nearly as great had the CSA become an independent nation.

For a considerable majority of freed slaves and their descendants, the next 130 to 150 years were much better than the years that came before. Things would have been much worse for African Americans if the CSA had gained its independence, even after such time that the CSA abolished slavery.

Asians. Because Asians had higher incomes than blacks, the income of black males/females was *less than* 41%/36% of the income of white males/females.

[96] Ibid.

[97] Franklin, *From Slavery to Freedom*, p. 579.

2. *Lincoln's Argument that a Very Bad Precedent for Democracy Would Have Been Set if the Confederacy Had Become Independent.* In his first Inaugural Address and other speeches he gave during the Civil War, Lincoln claimed that if the Confederacy was permitted to leave the Union, this would set a terrible precedent for democratic nations to splinter whenever one faction was unhappy with the outcome of an election.

Lincoln also thought that if the Confederacy became independent, it would seem to show that democracies were inherently unstable and tended to disintegrate, something that would discredit the very idea of democracy and greatly discourage democratic movements in other parts of the world.

On May 7, 1861, he told his secretary John Hay,

> For my own part, I consider the central idea pervading this struggle is the necessity that is upon us, of proving that popular government is not an absurdity. We must settle this question now, whether in a free government the minority have the right to break up the government whenever they choose. If we fail it will go far to prove the incapability of a people to govern themselves.[98]

Lincoln's other secretary, John Nicolay, was present during this conversation, and his recollection of what Lincoln said is roughly the same as Hay's.[99]

Lincoln said that if the precedent for secession set by the CSA stood and a minority seceded from a democracy whenever it was unwilling to accept the outcome of an election, that precedent would "divide and rule them." In other words, the smaller democratic states that would be created by secession would themselves be further divided by secession movements led by electoral minorities dissatisfied with the outcomes of future elections. This would lead to anarchy and

---

[98] Burlingame and Ettlinger, eds., *Inside Lincoln's White House*, p. 20.
[99] Ibid., p. 280.

the destruction of all large, strong, democratic nations.[100] He repeated this argument in his Special Message to Congress, July 4, 1861, delivered soon after the Civil War began:

No popular government can long survive a marked precedent, that those who carry an election, can only save the government from immediate destruction, by giving up the main point, upon which the people gave the election.[101]

It [the secession of the Confederate states] forces us to ask: "Is there, in all republics, this inherent, and fatal weakness?" "Must a government of necessity, be too *strong* for the liberties of its own people, or too *weak* to maintain its own existence?"[102]

No doubt, Lincoln was correct in saying that the successful secession of the Confederacy would create a very bad precedent for democracies to splinter when certain regions are unhappy with the outcomes of elections. But his further claim that this precedent would discredit the idea of democracy and show it to be "an absurdity" and thus have dire consequences for the cause of democracy throughout the world is extremely speculative. It is unclear what would have happened as a result of the independence of the CSA. Undoubtedly, it would have given aid and comfort to antidemocratic forces throughout the world, but Lincoln's claim that this would seriously harm the cause of democracy globally and his claim (in the Gettysburg Address) that it would have caused "government of the people, by the people and for the people" to "perish from the earth"[103] are questionable. The United

---

[100] Abraham Lincoln, *Speeches and Writings*, II, p. 220.

[101] Ibid., p. 261. According to Michael Lind, if the CSA had become independent, it is likely that Texas would have seceded from the CSA and that California would have seceded from the United States; Lind, *What Lincoln Believed*, p. 285. In January 1861, New York City Mayor Ferando Wood sent a message to the city alderman saying that the city should secede from the United States; McPherson, *Battle Cry of Freedom*, p. 247.

[102] Abraham Lincoln, *Speeches and Writings*, II, p. 250.

[103] Ibid., p. 536.

States might still have continued as a successful model for democracy, and it could have prevented the possibility of further instances of secession by amending the U.S. Constitution with explicit prohibitions against secession. Further, Britain, which was slowly but surely evolving into a democratic nation,[104] might have served as a model for democracy in the future. There is no reason to think that its very long and gradual evolution toward democracy was dependent on what happened to democracy in the United States. Finally, as Lincoln well knew, the existence of slavery in America greatly undermined the popular appeal and moral force of American democracy abroad. In his speech on the Kansas-Nebraska Act, October 16, 1854, Lincoln said,

I hate it [slavery] because of the monstrous injustice of slavery itself. I hate it because it deprives our republican example of its just influence in the world – enables enemies of free institutions, with plausibility, to taunt us as hypocrites – causes real friends of freedom to doubt our sincerity.[105]

The democratic United States practiced slavery and inflicted on its slaves what Lincoln called the worst injustice ever

---

[104] Here are some of the facts relevant to the issue of democracy in Britain. Before the reform act of 1832, the total British electorate was between 419,000 and 488,000 (C. Roberts and D. Roberts, *A History of England 1688 to the Present*, II, p. 558). The total British population was 24,028,000 at that time. This meant that only 1.7%–2.0% of the people were able to vote. (The percentage of adult men who were eligible to vote was considerably higher, but still a small percentage of the adult men.) "The Reform Acts of 1832 allowed one in five Englishmen, one in eight Scotsmen, and one in twenty Irishmen to vote" (p. 558). Later reform acts in 1867 and 1884 also greatly expanded the voting rights in Britain. In 1865, the total number of votes cast was 854,572; in 1868, 2,333,251 votes were cast. After the 1884 Reform Act, the electorate stood at 5,500,000. However, "an estimated 40% of all men still did not have the right to vote as a result of their status within society" (www.historylearningsite.co.uk/impact_1867_reform_act.htm). Britain gave all men and all women over age 30 the right to vote in 1918. Women under the age of 30 were not given the franchise until 1928 ("Universal Suffrage," Wikipedia).

[105] Abraham Lincoln, *Speeches and Writings*, I, p. 315.

suffered by any people (see Chapter 3.II), whereas undemocratic Russia and relatively undemocratic Britain had abolished slavery and serfdom within their empires by 1861.[106]

At the *very least*, however, Lincoln's arguments about harm to the cause of democracy have some force, and they strengthen the utilitarian arguments given earlier. If Lincoln was correct in claiming that Confederate independence would greatly harm the cause of democracy, then his arguments count for a great deal and *greatly strengthen* the earlier utilitarian arguments. So Lincoln's arguments about democracy strengthen the case presented earlier, but (at least for all that I have shown) it is uncertain to what degree. It is also unclear how we should weigh harms to the cause of democracy against the enormous badness of the death and suffering that were actually caused by the war. For my part, I think it doubtful that the harm to the institution of democracy that Confederate independence would have caused outweighs the enormous badness of the death and suffering caused by the war itself. But like Lincoln's claims about the effects of Confederate independence, this is very speculative. I leave the question of the strength of Lincoln's arguments about democracy to others who are more competent to assess it. It is not part of my larger purposes in this chapter to reject or discount Lincoln's arguments. Indeed, if his claims about the consequences of Confederate independence are correct, then that *supports and considerably strengthens* my arguments for thinking that the actual consequences version of utilitarianism implies that Lincoln and the Union were justified in fighting the war, from its very beginning.[107]

[106] Also recall Samuel Johnson's bitter quip from the time of the American Revolution: "How is it that we hear the loudest yelps for liberty among the drivers of negroes?"

[107] *A Speculative Digression about the Very Long-Term Consequences of Disunion.* Had the CSA become independent, it is possible that there would have been further splintering of the country (see note 101). Had that happened,

We should also briefly consider Lincoln's argument that his oath of office, in which he swore to preserve, protect, and defend the Constitution of the United States, required him to fight a war. Yet did his oath of office actually require him to fight to keep the country together? Lincoln's argument depends on his claim that the Constitution prohibits states from seceding. Is this claim true? Although the Constitution neither explicitly permits or prohibits secession, legal scholars continue to debate this question. For a good discussion of these issues, see Levinson and Amar, "What Do We Talk about When We Talk about the Constitution?" I offer no judgment about this extremely complex legal/constitutional question. In any case, even if the Constitution does prohibit secession and Lincoln's oath of office required him to try to keep the country together, this consideration counts for quite little, given the truth of utilitarianism. According to utilitarianism, it is morally permissible to break a promise or

the nations that emerged would not have been nearly as united or powerful as the United States actually was during the twentieth century. The United States played an essential role in defeating the Axis in World War II and a much more central role defeating totalitarian Marxism in the later half of the century. It is unclear that North America could have played such a role in defeating totalitarianism in the twentieth century had the CSA retained its independence. On balance, it was very good that the United States helped defeat totalitarianism, and it is likely that the United States had to be united to be able to accomplish this.

Other Counterfactual Histories. Roger Ranson speculates that the United States and the CSA would have been drawn into World War I on opposite sides and would have fought a very bloody war against each other. He thinks that the CSA would have been allied with Britain and the United States allied with Germany; Ransom, *The Confederate States of America: What Might Have Been*. DiLorenzo thinks it likely that if the CSA had become independent the United States would not have intervened in World War I and that European monarchies would have reached a peace agreement that would have spared the world the horrors of Nazism and World War II; DiLorenzo, *The Real Lincoln*, p. 273. McKinlay Kantor's *If the South Had Won the Civil War* speculates that the United States, the CSA, and the independent nation of Texas would have united to fight together in both world wars.

oath whenever it will have better consequences to break it rather than keep it.

3. *The Implications of the Probable Consequences Version of Utilitarianism.* This version of utilitarianism (see Chapter 2.III) asks us to weigh the antecedently probable consequences of the Union fighting the war against the antecedently probable consequences of allowing the Confederate states to secede peacefully.

Because the Union war aims changed over time and because the very heavy casualties caused by the war became clearer over time, the probable consequences of *continuing to fight* the war at later times were not the same as those of starting to fight the war at its beginning: the antecedently probable good and bad consequences of the war changed significantly throughout the war in light of new developments and new information. Throughout the war, Lincoln repeatedly decided to continue fighting, though ending the war was always an option for the Union. The CSA did not aim at conquering the United States; it only wanted to be left alone. These decisions to continue fighting are as much the proper subjects of moral scrutiny as Lincoln's initial decision to fight the war. We need to weigh the probable consequences of continuing the war against the probable consequences of ending the war and allowing the Confederacy to become independent at different times during the war.

We could ask about the probable consequences of the Union continuing the war for each different day of the war, but it is really not possible or helpful to do that. However, certain dates are salient. By July 1862, after the shockingly high casualties at the Battle of Shiloh and the Seven Days Battles, it was very probable that the Civil War would be long and bloody. The probable bad consequences of continuing to fight the war then were much greater than those that were probable at the beginning of the war. The Union war aims also changed during the war. After Lincoln decided to issue the Emancipation Proclamation in July 1862 (the proclamation went into effect on January 1, 1863), the Union planned to free all of the slaves in Confederate territory not occupied by the Union Army (see Chapter 2.I.5 for details). So Union war aims were different in July 1862 than they had been in April 1861. They changed again dramatically in June 1864 when Lincoln ran for reelection as a full-fledged abolitionist and publicly supported a constitutional amendment to totally abolish slavery. After this time, the Union aimed at a much greater good than it did at the beginning of the war. Two other salient times are November 1864 after Lincoln's reelection, when it was very clear that the Union would win the war, and January 1865 after the passage of the Thirteenth Amendment by both houses of Congress.

So let us examine the antecedently probable consequences of fighting and continuing to fight the Civil War at each of these salient times.

A. *April 1861 (the beginning of the war)*

The probable consequences of not fighting the war at this time were the independence of the CSA and the expansion and perpetuation of slavery in the South; it was also likely that not fighting would have led to the perpetuation of slavery in Latin America. The probable bad consequences of fighting the war were the predictable deaths and carnage of the war itself, but most people did not then foresee the full extent of the suffering and destruction. So on one reading, the antecedently probable good and bad consequences of the war were both considerably less than the war's actual good and bad consequences. In early 1865 Lincoln stated this view eloquently in his Second Inaugural Address: "Neither party expected for the war, the magnitude, or the duration which it has already attained. Neither anticipated that the *cause* of the conflict [slavery] might cease with, or even before, the conflict itself should cease."

But there is more to be said here. In his Second Inaugural Address Lincoln overstated, perhaps greatly overstated, his view. Perhaps a long bloody war was antecedently probable, and it might also have been antecedently probable that if there was a long war it would bring about the end of slavery. Shortly after Lincoln's election, Salmon Chase said that disunion would lead to a war and the abolition of slavery; Seward thought it likely that disunion would lead to the end of slavery.[108]

Because the liberty and basic rights of millions of people were at stake and it was likely that the war would end or greatly hasten the end of slavery, the kind of war that could have been reasonably expected was a lesser evil than the creation of a powerful and militant nation committed to slavery and its expansion and perpetuation.

However, we also need to factor in the probability of the success of the Union cause in the war. Given Lincoln's success in uniting public opinion in the North behind the war effort and the considerably greater manpower and industrial capacity of the Union, there was a high probability that the Union would win the war. But victory was not certain. The Confederacy had the advantage of being on the defensive and fighting on familiar ground. It only needed to repel the Union invasion to win its independence. When calculating the probable consequences of fighting the war, we need to consider both the probable good and bad consequences of Union victory and the probability of Union victory. If an action has a 50 percent chance of bringing about four units of good and a 50 percent chance of bringing about zero units of good, then the antecedently probable good consequences of the action are two units of good.

My case for saying that the probable consequences of fighting the war were good on balance depends on the claim that

---

[108] Oakes, *Freedom National*, pp. 332 and 67.

there was a fairly high probability that the Union would win the war and prevent the CSA from becoming an independent nation. If the probability of success had been sufficiently low (to take an extreme case, suppose that it had been less than 1 in 100), then the probable consequences version of utilitarianism implies that the Union was *not* justified in beginning to fight the Civil War. Still it is reasonable to suppose that, as the war began, the Union had *at least* a 50 percent chance of winning the war. Given that, the probable consequences of Lincoln deciding to fight the Civil War were good on balance. Given the arguments developed earlier in 4.II.1, it is reasonable to hold that the probable consequences of not fighting the war in 1861 were better than those of fighting the war only if we assume that the Union victory in the war was very improbable. But *that* assumption is untenable.

B. *July 1862*

As of this date, the war had produced shockingly high casualties. By then it was likely that it would be a long, bloody war and the probable bad consequences of continuing the war were very bad indeed. This made the case for the justice of the Union cause in the war much more doubtful.

But between the beginning of the war in April 1861 and this time, the aims of the war had shifted as well. Congress had passed and Lincoln had signed the Second Confiscation Act, which gave the president the power to proclaim the freedom of the slaves of all disloyal slave owners in the CSA if they did not cease in aiding and abetting the rebellion within sixty days after being given a public warning and proclamation by the president. Because the great majority of slave owners in the CSA were disloyal and supported the Confederacy, this act applied to the great majority of the slaves in the CSA (see Chapter 2.I.3 for details). Lincoln announced his intention to issue the Emancipation Proclamation to his cabinet on July 22, 1862 (he had announced this intention to Seward and Welles earlier on July 13, 1862[109]), but he delayed making this public until September 22, 1862. He acted on Seward's advice to wait until after an important victory on the battlefield so that the proclamation would not appear to be an act of desperation. The final version of the Emancipation Proclamation was issued on January 1, 1863. It declared the freedom of all slaves (not just the slaves of disloyal owners) in all of the parts of the CSA then in rebellion against the government of the United States. After this time, the Union war effort aimed at a much greater good than it had at the very beginning of the war. It was not clear whether the Emancipation Proclamation would stand after the war (see Chapter 2.I.5), but it and many of Lincoln's earlier actions were severe blows to the institution of slavery. Lincoln and the Union were justified in continuing to fight the war at this time, and clearly the stakes of the war were rising.

There are additional considerations that show that the war was becoming a war against slavery *before* July 1862 and that thus support the view that the probable consequences of the Union fighting the war were good on balance by then. Between the beginning of the war and July 1862, Lincoln, Congress, and the military adopted many policies that freed large numbers of slaves. In May 1861 Lincoln and his cabinet approved General Butler's "contraband" policy of seizing Confederate slaves who came to Union lines. In March 1862, Congress passed and Lincoln signed a law making it a crime for military personnel to enforce the Fugitive Slave Law (for more details, see Chapter 2.I.3 and Oakes, *Freedom National*).

C. *June 1864*

During the spring and summer of 1864 the war was bloodier than ever. Grant suffered horrific casualties attacking Lee

[109] Grimsley, *The Hard Hand of War*, p. 132.

with little apparent success; his army sustained 65,000 casualties in just seven weeks. Lee's casualties during that time were in excess of 35,000.[110] In June 1864, Lincoln ran for reelection as a full-fledged abolitionist and a supporter of a constitutional amendment to abolish slavery, which greatly increased the probable good consequences of Union victory. The main Union armies were pressing the Confederates very hard, and victory on the battlefield was only a matter of time if the war continued.[111]

However, it was doubtful that the war would continue to a successful conclusion unless Lincoln won reelection and the Republicans retained control of Congress, and the outcome of the election was very much in doubt.[112] For a brief time, Lincoln despaired of his chances of winning reelection and went so far as to prepare detailed plans to try to make sure that the Emancipation Proclamation would not be undone if he lost. This plan, which he discussed with Frederick Douglass, called for large numbers of slaves to escape to Union lines before the inauguration of the new president in March 1865.[113]

Lincoln's opponent in the election, General McClellan, wanted to reunite the country with slavery intact, but the Democratic party was deeply divided in 1864. The so-called peace Democrats wanted to end the war without any conditions, even if that meant recognizing the independence of the CSA; they saddled McClellan with an unpopular platform that he did not endorse (see Chapter 6.II). For a brief time, the probability of success in the war was greatly diminished because of the chance that Lincoln might lose the election – but the probable good involved in victory was greater than ever. The stakes of the war were extremely high after June

---

[110] McPherson, *The Battle Cry of Freedom*, pp. 742–3.
[111] Ibid., p. 743.
[112] Ibid.
[113] Stauffer, *Giants: The Parallel Lives of Frederick Douglass and Abraham Lincoln*, pp. 287–8.

1864. After the fall of Atlanta on September 2, 1864, Lincoln's reelection was assured, and the probability of a Union victory greatly increased.

This raises the question of whether Lincoln should have stopped fighting the war during the summer of 1864 and whether it would have been reasonable for him to have done so. The outcome of continuing the war was very uncertain at this time. A few months later, in the election of 1864, Lincoln received only 55 percent of the votes against McClellan, despite the fall of Atlanta, deep divisions among the Democrats, and Fremont's late withdrawal from the race.[114] There was a serious possibility that he would lose the election, and, for a time, before the capture of Atlanta, he thought that he would lose. But Lincoln might have been unduly pessimistic about his prospects for reelection. The Confederate military position was desperate, and there was reasonable hope that either Atlanta or Richmond would fall in time to shift popular opinion. There was also some hope that the Union military could achieve significantly good outcomes between the summer of 1864 and the time the new president would be inaugurated (March 1865), so that Lincoln's defeat in the election would not result in the nonfulfillment of his aim to reunite the nation and end (or at least greatly diminish) slavery. Therefore, the dire outcome of losing the election and having all his work undone was not sufficiently probable for a long enough time for it to have been reasonable for Lincoln to have given up fighting the war during this summer of 1864.

D. *November 1864*

After Lincoln's reelection in November 1864, it was clear that the Union would win the war. The Confederate

---

[114] Fremont ran as a third-party candidate for president in 1864. He withdrew from the race on September 22, 1864 (McPherson, *Battle Cry of Freedom*, pp. 715 and 776). Had he not withdrawn, he would have taken many votes away from Lincoln among the Radical Republicans.

economy was collapsing. The morale of the Confederate army was also collapsing, as evidenced by the very large number of Confederate soldiers who deserted.[115] During February 1865 alone, 8 percent of Lee's army deserted.[116] Because of Lincoln's reelection, there was no longer any chance that the Confederate states could gain their independence as a result of elections in the United States. By then, it was also very probable that the Thirteenth Amendment would be adopted. In November 1864, it was quite clear that the probable consequences of continuing to fight the war were better than those of ending it.

E. *January 1865*

Both Houses of Congress had passed the Thirteenth Amendment, and it seemed very likely that it would be ratified by three-quarters of the states (as is required for the adoption of a constitutional amendment). The CSA had been cut into three parts (see Map 4). By this time, the Union was very close to victory in the war: it was *very clear* that it would result in much better consequences if the Union would continue the war rather than end it and allow the Confederate states to maintain their independence and retain slavery. At this point, the probable good consequences of continuing the war were enormous, and the probable future costs of the war were very small by comparison.

Whatever force Lincoln's arguments about secession and democracy have from a utilitarian point of view also needs to be factored in at each of these times. They lend support to my arguments here, but how much support they provide is open to debate.

4. *Given the Truth of Utilitarianism, Was Lincoln Lucky that the Union Had Just Cause to Fight the American*

---

[115] Levine, *The Fall of the House of Dixie*, pp. 240–2, and 267.
[116] McPherson, *The Battle Cry of Freedom*, p. 821.

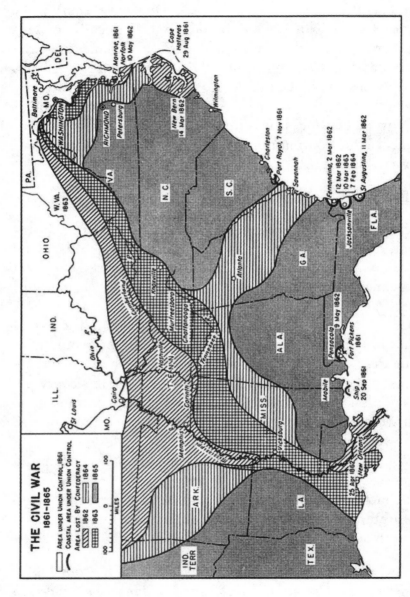

MAP 4. Map Showing the Progress of the Union Armies during the War

Civil War? This question suggests an objection that I first pose and then answer.

The Objection. Actions can be right or wrong on account of good or bad moral luck. For example, a careless and inattentive juror might act rightly in voting to acquit a defendant who is innocent of the crime he is accused of, and a very careful and conscientious juror might act wrongly by voting to convict the same defendant. Therefore, in addition to wanting to know whether a person acted rightly or wrongly (or justly or unjustly), we want to know whether her actions were reasonable or unreasonable from a moral point of view, given the information available to her. Lincoln did not accurately predict the outcome of the war, and he was just lucky that things turned out as well as they did. Therefore, he should not be given much credit for the fact that the Union was morally justified in fighting the war. The arguments he gave in support of the war were speculative, and he was lucky that the Union had just cause for fighting the Civil War.

Reply. The most salient antecedently probable good consequences of fighting the war as it began were much as Lincoln believed them to be. Most importantly, he correctly and reasonably regarded the creation of an independent CSA committed to expanding and perpetuating slavery as a very bad thing. In many speeches delivered before the war and in his debates with Stephen Douglas, he expressed the worry that slavery might spread throughout the United States and persist longer if it did. In his "House Divided Speech" he predicted that the United States could not long endure "half slave and half free." He also predicted that either all the states would become free or that all of them would adopt slavery:

"A house divided against itself cannot stand."
I believe this government cannot endure, permanently half *slave* and half *free*.

I do not expect the Union to be *dissolved* – I do not expect the house to *fall* – but I *do* expect it will cease to be divided.

It will become *all* one thing or *all* the other.

Either the *opponents* of slavery, will arrest the further spread of it, and place it where the public mind shall rest in the belief that it is in the course of ultimate extinction; or its *advocates* will push it forward, till it shall become alike lawful in *all* the States, *old* as well as *new* – *North* as well as *South*.

Have we no *tendency* to the latter condition?[117]

Then, he very pointedly went on to note ways in which the country was "tending to be" all slave. He said that, because of the Dred Scott decision, this might come about through the actions of the Supreme Court:

We shall *lie down* pleasantly dreaming that the people of *Missouri* are on the verge of making their state *free* [this is an allusion to Frank Blair's attempt to end slavery in Missouri in 1858 – see note 12]; and we shall *awake* to the *reality*, instead, that the *Supreme Court* has made *Illinois* a *slave* state.[118]

On other occasions, he expressed the worry that slavery was becoming "national and perpetual."[119]

Lincoln was alarmed by the militancy of Southern advocates of slavery. He claimed that the Dred Scott decision declared that the people in federal territories had "no constitutional power to exclude slavery during their territorial existence."[120] Lincoln also said that when "pushed to its legitimate consequences" that ruling would establish slavery "in all the States as well as in the Territories."[121] In his

---

[117] Abraham Lincoln, *Speeches and Writings*, I, p. 426.

[118] Ibid., p. 432; also see p. 430.

[119] Ibid., pp. 516, 574, 575, 604, and 718.

[120] Ibid., pp. 464.

[121] Ibid., p. 735. In the Dred Scott case, a slave, Dred Scott, sued his owner, John Sandford, for his liberty because Sandford had taken him to live in free territory in what later became the state of Minnesota. Scott claimed that he, his wife, and child (who was born in free territory) were all free for this reason. In its ruling on the case, the U.S. Supreme Court rejected Scott's

debates with Douglas, he repeatedly charged that there was a conspiracy, involving members of the Supreme Court and Douglas, to spread slavery throughout the entire nation.[122]

Clearly, the danger of the spread and perpetuation of slavery was much greater if the CSA became independent and pro-slavery interests were no longer checked and counterbalanced by antislavery forces in the North. This was all the more the case because antislavery views could not be freely expressed in Confederate states and those states suppressed the distribution of abolitionist writings (see 4.I.1). Although

claims. It ruled that Scott and others of African descent were not citizens of any state and therefore did not have legal standing to bring suit in federal court. According to Chief Justice Roger Taney, the authors of the Constitution viewed Negroes as "beings of an inferior order . . . so far inferior that they had no rights which the white man was bound to respect." The Court gave as a reason for siding against Scott the claim that to rule in favor of Scott

would give to persons of the negro race, . . . the right to enter every other State whenever they pleased, . . . to sojourn there as long as they pleased, to go where they pleased . . . the full liberty of speech in public and in private upon all subjects upon which its own citizens might speak; to hold public meetings upon political affairs, and to keep and carry arms wherever they went.

The Court also ruled that Congress had no authority to regulate slavery in federal territories created after the time of the signing of the U.S. Constitution. This decision overruled parts of the Missouri Compromise of 1820 that prohibited slavery in certain parts of the Louisiana Territory, which was acquired after the Constitution was signed. Two justices, Curtis and McLean, dissented from the Court's ruling. They said that there was no basis for its ruling that blacks could not be citizens and noted that, at the time that the Constitution was ratified, blacks were permitted to vote in five states. They also objected to its overturning of the Missouri Compromise on two grounds. First, because the Court ruled that Scott did not have legal standing, it should have simply dismissed his case and not ruled on the merits of his claims. Second, they noted that "none of the authors of the Constitution had ever objected on constitutional grounds to the United States Congress' adoption of the antislavery provisions of the Northwest Ordinance passed by the Continental Congress, or the subsequent acts that barred slavery north of 36 30'" (*Dred Scott* v. *Sanford*).

[122] Abraham Lincoln, *Speeches and Writings*, I, pp. 488, 519, 544, and 772.

he did not speak about it in his First Inaugural Address, Lincoln, like all of his contemporaries, was very well aware of Southern plans to annex and/or ally themselves with parts of Latin America. In 1858 Stephen Douglas expressed the hope that the United States would acquire Cuba and parts of Mexico and Canada.[123] Lincoln strongly objected to this and claimed that Douglas called for seizing more land from Mexico and invading parts of South America in order to create "additional slave fields."[124] In a letter written less than two months before he became president, Lincoln referred with dismay to the likelihood of future Southern demands that the United States annex Cuba as a condition of the South remaining in the Union.[125] He was clearly aware of these considerations, even though he did not emphasize them in his public statements at the time of the beginning of the Civil War.

As discussed in 4.II.3.A, Lincoln did not understand how bloody and horrible the war was likely to be. If it is the case that the magnitude and duration of the war were predictable *and* that it was improbable that even a long bitter war would end slavery, then actual consequences utilitarians must say that he was very lucky that the war he helped begin was morally justified, and probable consequences utilitarians must say that the war was not morally justified at the beginning. But it is much more reasonable to think that either (1) a long and terrible war was not probable/predictable in the spring of 1861 or (2) at that time it was probable that a long and bitter war would end or greatly diminish American slavery. If one or both of those is true, then it was not just a matter of luck that Lincoln and the Union were justified in choosing to fight the war in the spring of 1861.

---

[123] Ibid., I, p. 601.
[124] Ibid., I, p. 719.
[125] Abraham Lincoln, *Speeches and Writings*, II, p. 196.

Lincoln also clearly understood the probable consequences of the continuation of the war at later times. He understood that the war was proving to be much more terrible and costly than anyone imagined at the beginning. As the war continued, he and Congress changed the aims of the war numerous times; the good they sought to gain from the war kept growing along with the evil and carnage of the war itself. Throughout almost the entire war, they aimed at giving freedom to more and more slaves (for details see Chapter 2.I.3), and by the end of the war they aimed at completely eliminating slavery.

However, Lincoln seriously miscalculated other important things early in the war. He greatly exaggerated support for the Union in the Upper South, based on their votes against secession before the Civil War began.[126] This might be part of the reason why he failed to foresee the magnitude and duration of the war. He might also have underestimated the likelihood that the war would end slavery. In his First Inaugural Address, he stressed certain non-utilitarian reasons for fighting the war. He said that he felt bound by his oath of office, which he called an oath "registered in heaven," to execute and enforce the laws of the United States and protect federal property.[127] In the Gettysburg Address, he vowed not to let the Union dead die in vain (a policy that is sometimes opposed to utilitarianism). But none of this detracts from the fact that he was aware of and acted on the crucially important antecedently probable consequences at the beginning of the war and at later times in the war. Given the truth of utilitarianism, he was justified in thinking that the Union had just cause for fighting the war. However, as I argue later, he enjoyed good moral luck in that the Union eventually won

---

[126] Burlingame, *Abraham Lincoln: A Life*, II, p. 139.
[127] "First Inaugural Address," Abraham Lincoln, *Speeches and Writings*, II, p 224.

the war but not too soon, before it became a war to end slavery (see Chapter 6.II). After Lincoln issued the Emancipation Proclamation, he was clearly not simply lucky that the Union had just cause for fighting the Civil War. (This was very clear after he ran for reelection in 1864 as a supporter of a constitutional amendment to abolish slavery.) I also do not think that it was primarily a matter of luck that Lincoln and the Union were justified in fighting the war at the beginning, in April 1861, but this is less clear and more open to debate.

Finally, to the extent that Lincoln had reasonable grounds for claiming that the independence of the Confederacy would have greatly harmed the cause of democracy, that strengthens my reply to the current objection that he was simply lucky that the Union had just cause for fighting the war.

III. Standard Versions of Just War Theory Also Imply that the Union Had Just Cause for Fighting the American Civil War

1. *The Need to Consider Non-Utilitarian Theories of jus ad bellum.* Standard versions of utilitarianism imply that the Union had just cause for fighting the American Civil War. But demonstrating this is not sufficient for my purposes in this book.

Utilitarianism is a very controversial moral theory. Many think that it all too easily justifies fighting wars and all too readily permits ruthless actions that violate moral prohibitions against killing, lying, harming others, and violating people's moral rights. For classic statements of this view, see Ross, Rawls, Dworkin, and Hooker.

Various versions of what is called "just war theory" are the main alternatives to the utilitarian theory of just war. I discuss several of these versions in some detail, but before doing so, I want to briefly discuss two other theories of *jus ad bellum* and give my reasons for rejecting them. The two views in question are "national egoism," the view that any nation is justified in fighting a war whenever doing so promotes its own national interests (regardless of the war's effects on the rights and interests of people in other nations), and unconditional pacificism, the view that all killing of human beings and all wars are morally wrong under any circumstances. Very briefly, here is why these two views are untenable. National egoism is not defensible on any remotely plausible moral theory. It is a view that will sometimes justify immoral wars of conquest and ethnic cleansing by strong nations against weak nations. (This is so because it could sometimes promote the welfare of members of one nation to seize the land and resources of other nations and expel their inhabitants.) Unconditional pacifism is unacceptable because it does not permit states to fight against the most evil regimes bent on mass murder or mass slavery (e.g., Nazi Germany or the Interahamwee in Rwanda), even if fighting would *greatly* reduce killing and the loss of life. It is reasonable to hold that some wars are justified and that reasons of national self-interest *alone* are insufficient to justify the violence and killing involved in war, just as personal self-interest is not enough to justify acts of violence and murder.

In this brief discussion I have not done justice to unconditional pacifism, which unlike national egoism, is a morally respectable view. Many people throughout the ages have defended pacifism. It is noteworthy that many (most) pacifists have based their views on religious grounds (e.g., Mennonites, Quakers, Seventh-Day Adventists, Jainists, and some Hindus). On the assumption that there is a just God who absolutely forbids all killing of human beings and all acts of war (or on the assumption that the universe is governed by a principle of karma according to which it *always* tends for the best for people to refrain from all acts of violence), unconditional pacifism is a reasonable view. But in the absence of these kinds of religious justifications, I think that unconditional pacifism is an unreasonable view. For the purposes of this book, I am assuming that there is no good reason to think that there exists a God who unconditionally forbids all acts of war nor to think that the universe is governed by a principle of karma that renders all acts of violence counter-productive.

>   2. *Just War Theory and Utilitarianism.* "Just war theory" refers to a large family of non-utilitarian moral theories that address questions of *jus ad bellum* (justification for fighting wars, just cause for war) and *jus in bello* (justice in war, just means in fighting wars).

Standard canonical versions of just war theory include not only the quasi-utilitarian requirement that just wars must be "proportionate" but also several additional requirements for the justice or permissibility of wars and acts of war. So as a rule, just war theory is more restrictive about the permissibility of war and acts of war than utilitarianism. With few exceptions (exceptions that are not relevant to our present example), any war that just war theory permits will also be permitted by utilitarianism. But many wars that utilitarianism permits are not justified according to just war theory, and, for all that I have shown up to this point, the Civil War might be one of them.

Standard versions of just war theory imply that the Union was morally justified in fighting the Civil War by the time the Emancipation Proclamation was issued. By this time, when the Union was aiming to free most American slaves, it was fighting for the freedom of millions of people, and losing or ending the war would mean that those people would remain in slavery. From that time on, the Union cause in the war satisfied the additional conditions for *jus ad bellum* in just war theory. Just war theory also very clearly implies that the Union was justified in fighting the war at and after the time when Lincoln and the Republican Party intended to completely abolish slavery (June 1864) and the Confederates were fighting (among other reasons) to preserve the institution of slavery. These are clear cases morally speaking: every reasonable theory about the morality of war will agree that the Union was morally justified in fighting the war by the time of the Emancipation Proclamation.

I also try to show that standard versions of just war theory imply that the Union had just cause for fighting at the very beginning of the war. But my arguments for this are inconclusive, and some reasonable people might disagree with my conclusions. Although the Union cause at the beginning of the war satisfied most of the standard conditions of just war theory, it is very much open to question whether it satisfied the "just cause" condition.

3. *Requirements for jus ad bellum in Just War Theory.* Just war theory attempts to state conditions that are necessary and sufficient for *jus ad bellum.*

Almost all versions of just war theory include the requirement of "proportionality." They hold that, for a war to be justified, the good achieved by fighting the war (including the evils it prevents) must be greater than or equal to the evil of the war itself. Here is one statement of this condition from Brian Orend:

Proportionality. . . . mandates that a state considering a just war must weigh the expected *universal* (not just selfish national) benefits of doing so against the expected *universal* costs. Only if the projected benefits, in terms of securing the just cause, are at least equal to, and preferably greater than, such costs as casualties may the war action begin.[128]

Note that Orend states the proportionality condition in terms of *expected* costs and benefits. Alternatively, we could state the condition in terms of *actual* costs and benefits. The

---

[128] Orend, *The Morality of War,* p. 59.

proportionality requirement is not as strong as the utilitarian requirement that actions be *optimific* (i.e., have better expected consequences than any alternative courses of action). But if fighting a given war is optimific, it is also proportionate. So, any war that is justified according to the expected consequences version of utilitarianism will also satisfy Orend's proportionality condition.

But not all versions of just war theory make the proportionality principle so explicitly utilitarian. One important version of just war theory (Jeff McMahan's) excludes (or at least does not fully count) harms inflicted on enemy combatants whose cause is unjust from the determination of proportionality.[129]

A second important requirement for *jus ad bellum* in just war theory is "just cause." This condition is difficult to state clearly. One view is that a state, A, has just cause for war with another state, B, if and only if A is defending itself (or another state) against armed attack by B. But this view is too simple. Ending genocide within sovereign states that are not themselves attacking other states can be just cause for fighting a war, as can ending or greatly reducing other horrendous violations of human rights. For example, other nations would have been justified in attacking Rwanda in 1994 to end its genocide against the Tutsi people. Further, nations committing gross human rights violations against their own people are not justified in defending their borders against humanitarian interventions mounted by other states. As Orend argues, only minimally just societies have the right to national self-defense.[130]

Orend formulates the just cause condition as follows: a state A has just cause for fighting another state B if, and only, if (1) A is defending itself against the violent aggression of B (or coming to the aid of the victim of the aggression

---

[129] McMahan, "Proportionate Defense," pp. 7–8, and 10 (mss version).
[130] Orend, *The Morality of War*, pp. 35–7.

of B[131]), (2) A is minimally just, and (3) A does not violate human rights in so doing. James Murphy contends that for just cause to exist certain important values must be attacked or threatened with attack:

There is a range of act-types that generate the right kinds of grounds to warrant resort to armed force. They include such things as invasion, imminent threat of armed attack, gross violation of human rights on a large scale, criminal activities of certain kinds (e. g. international terrorism or piracy), and violations of international law.[132]

The U.S. Catholic Bishops formulate the "just cause" condition as follows: "War is permissible only to confront 'a real and certain danger,' i.e., to protect innocent life, to preserve the conditions necessary for decent human existence, and to secure basic human rights."[133]

A third central requirement for *jus ad bellum* in just war theory is "right intention." Roughly, this says that for a nation to have just cause in fighting a war its reasons for fighting must involve just aims, as defined by the just cause requirement. It cannot be fighting for some other reason. Orend writes, "It is commonly thought, by just war theorists, that it is not enough to have *objectively* just cause for going to war . . . you must also have the proper *subjective* intention, or state of mind, for your act to be moral."[134] In regard to this third requirement, McMahan says, "The traditional principle of *right intention* requires that war be intended to achieve a just cause – that is, that the just cause not be used merely as a pretext for fighting a war for other reasons."[135]

Just war theorists need to clarify this condition. Does it refer to the collective intentions of states or to the intentions

---

[131] For this to be plausible, Orend has to allow that groups within B (not just other states) can be the victims of B's aggression.
[132] Murphy, *War's Ends*, p. 71.
[133] U.S. National Conference of Catholic Bishops, *The Challenge of Peace*, p. 28.
[134] Orend, *The Morality of War*, p. 46.
[135] McMahan, "War Crimes and Immoral Action in War," p. 165.

of leaders of states? *Whose* right intention is required for *jus ad bellum*?

Three other conditions are frequently included in just war theory:

i. A reasonable probability of success – this condition is included in both Orend's theory and the theory of the U.S. Catholic bishops, but not in McMahan's theory.[136]

ii. Necessity or last resort – the war must be necessary to achieve the legitimate war aims of the warring party. "A war is ruled out if the just cause can be achieved by means that would involve the infliction of fewer or less serious wrongful harms" (fewer or less serious harms than those involved in fighting the war).[137]

iii. Proper authority – the war must be endorsed or entered into by the "proper authorities."[138]

4. *How Standard Versions of Just War Theory Apply to the Case of the Justice of the Union Cause in the American Civil War*

Proportionality. The lengthy application of the expected consequences version of utilitarianism to the justice of the Union cause in the Civil War earlier in this chapter (4.II.3) shows that the Union cause in the war satisfied Orend's version of the proportionality condition throughout the entire war. It was very clear that the war was proportionate at the end of the war, but that this condition was satisfied was not

---

[136] Orend, *The Morality of War*, pp. 58–9; U.S. National Conference of Catholic Bishops, *The Challenge of Peace*, p. 30. McMahan, "War Crimes and Immoral Action in War," p. 166.

[137] McMahan, "War Crimes and Immoral Action in War," p. 165; also see Orend, *The Morality of War*, pp. 57–8; U.S. National Conference of Catholic Bishops, *The Challenge of Peace*, p. 30.

[138] Orend, *The Morality of War*, pp. 50–1; U.S. National Conference of Catholic Bishops, *The Challenge of Peace*, pp. 28–9.

nearly as clear at the beginning of the war. The lengthy application of the actual consequences version of utilitarianism presented earlier in this chapter (4.II.1) shows that the Union cause satisfied a modified version of the proportionality condition (understood in terms of the total balance between *actual* good and bad consequences) throughout the entire Civil War. McMahan's version of the proportionality condition discounts the badness of harm suffered by killed and wounded Confederate soldiers (whose cause was unjust) for the purposes of determining proportionality. Construing proportionality in this way makes it easier to show that the Union war effort was proportionate.

Probability of Success. The evidence given in 4.II.3.A shows that the Union cause in the war clearly satisfied this condition throughout the entire war.

Proper Authority. Neither Orend nor the U.S. Catholic Bishops define what they mean by "proper authority." However, the meaning of this is reasonably clear in the case of constitutional governments such as the United States. Lincoln and the U.S. Congress were clearly the proper authorities for fighting the war (the U.S. Constitution gives them this authority). So the Union cause in the war clearly satisfies this requirement: on many occasions Congress voted to fund and support the war.

Last Resort/Necessity. This condition was satisfied at the beginning of the war and throughout the war. Fighting the war was necessary to keep the country together and defend the principle that slavery should not expand further. At the time Lincoln became president, seven states had already seceded from the United States, and there was no alternative other than war to keep the nation together and prevent the creation of a powerful nation dedicated to slavery and its expansion and perpetuation.

Now we come to the just cause and right intention conditions. Here, my argument becomes much more difficult.

There is a prima facie case for the view that the Union did not satisfy the just cause condition in just war theory. Even though the Confederates fired the first shots by attacking Fort Sumter, it is arguable that it was the Confederacy, not the Union, that was fighting a defensive war. The CSA had no intention to invade or attack other states outside of the territory it claimed. Fort Sumter was located in the middle of the harbor in Charleston, South Carolina, the epicenter of radical secessionism. By attacking Fort Sumter, the Confederates were only seizing what they claimed as their own sovereign territory. The Union armies invaded and conquered the CSA, and the Confederates fought against the Union invasion.

On the widely held but overly simplistic view that fighting a defensive war is sufficient for having just cause, there is even a prima facie case for the argument that the Confederates themselves satisfied the just cause consideration. Nonetheless, it is clear that the Confederates did *not* satisfy the just cause condition. The fact that they fought only to defend what was arguably their own territory is greatly outweighed by the immense evil and injustice of American slavery. The CSA was formed to protect, expand, and perpetuate slavery. The principal reason why the leaders of the CSA wanted to secede from the United States was Lincoln's avowed opposition to slavery and its expansion and perpetuation. The Union was led by someone who said that slavery was "a monstrous injustice" and wanted to begin what he thought would be a very long-term program to end it in the United States. Lincoln intended to fight slavery by keeping the country together and was unwilling to try to keep the country together by dropping his insistence on the non-expansion of slavery (but see Chapter 2.I.1 for a qualification).

Was the fact that Lincoln and the Republicans were fighting (in part) to oppose the spread of slavery sufficient to give the

Union just cause to fight the war in 1861? I *think* that their aim to oppose the further enlargement of the immense evil and injustice of slavery (and thereby prevent much greater violations of human rights) was sufficient to give the Union just cause for fighting the war from the beginning. But this is debatable, and reasonable people can and do disagree. The case for thinking that the Union had just cause for the war is clearer after the fall of 1862 and much clearer after June 1864. The Union aim of freeing most slaves at the time of the Emancipation Proclamation was sufficient to satisfy the just cause requirement.[139]

Did Lincoln and the other Union leaders satisfy the right intention condition at the beginning of the war? I speak primarily to Lincoln's intentions. (Note again that standard versions of just war theory are not very clear about *whose* intentions matter, and it is debatable whether the idea of collective

---

[139] We should also consider the following questions. Do Lincoln's arguments about secession and democracy support the view that the Union cause satisfied the just war theory's "just cause" requirement? Are these arguments sufficient to show that the Union satisfied the just cause requirement? For the sake of argument, let us assume that Lincoln was correct to say that successful secession by the CSA would greatly harm the cause of democracy. These questions are very difficult to answer, and the answers depend on which versions of just war theory we are considering. David Rodin would hold that Lincoln's aim of promoting the cause of democracy did not satisfy the just cause condition. He writes, "The 2003 invasion of Iraq would have been wrong even if it had turned out to have had good consequences by bringing democracy to the Middle East. For bringing democracy to the Middle East is not the kind of war aim that is capable, even in principle, of justifying the invasion under the laws of war and just war theory" (Rodin, "The Moral Inequality of Soldiers," p. 67). It is not clear to me how Orend's and Murphy's formulations of the just cause condition presented earlier apply to this issue. But arguably promoting the cause of democracy would satisfy this condition in the Catholic bishops' theory, because, to the extent that fighting the war promoted the cause of democracy, it also helped "secure basic human rights." The questions I pose here are best left to scholars in the just war tradition. But it seems that at least some versions of just war theory would take Lincoln's arguments about democracy to strengthen the case for thinking that the Union war effort satisfied the "just cause" requirement.

intentions makes any sense, at least not without a great deal of explanation.) It is unclear that Lincoln's aim to keep the nation together and prevent the creation of a precedent for the splintering of democracies was enough for the Union to satisfy the just cause conditions in this very bloody war (see 4.II.2). If we take this to be his only intention at the beginning of the war, then it is questionable whether the Union cause satisfied the right intention condition at the beginning of the war. But when the war began, Lincoln also had the intention to do *something else*: to prevent the creation of a large, powerful, and militant nation dedicated to preserving and expanding slavery. So from the beginning, he aimed at preventing the great enlargement of the evil of slavery, and he took the war to be the first step in a process that would end slavery. Because he and his administration had this aim, I think that they satisfied the right intention condition at the very beginning of the war, assuming that preventing the creation of a nation dedicated to expanding slavery constituted "just cause." (But, by the same token, if trying to prevent the creation of a nation dedicated to expanding slavery did not satisfy the "just cause" requirement, then Lincoln and the Union also failed to satisfy the "right intention" requirement.)

By July 1862, Lincoln aimed at freeing most American slaves. By June 1864, he aimed at completely ending American slavery. Clearly the war satisfied the right intention condition as of July 1862.

In sum, standard versions of just war theory imply that the Union was morally justified in fighting the Civil War as of July 1862. They very clearly imply that Lincoln and the Union were morally justified in fighting the war after June 1864 when he ran for reelection as an abolitionist. I *think* that just war theory also implies that he and the Union were justified in fighting the Civil War at its very beginning. But the argument for this is open to question, and reasonable people can and do disagree.

IV. Was the Union Morally Required to Fight the War?

I have argued that Lincoln and the Union were morally justified in fighting the Civil War. But were they morally obligated to fight the war? I do not have the space to address this question adequately, but let me very briefly give reasons why I think that the states of the Union were obligated to fight the war and to prevent the creation of a militant nation dedicated to the spread and perpetuation of slavery. In fact, the entire United States benefited from the very large exports of slave-produced goods. In 1850 cotton accounted for 50 percent of U.S. exports, and in 1860 the South accounted for most of America's exports.[140] The Northern states and their people benefited from and were complicit in American slavery. Much of the wealth of the North was derived directly or indirectly from slavery. The very large textile industry of the North used slave-produced cotton, and much of the very lucrative Atlantic slave trade was carried out on Northern ships. Those who enjoy the benefits of injustices have obligations of reparation and repair, even if they themselves did not perpetrate those injustices.[141] This makes a prima facie case for claiming that the states of the Union were obligated to fight the war, but much more needs to be said here. In particular, it needs to be shown that people in the North were obligated to risk their lives and limbs to fight in a very bloody war against the CSA. This is admittedly a very debatable assumption.

---

[140] Fogel and Engerman, *Time on the Cross*, p.166 and DiLorenzo, *The Real Lincoln*, p. 242.
[141] Ross, *The Right and the Good*, p. 27.

Conclusion

Lincoln and the Union had adequate moral justification for fighting the Civil War at the beginning of the war and thereafter as well. The case for saying that the Union War effort was morally justified is clearer at the end of the war than at the beginning, and given the truth of just war theory, the claim that the Union was justified in fighting the war at the very beginning is open to serious debate.

5

Jus in Bello

Did the Union Fight the War Justly?

Questions of *jus in bello* (literally "justice in war" – just means in fighting wars) are very crucial for an ethical assessment of Lincoln. The Union military's treatment of Confederate civilians has been widely criticized. The Civil War has often been characterized as a "total war" that imposed very harsh and ruthless treatment of Southern civilians on a very large scale. During the war Lincoln was commander in chief of the Army and Navy of the United States. In addition, he personally authorized and approved a new code of conduct for the U.S. military (formalized in the Lieber Code) that permitted much harsher treatment of civilians than some important Union leaders, most notably General McClellan, thought proper. In this chapter I argue that the Civil War was not a total war and that Lincoln's policies concerning the treatment of civilians during the war were largely, but not entirely, justified.

I. The Union Army's Treatment of Civilians

Early in the Civil War, both sides followed rules of war that required soldiers to give immunity to civilians and strictly respect the property of civilians, even when doing so hindered military operations.[1] One notable example of how this worked in practice occurred after the Battle of Shiloh, when the Union Army moved very deeply into Confederate territory. Union General Halleck advanced on Beauregard's shattered Confederate army of 70,000, the most important Confederate military unit outside of Virginia at the time.[2] Halleck had a chance to capture Beauregard's army if he laid siege to Corinth, Mississippi, but he refrained from doing that. Halleck allowed Beauregard's army an avenue of escape from the city because of his concern for the civilians in Corinth.[3] General McClellan, who commanded the Army of the Potomac for more than a year early in the war, also wanted to fight a limited war. He tried to keep the number of casualties down, and he wanted property and unarmed persons to be strictly protected.[4] McClellan said that the war "should be conducted upon the highest principles known to Christian Civilization" and that "all private property and unarmed persons should be strictly protected" (McClellan clearly meant that slave owners' property in human persons should be strictly protected).[5]

By the summer of 1862 Lincoln strongly questioned these policies and came to believe that the Union needed to employ harsher tactics against civilians in order to win the war.[6] In a letter to a New Orleans Unionist who protested his war policies, he said that he would not "give up the contest" without using all available means to save the government.[7] On July 22, 1862 (the same day that he informed his cabinet

---

[1] Stout, *Upon the Altar of the Nation*, p. 21.
[2] McPherson, *The Battle Cry of Freedom*, p. 416.
[3] Stout, *Upon the Altar of the Nation*, p. 121.
[4] Ibid., p. 137.
[5] Witt, *Lincoln's Code*, p. 211.
[6] Grimsley, *The Hard Hand of War*, pp. 2–3, 23, and 67; also see Stout, *Upon the Altar of the Nation*, p. 139.
[7] Stout, *Upon the Altar of the Nation*, p. 139. Abraham Lincoln, *Speeches and Writings*, II, p. 346.

about his intention to issue the Emancipation Proclamation), he approved an executive order that authorized Union commanders anywhere in the Confederacy to "seize and use any property real or personal which may be necessary or convenient...for supplies, or other military purposes."[8]

In December 1862, General Halleck and Secretary of War Stanton commissioned Columbia University law professor Francis Lieber to draft a code of conduct for the Union military. Halleck then revised Lieber's draft. The Lieber Code, "Instructions for the Government of the Armies of the United States in the Field," was approved by the president and issued as General Orders Number 100 in May 1863.[9]

Lincoln's executive order of July 22, 1862, and Article 15 of the Lieber Code permitted the Union Army to live off of the land and seize food and fodder from civilians in Confederate territory. During the Vicksburg campaign Grant intentionally cut himself off from his supply lines, and his army lived off the land in Mississippi; Sherman's forces did the same in Georgia and the Carolinas in 1864–5.

The Union Army imposed collective punishments on civilians; among other things, it often burned the homes of civilians in areas where guerrilla attacks occurred. These actions were permitted by Articles 27–8 of the Lieber Code that allow acts of retaliation and Article 15 that "allows of all destruction of property, and obstruction of the ways and channels of traffic, travel, or communication, and of all withholding of sustenance or means of life from the enemy." In October 1862, when Sherman's gunboats were attacked by guerrillas near Memphis, Sherman destroyed the town of Randolph, Tennessee, and ordered that, in the future, ten families be expelled from their homes for every gunboat that was fired on. After the next attack, he expelled ten more people from

---

[8] McPherson, *This Mighty Scourge*, p. 126.
[9] Witt, *Lincoln's Code*, pp. 226–7 and p. 237.

Randolph and destroyed houses, farms, and crops in a fifteen-mile stretch of Tennessee along the Mississippi River.[10]

In response to the August 1863 massacre of all the men and boys in the antislavery, pro-Union town of Lawrence, Kansas, by Confederate irregulars led by the notorious guerrilla fighter Quantrill, Union general Ewing issued General Orders Number 11.[11] These orders

authorized Federal forces to first drive from their homes ten thousand Missouri citizens in suspected guerilla territories that bordered on Kansas, then commanded them to burn to the ground the homes of suspected abettors. The orders were followed to the letter, leaving as many dead civilians in their wake as Quantrill had murdered.[12]

Lincoln approved this order.[13]

In the late summer of 1864, General Sherman shelled Atlanta without warning (as permitted by Article 19 of the Lieber Code[14]); he later burned much of the city and expelled all civilians, which resulted in at least five hundred civilian deaths.[15]

The Lieber Code permitted the Union Army to kill Confederate prisoners in retaliation for the killing or enslaving of black Union prisoners. Article 27 reads:

The law of war can no more wholly dispense with retaliation than can the law of nations, of which it is a branch. Yet civilized nations

[10] Stout, *Upon the Altar of the Nation*, p. 155.
[11] McPherson, *The Battle Cry of Freedom*, p. 786.
[12] Stout, *Upon the Altar of the Nation*, p. 261.
[13] Neely, *The Fate of Liberty*, p. 48.
[14] Article 19 reads as follows, "Commanders, whenever admissible, inform the enemy of their intention to bombard a place, so that the noncombatants, and especially the women and children, may be removed before the bombardment commences. But it is no infraction of the common law of war to omit thus to inform the enemy. Surprise may be a necessity."
    The Lieber Code is included in Witt, *Lincoln's Code*, pp. 375–94; it is also available online.
[15] Stout, *Upon the Altar of the Nation*, pp. 368–9.

acknowledge retaliation as the sternest feature of war. A reckless enemy often leaves to his opponent no other means of securing himself against the repetition of barbarous outrage.

Article 58 reads:

The law of nations knows of no distinction of color, and if an enemy of the United States should enslave and sell any captured persons of their army, it would be a case for the severest retaliation, if not redressed upon complaint. The United States cannot retaliate by enslavement; therefore death must be the retaliation for this crime against the law of nations.

But Article 58 was contradicted by Lincoln's July 30, 1863, "Order of Retaliation," which called for the killing of Confederate prisoners only in retaliation for the killing of Union prisoners. It ordered that Confederate prisoners be put to hard labor in retaliation for the enslavement of black soldiers.[16]

Despite Articles 27 and 58 of the Lieber Code and his order of July 30, 1863, Lincoln did not want the Union to retaliate by killing innocent Confederate POWs who were not responsible for the mistreatment of black Union POWs. After the massacre of black prisoners by Confederate general Nathan Bedford Forrest's troops at Fort Pillow in April 1864, the president came under pressure to retaliate against the Confederates by killing an equal number of Confederate prisoners. This issue was discussed at two cabinet meetings. Naval Secretary Gideon Welles said that it would be "barbarous" and "inhumane" to punish innocent Confederate prisoners in this way. Lincoln agreed and refused to order the killing of Confederate prisoners.[17] He told Frederick Douglass that, "if once begun, there was no telling where [retaliation] would

[16] Abraham Lincoln, *Speeches and Writings*, II, pp. 484–5.
[17] McPherson, *The Battle Cry of Freedom*, p. 794.

end."[18] However, the Union did retaliate when the Confederates put black POWs to work on fortifications near Richmond that were under fire from the Union Army. Union generals "promptly placed an equal number of rebel prisoners at work on Union facilities under fire. This ended the Confederate practice."[19] The policy of putting Confederate prisoners to work under fire seems permissible, because it worked to save black POWs and also because it left it to the Confederates to decide whether they would fire on their own soldiers. The Lieber Code and Lincoln's order that Confederate prisoners be put to hard labor in retaliation for the enslavement of black soldiers caused the Confederates to modify and soften their treatment of *some* other black POWs. The Confederate secretary of war then decided that the CSA would treat black POWs who had been free people in the North before the war like other POWs.[20]

Article 156 of the Lieber Code calls for the use of oaths of loyalty to the government and the punishment of civilians who refused to take them:

Common justice and plain expediency require that the military commander protect the manifestly loyal citizens, in revolted territories, against the hardships of the war as much as the common misfortune of all war admits.

The commander will throw the burden of the war, as much as lies within his power, on the disloyal citizens, of the revolted portion or province, subjecting them to a stricter police than the noncombatant enemies have to suffer in regular war; and if he deems it appropriate, or if his government demands of him that every citizen shall, by an oath of allegiance, or by some other manifest act, declare his fidelity to the legitimate government, he may expel, transfer, imprison, or fine the revolted citizens who

---

[18] Ibid.
[19] Ibid, p. 795. Some black soldiers retaliated by killing Confederate prisoners, but this was done informally and was not sanctioned by either Lincoln or the Union Army.
[20] Witt, *Lincoln's Code*, p. 248.

refuse to pledge themselves anew as citizens obedient to the law and loyal to the government.

Article 17 of the Lieber Code also says that it is lawful to *starve* hostile belligerents whether armed or unarmed:

War is not carried on by arms alone. It is lawful to starve the hostile belligerent, armed or unarmed, so that it leads to the speedier subjection of the enemy.

On August 1, 1864, Grant ordered General Sheridan, commander of the Union Army in the Shenandoah Valley, to take all the men in the valley who were younger than fifty years of age as POWs and to "take all provisions, forages, and stock wanted for the use of your command. Such as cannot be consumed, destroy."[21] Grant also commanded Sheridan to turn "the Shenandoah Valley [into] barren waste so that crows flying over it for the balance of the season will have to carry their provender with them."[22] These are dreadful orders, but Grant's order to turn the Shenandoah Valley into a barren waste was not carried out. He issued this order in a moment of anger after Confederate general Early (who operated out of the Shenandoah Valley) burned Chambersburg, Pennsylvania, and threatened Washington, D.C.; Grant did not seriously intend that the order be carried out.[23] The Union Army did *not* starve the residents of the Shenandoah Valley: it destroyed less than one-third of the valley's wheat and hay crops and less than 10 percent of the corn crop.[24]

Generals Grant, Sherman, and Sheridan said some very harsh and terrible things about how they intended to treat Confederate civilians, but there was a substantial element of bluff and bluster in these statements: their deeds did not

---

[21] Stout, *Upon the Altar of the Nation*, p. 376.
[22] Ibid., p. 380.
[23] Neely, *The Civil War and the Limits of Destruction*, p. 116.
[24] Ibid., pp. 110–11.

match their sometimes infamous words. Similarly, Lincoln's policies regarding acts of retaliation against Confederate prisoners were considerably milder than those stated in the Lieber Code and his order of July 30, 1863. He was reluctant to explicitly state his views because he did not want the Confederates to know his actual policies, lest they cease to be restrained by fear of Union retaliation.[25] We should also remember that the Lieber Code set limits on what could be done, but did not prescribe that soldiers must always employ the harshest means permitted by it.

By the middle of the war, the Union military operated according to rules of war that permitted considerably harsher treatment of civilians than those sanctioned by the leaders of the Confederacy. During the Gettysburg campaign, Lee ordered that his army refrain from stealing and burning homes in Pennsylvania;[26] Jefferson Davis supported these policies.[27] However, those milder policies only applied to whites. Black Union soldiers captured by the Confederates were routinely killed or enslaved. When Lee invaded Pennsylvania in 1863, his army kidnapped scores of former slaves and free blacks and brought them back to slavery in the CSA.[28] In addition, Confederate irregulars committed terrible atrocities. As mentioned earlier, the worst of these occurred in Lawrence, Kansas, when Quantrill's Confederate raiders murdered all of the town's 183 men and boys and burned the town.[29] Lee and Davis strongly disapproved of this action, and the Confederate government repealed the Confederate "Ranger Act" that gave considerable latitude and freedom to Confederate irregulars.[30]

[25] On this point see ibid., pp. 195–8.
[26] Stout, *Upon the Altar of the Nation*, pp. 231–2.
[27] Ibid., p. 259.
[28] McPherson, *The Battle Cry of Freedom*, p. 649 and Stout, *Upon the Altar of the Nation*, p. 232.
[29] McPherson, *The Battle Cry of Freedom*, p. 786.
[30] Stout, *Upon the Altar of the Nation*, p. 261.

Later in the war, the Confederates changed their policies and retaliated in kind against Union civilians, most notably when Jubal Early's army burned the town of Chambersburg, Pennsylvania, in July 1864.[31] However, they had little opportunity to retaliate in kind because they were losing the war by then and their armies were seldom operating in Union territory.

II. A Moral Assessment of the Union's Treatment of Confederate Civilians

With one qualification (see the later discussion), I contend that the harsh measures taken against Confederate civilians that were *necessary* to win the war were justified, and those that were not necessary to win the war were not justified. To be clear, I am talking about actions *actually taken* by the Union that were necessary to win the war. I am not claiming that whatever would have been needed to win the war in every imaginable hypothetical situation (e.g., the mass murder of civilians) would have been justified.

What the Union did to Confederate civilians was not *nearly* as bad as what Confederates did to their slaves. The war-related deaths of fifty thousand civilians (the overwhelming majority of whom lived in the Confederacy and the border states) and the very extensive destruction of property caused by the Union Army were extremely small violations of human rights compared to the enslavement of 3.5 million people and their descendants and the greatly diminished rights and status that free blacks would have eventually had in the CSA if the Confederacy had gained its independence. Because the harm to civilians was so very small compared to the immense suffering and injustices of slavery that were ended by the war, those actions and the harm that they caused clearly seem proportionate, in the aggregate. Given this, it seems that the

[31] Ibid.

harm to civilians that was necessary to win the war and free the slaves was morally justified.

Utilitarians will accept these conclusions. But utilitarianism is a very controversial moral theory, and I cannot assume its truth for our purposes in this book. The main alternative views are found in the just war theory tradition. Just war theory includes strict rules that require immunity and protection for noncombatants. It holds that belligerents must not aim to deliberately harm or kill noncombatants, but given that certain other conditions (including proportionality) are met, it permits belligerents to do things that will foreseeably result in civilian deaths. For example, according to just war theory, it is wrong to bomb a city in order to kill civilians and terrorize the enemy and cause it to surrender, but it is not wrong to bomb an armaments factory, even though that will foreseeably result in many civilian casualties.[32]

According to just war theory, to be morally permissible, the means used in war must satisfy three conditions.[33] First, they must be discriminating. Second, the harm they inflict must be proportionate to the good they aim at. Third, they must be necessary to achieve legitimate war aims.

According to Jeff McMahan, the discrimination condition "incorporates both a permission and a prohibition. The permission is that all combatants may kill enemy combatants at any time during a state of war. The prohibition forbids intentional attacks on non-combatants."[34] McMahan thinks that the discrimination condition, as generally understood, is too permissive, because he claims that it is impermissible for

---

[32] Walzer, *Just and Unjust Wars*, pp. 153–6; Article 15 of the Lieber Code says something similar: "Military necessity ["the necessity of those measures which are indispensable for securing the ends of the war" Article 14] admits of all direct destruction of life or limb of armed enemies, and of other persons whose destruction is incidentally unavoidable in the armed contests of the war."

[33] McMahan, "War Crimes and Immoral Action in War," p. 152.

[34] Ibid., p. 154.

soldiers fighting for an unjust cause to kill enemy combatants whose cause is just.[35] He thinks that this condition should be modified roughly as follows: it is permissible to intentionally attack "legitimate targets" and impermissible to attack people who are not legitimate targets.[36]

The necessity condition in traditional just war theory permits acts that harm civilians as foreseeable side effects of otherwise impermissible actions for the sake of military advantage unless "there is an alternative act that would yield at least an equivalent military advantage, would not be costlier to the combatants, and would cause less harm to non-combatants."[37] McMahan rejects this formulation of the necessity condition because it permits acts that both harm civilians and do not promote the achievement of just aims. According to him, all acts of war that foreseeably harm civilians are impermissible unless one is morally justified in fighting the war in question. He proposes the following alternative version of the necessity requirement:

The correct *in bello* requirement of necessity thus asserts that an act of war may permissibly harm innocent people as a side effect only if there is no alternative act of war that would make an equal or greater contribution to the just or justifying aims of the war. That an act of war is necessary for a certain degree of military advantage is insufficient to make it necessary in the relevant sense. The military advantage must itself be instrumental to the achievement of an aim that is morally justified.[38]

---

[35] Ibid.

[36] I cannot fully explain what McMahan means by "legitimate targets," because his account of this term is very complicated. The crucial point for our present purposes is that he says that enemy soldiers are not legitimate targets unless one's cause (in the war) is just. He claims that all acts of killing in war are wrong unless the army in which one fights is morally justified in fighting (ibid., p. 158; also see McMahan's *Killing in War*).

[37] McMahan, "War Crimes and Immoral Action in War," p. 155.

[38] Ibid., p. 160.

Roughly, and at a minimum, the proportionality requirement says that attacks on legitimate targets that are necessary to achieve legitimate war aims must not cause harm that exceeds the good they achieve.[39]

Some of the most notable anti-utilitarian thinkers in the just war tradition hold that the rules that provide immunity for noncombatants are overridable in extreme cases.[40] For example, Michael Walzer is very strongly opposed to utilitarianism. Nonetheless, his version of just war theory permits combatants to deliberately harm civilians in what he calls "supreme emergencies" (i.e., situations in which [1] a nation is in grave danger of losing a war and intentionally harming civilians is necessary to avoid that outcome and [2] the triumph of the enemy would lead to an abhorrent moral catastrophe such as the extermination or enslavement of a nation.[41] Other recent proponents of just war theory, including Jeff McMahan and John Rawls, also permit overriding the standard rules of war in extreme cases.[42] Walzer's "supreme emergency" exception is a significant improvement on traditional just war theory.[43]

---

[39] McMahan qualifies this in ways that are not relevant for our purposes here. His notion of proportionality is "moralized." "Proportionality does not simply weigh good and bad effects independently of how they are produced, how they are distributed, and whether people are entitled to them, deserve them, or are liable to them" (ibid., p. 157).

[40] Walzer, *Just and Unjust Wars*, p. 132.

[41] Ibid., pp. 251–5.

[42] McMahan, "War Crimes and Immoral Action in War," p. 162 and Rawls, *The Law of Peoples*, pp. 98–105.

[43] *A Philosophical Digression in Support of the Supreme Emergency Exception.* Thomas Nagel and Brian Orend are two notable philosophers who reject the supreme emergency exception. (Nagel does not explicitly reject the supreme emergency exception. His 1971 essay "War and Massacre" [included in *Mortal Questions*] to which I refer was written before Walzer formulated the exception in *Just and Unjust Wars*. But Nagel's view is clearly inconsistent with this exception.) Nagel's and Orend's heavily qualified rejections of the exception show how difficult (and, to my way of thinking, unreasonable) it is to consistently reject it. Neither can bring himself to say that intentionally killing innocents in situations in which the supreme emergency condition

The continued enslavement of millions of people was a morally abhorrent catastrophe, and the independence of a

permits it is morally wrong "full stop." Orend says that doing so is wrong, but "excusable" for reasons of duress and tragedy; *The Morality of War*, p. 158. Nagel says that in situations in which violating strict deontological rules of war is overwhelmingly justified on utilitarian grounds and abiding by those rules is almost certain to have horrifically bad consequences, then one must choose between "morally abominable actions," and it would be wrong to take either course of action. In such cases, he thinks that it would be wrong either to violate or not violate the rules of war in question. Nagel notes that this view commits him to rejecting the principle that "ought implies can." He holds that, although we ought to refrain from performing wrong actions, in these kinds of cases it is impossible to avoid acting wrongly; *Mortal Questions*, pp 73–4.

Let me clarify what *I* mean by saying that an action is morally wrong "full stop." If an action is morally wrong full stop that means (1) one should not do it, *period*; (2) there is *something else* that one should do instead; and (3) the action, when done with full knowledge and full understanding, is presumptively blameworthy and inexcusable. Neither Orend nor Nagel is willing to say that violating deontological rules of war in supreme emergency situations is wrong full stop. Orend will not call these actions blameworthy, and Nagel will not say that there is something else one should do instead.

Nagel and, to a lesser extent, Orend reject fundamental and well-grounded understandings of the logic of moral concepts. These kinds of cases, as agonizing and horrible as they are, do not provide us good enough reasons to revise our understanding of the logic of moral concepts. It would be preferable for Nagel and Orend to say instead that, in such cases, it is permissible to violate or not violate the deontological rules of war. That is, it would be preferable for them to say that it is permissible to do morally abominable things in situations in which all possible alternatives are also abominable. Saying this falls short of what utilitarians would say. Utilitarians do not just acknowledge the permissibility of violating deontological rules of war in supreme emergency conditions: they hold that it is *obligatory* to violate the rules of war under those conditions.

Here, it is relevant to add that the two most important rule-utilitarian philosophers, Brad Hooker and Richard Brandt, endorse a "prevent disaster rule" very similar to the supreme emergency condition in Walzer, Rawls, and McMahan. As rule-utilitarians, Brandt and Hooker agree that traditional forms of utilitarianism permit far too many violations of ordinary moral prohibitions. They want to defend moral theories that are much more compatible with most people's moral intuitions about these cases than traditional utilitarianism. Their prevent disaster rule is much broader in scope than Walzer's supreme emergency exception, and it applies to all situations, not just wars. It permits actions that violate ordinary moral prohibitions (against lying, etc.) to prevent disasters (see Hooker, *Ideal Code: Real World*, pp. 98–9 and 129–36 and Brandt, *Morality, Utilitarianism, and Rights*, pp 87–8, 151, and 156).

powerful and militant Confederate States of America – a nation dedicated to the enlargement and perpetuation of slavery and the proposition that all people are not created equal – would have been a catastrophe. Therefore, the Civil War was a supreme emergency, at least after the time the Union aimed to free most American slaves.

The principle that noncombatants are not subject to attack was generally upheld in the Civil War.[44] Union military policies strictly prohibited acts of violence against innocent Confederate civilians. Union soldiers intentionally killed or murdered very few noncombatants, and when they did directly kill noncombatants[45] it was *always* contrary to the policies of Lincoln and other Union leaders. However, Union policies sanctioned very extensive destruction of civilian property to punish and deter guerrilla attacks on Union soldiers and supply lines. Union policies also permitted the seizure of food and fodder for the use of the Union Army (and to prevent it from being used by the Confederate Army) and the expulsion of civilians from their homes. Overall, the harm that the Union inflicted on Confederate civilians (very extensive loss of property, but less than fifty thousand deaths) was *very* small and proportionate compared to the enormous good achieved by winning the war and ending slavery. Roughly eighty slaves were freed as a result of war for each civilian who died in the war, and if we count the freedom of their descendants who would have lived as slaves had the war not been fought, then that ratio is much greater.

Both utilitarianism and traditional versions of just war theory will agree that most of the harm done to Confederate property to punish and deter guerrilla attacks was morally permissible. In the aggregate, this harm was quite proportionate, even if not in every instance.

---

[44] Grimsley, *The Hard Hand of War*, p. 6.
[45] I am counting guerillas and spies who were executed as combatants.

However, three Union policies/actions concerning civilians seem morally questionable: (1) the policy that it was lawful to starve civilians, (2) the policy of expelling civilians from their homes and the policy that permitted this if they refused to take an oath of loyalty to the United States, and (3) Sherman's devastating march through Georgia and the Carolinas beginning in November 1864. Because Sherman began his march after Lincoln's reelection and because the Confederate military and economic situation was already dire, the march was probably not necessary for the Union to win the war.

Given the limited war aims of the Union in April 1861, it is debatable whether the Civil War constituted a "supreme emergency" at the beginning. The Union did not aim to free the slaves then. But this is not an objection to the view I am defending here, because the Union's "hard war" policies did not begin until the summer of 1862[46] at almost the same time that Lincoln told members of his cabinet of his intention to issue the Emancipation Proclamation (which aimed at freeing the great majority of the 3.5 million slaves in the CSA). Further, the hard war policies were not *fully implemented* until after the summer of 1864 when Lincoln and the Union aimed to completely abolish slavery in the United States. Sheridan's campaign in the Shenandoah Valley and Sherman's march through Georgia and the Carolinas took place after June 1864. So the morally questionable actions of the Union military against Confederate civilians occurred *after* the war became a war for freedom against slavery.[47]

---

[46] Grimsley, *The Hard Hand of War*, pp. 2–3, 23, and 67; also see Stout, *Upon the Altar of the Nation*, p. 139.

[47] Only very unreasonable views, bordering on moral absolutism, will condemn those actions of the Union Army that were necessary to avert the moral catastrophe of Confederate independence. As many anti-utilitarians agree, in *very extreme* cases, it can be morally right to violate some people's rights, provided

Which of the actions of the Union Army at issue were, in fact, justified according to this modified and improved version of the *jus in bello* conditions of just war theory? If the Union Army was to invade deep into Confederate territory, it was necessary for it to live off the land and seize food and provisions from civilians, because long supply lines were almost impossible to defend and could easily be cut by small numbers of guerrillas. Those actions were clearly justified. Armies have had to seize food and other resources when operating in enemy territory in almost all wars until quite recently in history. Many of the collective punishments of civilians involving the destruction of their property in areas where the Union Army was attacked by guerrillas were justified in order to deter and restrain guerrilla attacks.

It is much more difficult to justify the stated policies of the Union military that permitted deliberately starving civilians and expelling civilians from their homes (sometimes for refusing to take loyalty oaths). In my view, those policies were wrong – I say this on the assumption that carrying out these policies was not necessary for winning the war. The great majority of whites in the CSA were not loyal to the Union. That itself was not sufficient reason to expel them from their

that doing so is necessary to prevent an *enormously* greater violation of rights. I appeal to the following principle from Chapter 2.IV:

P3.Other things equal, it is morally permissible to do something that violates certain people's moral rights, provided that doing so is *necessary* to prevent an *enormously greater* violation of moral rights.

P3 is admittedly a very dangerous moral principle that is likely to be misused and misapplied in practice. Nonetheless, P3 is true. It *is* permissible to violate people's moral rights, provided that doing so *really is necessary* to prevent an *enormously greater* violation of moral rights. But it is also true that leaders who endorse this principle are likely to misapply it and use it to justify and rationalize very wrong acts. We need to distinguish between correct standards of right and wrong and useful practical guides to decision making that we would want our leaders to use as guides to action. On the distinction between ultimate standards of right and wrong and useful guides for decision making, see Carson, "Strict Compliance and Rawls's Critique of Utilitarianism" and *Lying and Deception: Theory and Practice*, pp. 91–4.

homes. The Union army could legitimately demand a promise of nonviolence or nonbelligerence of civilians in occupied territory, but it was too much to demand loyalty to the United States.[48] These were morally objectionable policies, and it would have been very wrong to carry them out on a large scale. But it seems that they were *not* carried out on a large scale.

Although the Lieber Code permitted the starving of hostile Confederate civilians, this was clearly not done on a large scale. The total number of civilians who died in the war was fifty thousand, and few of those civilians died because of this policy. In practice, the actions of the Union military were generally proportionate to the legitimate Union war aims of feeding its own armies and depriving the Confederate armies of food and fodder. But what about the policies that permitted expelling civilians from their homes (particularly those civilians who refused to take loyalty oaths)? The only case in which this was done on a large scale was when General Ewing expelled ten thousand people from their homes in Missouri in retaliation for Quantrill's murder of all the men and boys in Lawrence, Kansas. In July 1864, Sherman expelled the approximately four hundred civilians living in Roswell, Georgia.[49] A few months later after the fall of Atlanta, Sherman turned the city into a military base and expelled the remaining 1,560 civilians from the city.[50]

Although, to my knowledge, aggregate figures about the number of people expelled from their homes by the Union Army do not exist, it seems that it expelled relatively few civilians from their homes. The total number of civilians expelled from their homes by the Union Army was a very small percentage of the total number of Confederate

[48] This raises the question of whether it would have been reasonable to hold civilians responsible for the actions of guerillas and/or require them to report guerilla activity.

[49] Stout, *Upon the Altar of the Nation*, p. 356.

[50] Ibid., pp. 368–70.

civilians, and many (most?) of those who were expelled were hostile civilians who aided and abetted Confederate guerrillas in areas occupied by the Union Army. On the whole, the Union military was very restrained in expelling civilians from their homes. It was far more restrained than the U.S. military during the Vietnam War when its relocation policies and battles that it fought forced millions of people from their homes.

Sherman's march through Georgia and the Carolinas began on November 14, 1864, *after* Lincoln's reelection. That election made Union victory overwhelmingly probable (see Chapter 4.II.3. D). Therefore the march was not necessary to win the war, and there is a strong case for saying that it was *not justified*. This line of reasoning parallels Walzer's argument that, once it became clear that the Allies would win World War II, Allied air attacks aimed at killing and terrorizing German civilians were not justified.[51]

Utilitarians do not agree with Walzer's principle: they permit attacks on civilians and civilian property that are not necessary for victory, provided that those attacks hasten victory and reduce the overall badness of war. It is possible that Sherman's march was not necessary for Union victory, but that it nonetheless shortened the war and thus saved many lives by weakening the will of the Confederacy to continue fighting. Sherman defended his actions on similar grounds – he claimed that they would cause civilians to bring about the end of the war and that the Confederate civilians were the ones who had to stop the war.[52] Mark Grimsley thinks that the destruction and harm to Confederate civilians caused by Sherman and other Union generals brought about the end of the war:

Ultimately these marches, more than anything else, destroyed the Confederacy. They smashed the remainder of the Confederate rail

---

[51] Walzer, *Just and Unjust Wars*, p. 261.
[52] Stout, *Upon the Altar of the Nation*, p. 370.

network, eliminated foodstuffs and war resources, completed the ruin of Southern morale, and caused the desertion of thousands of Confederate soldiers who had resisted valiantly for years.[53]

Even at the end of the war, Confederate troops still possessed weapons and ammunition. Rations had been bad for a year but they still had food to eat. What they did not possess was the confidence that they could continue the struggle effectively. They could not prevent Union troops from roaming at will and visiting hardship and destruction upon places throughout the South. This sense of helplessness accelerated – although it did not begin – the wave of desertions that plagued the Confederate army during the war's final year. Many rebel soldiers, recognizing that their presence in the ranks could no longer protect their families, simply went home.[54]

Similarly, Sheridan said that reducing Confederate civilians to poverty would hasten the end of the war.[55] Given this understanding of the facts, reasonable people can disagree about this issue, and I am uncertain what to say about it.

Southern Bitterness in the Wake of the War. These issues are further complicated by the fact that the Union Army's treatment of Confederate civilians left a lingering bitterness after the war, a bitterness that continues to this day. The bad consequences of this bitterness, which very adversely affected the treatment of black people in the South after the war, need to be taken into account: they weaken the case for saying Sherman's actions were justified.

But although it is understandable, Southern bitterness about the war was, and, in some quarters still is, very excessive. It was inflamed by infamous statements by certain Union generals (e.g., Grant's order to reduce the Shenandoah Valley to a barren waste, Sherman's telegram to Grant in which he said that he "could make Georgia howl,"[56] and Sheridan's stated desire to reduce Confederate civilians to poverty). But,

[53] Grimsley, *The Hard Hand of War*, pp. 169–70.
[54] Ibid., pp. 203–4.
[55] Stout, *Upon the Altar of the Nation*, p. 376.
[56] Grimsley, *The Hard Hand of War*, p. 190.

as we have seen, the Union Army did not carry out anything nearly as bad as the actions its generals urged: its deeds did not match the generals' words.

Southern bitterness has also been fanned by distorted and dishonest accounts of history (see Chapter 4.I.1). This process started just after the war began. In his message to the Confederate Congress on July 20, 1861, *before* the Union began its invasion of the Confederacy, Confederate president Jefferson Davis said that the United States was

waging an indiscriminate war on them all, with a savage ferocity unknown to modern civilization. In this war, rapine, is the rule: private residents in peaceful rural retreats are bombarded and burnt: Grain crops in the field are consumed by the torch: and when the torch is not convenient, careful labor is bestowed to render complete the destruction of every article of use or ornament remaining in private dwellings, after their inhabitants have fled from the outrages of brutal soldiery.

Mankind will shudder to hear of the tales and outrages committed on defenseless females by soldiers of the United States now invading our homes.[57]

These claims were false. The Union army had not treated Confederate civilians with "a savage ferocity unknown to modern civilization," and acts of rape by Union soldiers against white women were very rare. Surely Davis knew that what he said was false. He knew that the Union was still preparing for war and had not yet begun a large-scale invasion of the Confederacy. Davis lied.

Even earlier, in June 1861, Confederate general Beauregard wrote to the people of northern Virginia saying that Lincoln had sent "abolition hosts" there who were murdering innocent civilians "and committing other acts of violence

---

[57] Neely, "Was the Civil War a Total War?," pp. 455–6.

and outrage too shocking to humanity to be enumerated."[58]
These claims were also false.

Davis spoke of "outrages" (rapes) committed by Union soldiers against Southern women, and it is safe to assume that he
was referring to outrages against (rapes of) white women. But
even later in the war, Union soldiers raped very few Southern
white women.[59] Sherman's forces in Georgia committed very
few rapes or murders of civilians.[60] However, his army was
somewhat out of control when it wreaked special vengeance
on South Carolina, the state they correctly believed to be
most responsible for starting the war.[61] Although there was
considerable looting and widespread deliberate destruction
of property in South Carolina, the soldiers committed few
assaults on white civilians and rapes of white women were
rare.[62] However, soldiers in Sherman's army did rape many
black women in South Carolina. The number of victims is difficult to determine because many women were too frightened
to testify against Union soldiers.[63] Lincoln and the leaders of
the Union army did not condone the rape of anyone, black or
white, but punished rapists severely. Several Union soldiers
were executed for rape (most of those executed in South Carolina were executed for the rape of black women).[64] Lincoln
was inclined to be lenient to Union soldiers, but he rarely par-
doned rapists.[65] According to Article 44 of the Lieber Code,
"all rape, wounding, maiming, or killing" of inhabitants of
enemy territory "are prohibited under the penalty of death,
or such other severe punishment as may seem adequate for

---

[58] Grimsley, *The Hard Hand of War*, p. 7.
[59] Neely, "Was the Civil War a Total War?," p. 445.
[60] Stout, *Upon the Altar of the Nation*, p. 400.
[61] Ibid., pp. 413–17.
[62] Ibid., p. 416.
[63] Ibid., p. 417.
[64] Ibid.
[65] Burlingame, *Abraham Lincoln: A Life*, II, p. 493.

the gravity of the offense." It also provides that soldiers in the act of committing such violence who disobey orders to stop "may be lawfully killed on the spot."

As mentioned earlier, although many describe the Civil War as a "total war" and some call it the first total war, this characterization is greatly overstated and very misleading. "Total war" suggests a war conducted "without scruple or limitations."[66] The Union did not fight such a war: it was very constrained in its treatment of Confederate civilians, especially whites. Despite the fact the Union Army operated in the midst of frequent guerrilla attacks and very hostile civilians, in total only about fifty thousand American civilians died as a result of the war and very few of them were intentionally killed or murdered by Union soldiers. Most of these fifty thousand civilians died from disease and malnutrition.[67] Many of them died because of the actions of the *Confederate* Army. Many Unionists in Missouri and East Tennessee were driven from their homes by the Confederates.[68] Both sides had to contend with irregulars, and Confederate guerrillas often preyed on Unionists and enforced secessionist order behind Union lines.[69] The Confederate Army also foraged and seized food and fodder in Confederate territory, and the Union Army's foraging practices were no worse than those of the Confederate Army.[70]

Lincoln and the Union made many efforts to encourage slaves to escape from their masters and come to Union lines. But the president and the other leaders of the Union scrupulously avoided exploiting the potential rage of freed slaves against their former masters or Southern whites in general, something that might have led to a great deal of violence and

---

[66] Neely, "Was the Civil War a Total War?," p. 440.
[67] McPherson, *The Battle Cry of Freedom*, p. 619.
[68] Grimsley, *The Hard Hand of War*, p. 50 and Donald, *Lincoln*, p. 384.
[69] Grimsley, *The Hard Hand of War*, p. 112.
[70] Ibid., pp. 105 and 204.

would have aided the Union war effort.[71] Although hundreds of thousands of slaves escaped to Union lines and freedom, there were remarkably few acts of violence by slaves against white civilians during the war.

World War II and the wars fought by Genghis Khan and Tamerlane involved the deliberate murder of millions of people: they were total wars. The Korean War is not generally regarded as a total war, but resulted in the death of two million civilians, mostly from the massive American bombing campaign during the war.[72] The Union Army's treatment of Confederate civilians was *far milder* than the U.S. military's treatment of Vietnamese civilians during the Vietnam War when the American military designated certain areas as "free fire zones" and used massive firepower to try to kill all people (both civilians and combatants) within those zones. The American military attempted to warn civilians to leave those zones and go to refugee camps, but all civilians who failed to leave their homes were deemed legitimate targets and were attacked with massive amounts of firepower.

At the end of the Civil War, there was considerable worry that the fighting would continue as a guerrilla war. Jefferson Davis wanted the Confederacy to continue waging a guerrilla war and for Lee's soldiers to disperse and melt into the countryside before they could be captured by the Union.[73] It is likely that, had that happened, the war could have continued for a very long time: the Confederacy had extensive

---

[71] Ibid., p. 212.

[72] Cumings, *The Origins of the Korean War*, II, p. 748. The United States used napalm on a very large scale and destroyed massive dams to flood Korea's northern valleys. Nor were Korean cities spared. The urban destruction in Korea (measured by the percentage of city areas destroyed) caused by U.S. bombing was greater than that inflicted on Japanese and German cities in World War II. The weight of the bombs dropped by the United States in the Korean War exceeded the weight of the bombs used in the Pacific theater during World War II; Cumings, *The Korean War*, pp. 159–60.

[73] Winik, *April 1865: The Month that Saved America*, p. 150.

mountains, forests, and swamps in which guerrillas could operate.[74] Just before he surrendered his army to Grant, Lee was urged to send his soldiers into the woods to keep fighting, but he rejected that proposal.[75] In his last orders to his soldiers Lee urged them to refrain from further fighting and return to their homes.[76] To his great credit, Robert E. Lee urged the Southern people to accept the outcome of the war and cease fighting.

Even though Lincoln apparently never intended that innocent Confederate prisoners be killed in retaliation for the Confederate abuse and murder of black Union prisoners, his approval of those provisions of the Lieber Code that permitted this killing and his order of July 30, 1863 could have led to the wrongful killing of innocent Confederate prisoners of war. In my view, these were justifiable bluffs to try to protect black prisoners. To some extent, they worked, and these bluffs were less dangerous than they appeared. Because Lincoln insisted that no prisoners could be executed without presidential review, soldiers in the field did not have the authority to execute prisoners without his permission – permission he was unwilling to grant.[77]

In sum, the Union military's treatment of Confederate civilians has been greatly distorted and falsified in popular imagination and memory. The Civil War was, most decidedly, not a total war. Lincoln and the Union did not begin their "hard war" treatment of Confederate civilians until the summer of 1862 when the war was becoming a fight for freedom against slavery. At a minimum, all those means used by the Union Army that were necessary to win the war and free the slaves were morally justified – although there is some uncertainty

[74] Ibid.
[75] McPherson, *The Battle Cry of Freedom*, p. 848.
[76] Stout, *Upon the Altar of the Nation*, p. 442.
[77] Neely, *The Civil War and the Limits of Destruction*, pp. 194–5.

about the justification of certain actions and policies (e.g., Sherman's march). Lincoln's policies concerning the treatment of civilians during the war were largely, but not entirely, justified.

III. The Treatment of Prisoners of War

One of the more shameful aspects of the Civil War was the treatment of prisoners of war. Thirty thousand of the 194,000 Union soldiers held as prisoners by the Confederates died in captivity, as did 25,000 of the 214,000 Confederate prisoners held by the Union.[78] Most died of diarrhea and other diseases.[79] Death rates for Union POWs held by the Confederates (15.5%) were higher than death rates for Confederate POWs held by the Union (12.1%), but this latter statistic is misleading and suggests greater Union responsibility for the deaths of Confederate prisoners than was actually the case. Confederate prisoners were in considerably worse health than Union prisoners before they entered POW camps. Union soldiers were 68 percent more likely to die in Confederate prisons than they were to die of disease while serving in the Union Army, whereas Confederate soldiers were 29 percent *less* likely to die while in Union prisons than they were to die of disease while serving in the Confederate Army.[80] On average, Confederate soldiers were considerably healthier as POWs than they were while serving in the Confederate Army.

The Lieber Code calls for humane treatment of prisoners of war. Article 76 reads as follows: "Prisoners of war shall be fed upon plain and wholesome food, whenever practicable, and treated with humanity."

---

[78] Stout, *Upon the Altar of the Nation*, pp. 295 and 299.
[79] Ibid., pp. 297–8.
[80] McPherson, *Ordeal by Fire*, p. 451.

Until 1863, both sides exchanged prisoners of war. The exchange was stopped in 1863, because Lincoln insisted that black prisoners be also exchanged and he objected to the vicious treatment they suffered at the hands of the Confederates. Black prisoners were often killed or returned to slavery; white officers who led black units were often killed as well. Early in the war prisoners were often "paroled" (i.e., released after taking an oath not to fight again). At Chattanooga in November 1863, Grant recaptured Confederate prisoners who had been paroled during the Vicksburg campaign.[81] He was outraged that they had violated their oath. This contributed further to the breakdown of the prisoner exchange system, which caused many prisoners to be held for a very long time. The Confederates were also to blame for this turn of events.

Because the programs to exchange and parole prisoners broke down and because leaders did not foresee the magnitude and duration of the war, neither side made adequate preparations to care for large numbers of prisoners of war. Grant maintained that the breakdown of the prisoner exchange benefited the Union because the well-fed Confederate prisoners who had been returned in the exchanges were ready to fight again, but the malnourished Union prisoners released by the Confederates were not in good fighting condition.[82] But this was *not* the reason for the breakdown of the prisoner exchange. Grant made this remark more than a year after the prisoner exchange broke down. In October 1864, Lee offered to exchange prisoners with Grant. Grant agreed, subject to the additional condition that black soldiers be exchanged the same as white soldiers, but Lee refused to exchange prisoners on those terms.[83] Once the Confederates

---

[81] McPherson, *The Battle Cry of Freedom*, p. 792.
[82] Ibid., p. 799.
[83] Ibid., p. 800.

agreed to exchange all prisoners, including blacks, in January 1865, the exchange was renewed. It is clear that Lincoln and the Union were willing to exchange prisoners on those terms all along.

At the end of the war the Confederacy's mistreatment of Union prisoners became well known with the release of shocking photographs of skeletal Union prisoners from Andersonville (see photo plates). This sparked many heated demands for retaliation. Congress discussed a proposal to feed Confederate prisoners in the way the Confederates were feeding Union prisoners (i.e., starving them). Lincoln resisted those pressures to mistreat Confederate prisoners.[84]

---

[84] Neely, *The Civil War and the Limits of Destruction*, pp. 174–93.

6

Moral Luck and Lincoln's Good Moral Luck

Here I explain the concept of moral luck and attempt to show that moral luck is a genuine and widespread phenomenon. I argue that, in many respects, Lincoln profited from good moral luck. However, he also suffered bad moral luck.

I. The Concept of Moral Luck and the Widespread Existence of Moral Luck

The rightness and wrongness of our actions depend at least partly on things beyond our control, such as the truth or falsity of the beliefs on which we act and the future consequences of our actions. Sometimes people act rightly or wrongly primarily as a matter of chance and because of things that happen beyond their control. These are cases of what philosophers call good and bad moral luck. Moral luck and things beyond one's control can also affect the goodness or badness of one's character.

Here are some clear examples of cases in which moral luck largely determines the rightness and wrongness of what someone does. Two people are members of a jury in a murder trial. The defendant is innocent, but he is the victim of a diabolically clever frame-up. Many honest and reliable eyewitnesses to the crime who know the defendant well say that he did it, and there is considerable forensic and circumstantial evidence of his guilt. But unbeknownst to the police and members of the court, the defendant has an identical twin separated at birth who committed the crime. Juror 1 is extremely conscientious and weighs the evidence very carefully and comes to the reasonable, though mistaken, conclusion that the defendant is guilty beyond any reasonable doubt. Though the defendant is innocent, this is the only reasonable conclusion to draw, given the evidence. Juror 2 is lazy and inattentive; she does not listen carefully to the evidence presented at the trial. She votes to acquit the defendant only because she thinks he looks cute, and she has strong racial prejudices against the victim of the murder. Juror 1 acts wrongly in voting to convict the innocent person on account of bad moral luck; juror 2 acts rightly in voting to acquit the innocent person on account of good moral luck.

Here is a different example of moral luck. Lars becomes very angry with his wife and screams at her, but he calms down and does not do anything more because the front door to their house is open and the neighbors notice them. Astrid and her husband are visiting a friend's summer home, and Astrid becomes very angry with her husband. No one is around to hear them, and she gets angrier and angrier; she then shoots and kills him with a loaded gun that she finds lying near her. Their friend is largely to blame for leaving a loaded gun in the living room of his house. But Astrid is a murderer and does something that is very seriously morally wrong. Lars is not a murderer, and he does nothing that is seriously wrong. This difference is a matter of luck. If Astrid had been in Lars's position (with the neighbors looking on and no loaded gun around), she would not have shot her husband. If Lars had been in Astrid's position (with no one else around and a loaded gun in sight), he would have shot and killed his wife. Both Lars and Astrid have chosen not to own guns because they know that they have very bad tempers and do not want to have guns lying about when they become angry. They were both aware of their own weaknesses and they compensated for them, but Astrid had bad moral luck in that her friend carelessly and irresponsibly left a loaded gun lying around, while Lars had good moral luck.

Sometimes people's circumstances create bad moral luck that makes it more difficult for them to do what is morally right. For example, Larry is a physically unattractive man who never travels on business. He remains faithful to his wife and never commits adultery. Stan is a stunningly handsome man who frequently takes business trips. Most of his business associates are attractive women. Many of those women make sexual overtures to him. He frequently commits adultery. It is much more difficult for Stan to do what is right than Larry.

Sometimes bad moral luck can affect both one's actions and character. Living in a society in which grossly unjust and morally wrong actions are permitted and condoned can make for bad moral luck. We should ask ourselves what we would have done had we been soldiers in one of the *great many* armies all over the world (in many times and places in human history) that slaughtered, raped, and enslaved captured enemy soldiers and civilians. We should also ask ourselves what we would have done had we been forced to join such an army as a child, as were the child soldiers of Sierra Leone in recent times. It is good moral luck not to have been placed in such situations, situations that would cause most people to act very immorally and thereby corrupt their characters.

The institution of slavery often causes slave owners both kinds of bad moral luck (bad luck that harms someone's character and bad luck that causes someone to act wrongly). What would you have done if you had grown up as a slave owner in a society that practiced slavery? Would you have emancipated the people you own at considerable financial cost to yourself? If you owned another person and could do almost anything to her that you wanted, with complete impunity, would you refrain from mistreating and exploiting her? Think of a sixteen-year old with raging hormones who owns physically attractive slaves and recall Lincoln's statement, "No man is good enough to govern another man without the other man's consent."[1] Very few, if any, people are morally good enough to deal with the temptations to wrongdoing that come with having that kind of power over another person; most of us have the good moral luck not to have this sort of power over others.

Here are some examples in which good and bad moral luck can affect one's character for better or worse. A person who has a loving home and good moral examples as a child will find it much easier to be morally virtuous than a person who is cruelly treated by morally bad parents who provide him with horrible role models.

The movie *Monster*, starring Charlize Theron, is based on the true story of a woman who has an appallingly bad childhood and becomes a prostitute as a young girl. She has many terrible experiences with her clients, some of whom abuse and torture her. She grows to hate men and begins to kill many of her clients. She also kills a kindly old man who picked her up while she was hitchhiking. She becomes a cruel and vicious person, a "monster." Horrible luck and circumstances over which she had no control make her a very bad person.

Cases such as these raise questions about issues of praise, blame, and responsibility. In principle, there is a distinction between the goodness or badness of one's character and the extent to which one deserves praise or credit for it. One person could have a better, more virtuous character than another, although the other person might deserve more praise

[1] Abraham Lincoln, *Speeches and Writings*, I, p. 328.

or credit for her character because of the difficulty of her circumstances. It seems to me that the protagonist of *Monster* was not greatly to blame for having become a very bad person with a very bad character, but I do not pursue this issue here, because doing so would compel me to digress and address the very difficult question of free will.

II. Lincoln's Good Moral Luck

Lincoln enjoyed a great deal of good moral luck in that his policies succeeded. His historical reputation is dependent on his having been successful in winning the war, restoring the Union, and abolishing slavery. It would be difficult to claim that his compromises with slavery were justified if the Civil War had not turned out so well. He was also lucky that the Union did not win the war *too easily* or *too soon*, because in that case the war and Lincoln would not have ended American slavery.

He was also very lucky that much good came from his silence about Illinois's extremely unjust black exclusion laws and his active support for other unjust provisions of Illinois's black codes. Early in his political career, it was quite improbable and unforeseeable that any great good would result from this. But his silence about and his support for these laws enabled him to be a viable political candidate in Illinois and later become president and accomplish the great things that he did.

He was lucky that the South was *not* conciliated by his many compromises and attempts to avert a civil war at the beginning of his presidency: he could not have brought about the very great good of ending American slavery if the Civil War had not been fought. Therefore, he was lucky that he failed to do what he was trying to do at that time. He was also lucky that the state of Virginia did not take him up on his offer to abandon Fort Sumter in exchange for a promise from Virginia to remain in the Union, because it is unclear that there would have been sufficient support in the North to fight the war if Fort Sumter had not been attacked.

Lincoln was very lucky that the Union eventually won the Civil War. It was lucky for him that Confederate general Leonidas Polk made the very bad mistake of invading Kentucky in 1861 and that Jefferson Davis did not force Polk to withdraw, even after the Kentucky legislature denounced the invasion. Lincoln was lucky that his best generals were not killed on the battlefield during the war and also that he was not voted out of office in 1864 with his work undone.

Two major pieces of good luck were necessary for his reelection. First, the Democrats were deeply divided during the 1864 presidential election. Their platform included an unpopular provision calling for an immediate end of the war without any conditions; it very likely cost them the election.[2] However, the Democratic candidate for president, General McClellan, announced that he had no intention of abiding by that platform provision and ending the war, unless the Confederate states returned to the Union. McClellan wanted to revoke the Emancipation Proclamation and hoped to restore the Union by promising the Confederate states that they could keep slavery in place. Because many Northern voters wanted to restore the Union, but did not care at all about the freedom of the slaves, McClellan should have been their clear choice in the election. However, the peace plank in the Democratic platform pushed many of them to vote for Lincoln, who ended up winning 55 percent of the popular vote. Very likely, this division among the Democrats allowed Lincoln to win reelection. He himself believed this. He told a cabinet member, "I am here [reelected] by the blunders of the Democrats," and added, "If, instead of resolving that the war was a failure,

---

[2] Guelzo, *Abraham Lincoln: Redeemer President*, p. 396.

they had resolved that I was a failure...I should not have been reelected."[3]

The second piece of good luck for Lincoln was Sherman's capture of Atlanta on September 2, 1864. Had his advance on Atlanta been delayed by only a few months, it is likely that Lincoln would have lost the election. By giving people in the North confidence that the Union would win the war, Sherman's victory virtually ensured Lincoln's reelection, which had been very much in doubt, despite the divisions among the Democrats. During the summer of 1864, Lincoln, thinking that he would be defeated, made plans for that contingency.[4] He met with Frederick Douglass to discuss a plan to help slaves escape from the Confederacy and reach Union lines before he left office if, as it seemed likely, he was not reelected.[5]

Lincoln was also lucky that the Union did not win the war too easily or quickly, before it became a war for abolition, because in that case he would not have had the opportunity to end American slavery. There are many ways in which the Union could have won the war too soon; for example, if General McClellan had pressed the attack on Richmond after the Seven Days Battles in July 1862;[6] or if McClellan had attacked Lee during Lee's invasion of Maryland in September 1862 when he came into possession of Lee's orders and could have destroyed Lee's divided army; or if, a few

---

[3] Ibid.
[4] Abraham Lincoln, *Speeches and Writings*, II, p. 624.
[5] Stauffer, *Giants*, pp. 286–8.
[6] Burlingame, *Abraham Lincoln: A Life*, II, pp. 322 and 333. One of McClellan's generals, Phil Kearny, told some of his fellow officers that McClellan's order to retreat from Richmond after this battle in which Lee had suffered considerably greater casualties than McClellan could only have been "prompted by cowardice or treason" (McPherson, *Battle Cry of Freedom*, p. 470). McPherson thinks that "if McClellan's campaign had succeeded, the war might have ended.... [and] Slavery would have survived in only slightly modified form, at least for a time" (p. 490).

days later, McClellan had taken advantage of the chance to destroy Lee's army when it was greatly outnumbered and trapped north of the Potomac after the Battle of Antietam. If any of these things had happened, then the Union probably would have won the war and reunited the nation without abolishing slavery. It is also possible that Lincoln was lucky that General Meade did not end the Civil War by trapping Lee's army north of the Potomac after the Battle of Gettysburg, as he probably could have. If that had happened, it is unclear that the Emancipation Proclamation would have stood.[7] Further, it is likely that many of the slaves not freed by the Emancipation Proclamation would have remained in bondage. As Lincoln strongly suggested in his Second Inaugural Address, American slavery was a deeply entrenched and powerful institution that could only have been abolished at that time after a terrible and bloody war.

Lincoln and the nation were also lucky that there was not a bloody guerrilla war in the aftermath of the Civil War. Jefferson Davis wanted the Southern people to continue fighting a guerrilla war against the Union, even after the surrender of the main Confederate armies. To his great credit, Robert E. Lee urged the Southern people to accept the outcome of the war and cease fighting.

The rightness and wrongness of what Lincoln did depended on many things that were beyond his control. He enjoyed very good moral luck in that some important things he did turned out well. Despite this, he did not have the kind of moral luck that is involved in cases in which one's actions turn out well

---

[7] The Chief Justice of the Supreme Court, Roger Taney, held that, although the Emancipation Proclamation was constitutional as a war measure, it would become null and void at the end of the war and that those who were freed by the proclamation were only freed temporarily for the duration of the war, (Guelzo, *Abraham Lincoln: Redeemer President*, p. 344). There was considerable uncertainly about how the Supreme Court would rule about the constitutionality of the Emancipation Proclamation after the war ended.

when there was no reasonable expectation that they would, as in my earlier example of the inattentive and prejudiced juror. Lincoln was justified in thinking that his actions and policies would turn out for the best. He correctly and justifiably believed that if he did not make the compromises he made (those discussed in Chapter 2.I), the South would win the Civil War and gain its independence. He was also justified in believing that an independent Confederate States of America would strengthen, enlarge, and perpetuate the institution of slavery, and that made it reasonable for him to think that the Union had just cause to fight the Civil War.

Lincoln did not just make lucky guesses about what would happen in the future: he was an *extraordinarily* farsighted and prescient leader. Here are several cases that illustrate this point. In 1858 he foresaw that Stephen Douglas's answer to his question in the Freeport debate – "Does Douglas's principle of popular sovereignty allow states to choose to prohibit slavery?" – would greatly weaken Southern support for Douglas as a presidential candidate in 1860. He foresaw that the Democrats would be divided in the 1860 presidential election because of widespread opposition to Douglas in the South.[8] He realized that this meant that the Republicans had a good chance of winning the election. He also understood that he had a good chance of being nominated as the Republican candidate for president if he could be many people's second choice. During the Fort Sumter crisis he understood that his order to re-provision the fort would likely cause South Carolina to attack the fort and begin a civil war. He also understood that, for the purposes of uniting the North behind the war effort, it was vital that the Confederates, and not he, start the war (see Chapter 2.I.2).

---

[8] Burlingame, *Abraham Lincoln: A Life*, I, pp. 559.

III. Lincoln's Bad Moral Luck

It is bad moral luck to grow up in a time and place in which almost all of one's associates have strong prejudices (or even hatred) against other groups of people. Lincoln had this kind of bad moral luck because he lived in a time and place in which very strong racial prejudices against blacks were nearly universal among whites. He absorbed some of those prejudices when he came of age, and he had to pander to (and refrain from condemning) the very strong racial prejudices of the Illinois electorate to be a viable politician in the state of Illinois. (Chapters 3, 10, and 11 give many more details of this bad moral luck.) We need to keep his bad moral luck firmly in mind when we address the issue of his racism in Chapter 10.

PLATE 1: Lincoln's Father Thomas Lincoln. *Source:* Photographer and date unknown. Courtesy of the Library of Congress, Prints and Photographs, Division, LC-DIG-ppmsca-19418.

PLATE 2: Lincoln's Stepmother Sarah Bush Johnston Lincoln. *Source:* Photographer and date unknown. Courtesy of Chicago Historical Society.

PLATE 3: Lincoln's Wife Mary Todd Lincoln (1846 or 1847). *Source:* Photograph Nicholas Shepard, 1846 or 1847. Courtesy of the Library of Congress, Prints and Photographs, Division, LC-USZ62-12458.

PLATE 4: Lincoln's Oldest Son, Robert Todd Lincoln around 1865. *Source:* Brady's National Photographic Portrait Galleries, ca. 1865. Courtesy of the Library of Congress, Prints and Photographs, Division, LC-DIG-ppmsca-19230.

PLATE 5: Lincoln's Sons, Willie and Tad Lincoln, with their cousin Lockwood Todd. *Source:* Brady's National Portrait Galleries, 1861. Courtesy of the Library of Congress, Prints and Photographs, Division, LC-DIG-ppmsca-32298.

PLATE 6: Lincoln 1860. "That looks better and expresses me better than any I have ever seen; if it pleases the people I am satisfied." *Source:* Alexander Hesler, June 3, 1860. Courtesy of the Library of Congress, Prints and Photographs, Division, LC-DIG-ppmsca-19195.

PLATE 7: Lincoln 1860. *Source:* Photograph unknown, Spring or Summer 1860. Courtesy of the Library of Congress, Prints and Photographs, Division, LC-USZ62-7992.

PLATE 8: Candidate for President August 1860. *Source:* Photograph by Preston Butler, August 13, 1860. Courtesy of the Library of Congress, Prints and Photographs, Division, LC-DIG-ppmsca-17159.

PLATE 9: The Toll and Burdens of Lincoln's Office (this photo was taken less than 5 years after the photo on the facing page). *Source:* Photograph by Alexander Gardner, February 5, 1865. Courtesy of the Library of Congress, Prints and Photographs, Division, LC-USZ62-11896.

PLATE 10: Lincoln and General McClellan on the Battlefield at Antietam, Maryland. *Source:* Photograph by Alexander Gardner, October 2, 1862. Courtesy of the Library of Congress, Prints and Photographs, Division, LC-USZ62-2276.

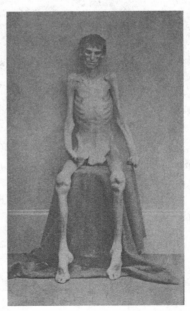

PLATE 11: Union Prisoner of War, Andersonville Prison. *Source:* Photograph by A. Hill Messinger, (between 1861–1865). Courtesy of the Library of Congress, Prints and Photographs, Division, LC-DIG-ppmsca-33758.

PART TWO

LINCOLN'S MORAL CHARACTER

7

Lincoln's Virtues

Lincoln possessed many important moral virtues. He possessed some of these virtues to a very high degree, but he might have lacked other virtues.

I. Some Important Moral Virtues that Lincoln Possessed to a High/Very High Degree

1. Lincoln was an unusually kind, benevolent, compassionate, and tender-hearted person in both his feelings and actions. He was deeply moved and distressed by human and animal suffering. His kindness was a virtue, and it was the foundation of his opposition to slavery. This trait was very pronounced from his childhood on and was observed by many people on many occasions.

He was exceptionally kind to animals. His stepsister recalled that "he once preached a youthful sermon defending the right to life of ants."[1] As a ten-year-old boy he upbraided his companions for putting hot coals on the backs of turtles.[2] Once

---

[1] Miller, *Lincoln's Virtues*, p. 27.
[2] Ibid., p. 28.

he went to great trouble to rescue a hog from drowning in the mud.[3] He plunged barefoot into a cold icy swamp to rescue his dog during the bitterly cold winter of 1830 when he and his family were moving from Indiana to Illinois.[4] In 1855, while traveling in a buggy, he heard the loud squealing of a small pig. He leapt out and drove off an old sow who was eating one of her young.[5] His very close friend Joshua Speed recalled that while riding on horseback through the woods with a number of other men Lincoln fell behind, and the others wondered why. Here is Speed's account as recorded by Herndon:

After waiting for some time Hardin came up and we asked him where Lincoln was. "Oh," said he, "when I saw him last" (there had been a severe wind storm), "he had caught two little birds in his hand, which the wind had blown from their nest, and he was hunting for the nest" ... He finally found the nest, and placed the birds, to use his own words, "in the home provided for them by their mother." When he came up with the party they laughed at him. Said he, earnestly, "I could not have slept tonight if I had not given those two little birds to their mother."[6]

Lincoln was equally kind and benevolent to humans. He was deeply moved and distressed by the suffering of slaves on his trips to the South as a young man. Many years later, in a letter to Speed, a man who owned slaves and defended slavery, he wrote that the sight of shackled slaves "was a continual torment to me" and that slavery "continuously exercises the power of making me miserable."[7] As a young man in Indiana, he would visit and comfort sick children who lived near him.[8] A neighbor from Indiana describes an

---

[3] Ibid., p. 28.
[4] Wilson and Davis, *Herndon's Informants*, pp. 718–19.
[5] Ibid., pp. 423–4.
[6] Statement by Joshua Speed to William Herndon, 1882, in ibid., p. 590.
[7] Abraham Lincoln, *Speeches and Writings*, I, pp. 360–1.
[8] Wilson and Davis, *Herndon's Informants*, p. 126.

incident in which Lincoln found a man lying dead drunk in a mud hole on a very cold night. He picked the man up and carried him to a house, built a fire to warm him, and stayed up with him all night, even though Lincoln had worked very hard threshing wheat during the day.[9]

His kindness and compassion for wounded Union soldiers were well known and made him beloved by the soldiers. The soldiers knew that he cared for them, and many of them loved him for that reason. He and Mary often visited wounded soldiers in hospitals. Burlingame recounts a firsthand report of one of his visits:

Noah Brooks reported that as he "moved softly from between the beds, his face shining with sympathy and his voice often low with emotion," many patients "shed a tear of pleasure as they returned the kind salutation of the President and gazed after him with a new glow on their faces." To Brooks it was no wonder that "a thundering cheer burst from the long lines of men" as Lincoln rode past them on his way back to headquarters.[10]

During the Civil War, the president told Congressman Daniel Voorhees, "Doesn't it seem strange that I should be here – I, a man who couldn't cut a chicken's head off – with blood running all around me."[11]

There is a great deal of additional evidence for thinking that Lincoln was an unusually kind, compassionate, benevolent, and tender-hearted person. Many people who knew him described him as extremely kind.[12] His passionate hatred of slavery and many efforts on behalf of the antislavery cause sprang largely from his benevolence and concern for the welfare of others.

---

[9] Ibid., p. 122.

[10] Burlingame, *Abraham Lincoln: A Life*, II, p. 492.

[11] Fehrenbacher and Fehrenbacher, eds., *Recollected Words of Abraham Lincoln*, p. 458.

[12] Wilson and Davis, *Herndon's Informants*, pp. 9, 18–19, 120, 166, 184, 204, 264, 357, 373, 445, 453, 474, 485, and 720.

His benevolence was closely tied to his ambition. His intense desire to do things that would redound to the benefit of his fellow humans drove his political ambitions (see 7.I.7).

One important qualification needs to be added here. As a young man, Lincoln enjoyed mocking and ridiculing his political opponents and often did this in anonymous letters to newspapers. He also attacked his opponents very harshly and personally. Once, on the political stump, he reduced a local Democratic politician to tears, and on another occasion an anonymous letter he wrote led the Democratic auditor of the State of Illinois to challenge him to a duel. He did not give up his penchant for denigrating his political opponents until middle age – roughly from about 1849 to 1854. But for the last eleven to sixteen years of his life, he was an extremely kind person without qualification (for more details about his personal attacks on political opponents see Chapter 8.3 and 8.4).

> 2. Lincoln's second salient moral virtue was magnanimity. To be magnanimous in the sense I am concerned with means roughly to be "generous in overlooking injury and insult" and "rising above pettiness or meanness."[13] Alternatively, magnanimity is "superiority to petty resentment or jealousy, generous disregard of slights."[14] He possessed the virtue of magnanimity to an extraordinary, almost superhuman,[15] degree. Magnanimity is an important virtue for a leader as I explain, and Lincoln's magnanimity was central to his greatness as a leader.

Lincoln did not engage in petty quarrels with others, and he freely admitted his errors. For example, he wrote a letter to

---

[13] *Webster's New World Dictionary of American English*, third college edition.
[14] *The New Shorter Oxford English Dictionary*.
[15] Secretary of State William Seward said that Lincoln's magnanimity was "almost superhuman;" Kearns Goodwin, *A Team of Rivals*, p. 364.

General Grant after Grant's great victory at Vicksburg, in which he captured a Confederate fortress on the Mississippi River and a very sizable Confederate army. His letter included the following admission:

I write this now as grateful acknowledgment for the almost ines-timable service you have done the country. I wish to say a word further.... When you got below, and took Fort-Gibson, Grand Gulf, and vicinity, I thought you should go down the river and join General Banks; and when you turned Northward East of Big Black, I feared it was a mistake. I now wish to make the personal acknowledgment that you were right and I was wrong.[16]

He also did not withhold praise or take undue credit when things went well. Neither did he hold grudges against oth-ers, even when he was badly insulted and mistreated. In this section I discuss four of the most well-known illustrations of this; there are many other instances as well.

Several years before the start of the war, Lincoln and Edwin Stanton were both members of a team of lawyers working on an important case involving the patent on the McCormick reaper. Stanton treated Lincoln very badly, refusing to talk to him or to allow him to take an active role in the trial; he was also openly contemptuous of him. At their initial meet-ing, Lincoln wanted to discuss his ideas for the case. Stanton walked away, muttering to another companion, "Why did you bring that damned long-armed Ape here ... he does not know any thing and can do you no good."[17] Stanton was a Democrat and was briefly attorney general at the end of the Buchanan administration. He did not support Lincoln during the 1860 election. Stanton's disdain for Lincoln was clear. Nonetheless, Lincoln greatly admired Stanton's abil-ities. When he had to find a successor to Simon Cameron as secretary of war, Lincoln consulted George Harding, a

---

[16] Abraham Lincoln, *Speeches and Writings*, II, pp. 477–8.
[17] Kearns Goodwin, *A Team of Rivals*, p. 174.

Philadelphia patent attorney whom he had met at the Reaper trial in Cincinnati. Harding told him that Stanton would be best for the job, but said "but I know that you could not and would not appoint him after the outrageous way he has insulted you and behaved towards you in the Reaper case." Lincoln replied, "Now, Mr. Harding, this is not a personal matter. I simply desire to do what is best for the country."[18] And so he did, appointing Stanton as secretary of war in early 1862. Stanton was a superb secretary of war and played a crucial role in the Union war effort. He also grew to greatly love and admire the president.

Lincoln also showed great patience and forbearance with several other members of his cabinet who were extremely difficult people. Treasury Secretary Salmon P. Chase gave Lincoln no end of trouble and proved to be personally disloyal to Lincoln by seeking the Republican nomination for president in 1864. Although it pained him greatly to do so, Lincoln appointed Chase chief justice of the U.S. Supreme Court.[19] He preferred Chase to the other likely candidates, in part, because he was confident that Chase would help prevent the abolition of slavery from being overturned by the court.[20]

The third example is that of Lyman Trumbull. In 1854 Lincoln ran for the U.S. Senate. The big issue in the election was the Kansas-Nebraska Act, which permitted new states entering the Union to vote on the question of whether they would permit slavery within their borders. He and one of his

---

[18] Burlingame, *Abraham Lincoln: A Life*, II, pp. 243–4. Burlingame writes, "Stanton's appointment was one of the most magnanimous acts of a remarkably magnanimous president" (p. 244).

[19] Fellow cabinet member Montgomery Blair said that Chase "was the only human being that I believe Lincoln actually hated" (Burlingame, *The Inner World of Abraham Lincoln*, p. 173).

[20] Donald, *Lincoln*, pp. 551–2; also see Kearns Goodwin, *A Team of Rivals*, pp. 676–81.

rivals, the Democrat Lyman Trumbull, were both opposed to the Kansas-Nebraska Act and any extension of slavery into new states. On the first ballot in the state legislature, Lincoln received forty-five of the fifty-one votes needed to win the election, and Trumbull received five votes. Together they controlled almost enough votes to win the election. In subsequent ballots, Trumbull and his supporters refused to back Lincoln because Lincoln was a Whig, and Lincoln's votes began to slip away. After nine ballots, when it appeared that a candidate who supported the Kansas-Nebraska Act would win the election, Lincoln urged his supporters to help the antislavery cause by voting for Trumbull, despite his great personal disappointment with the outcome and his reasons to feel bitter toward Trumbull for his intransigence and unwillingness to support Lincoln. Trumbull was subsequently elected to the Senate. Mary Lincoln was very bitter about this episode; she was never again on speaking terms with Trumbull's wife, who had been her close intimate friend. Yet Trumbull became an important Republican Senator and later helped engineer Lincoln's nomination for president in 1860.

Lincoln also exhibited extraordinary magnanimity in his relations with General George McClellan. He tolerated great rudeness and insolence on McClellan's part because he thought that he needed McClellan. In one well-known incident, he came to McClellan's home at night to talk with him, but McClellan was not home. After Lincoln waited a long time for him, McClellan returned home and went upstairs without speaking to the president, and it was not until a half-hour later that Lincoln was informed that the general had gone to bed. Early in the war, McClellan met with Lincoln and a number of the president's advisors to discuss strategy for the war. When asked about the details of his plans for attacking the Confederates, McClellan refused to answer; then, when pressed for an answer by Montgomery Meigs (quartermaster general of the U.S. Army during the

Civil War), McClellan told Meigs, "If I tell him [Lincoln] my plans they will be in the *New Herald Tribune* tomorrow morning. He can't keep a secret."[21] Many people close to Lincoln were outraged by McClellan's treatment of the president, but Lincoln said that he was not upset on his own account and that he would even hold McClellan's horse if McClellan gave him victories.[22] McClellan's record as a general was very mixed, and Lincoln was rightly exasperated by McClellan's reluctance to attack Lee's army and by McClellan's totally unfounded fears that he was greatly outnumbered by the Confederate armies he faced. However, by all accounts, McClellan did a splendid job of organizing and training the Army of the Potomac. He also stopped Lee's first invasion of the North at the Battle of Antietam and thus gave the Union the victory that Lincoln thought was necessary for him to be able to issue the Emancipation Proclamation.[23]

In a letter from July 1862, Lincoln aptly described himself when he wrote, "I shall do nothing in malice. What I deal with is too vast for malicious dealing."[24]

Magnanimity is an important moral virtue and a *very important* virtue for any leader, as Michael Burlingame writes,

Most politicians, indeed, most people, are dominated by their own petty egos. They take things personally, try to dominate one

[21] Donald, *Lincoln*, p. 330.
[22] Ibid.
[23] There is a case for thinking that Lincoln diminished the office of the president and the institution of civilian control of the military by tolerating McClellan's behavior. Perhaps he should have removed McClellan earlier, just as Harry Truman removed General Douglas MacArthur during the Korean War. Like McClellan, MacArthur was an egomaniac who enjoyed considerable political support. In this instance, we need to distinguish between saying that Lincoln acted magnanimously and saying that he acted rightly. Although we can question Lincoln's actions regarding McClellan, his actions in this case still support the view that he was extremely magnanimous.
[24] Abraham Lincoln, *Speeches and Writings*, II, p. 346.

another, and waste time and energy on feuds and vendettas . . . and put the needs of their own egos above all other considerations.[25]

Had he acted on the promptings of a normal human ego, Lincoln would not have enjoyed the services of the best people working for him, he would have been greatly distracted by the numerous slights and slanders that assailed him, and he would not have succeeded in the tremendously difficult tasks of his presidency. Lincoln's magnanimity was essential for his success as president. From the foregoing, it is clear that Lincoln was an extremely outstanding exemplar of the Christian virtues of forgiveness and turning the other check.

3. Some underappreciated features of Lincoln's character are his nonconformity, skepticism, independence of mind, and openness to criticism.

He questioned and rejected many of the conventional values of his own time and place. He was a singular and extremely unconventional person. As William Lee Miller writes,

In a society of hunters, Lincoln did not hunt; . . . among many who were cruel to animals, Lincoln was kind . . . in a social world in which fighting was a regular male activity, Lincoln was a peacemaker; in a hard-drinking society, Lincoln did not drink; when a temperance movement condemned all drinking, Lincoln the nondrinker did not join it; in an environment soaked with hostility to Indians, Lincoln resisted it; in a time and place in which the great mass of common men in the West supported Andrew Jackson, Lincoln supported Henry Clay; surrounded by Democrats, Lincoln became a Whig; in a political party with a strong nativist undercurrent, Lincoln rejected that prejudice; in a southern flavored setting soft on slavery, Lincoln always opposed it; in a white world with strong racial antipathies, Lincoln was generous to blacks; in an environment indifferent to education, Lincoln cared about it intensely; in a family active in church, Lincoln abstained; when

[25] Burlingame, *Abraham Lincoln: A Life*, II, p. 833.

evangelical Christianity permeated the western frontier, Lincoln raised questions – and gave different answers than his neighbors.[26]

Lincoln was very skeptical about the common prejudices of his own time and place, including the prevailing racial prejudices against African Americans. When he alluded to those prejudices, he stressed that they might be ill founded (see Chapters 3.II.2 and 10.IV). He was willing and able to alter his views and abandon prejudices in light of evidence. Here is one notable instance. He was initially reluctant to permit black soldiers to serve in the Union Army. In part, he was motivated by his well-founded worries about the attitudes of white soldiers and the general public, but he also worried that blacks might not make good soldiers.[27] However, once it became clear that black soldiers were acquitting themselves very well in battle, he went out of his way to acknowledge their valor and crucial role in the Union war effort.[28]

---

[26] Miller, *Lincoln's Virtues*, pp. 43–4.

[27] Foner, *The Fiery Trial*, pp. 229–30.

[28] See, for example, Lincoln's public letter to James Conkling; Lincoln, *Speeches and Writings*, II, pp. 495–9. Conkling was a conservative Unionist who criticized Lincoln for issuing the Emancipation Proclamation. Here are the relevant parts of Lincoln's response:

> But to be plain, you are dissatisfied with me about the negro. . . . I certainly wish that all men could be free, while I suppose you do not. Yet I have neither adopted, nor proposed any measure, which is not consistent with even your view, provided you are for the Union. . . .
>
> You dislike the emancipation proclamation; and, perhaps, would have it retracted. You say it is unconstitutional – I think differently. I think the constitution invests its Commander-in-chief, with the law of war, in time of war. . . .
>
> The war has certainly progressed as favorably for us, since the issue of proclamation as before. I know, as fully as one can know the opinions of others, that some of the commanders of our armies in the field who have given us our most important successes believe the emancipation policy and the use of the colored troops constitute the heaviest blow yet dealt to the Rebellion, and that at least one of these important successes could not have been achieved when it was but for the aid of black soldiers. . . .
>
> You say you will not fight to free negroes. Some of them seem willing to fight for you; but, no matter. Fight you, then exclusively to save the Union. . . .

As president, Lincoln continuously subjected his views to criticism and sought to improve them. He appointed strong and able people to his cabinet and sought their frank criticisms of his ideas. He listened to and learned from the criticisms of the abolitionists, even though they criticized him very harshly and often unfairly. Some abolitionists even made bigoted remarks about his family background, calling his family "poor white trash" (see Chapters 2.I.4, 3.II.2, and 10.VII). He exemplified these words of his 1862 letter to Horace Greeley: "I shall try to correct errors when shown to be errors; I shall adopt new views so fast as they appear to be true views."[29] In his first written political statement, Lincoln wrote, "Upon the subjects of which I have treated, I have spoken as I thought. I may be wrong in regard to any or all them. . . . so soon as I discover my opinions to be erroneous, I shall be ready to renounce them."[30]

Lincoln wanted to learn the answers to questions, and he did not let his ego get in the way of his pursuit of knowledge. He was not ashamed to admit his ignorance, nor to admit that he did not know the meaning of a word.[31]

> I thought that in your struggle for the Union, to whatever extent the negroes should cease helping the enemy, to that extent it weakened the enemy in his resistence to you. Do you think differently? . . . . But negroes, like other people, act upon motives. Why should they do any thing for us, if we will do nothing for them? If they stake their lives for us, they must be prompted by the strongest motive – even the promise of freedom. And the promise being made, must be kept. . . .
>
> Peace does not appear so distant as it did. . . . And then, there will be some black men who can remember that, with silent tongue, and clenched teeth, and steady eye, and well-poised bayonet, they have helped mankind on to this great consummation; while, I fear, there will be some white ones, unable to forget that, with malignant heart, and deceitful speech, they strove to hinder it.

Lincoln came to greatly appreciate the bravery of black soldiers and their contributions to the Union cause, and he frequently paid tribute to black soldiers in his public and private statements.

[29] Abraham Lincoln, *Speeches and Writings*, I, p. 358.
[30] Ibid., pp. 4–5.
[31] Wilson and Davis, *Herndon's Informants*, p. 589.

His capacity for self-criticism came to be appreciated by many of his abolitionist critics. Wendell Phillips described him as "a growing man" whose views changed and might well change again.[32] Shortly before his death, the abolitionist Lydia Child wrote,

I think that we have reason to thank God for Abraham Lincoln. With all his deficiencies, it must be admitted that he has grown continuously; and considering how slavery had weakened and perverted the moral sense of the whole country, it was great good luck to have the people elect a man who was *willing* to grow.[33]

Lincoln's openness to criticism was closely connected with his magnanimity. He was able to learn even from people who spoke harshly and unfairly of him, people he had reason to be angry with and to resent.

4. William Lee Miller aptly describes Lincoln as someone who had strong moral convictions and gave strong moral arguments about the morality of slavery without being moralistic or self-righteous.[34]

Lincoln frequently made judgments about the rightness or wrongness of actions and the justice or injustice of institutions, but he was very reluctant to make moral judgments that condemned *other people*.[35]

Although Lincoln condemned slavery in the strongest terms, called it a "monstrous injustice," and said that he "hated" it, he did not condemn slave owners or Southerners. Two paragraphs from his Peoria speech on the

---

[32] Foner, *The Fiery Trial*, p. 291.

[33] Ibid., p. 336.

[34] Miller, *Lincoln's Virtues*, p. 286. Also see Wolf, *The Almost Chosen People*, p. 139 and Trueblood, *Abraham Lincoln: Theologian of America's Anguish*, pp. 5 and 23.

[35] This is not to say that making moral judgments about people is always contrary to virtue. However, not making such judgments helped Lincoln avoid the vice of self-righteous disdain for others.

Kansas-Nebraska Act illustrate this. He said that he hated the "*declared* indifference" of supporters of the act to the spread of slavery:

I hate it because of the monstrous injustice of slavery itself. I hate it because it deprives our republican example of its just influence in the world – enables enemies of free institutions, with plausibility, to taunt us as hypocrites – causes real friends of freedom to doubt our sincerity.

But in the next paragraph Lincoln said,

Before proceeding, let me say I think that I have no prejudice against the Southern people. They are just as we would be in their situation. If slavery did not now exist amongst them, they would not introduce it. If it did now exist amongst us, we should not instantly give it up.[36]

In his Second Inaugural Address, Lincoln said that American slavery was an "offense" for which both the North and South were punished in the Civil War. He hated the sin of slavery, but unlike many abolitionists, he did not hate or disdain the sinners.

Because so many people who have strong moral convictions are self-righteous and betray considerable hostility in condemning others, Lincoln's non-moralistic, non–self-righteous concern for moral questions was morally virtuous; indeed, it was very virtuous. He avoided vices often possessed by people with strong moral convictions. This feature of Lincoln's character was clearly connected with his belief in what he called the "the doctrine of necessity." He was a fatalist who rejected belief in free will, something that is a presupposition of judgments of moral blame.[37]

---

[36] Abraham Lincoln, *Speeches and Writings*, I, p. 315. I follow Miller in making this connection; *Lincoln's Virtues*, p. 287.

[37] Guelzo, *Abraham Lincoln as a Man of Ideas*, pp. 27–48.

This general feature of his character is powerfully conveyed in the following memorable sentence from his Second Inaugural Address:

It may seem strange that any men should dare to ask a just God's assistance in wringing their bread from the sweat of other men's faces; but let us judge not that we not be judged.

But we should also note his 1854 Peoria speech in which he harshly condemned those who treated blacks as property and "mere merchandise":

In all these cases it is your sense of justice and human sympathy, continually telling you, that the poor negro has some natural right to himself – that those who deny it, and make mere merchandise of him, deserve kickings, contempt, and death.[38]

This statement is quite out of character and is, to my knowledge, the harshest and angriest language Lincoln ever used in a public statement.

5. Lincoln was an extremely temperate and self-controlled person.

He abstained from alcohol and tobacco, and he was very moderate in his eating habits.[39] He was faithful to his wife and self-controlled in his sexual activity, despite having very strong sexual desires and many opportunities to stray from his marriage vows while traveling on the circuit court and as a politician (see Chapter 9.I.2). He also was very moderate in his desires to acquire and spend money (see Chapter 8.5).

Lincoln was exceptionally self-controlled in his expressions of anger. Contrary to his popular image, he had a temper. He

---

[38] Speech at Peoria, Illinois, October 16, 1854, Abraham Lincoln, *Speeches and Writings*, I, p. 327.

[39] Burlingame, *Abraham Lincoln: A Life*, I, p. 327.

could be irritable and harsh when he was tired, and he sometimes lost control when bad news about the war arrived.[40]
However, he was also quick to apologize when he lost his
temper.[41] Despite the tremendous and unrelenting pressures
of his office, the vicious criticism to which he was subjected
from all quarters, and the blunders and incompetence of some
of his generals, Lincoln kept his anger out of important decisions and policies – a very important virtue in a leader. He
also tightly controlled his anger with his wife, who frequently
tried his patience (see Chapter 9.I).

One of the secrets of his mastery over his anger was that he
would write, but not send, angry letters to people who had
annoyed him. He did this on four occasions that we know
of.[42] The most well-known example is the letter he wrote
to General Meade after the Battle of Gettysburg. Although
Meade held off the Confederate attacks at Gettysburg and
won an extremely important victory for the Union, Lincoln was bitterly disappointed by Meade's failure to try to
destroy Lee's Army when it was trapped north of the Potomac
River during its retreat from Pennsylvania after the battle. He
thought that Meade had failed to seize an opportunity to end
the war. Here is part of his letter written to Meade but not
sent:

I had been oppressed nearly ever since the battles at Gettysburg, by
what appeared to be evidences that yourself, and Gen. Couch, and
Gen. Smith, were not seeking a collision with the enemy, but were
trying to get him across the river without another battle.... The
case, summarily stated is this. You fought and beat the enemy
at Gettysburg; and, of course, to say the least, his loss was as
great as yours. He retreated; and you did not, as it seemed to
me, pressingly pursue him; but a flood in the river detained him,
till, by slow degrees, you were again upon him. You had at least

---

[40] Burlingame, *The Inner World of Abraham Lincoln*, pp. 206–7.
[41] Ibid., pp. 207–8.
[42] Ibid., pp. 189–90.

twenty thousand veteran troops directly with you, and as many more raw ones within supporting distance, all in addition to those who fought with you at Gettysburg; while it was not possible that he had received a single recruit; and yet you stood and let the flood run down, bridges be built, and the enemy move away at his leisure, without attacking him. . . .

Again, my dear general, I do not believe you appreciate the magnitude of the misfortune involved in Lee's escape. He was within your easy grasp, and to have closed upon him would, in connection with our other late successes, have ended the war. As it is, the war will be prolonged indefinitely. . . . Your golden opportunity is gone, and I am distressed immeasurably because of it.[43]

Lincoln wisely decided not to send this letter. Although his criticisms and anger were entirely justified, he did not, at that time, have a better alternative to Meade as a commander of the Army of the Potomac.

Burlingame makes the following apt comment on Lincoln's anger and his ability to control it:

The remarkable thing about Lincoln's temper is not how often it erupted, but how seldom it did, considering how frequently he encountered the insolence of epaulets, the abuse of friends and opponents alike, and the egomaniacal selfishness of editors, senators, governors, cabinet members, generals, and flocks of others who pestered him unmercifully about their own petty concerns. It is no wonder that John Hay marveled in 1863, "While the rest are grinding their little private organs for their own glorification [,] the old man is working with the strength of a giant and the purity of an angel to do this great work."[44]

6. Lincoln possessed the virtue of courage. He was willing to risk his life and physical safety when important matters were at stake.

---

43 Abraham Lincoln, *Speeches and Writings*, II, pp. 478–9.
44 Burlingame, *The Inner World of Abraham Lincoln*, p. 208.

During the Blackhawk War, Captain Lincoln risked his life to save an old Indian man who wandered into his camp. His men, who were armed, wanted to kill the old man. Lincoln interposed himself between his men and the old man and said that they would have to fight him if they tried to kill the man. His men backed down, and the old man was spared. Two eyewitnesses, William Greene and Royal Clary, reported this incident.[45] We might try to minimize the importance of this action by noting that Lincoln was the commanding officer of his unit, but that would be a mistake. He was a member of an ill-disciplined militia that elected its own officers. On another occasion, he stepped into an angry mob that was menacing his friend E. Baker, who had been speaking to them; he threatened to fight anyone who tried to stop Baker from speaking.[46]

Lincoln lived continually under the threat of assassination during his time as president. He received many anonymous death threats[47] and showed great courage in calmly going about his business, meeting with many ordinary citizens in the White House, and frequently appearing in public. He had reason to think that his actions to end slavery would make many people want to kill him and that he was likely to be assassinated. In August 1864, a would-be assassin shot his hat off while he was riding alone on a horse in Washington, D.C.[48]

Many people called Lincoln a coward because he secretly passed through Baltimore at night on his way to be inaugurated in Washington to avoid hostile pro-Confederate mobs in the city. He was widely criticized and ridiculed for this. But this incident is not evidence of lack of courage on his part. He

---

[45] Wilson and Davis, *Herndon's Informants*, pp. 18–19 and 372; also see Miller, *Lincoln's Virtues*, p. 256.
[46] Wilson and Davis, *Herndon's Lincoln*, pp. 129–30.
[47] Burlingame, *Abraham Lincoln: A Life, II*, pp. 807–8.
[48] Ibid., p. 808.

was acting on the advice of the detective Allan Pinkerton and others who accompanied him on his journey to the capital. They worried that Lincoln's presence in the city might incite violence between rival groups.[49] In the recent past, many people in Baltimore had died in civil disturbances. Lincoln later regretted this action as one of his worst mistakes.[50]

Aristotle defines courage as a virtue involving the fear of sudden death, which arises most commonly in war.[51] In English, there is a broader sense of the word "courage" in which one can display courage in situations that do not involve physical danger. In this broader sense, we say that some people have "moral courage": they can show moral courage by stating and holding unpopular beliefs. Lincoln had considerable moral courage. He was a very unconventional person who defended very unpopular views about politics, animal rights, and religion (see Chapters 7.I.3 and 8.6). He showed moral courage in being one of a small minority of Illinois legislators who opposed an anti-abolitionist resolution in 1837.[52]

As a member of Congress he fiercely denounced the Mexican War, even though he had reason to think that this stance would be very harmful to him politically. He voted in favor of a congressional resolution that said that "the war was unnecessary and unconstitutionally commenced by the president."[53] Herndon wrote to Lincoln criticizing his position on the war and warning him that this stance would make him unelectable in the future;[54] others shared Herndon's view that this vote would ruin Lincoln's political career. Lincoln's

---

[49] Wilson and Davis, *Herndon's Informants*, pp. 267–314, and 317–25.

[50] Burlingame, *Abraham Lincoln: A Life*, II, p. 39.

[51] *Nicomachean Ethics*, Rowe translation, 1115a25–35; also see 1116 a10.

[52] "Protest in the Illinois Legislature on Slavery," in Abraham Lincoln, *Speeches and Writings*, I, p. 18; also see Miller, *Lincoln's Virtues*, pp. 119–29.

[53] Greenberg, *A Wicked War*, p. 250.

[54] Ibid. and Wilson and Davis, *Herndon's Lincoln*, pp. 176–7.

position on the Mexican War was very unpopular in Illinois and his home congressional district. An Illinois newspaper called him a new "Benedict Arnold."[55] Later he told Herndon that he had committed political suicide by taking the positions he took on the war; he expressed the desire to leave Illinois and was tempted to move to Oregon where he was offered the position of territorial governor.[56] It is likely that he would have moved to Oregon were it not for Mary's strong objections to this idea.[57] Stephen Douglas made a major issue of Lincoln's stance of the Mexican War in the 1858 Illinois senate race, charging that Lincoln had sided with his country's enemies during the war.[58]

All of this is evidence of moral courage on Lincoln's part, but we might take some of his later political pandering and compromises to indicate the absence of moral courage. This is a serious issue that I cannot do justice to here. There is a case for the view that he changed in this respect and became much less morally courageous than he had been earlier. For a number of years he believed that his outspoken position on the Mexican War had destroyed his political career. He clearly *was* much more cautious and circumspect about expressing unpopular views in the 1858 and 1860 campaigns. He went so far as to conceal his views and pander to the prejudices of the voters (see 7.II.2 and 10.V). But his motives for doing this are unclear. It is likely that Lincoln's ambition and desire to win elective office caused him to be less courageous than he had been before. But it is also possible that his pandering and compromises were motivated primarily by his desire to do good by being an electable and effective politician; in that case, they should not be taken to be evidence of a lack of moral courage.

---

[55] Greenberg, *A Wicked War*, p. 254.
[56] Wilson and Davis, *Herndon's Lincoln*, p. 192.
[57] Ibid.
[58] Burlingame, *Abraham Lincoln: A Life*, I, p. 526.

7. Lincoln's remarkable self-education and rise to success and prominence, despite his extreme poverty and lack of social connections, are evidence of great ambition and diligence on his part.

His law partner William Herndon described him as "inordinately ambitious" and "the most ambitious man in the world."[59] Herndon also wrote,

The man who thinks Lincoln calmly sat down and gathered his robes about him, waiting for the people to call him, has a very erroneous knowledge of Lincoln. He was always calculating, and always planning ahead. His ambition was a little engine that knew no rest.[60]

Many of his close friends and associates, including Lyman Trumbull, Joseph Gillespie, Orville Browning, William Jayne, and David Davis, also described him as a very ambitious person.[61]

Ambition often leads people to act wrongly: it is a vice in many people. But Lincoln's ambition was morally virtuous. He was not ambitious for wealth; rather, he was ambitious for the honor and esteem of others and to be remembered in history. He wanted to gain the honor and esteem of others by rendering himself *worthy* of their esteem. In his first political statement from his campaign for the state legislature in 1832, he wrote, "Every man is said to have his peculiar ambition. Whether it be true or not, I can say for one that I have no other so great as that of being truly esteemed of my fellow men, by rendering myself worthy of that esteem."[62] During the deep depression that he experienced after breaking off his

59 Burlingame, *The Inner World of Abraham Lincoln*, p. 236.
60 Wilson and Davis, *Herndon's Lincoln*, p. 231.
61 Burlingame, *The Inner World of Abraham Lincoln*, p. 236.
62 Abraham Lincoln, *Speeches and Writings*, I, p. 5.

engagement with Mary Todd, he seriously contemplated suicide, but his ambition saved him. Lincoln told Joshua Speed
that he was willing to die except that "he had done nothing
to make any human being remember that he had lived."[63]
In a similar vein, he told his friend Mentor Graham that
he thought frequently of suicide, but thought that God had
a plan for him.[64] Lincoln did not just want to be remembered; he wanted to be remembered for doing things that
were good. He said that he wanted to "connect his name with
the events transpiring in his day & generation and so impress
himself upon them as to link his name with something that
would redound to the interest of his fellow man" and that
this "was what he desired to live for."[65] Many years later, he
reminded Speed of their earlier conversation about his ambition to be remembered and said that he believed that in the
Emancipation Proclamation his "fondest hopes" would be
realized.[66]

His ambition, which involved wanting to be honored and
remembered for doing great things that made him worthy of
the esteem of others, closely resembles what Aristotle calls
the virtue of "greatness of soul": "Greatness of soul seems
to belong to the sort of person that thinks himself, and is,
worthy of great things."[67] According to Aristotle greatness
of soul is a mean between the vices of being conceited and
being "little souled."

Someone actually unworthy who thinks himself worthy of great
things is conceited . . . As for the person who thinks himself worthy
of less than he is, he is little-souled.[68]

---

[63] Wilson and Davis, *Herndon's Informants*, p. 197.
[64] Ibid., p. 243.
[65] Ibid., p. 197.
[66] Ibid., p 197.
[67] Aristotle, *Nicomachean Ethics*, Rowe translation, 1123b 2–3.
[68] Ibid., 1123b 7–11.

Honor is the primary good that the great-souled person seeks for herself.[69]

During most of his life, Lincoln aspired to receive great honor and be worthy of receiving it. Because he undoubtedly wanted to know that he received and was worthy of receiving great honor, he wanted to be the sort of person Aristotle calls "great-souled." By the end of his life, he had fulfilled this ambition. He knew that he had done things that made him worthy of great honor, and he knew that he was beginning to receive great honor.

Most people are not capable of doing things that make them worthy of great honor and should not aim at doing great things. But Lincoln had a great and justified confidence in his abilities and great determination to use them.

As we see in Chapter 9.I.2 and 9.I.5, during the late 1850s Lincoln put his political ambitions ahead of his duties as a father. Normally that kind of ambition is contrary to virtue and the demands of morality. In his case, this was probably justified by the great good he did as president.

8. Lincoln was a just person. He had a strong sense of justice and was strongly motivated to act justly and fight injustice. He could become greatly roused and angered by what he took to be injustice and sometimes became extremely angry and indignant when representing clients whom he thought had been treated unjustly.[70]

Once, while representing a poor Revolutionary War widow in court, he became extremely angry with the man he thought had swindled his client.[71] By contrast, he was a very ineffectual attorney when representing clients he thought were in the wrong. Samuel Parks stated that when Lincoln "thought

[69] Ibid., 1123b 15–25.
[70] Burlingame, *Abraham Lincoln: A Life*, I, pp. 348–9.
[71] Ibid., p. 349.

he was in the wrong he was the weakest lawyer I ever saw."[72] Others who observed him in the courtroom made similar reports.[73] Many who knew Lincoln described him as a very just and fair person. One person described him as "the fairest man I have ever had to deal with."[74] William Thomas described him as remarkable for his honesty and fairness as an attorney.[75] Joseph Gillespie referred to Lincoln's "extreme fairness."[76] David Davis said that Lincoln was "eminently just"[77] and that "justice was Lincoln's leading characteristic, modified by mercy – when possible."[78]

However, Lincoln's own sense of justice was imperfect. He was legalistic, and before becoming president, he endorsed Illinois laws that were very unjust to blacks (see Chapter 3.IV). Nonetheless, he had a strong sense of justice and was strongly motivated to act on it.

II. Mercy and Honesty

There is no doubt that Lincoln was merciful, but it is debatable whether his mercy was entirely virtuous. And in the case of honesty, we need to qualify the statement that he was honest. He was *not* honest in what I call the positive sense of being candid, open, and willing to reveal information about himself and his intentions. However, he was honest in the more familiar negative sense of the term: he had a strong

[72] Ibid., p. 321.
[73] Ibid. It is notable that in 1847 he represented a Kentucky slave owner who was trying to recover runaway slaves in Coles County, Illinois. Lincoln lost the case and his client never paid him. In 1841 he successfully represented a black woman suing for her freedom in Tazwell County, Illinois, after someone tried to sell her; Donald, *Lincoln*, p. 103; also see Burlingame, *Abraham Lincoln: A Life*, I, pp. 250–2.
[74] Wilson and Davis, *Herndon's Informants*, p. 14.
[75] Ibid., p. 47 and see p. 392.
[76] Ibid., p. 507 and see p. 181.
[77] Ibid., p. 529.
[78] Ibid., p. 350.

principled disposition not to lie, steal, or engage in fraud or deception. On balance, he deserved the name "Honest Abe," and his honesty was a very significant moral virtue.

1. *Mercy*. Lincoln was very averse to punishing people who ostensibly deserved it. He spent a great deal of time investigating the cases of Union soldiers and Sioux warriors who had been sentenced to death and looked for reasons to spare them from execution. He planned to be lenient and merciful to the leaders and people of the Confederacy, despite their treason and their role in plunging the nation into a terrible civil war. He was clearly merciful according to the following two definitions of "mercy": "refraining from harming or punishing offenders, enemies, persons in one's power, etc." and "kindness in excess of what may be expected or demanded by fairness."[79]

There is no doubt that Lincoln was very merciful, but it is debatable whether his mercy was virtuous because it arguably led him to do things that were wrong. Some of Lincoln's contemporaries thought that his mercy undermined the discipline and fighting ability of the Union Army, and it is possible that had he lived longer, his mercy for the defeated CSA would have come at the expense of the future rights and welfare of African Americans.

A. *Union Soldiers*. During the Civil War, many soldiers deserted, and many fled from the enemy in battle. The standard penalty for desertion or cowardice in the face of the enemy was death. As president, Lincoln had the power to grant clemency. He spent a great deal of time reviewing individual cases and looked for reasons to pardon soldiers who had been condemned to die.

[79] *Webster's New World Dictionary*, third edition.

He was inclined to pardon soldiers accused of cowardice or falling asleep while on sentry duty[80] and took great pleasure in pardoning condemned soldiers.[81] He was especially inclined to pardon soldiers when entreated by tearful women – a weakness that he guarded against.[82] However, he did not pardon those who were found guilty of cruelty, and he "never hesitated" to approve the death sentence for those accused of rape.[83]

Secretary of War Edwin Stanton and many Union military leaders thought that President Lincoln's frequent pardons for soldiers undermined the discipline of the Union Army; this was a source of friction between Lincoln and Stanton.[84] If Stanton's view is correct, Lincoln's pardoning of condemned soldiers was a very serious matter, because these actions might have prolonged the war and thus led to unnecessary suffering. There is some truth in this charge, but Lincoln's mercy toward soldiers also enhanced his popularity with the troops and the morale of the army. In September 1861 William Scott, a Union private who had fallen asleep on sentry duty, was sentenced to death. At Lincoln's request, General McClellan granted Scott a pardon. Seven months later Scott was killed on the battlefield. As he lay dying, Scott asked a comrade to tell the president,

"That I thank him for his generous regard for me, when a poor soldier under the sentence of death. Tell him that I died for my country with six bullets shot into me, by my enemies and his enemies and my country's enemies. And oh, tell him that I hope that God will guide and direct him and take care of him in all the scenes through

[80] Burlingame, *Abraham Lincoln: A Life*, II, pp. 492–3.
[81] Kearns Goodwin, *A Team of Rivals*, p. 539.
[82] Wilson and Davis, *Herndon's Lincoln*, p. 203.
[83] Kearns Goodwin, *A Team of Rivals*, p. 539 and Burlingame, *Abraham Lincoln: A Life*, II, 493.
[84] Kearns Goodwin, *A Team of Rivals*, pp. 730–1.

which he may be called to pass. Yes, God bless President Lincoln for he will one day give him victory over all our enemies."[85]

Stanton and others to the contrary, Lincoln's actions were not seriously harmful to the Union war effort, on balance. His great popularity with the soldiers and his very clear concern for them (see 7.I.1) contributed greatly to the morale of the Union Army.

When a Massachusetts congressman asked Lincoln to save the life of a nineteen-year-old soldier who had deserted from the army, Lincoln replied "that the War Department insisted that the severest punishment for desertion was absolutely necessary to save the army from demoralization." But he also added,

But when I think of these mere lads, who had never before left their homes, enlisting in the enthusiasm of the moment for a war of which they had no conception and then in the camps or on the battle field a thousand miles from home, longing for rest and safety, I have so much sympathy for him that I cannot condemn him to die for forgetting the obligations of the soldier in the longing for home life. There is death and woe enough in this war without such a sacrifice.[86]

It is instructive to compare the views and sentiments of Lincoln and Stanton on the matter of pardoning condemned soldiers. Doris Kearns Goodwin recounts the following incident:

A clerk recalled finding Stanton one night in his office, "the mother, wife, and children of a soldier who had been condemned to be shot as a deserter, on their knees before him pleading for the life of their loved one. He listened standing, in cold and austere silence, and at the end of their heart-breaking sobs and prayers answered briefly that the man must die. The crushed and despairing little family left and Mr. Stanton turned, apparently unmoved, and walked into

---

[85] Burlingame, *Abraham Lincoln: A Life*, II, p. 492.
[86] Ibid., pp. 492–3.

his private room." The clerk thought Stanton an unfeeling tyrant, until he discovered him moments later, "leaning over a desk, his face buried in his hands and his heavy frame shaking with sobs. 'God help me to do my duty; God help me to do my duty!' he was repeating in a low wail of anguish."[87]

This incident shows Stanton's character in a very admirable light. He was a man with deeply humane impulses who did his duty as he saw it, despite those admirable impulses to the contrary, and despite the great suffering and anguish that it caused him. It is important to stress that Stanton's views about what his duty required were at least *reasonable*. Sometimes *unreasonable* moral views cause otherwise humane people to do heinous things contrary to their humane impulses. For example, an otherwise humane man might act against his sympathetic impulses and sentiments to kill his sister because she was raped because he thinks that it is his duty to preserve his family's honor by killing her.[88]

By contrast, Lincoln's time and attention to pardoning a relative handful of soldiers amidst the mass carnage that he oversaw and directed smacked of moral self-indulgence. Although he was responsible for the deaths of hundreds of thousands of people in the war, he wanted to enjoy the pleasure of pardoning a relatively small number of soldiers. But, that said, it is possible that this was a necessary indulgence for someone so overwhelmed by sorrow, overwork, pressure, and compassion for those harmed by his own actions. If pardoning a few individuals helped him retain his sanity and equilibrium, it was for the good. Joshua Speed recalled witnessing an incident late in Lincoln's presidency. He was visited by two women – the wife and the mother of men imprisoned for resisting the draft. He looked into the cases and decided that the men had been punished long enough and

---

[87] Kearns Goodwin, *A Team of Rivals*, p. 671.
[88] See Appiah, *The Honor Code*, chapters 4 and 5.

granted the women their request that he release their men; the two women were very happy and very grateful. Afterward, Lincoln and Speed talked. Speed described their conversation as follows [I have not corrected Speed's many stylistic errors]:

I said to him – Lincoln with my knowledge of your nervous sensibility it is a wonder that such scenes don't kill you – I am said he very unwell – my feet and & hands are always cold – I suppose I ought to be in bed –

But things of that sort dont hurt me – For to tell you the truth – that scene which you witnessed is the only thing I have done today which has given me any pleasure – I have in that made two people happy. . . . It is more than we can often say that in doing right we have made two people happy in one day – "Speed die when I may I want it said of me by those who know me best to say that I always plucked a thistle and planted a flower where I thought a flower would grow."[89]

B. *The Sioux in Minnesota*. In the fall of 1862, the Sioux staged a very large uprising in Minnesota.

They killed and captured hundreds of whites and drove thirty thousand people from their homes. There was widespread panic and anger in the state,[90] and General Pope was dispatched to Minnesota to put down the uprising. The uprising was quickly suppressed, and 303 captured Sioux were tried and sentenced to death. Lincoln asked to review the convictions. Burlingame writes,

In response the general [Pope] warned that white Minnesotans "are exasperated to the last degree & if all the guilty ones are not executed I think it nearly impossible to prevent the indiscriminate massacre of all the Indians."[91]

[89] Wilson and Davis, *Herndon's Informants*, pp. 157–8.
[90] Burlingame, *Abraham Lincoln: A Life*, II, p. 480.
[91] Ibid., p. 481.

The Minnesota congressional delegation communicated similar views to the president.[92] Lincoln ignored these warnings and with the help of two lawyers carefully looked at the evidence from the trials of the 303 condemned men. They discovered that the trials had been deeply flawed – some lasted only fifteen minutes, and some admitted hearsay evidence.[93] He granted clemency to all but 37 (35 who were charged with murder and 2 with rape) of the 303 Indians. In 1864 the governor of Minnesota told Lincoln that if he had executed all 303 Sioux he would have enjoyed more support in his reelection bid. Lincoln replied, "I could not afford to hang men for votes."[94] In this case, his mercy was virtuous and helped him do the right thing.

C. *Lincoln's Intention to Be Merciful to the Confederacy.* Lincoln wanted to "Let em up easy."[95]

It was good that he was not malicious or vengeful toward the South. However, had he lived, his mercy for the South might have proven to be excessive, coming partly at the expense of the rights and status of the newly freed slaves, although this is uncertain. We do not know what he would have done if he had lived longer (see Chapter 3.V). Lincoln's mercy to the South might also have had positive effects. Very late in the war, he wanted to appropriate a large amount of money to compensate slave owners for their financial loses due to emancipation.[96] Had he lived out his second term of office, he probably would have offered considerable economic aid to the Confederate states to help them recover from the war. It is also likely that he would have given them financial aid to help bury the Confederate dead. The fact that the federal

---

[92] Ibid., pp. 481–2.
[93] Ibid., p. 482.
[94] Ibid., p. 483.
[95] Ibid., p. 793.
[96] Ibid., pp. 757–8.

government spent a great deal of money to find and properly
bury the Union dead but spent nothing for the Confederate
dead caused a great deal of bitterness in the South.[97] Lincoln's
actions would have reduced poverty and bitterness in the
South and directly and indirectly improved the situation of
African Americans.[98]

> 2. *Was Lincoln Really "Honest Abe?"* Lincoln developed a
> reputation for honesty as a young man and was known
> to many of his contemporaries as "honest Abe" and
> "honest old Abe."

His stepmother said of Lincoln that "he never told me a lie
in his life – never Equivocated never dodged – nor turned a
Corner to avoid any chastisement or responsibility."[99] This
is confirmed by his stepsister Matilda Johnston Moore, who
recounted a case in which she jumped on Lincoln's back and
cut her foot on an axe he was carrying. She talked with him
about how they would explain it to their mother. She wanted
to simply tell her mother, "I cut my foot on the axe." He said
that he thought that would not be a lie, but he insisted that
they tell their mother the whole truth.[100]

Lincoln was, by every account, extremely honest and
upright in his business dealings and in his work as a lawyer.
In New Salem he owned a small store in 1832 with William
Berry. The business went broke the next year, largely on
account of Berry's drinking. When Berry died not long afterward, leaving practically no estate, Lincoln was saddled with
the burden of paying off the store's debts by himself. These
debts totaled $1,100 – a very large sum of money at the time.
This debt was a huge burden to a young man trying to rise in

[97] Faust, *This Republic of Suffering*, pp. 233–8.
[98] For a helpful discussion of related issues see Meyers, "The Virtue of Cold-
Heartedness."
[99] Wilson and Davis, *Herndon's Informants*, p. 108.
[100] Ibid., p. 110.

the world. He jokingly referred to his debts from the store as his "national debt."[101] After the store went under, he worked as a surveyor. His surveyor's tools were later seized by a creditor and then given back to him by a friend.[102] According to Herndon, Lincoln was paying off his debts as late as 1848.[103] His determination to pay the debts fully earned him the respect of his contemporaries and contributed to his reputation for honesty and fairness.[104]

Lincoln was an extremely honest attorney.[105] He was fair and honest with his clients and often advised them not to litigate.[106] He did not overcharge clients and sometimes returned their money when he thought that they had overpaid him.[107] Judges and other lawyers trusted his word and did not question factual claims he made in court.[108] Often he served as a judge when regular judges were unable to be in court because the other members of the court trusted him to be fair.[109]

But in politics, Lincoln was sometimes slippery and evasive in his public statements. On a number of occasions, he tried to keep his actual views secret from the public because he thought that this would be politically advantageous. His friend Albert Bledsoe said that Lincoln was "honest and

---

[101] Donald, *Lincoln*, p. 54.

[102] Ibid., pp. 54–5.

[103] Wilson and Davis, *Herndon's Lincoln*, p. 78.

[104] Thomas, *Abraham Lincoln: A Biography*, p. 38. According to David Donald, Lincoln was not legally required to pay Berry's share of their debts; Donald, *Lincoln*, p. 54. But Kenneth Winkle claims that because Lincoln and Berry were "unlimited partners," they were legally liable to pay each other's debts; Winkle, *The Young Eagle*, p. 97. Harry Pratt's book on Lincoln's finances discusses this case in some detail, but does not directly address the question of whether Lincoln was legally required to pay off Berry's share of the store's debts; Pratt, *The Personal Finances of Abraham Lincoln*, pp. 12–15.

[105] Wilson and Davis, *Herndon's Informants*, p. 47.

[106] Burlingame, *Abraham Lincoln: A Life*, I, pp. 311–12.

[107] Ibid., pp. 332–3.

[108] Donald, *Lincoln*, p. 149.

[109] Ibid., p. 147; also see Burlingame, *Abraham Lincoln: A Life*, I, p. 352.

truthful in all the ordinary affairs of life," but he also said that "Mr. Lincoln was no stickler for the truth in contests before the people for political office and power. On the contrary, he entertained the opinion that 'all is fair in politics.' It was one of his favorite maxims, that 'we must fight the devil with fire': that is, with his own weapons."[110]

After leaving Congress in 1849, Lincoln became very active in politics again in 1854 when he very badly wanted to be elected to the U.S. Senate. During that year, an abolitionist meeting was planned in Springfield. His law partner William Herndon learned that the radical abolitionist, Owen Lovejoy, wanted Lincoln to speak at the meeting. Although Herndon himself was an abolitionist, he knew that it would greatly harm Lincoln's political prospects to be associated with abolitionism. Herndon recalled,

Strong as I was in the faith [abolitionism], yet I doubted the propriety of Lincoln's taking any stand yet. As I viewed it, he was anxious to climb to the United States Senate, and on grounds of policy it would not do for him to occupy at that such advanced ground as we [the abolitionists] were taking.[111]

Herndon and Lincoln also knew that Lincoln needed the support of abolitionists and that it would harm him to decline to speak to the abolitionists. Herndon continued,

On the other hand, it was equally dangerous to refuse a speech for the Abolitionists.... on learning that Lovejoy intended to approach him with an invitation, I hunted up Lincoln and urged him to avoid meeting with the enthusiastic champion of Abolitionism. "Go home at once," I said. "Take Bob with you and drive somewhere into the country and stay till this thing is over." ... under the pretence of having business in Tazewell county he drove out of town in his buggy, and did not return till the apostles of Abolitionism had separated and gone to their homes. I have

---

[110] Wilson, *Honor's Voice*, pp. 315–16.
[111] Wilson and Davis, *Herndon's Lincoln*, p. 229.

always believed that this little arrangement...saved Lincoln. If he had endorsed the resolutions passed at the meeting, or spoken simply in favor of freedom that night, he would have been identified with all the rancor and extremes of Abolitionism. If, on the contrary, he had been invited to join them, and then had refused to take a position as advanced as theirs, he would have lost their support. In either event he was in great danger.[112]

A similar case in which Lincoln sought to avoid revealing his views and answering questions for political purposes involved the anti-immigrant, anti-Catholic "Know-Nothing" organization (so named because it was a secret society and its members were told to answer questions about it by saying "I know nothing"). Lincoln was not a "Know-Nothing," and he deplored the prejudice and hostility of many native-born Protestant whites against immigrants and Catholics. His most well-known statement about the Know-Nothings is part of a letter to Joshua Speed in 1855:

I am not a Know-Nothing. That is certain. How could I be? How can any one who abhors the oppression of negroes, be in favor of degrading classes of white people?...As a nation, we began by declaring that "*all men are created equal.*" We now practically read it "all men are created equal, *except negroes.*" When the Know-Nothings get control, it will read "all men are created equal, except negroes, *and foreigners, and catholics.*" When it comes to this I should prefer emigrating to some country where they make no pretense of loving liberty – to Russia, for instance, where despotism can be taken pure, and without the base alloy of hypocrisy.[113]

However, nativists and Know-Nothings were an important voting block within the Whig and Republican parties, and many nativists were strongly opposed to slavery. Lincoln wanted their votes and knew he needed to conceal his disdain for their views so as not to lose their support. During the

---

[112] Ibid.
[113] Abraham Lincoln, *Speeches and Writings*, I, p. 363.

presidential election, the Democrats alleged that Lincoln had visited Know-Nothing or American Party lodges (the American Party was a nativist political party that descended from the Know-Nothings). Lincoln knew that this charge was false, but he also knew that it would offend nativist voters for him to deny it. In a confidential letter to a political supporter, he explained this and wrote that he would not answer the charge publicly but would pretend not to be paying any attention to it. He concluded his letter by writing,

And now, a word of caution. Our adversaries think that they can gain a point, if they could force me to openly deny this charge, by which some degree of offense would be given to the Americans. For this reason, it must not publicly appear than I am paying any attention to this charge.[114]

Lincoln also discussed the Know-Nothings in a letter from 1855. He deplored their principles and expressed the hope that they would die out, but he noted that the Know-Nothings were his political friends and he did not want to openly oppose them:

About us here, they [the Know-Nothings] are mostly my old personal and political friends; and I have hoped that their organization would die out without the painful necessity of my taking an open stand against them. Of their principles I think little better of them than I do of those of the slavery expansionists. Indeed I do not perceive how any one professing to be sensitive to the wrongs of negroes, can join a league to degrade a class of white men.[115]

In a very important case portrayed in the Spielberg film *Lincoln*, Lincoln deceived members of Congress without lying to them. This happened in early 1865 when the House of Representatives was debating the proposed Thirteenth Amendment, which totally abolished slavery. As explained

[114] Abraham Lincoln, *Speeches and Writings*, II, p. 173.
[115] Abraham Lincoln, *Speeches and Writings*, I, p. 358.

earlier, constitutional amendments must be "proposed" to the states and then ratified by three-quarters of them (see Chapter 2.I.1). One way to propose an amendment is to approve it by a two-thirds vote of each house of Congress. In June 1864 more than two-thirds of the Senate voted for the Thirteenth Amendment, but in the House of Representatives, the amendment fell a few votes short of the needed two-thirds majority. In January 1865, supporters of the Thirteenth Amendment still needed a few more votes in the House to pass it. At this time, "peace commissioners" from the United States and the CSA were discussing terms for ending the war. The Confederate representatives wanted the Union to rescind the Emancipation Proclamation, but Lincoln refused to compromise about this. There was pressure from people who wanted the war to end as soon as possible for him to negotiate an end to the war by abandoning the Emancipation Proclamation or at least giving up his attempt to pass the Thirteenth Amendment. Some members in the House were wavering in their support for the amendment and wanted to delay voting for it until after the peace conference, and it is likely that some of them would have voted against the Thirteenth Amendment if the Confederates had agreed to peace on that condition. While the House was considering the amendment, the president received the following short note from a leader of the House effort to pass the amendment:

Dear Sir,

"The report is in circulation in the House that the peace commissioners are on their way or are in the city, and being used against us. If it is true, I fear that we shall lose the bill. Please authorize me to contradict it if it is not true."

J M Ashley[116]

---

[116] Wilson and Davis, *Herndon's Informants*, pp. 413–14.

Lincoln responded to Ashley as follows:
"So far as I know, there are no peace commissioners in the City,
or are likely to be in it."
Jan 31 1865
A. Lincoln[117]

Lincoln's statement was true, and he knew that it was true.
The peace commissioners were not meeting in Washington,
D.C., and they were not likely to be in Washington for the
foreseeable future. Thus, his statement was not a lie. But
he knew that the peace commissioners were about to meet
somewhere else – in Fort Monroe, Virginia. Therefore, his
statement was deceptive: the commission *was* about to meet
and his statement suggested that it was not. The members
of Congress in question did not care *where* the meeting was
taking place; they just wanted to know if there was a meeting
being held or about to be held.

In a later letter to William Herndon, Ashley wrote,

I send you this note because it is connected with a historical event of
great importance. I had given notice that at one oclock [sic] on the
31" of January I would call a vote on the proposed constitutional
amendment abolishing slavery.

The opposition caught up a report which had been put into
circulation that evening that the Peace Commissioners wer [sic.]
on the way to the City or were in the City. Had this been true I
think that the proposed amendment would have failed, as a number
of those who voted for it could easily have been prevailed upon to
vote against it, on the ground that the passage of such a proposition
would be offensive to the Commissioners.

Mr. Lincoln *knew* that the commissioners were *then* on their
way to Ft Monroe where he expected them to meet afterwards and
afterwards did meet them. You see how admirably he answered
my note for my purposes and yet how *truly*.[118]

[117] Ibid., p. 414.
[118] Ibid.

Another issue concerning Lincoln's honesty is that he authorized his political operatives to make bribes in the form of patronage offers to induce congressmen to change their votes to support the amendment.[119] The president told Congressman John Alley of Massachusetts to procure votes for the Thirteenth Amendment "any way he chose,"[120] and he promised that "whatever [Congressman] Ashley had promised [to do to obtain votes from other congressmen] should be performed."[121] One border state congressman who voted for the Thirteenth Amendment was subsequently appointed ambassador to Denmark.[122] Because of Republican gains in the 1864 congressional elections, Lincoln would have had little trouble passing the Thirteenth Amendment in the House once the new congress was seated in March 1865.

How should we evaluate Lincoln's honesty in light of these actions? It is useful to distinguish between "honesty in the negative sense," which means roughly having a strong principled disposition not to tell lies, deceive others, steal, break promises, or engage in fraud or bribery, and "honesty in a positive sense," which, in addition to requiring being honest in the negative sense, involves being candid, open, and willing to reveal information.[123] A strong case can be made for the view that he was honest in the negative sense but not in the positive sense.[124]

[119] Burlingame, *Abraham Lincoln: A Life*, II, pp. 745–50.
[120] Foner, *The Fiery Trial*, p. 312.
[121] Guelzo, *Lincoln's Emancipation Proclamation*, p. 231.
[122] Foner, *The Fiery Trial*, p. 313.
[123] For more details see my book, *Lying and Deception: Theory and Practice*, chapter 14.
[124] I rely heavily on Douglas Wilson's unpublished paper, "Character or Calculation," which describes Lincoln as honest despite his secretiveness and lack of candor. Although Wilson does not use my distinction between being honest in the positive and negative senses, his description of Lincoln implies that Lincoln was honest in the negative sense, but not in the positive sense.

Lincoln was not honest in the positive sense – he was not open, candid, or forthcoming. Many of his closest associates described him as "secretive" and "reticent." Herndon said that Lincoln was secretive about his religious views and reluctant to talk about religion, because he knew that if his unorthodox religious views came to light it would hurt him politically.[125] Judge David Davis, a long-time member of the circuit court who frequently roomed with Lincoln, confirmed that Lincoln was very reluctant to talk about his religious views. Davis said, "I don't know anything about Lincoln's Religion – I don't think anybody Knew." He added that Lincoln "was the most reticent – Secretive man I ever Saw – or Expect to See."[126] Herndon agreed, saying that Lincoln was the most "shut-mouthed man that ever existed."[127] Herndon also said that his partner was "terribly secretive, confiding his plans and purposes, ambitions, and ends, to no man."[128] Herndon further drew attention to his partner's "irritability when anyone tried to peep into his own mind's laboratory."[129] Leonard Swett, who was one of Lincoln's closest associates, wrote the following of Lincoln:

He is considered by the people of this country as a frank, guileless unsophisticated man. There was never a greater mistake. Beneath a smooth surface of candor and apparent declaration of all his thoughts and feelings, he exercised the most exalted tact and the wisest discrimination. He handled and moved man *remotely* as we do pieces on a chessboard.... He always told enough only of his plans and purposes to induce the belief that he had communicated all; yet he reserved enough, in fact to have communicated nothing.

---

[125] Wilson and Davis, *Herndon's Lincoln*, p. 265.
[126] Wilson and Davis, *Herndon's Informants*, p. 348.
[127] WHH to J. E. Remsburg, Sept. 10, 1887; cited in Wilson, "Character or Calculation."
[128] Ibid. Wilson quotes from Herndon's letter to an unknown recipient, Nov. 24, 1882. This letter was printed in several newspapers, including the *New York Tribune* (Jan. 21, 1883) and *The Truth Seeker* (March 10, 1883).
[129] Ibid. Wilson's source is Remsburg, *Six Historic Americans*.

He told all that was unimportant with a gushing frankness; yet no man ever kept his real purposes more closely, or penetrated the future further with his deep designs.[130]

These reports about Lincoln's secretiveness and the cases discussed earlier in which he sought to withhold or conceal his views about various political issues provide strong evidence that he was not honest in the positive sense of being candid, open, and forthright. But his secretiveness about his personal life was not contrary to virtue. Virtue does not require the kind of candor and openness about one's personal life that he lacked. There is no duty as such to reveal to others facts about one's personal life. Openness about such matters is optional and something to be negotiated in personal relationships.[131] His concealment of some of his political views that he knew would be unpopular with the public violated the public's right to know relevant information. But it was also politically expedient and helped him do the great good that he did; it is at least arguable that it was permissible for him to conceal this information. His secretiveness and lack of candor in the service of very good ends do not count very much, if at all, against the goodness of his character.

Lincoln was honest in the negative sense of having a strong principled disinclination to tell lies, deceive others, steal, break promises, or engage in fraud or bribery. He was, for the most part, extremely honest in this sense. It is very hard to find any clear cases of him telling a lie, but see Chapter 8.6 for a discussion of a case in which it is likely that he told a lie; during his successful campaign for the U.S. House in 1846 he answered charges of "religious infidelity" by saying, "I have never denied the truth of the Scriptures."

The few cases in which he engaged in deception and bribery are perfectly compatible with his having a very strong and

---

[130] Wilson and Davis, *Herndon's Informants*, p. 168.
[131] See my *Lying and Deception: Theory and Practice*, pp. 264–5.

principled compunction against such acts and are not sufficiently frequent or characteristic of him for us to decline to
call him honest in the negative sense. If we say that he was
not honest in the negative sense because of what he did in
these cases, then we are setting the bar for honesty much too
high, and it is not clear that anyone is honest in that sense.
Further, his deception and bribery to promote the Thirteenth
Amendment were *morally justified* and not contrary to virtue.
Because his actions in these cases were justified, it is unclear
that we should say that these cases count at all against the
view that he was honest in the negative sense. The fact that a
person is prepared to lie, deceive, or bribe others when doing
so is morally permissible because it is necessary to achieve a
very great good, such as saving many lives or freeing many
people from slavery, does not count against the view that he
or she is honest. Being an honest person in the negative sense
does not require that one never, under any circumstances, lie
or deceive others. (If *that* were a requirement for being an
honest person in the negative sense, then it would follow that
no one, or almost no one, is honest in the negative sense.)
Similarly, the fact that someone flees from physical danger
when that is the right thing to do – for example, if someone
declines to risk her life or safety in order to achieve trivial
goods – does not count against her being courageous.

III. Was Lincoln Generous?

As a young man in Springfield, Lincoln acquired a reputation
for being generous and charitable.[132] Was this reputation
justified?

There is no evidence that he ever donated large sums of
money to charity, and because we have a very detailed record

---

[132] Burlingame, *Abraham Lincoln: A Life*, I, p. 77.

of his finances, there is reason to think that he did not contribute much to charity.[133] This is significant, but we should not attach too much importance to it, because few large organized charities solicited contributions then in the way that is common now. Also, during most of his life, Lincoln was in strained financial circumstances and had limited ability to be generous with money. He started his marriage deeply in debt, and as late as 1848 he was still paying off debts from the general store he ran with William Berry.[134] As mentioned earlier he became Berry's partner in a New Salem general store in 1832. Their store went bankrupt in 1833. Burlingame thinks that he was still being dunned for payment of his New Salem debts in 1860.[135]

In the 1850s he became a very prominent attorney and earned some very large fees, but he also lost a considerable amount of income because of the time he took off from his law practice to devote to politics. After the 1858 Senate race, he was nearly broke; he wrote his friend Norman Judd that he was "absolutely without money now for even household purposes."[136] In addition, to keep peace at home, he had to be willing to allow his wife to spend a good deal of money on luxuries for herself.[137] Mary also spent a good deal of money to add a second floor to their house in 1856 (without her husband's knowledge while he was away on business).[138]

Lincoln often helped individuals in need. He helped his parents financially. He purchased forty acres of land on his parents' farm for much more than it was worth and allowed

---

[133] Pratt, *The Personal Finances of Abraham Lincoln.*

[134] Wilson and Davis, *Herndon's Lincoln*, p. 78. But Pratt thinks that Lincoln had paid off his debts from the store with Berry by 1844; *The Personal Finances of Abraham Lincoln*, p. 15.

[135] Burlingame, *Abraham Lincoln: A Life*, I, p. 76.

[136] Abraham Lincoln, *Speeches and Writings*, I, p, 829. See Thomas, *Abraham Lincoln: A Biography*, p. 194.

[137] Burlingame, *Abraham Lincoln: A Life*, I, p. 208.

[138] Ibid., p. 221.

his parents to retain "a life estate" on the land (they could use the land rent-free for the rest of their lives). He paid his father money to prevent the sale of additional land on the family farm when Thomas Lincoln was threatened by a creditor.[139] When Thomas Lincoln died, "Lincoln as his father's heir, conveyed his interest" in eighty acres of land to his stepbrother John Johnston "for a nominal consideration subject to Sarah Lincoln's dower right."[140]

Lincoln's generosity extended beyond his family members. Burlingame notes the following cases of Lincoln's generosity:

In 1857, Lincoln responded positively to the appeal of a free black woman whose son faced enslavement in New Orleans. The...young man had worked on a steamboat and was seized...because he lacked free papers. Lincoln asked his old friend Alexander P. Field...to represent the accused, [who was] a native of Springfield, and offered to pay all costs....Lincoln eventually raised money to secure the young man's freedom.[141] As president, he similarly tried to cut through red tape to save a young slave by offering to pay the owner up to $500 for his freedom.[142]

As president, Lincoln earned a very large salary, but he was far too busy with the duties of his office to think much about charity. In addition, he had to hold on to his money to cover the huge debts caused by his wife's extravagance, something that caused him a great deal of worry during his time as president (see Chapter 9.I.1.C).

---

[139] Pratt, *The Personal Finances of Abraham Lincoln*, pp. 60–1.

[140] Ibid., p. 61.

[141] Burlingame also recounts that during this episode, Lincoln and Herndon called on the governor of Illinois to help him secure the freedom of the young man from Springfield. The governor said that he had no power to help. This angered Lincoln. Herndon reports that Lincoln "exclaimed with some emphasis" "By God, Governor, I'll make ground in this country too hot for the foot of a slave whether you have the legal power to secure the release of the boy or not" (Burlingame, *Abraham Lincoln: A Life*, I, p. 381).

[142] Ibid.; on the later case during the Civil War, see Burlingame, *Abraham Lincoln: A Life*, II, p. 351.

He was generous in ways that did not involve giving away money. He was generous with his time and served as a mentor and advisor to many young attorneys.[143] He treated his household servants generously and paid them more than Mary wanted to pay them.[144] He was generous and fair in charging fees to clients, and he sometimes did legal work for free. In one case, he charged a client only $2 for his work in a case in which he earned the client a $2,000 settlement. He often returned money to clients whom he thought had overpaid him, and he generously split all legal fees equally with his younger and less prominent law partner Herndon.[145] He did these things despite considerable pressure from his wife to earn more money.[146]

Lincoln was a very soft-hearted man who was strongly inclined to help people in need whom he met in face-to-face encounters. Herndon wrote that Lincoln could "never say 'No' to any one who puts up a poor mouth, but will hand out the last dollar he has, sometimes when he needs it himself and needs it badly."[147] But, as a self-made man, he thought that other people should be as self-reliant as he was, and he was disinclined to help others he thought were capable of helping themselves. Some good illustrations of this attitude are found in several letters he wrote to his stepbrother John Johnston. In December 1848, he wrote to Johnston declining to send him $80. He called Johnston "an idler" and advised him to work for wages in order to pay off his debts, but he also promised to pay Johnston a dollar for every dollar that he earned.[148] In 1851, he wrote Johnston a series of letters in which he declined to give his stepbrother permission to sell

---

[143] Burlingame, *Abraham Lincoln: A Life*, I, pp. 346–8.
[144] Ibid., pp. 208–9.
[145] Ibid., pp. 332–3.
[146] Ibid., p. 207.
[147] Ibid., p. 208.
[148] Abraham Lincoln, *Speeches and Writings*, I, pp. 224–5.

land to which he (Lincoln) held the title. He also objected to Johnston's proposal that his mother sell land belonging to her and to give him one-third of the proceeds. He rebuked Johnston for not planting a crop on the family's land. He described Johnston's plan to move to Missouri as "utterly foolish" and scolded him harshly for his idleness:

Now do not misunderstand this letter. I do not write it in any unkindness. I write it in order, if possible, to get you to *face* the truth – which truth is, you are destitute because you have *idled* away all your time. Your thousand pretenses for not getting along better, are all non-sense – they deceive no body but yourself. *Go to work* is the only cure for your case.[149]

It is open to debate how we should interpret this evidence. One might conclude that Lincoln lacked the virtue of generosity. But I think that it makes more sense to say that he was a moderately generous person. He was probably not as generous as he would like to have been. He married a woman who came from a wealthy family and who lived for most of their marriage at a much lower standard of living than she had enjoyed earlier. He had to spend money on servants and a large house to keep peace at home. Mary Lincoln spent a considerable amount of money on clothing and jewelry for herself; when her husband died, Mary owed the New York firm of Ball, Black & Company $64,000 – roughly equivalent to $900,000 in 2014 dollars (see Chapter 9.I.1.C). It is possible that Lincoln would have been considerably more generous if he had not been forced to spend a great deal of money to keep the peace with his wife, but we cannot know for sure.

IV. Two Alleged Vices

There are two vices of which Lincoln is sometimes accused: ingratitude and cold-heartedness. Despite the claims of some

[149] Abraham Lincoln, *Speeches and Writings*, I, p. 255–8.

people to the contrary, he was neither ungrateful nor cold-hearted.

Joshua Speed said that Lincoln never forgot a personal kindness. In this connection, he mentioned that Lincoln wrote to Speed's mother, thanking her for a gift she gave him twenty years earlier when he stayed with her and Joshua Speed while suffering from his second round of deep depression after he ended his engagement to Mary Todd.[150] Lincoln showed considerable gratitude to those who helped him in times of need early in his life.[151] But some of his close friends and associates complained that he did not show gratitude to his friends. His former law partner John Stuart wrote, "L did forget his friends – That there was no part of his nature which drew him to do acts of gratitude to his friends."[152] David Davis complained that Lincoln never thanked him for anything he did for him and added that Lincoln had "no Strong Emotional feelings for any person – Mankind or thing."[153] Davis also complained that Lincoln would not support him when he wanted to run to be judge of the Eighth Judicial Circuit Court:

Lincoln hadn't the manhood to come for me in preference to Ben Edwards whom he despised – wouldn't do so because Ben was in the family – that is Ben Edward's bro Nin married Lincoln's wife's sister. I had done Lincoln many, many favors – Electioneered for him – toiled for him – still he wouldn't move.[154]

Some of his Springfield friends complained that he ignored them and did not pay them attention after he became president.[155]

---

[150] Wilson and Davis, *Herndon's Informants*, p. 158.
[151] Burlingame, *Abraham Lincoln: A Life*, I, p. 77.
[152] This is from Herndon's notes from an interview with Stuart, in Wilson and Davis, *Herndon's Informants*, p. 63.
[153] Ibid., p. 348.
[154] Ibid., p. 349.
[155] Wilson and Davis, *Herndon's Lincoln*, pp. 299–300.

These complaints are unjustified. While he was president, Lincoln was much too busy and overburdened to give much time or attention to his Springfield friends. His failure to pay them much attention then is not evidence of cold-heartedness on his part.[156] What some call ingratitude to friends for not helping them enough was not ingratitude, but rather evidence of his fairness and justice in not wanting to play favorites. His friend Leonard Swett wrote,

Some of Mr. Lincoln's friends insisted that he lacked the strong attribute of personal affection which he ought to have exhibited. I think that this is a mistake. Lincoln had too much justice to run a great government for a few favorites, and the complaints against him in this regard when properly digested amount to this, and no more: that he would not abuse the privileges of his situation.[157]

Joseph Gillespie was of the same view:

He [Lincoln] was by some considered cold hearted or at least indifferent towards his friends. This was the result of his extreme fairness. He would rather disoblige a friend than do an act of injustice to a political opponent.[158]

Davis's complaint that Lincoln did not support him for the circuit court judgeship bears special comment. Friends should not expect their friends to favor them in ways that are likely to cause them to have family problems. There is no merit in Davis's complaint – it is all the more curious and obtuse because Lincoln had already nominated Davis to become a member of the U.S. Supreme Court four years earlier. Thanks to Lincoln, Davis was a Supreme Court justice at the time he complained about Lincoln's failure to support him for the circuit court judgeship. The two men had a close professional and political relationship. They worked and traveled together

---

[156] Ibid.
[157] Wilson and Davis, *Herndon's Informants*, p. 166.
[158] Ibid., p. 507.

on the circuit court. Davis led the attempt to get Lincoln nominated for president in 1860, and he served as the executor of Lincoln's will. But some think that Lincoln did not like Davis all that much personally.[159] Perhaps Davis correctly perceived that Lincoln did not have strong emotional feelings for *him*, but that is hardly evidence of Lincoln's lack of feeling for others.

The complaint that Lincoln was a cold, unfeeling man, lacking in proper affection for his family and friends, is even more unjust. There is a great deal of evidence of his deep love and affection for a number of individuals. Davis to the contrary, he had a deep emotional attachment to certain people. Here is just some of the evidence:

1. Lincoln felt immense grief and sorrow when Anne Rutledge died (see Chapter 8.1).
2. While trying to give the eulogy for his close friend Bowling Green at Green's funeral, Lincoln spoke a few words, then choked up and sobbed, and could not continue.[160]
3. Lincoln was deeply grieved by the death of his friend and protégé Elmer Ellsworth at the very beginning of the Civil War. On learning of Ellsworth's death, he burst into tears and mourned Ellsworth as if he had been his own son.[161]
4. He very deeply loved his children and was profoundly grieved by the death of his son Willie. The day after Willie's death, Lincoln saw Elihu Washburn who described him as "completely prostrated with grief."[162] Washburn said that Lincoln was "one of the most tender-hearted of men and devotedly attached to his

---

[159] Ibid., pp. 626–7.
[160] Ibid., p. 173; also see p. 366 – two eyewitnesses attest to this.
[161] Burlingame, *Abraham Lincoln: A Life*, II, p. 177.
[162] Burlingame, *Abraham Lincoln: A Life*, I, p. 298.

children."[163] Burlingame described Lincoln's behavior at Willie's funeral in the White House two days later:

> The president stood with his eyes full of tears and his lips aquiver, gazing at his boy's corpse, a look of utmost grief came over his face, and he exclaimed that Willie "was too good for this earth... but then we loved him so. It is hard, hard to have him die!" He said repeatedly, "This is the hardest trial of my life. Why is it? Why is it?" His body shock convulsively as he sobbed and buried his face in his hands. Elizabeth Keckley, Mrs. Lincoln's modiste and close friend, never observed a man so grief stricken."[164]

LeGrand Cannon, who was a military officer during the war, recalled Lincoln's grief over Willie's death [uncorrected]:

> He [Lincoln] read by himself in one my offices.... He interrupted & wished me to rest, & he would read to me. He read from... King, John & in reading the passage where Constance bewails the loss of her child to the King. I noticed that he was deeply move, his voice trembled, laying the Book on the table, he said, did you every dream of a lost friend & feel that you were having direct communication with that friend & yet a consciousness that it was not a reality. My reply was yes... He repleyed so do I dream of my Boy Willey. He was utterly overcome. His great frame shook & Bowing down on the table he wept as only a man in the breaking down of great sorrow could weep.[165]

Lincoln was a very reserved man. He did not reveal his feelings to everyone, and it is not surprising that he gave some people the mistaken impression that he was cold and unfeeling.

In this connection, it would be relevant to know his true feelings and views about his wife and whether he still loved her by the end of their marriage. But we simply do not know how he felt then. There is very little evidence, in part because

---

[163] Ibid.
[164] Ibid.
[165] Wilson and Davis, *Herndon's Informants*, p. 679.

very few letters between Abe and Mary survive (it is possible that Mary and Robert Todd Lincoln destroyed some of these letters).[166]

To summarize very briefly, Lincoln possessed many important moral virtues. He possessed some of these virtues to a very high degree, but he might have lacked other virtues.

[166] Burlingame, *The Inner World of Abraham Lincoln*, p. 320.

8

Other Salient Features of Lincoln's Character and Personality

This chapter attempts to give a more complete picture of Lincoln than the one presented in Chapter 7 by describing other salient features of his character and personality. Some of these characteristics were morally virtuous, and some enhanced or diminished other virtues that he possessed. This chapter shows that he was immature and had many rough edges as a young man, but it also reveals his capacity for growth and self-improvement.

> 1. Lincoln was melancholy and given to depression. His melancholy was closely connected with his keen awareness of human mortality.

When he was nine years old, he suffered greatly from the death of his mother soon after his great-aunt and great-uncle Betsy and Thomas Sparrow died. The Sparrows were a childless couple who raised his mother and were his neighbors and surrogate grandparents.[1] He also grieved the death of his

---

[1] Burlingame, *Abraham Lincoln: A Life*, I, pp. 12 and 25. The Sparrows died shortly before Lincoln's mother. All three suffered long agonizing deaths from "milk sickness." Milk sickness is caused by drinking the milk of cattle who have eaten poisonous snakeroot, which kills them and makes their milk extremely poisonous to humans.

sister Sarah when he was eighteen and the death of his first (and perhaps greatest) love, Anne Rutledge, when he was twenty-six. Later, he was heartbroken by the deaths of his sons Edward and Willie. Willie's death in the White House at the age of eleven from a lingering illness was particularly hard on him (see Chapter 7.IV).

His preoccupation with human mortality was reflected in his taste in poetry. He loved poetry, and his favorite poem was said to be William Knox's "Mortality."[2] Here is part of that poem:

> Oh! why should the spirit of mortal be proud?
> Like a swift-fleeting meteor, a fast-flying cloud
> A flash of the lightning, a break of the wave
> He passeth from life to his rest in the grave....

'Tis the wink of an eye – 'tis the draught of a breath–

> From the blossom of health to the paleness of death,
> From the gilded saloon to the bier and the shroud:–
> Oh! why should the spirit of mortal be proud?

Lincoln also greatly loved Poe's poem "The Raven," which describes a lover's sorrow over the death of his "lost Lenore." His own poem "My Childhood Home," written after his 1844 visit to his childhood home in Indiana, vividly conveys his strong sense of human mortality, as seen in this excerpt:

> The friends I left that parting day,
> How changed, as time has sped!
> Young childhood grown, strong manhood gray,
> And half of all are dead.
> I hear the loved survivors tell
> How nought from death could save,
> Till every sound appears a knell,
> And every spot a grave.
> I range the fields with pensive tread,

---

[2] Wolf, *The Almost Chosen People*, p. 80.

And pace the hollow rooms,
And feel (companion of the dead)
I'm living in the tombs.[3]

The poem "The Suicide's Soliloquy" was probably written by Lincoln. It was published anonymously in the *Sangamo Journal* on August 25, 1838.[4] Here is part of this poem:

Here, where the lonely hooting owl
Sends forth his midnight moans,
Fierce wolves shall o'er my carcase growl,
Or buzzards pick my bones.
Yes! I've resolved the deed to do,
And this the place to do it:
This heart I'll rush a dagger through,
Though I in hell should rue it!
Hell! What is hell to one like me
Who pleasures never know;
By friends consigned to misery,
By hope deserted too?
To ease me of this power to think,
That through my bosom raves,
I'll headlong leap from hell's high brink,
And wallow in its waves.
Yes! I'm prepared, through endless night,
To take that fiery berth!
Think not with tales of hell to fright
Me, who am damn'd on earth!
Sweet steel! come forth from out your sheath,
And glist'ning, speak your powers;

---

[3] Abraham Lincoln, *Speeches and Writings*, I, pp. 138–9. See Burlingame, *Abraham Lincoln: A Life*, I, pp. 241–7 for other similar poems and songs that Lincoln loved.

[4] Here is the evidence that the poem is his work. Joshua Speed told William Herndon that Lincoln had published a suicide poem in the *Sangamo Journal*, but was not sure about the date. He said that it might have been 1840, 1841, or 1838. Many years later, Richard Lawrence Miller found the poem exactly where Speed said it was. This poem is similar in meter and style to Lincoln's published poetry. Douglas Wilson says that he does not have many doubts that this is Lincoln's work; see Wolf Shenk, "The Suicide Poem."

> Rip up the organs of my breath,
> And draw my blood in showers!
> I strike! It quivers in that heart
> Which drives me to this end;
> I draw and kiss the bloody dart,
> My last – my only friend!

As a young man, Lincoln often sang "John Adconsons Lementation," a very grim song about a man condemned to die for killing his wife. This song includes the following verses:

> much in toxication my ruin has bin
> and my dear companion have barberly slain
> in yanders cold grave yard her body doth lay
> whilest I am condemned and Shortly must die
> remember John adconsons death and reform
> before deth overtakes you and vengeance comes on
> my griefs overwhelming in god I must trust
> I am Justly condemned my Sentance is just[5]

As a young man, Lincoln suffered from two bouts of severe depression during which he was unable to work regularly and seriously contemplated suicide. The first episode of depression followed the death of Anne Rutledge to whom he was then engaged.[6] His friend and neighbor Hannah Armstrong said that he wept like a baby over Anne's death.[7] His friends worried about him and watched him closely to see that he did not harm himself. Lincoln was afraid then to carry a knife for fear that he would use it on himself.[8] He was unable to work for a time.[9]

---

[5] Wilson and Davis, *Herndon's Informants*, pp. 215–16. Carl Sandburg thinks that Lincoln himself wrote these two verses of the song. Sandburg titles the song "John Anderson's Lamentations;" Sandburg, *Abraham Lincoln: The Prairie Years*, I, p. 53.

[6] Burlingame, *Abraham Lincoln: A Life*, I, p. 99

[7] Ibid., p. 100.

[8] Wolf Shenk, *Lincoln's Melancholy*, p. 23.

[9] Ibid.

His second round of deep depression occurred after he broke off his engagement with Mary Todd.[10] Afterward, he felt horribly about having hurt Mary Todd so much. At this time, he wrote to his very close friend Joshua Speed as follows:

I am now the most miserable man living. If what I feel were equally distributed to the whole human family, there would not be one cheerful face on earth. Whether I shall ever be better, I cannot tell; I awfully forebode I shall not. To remain as I am is impossible. I must die or be better . . . [11]

During this depressive episode he was unable to work for a time and missed sessions of the state legislature for almost three weeks.[12]

At this time Lincoln was saved by his ambition. He told Joshua Speed that he was willing to die except that "he had done nothing to make any human being remember that he had lived."[13] He wanted to be remembered for doing things that benefited humanity (see Chapter 7.I.7). In a similar vein, he told his friend Mentor Graham that he thought frequently of suicide, but thought that God had a plan for him.[14] He suffered no further instances of debilitating depression after he married.

2. Despite his melancholy and preoccupation with death and mortality, Lincoln had a remarkable sense of humor. His contemporaries thought that he was hilarious; his stories could make people laugh until they cried.[15]

---

[10] Wilson and Davis, *Herndon's Lincoln*, p. 137.
[11] Ibid., pp. 137–8.
[12] Ibid., p. 138.
[13] Ibid., p. 197.
[14] Ibid., p. 243.
[15] Wolf Shenk, *Lincoln's Melancholy*, p. 114.

Joseph Gillespie said that Lincoln was "the most entertaining person I ever knew."[16] One of the things that made him so extremely funny was that he was a very talented mimic – "he could mimic any accent or vernacular."[17] His humor was often crude and he was fond of smutty stories.[18] Many people who remembered his jokes and stories did not write them down for fear that they would reflect badly on Lincoln. Herndon said that he would not repeat Lincoln's stories for that reason.[19] Aside from a few stories that were sent to Herndon and published much later in Davis and Wilson's *Herndon's Informants*, almost all of them were thought to be lost to history. But recently Michael Burlingame discovered documents collected by Carl Sandburg but not included in his biography of Lincoln; among them were many off-color stories.

Here is Lincoln's story about the Revolutionary War hero Ethan Allen, recently made famous by Doris Kearns Goodwin and Spielberg's film *Lincoln*:

[uncorrected letter from Abner Ellis to William Herndon] It appears that Shortly after we had pease with England Mr Allen had occasion to visit England, and while the English took great pleasure in teasing him, and trying to Make fun of the Americans and General Washington in particular and one day they got a picture of General Washington and hung it up in the Back House [outhouse] where Mr Allen Could see it and they finally asked Mr A if he saw that picture of his friend in the Back House.

Mr Allen said no. but said he thought that it was very appropriate for an Englishman to keep it Why they asked, for said Mr Allen there is Nothing that Will Make an Englishman Shit so quick

---

[16] Wilson and Davis, *Herndon's Informants*, p. 180.
[17] Wolf Shenk, *Lincoln's Melancholy*, p. 115.
[18] Wilson and Davis, *Herndon's Informants*, pp. 443 and 651.
[19] Wilson and Davis, *Herndon's Lincoln*, p. 76. However, Herndon did receive a few of Lincoln's stories and jokes from others, which are included in *Herndon's Informants*.

as the Sight of Genl Washington And after that they let Mr Allens Washington alone.[20]

Here is another one of his stories as recalled by John Webster:

When I was a little boy, I lived in the state of Kentucky, where drunkenness was very common on election days, At an election said he, in a village near where I lived, on a day when the weather was inclement and the roads exceedingly muddy, A toper named Bill got brutally drunk and staggered down a narrow alley where he layed himself down in the mud, and remained there until the dusk of the evening, at which time he recovered from his stupor, Finding himself very muddy, immediately started for a pump (a public watering place on the street) to wash himself. On his way to the pump another drunken man was leaning over a horse post, this, Bill mistook for the pump and at once took hold of the arm of the man for the handle, the use of which set the occupant of the post to throwing up, Bill believing all was right put both hands under and gave himself a thorough washing, He then made his way to the grocery for something to drink, On entering the door one of his comrades exclaimed in a tone of surprise, Why Bill what in the world is the matter Bill said in reply, I G–d you ought to have seen me before I was washed.[21]

Here is one of the stories that Burlingame found:

[There was a man] who had great veneration for Revolutionary relics. He heard tha[t] an old lady . . . had a dress which she had worn in the Revolutionary War. He made a special visit to this lady and asked her if she could produce the dress as a satisfaction to his love of aged things. She obliged him by opening a drawer and bringing out the article in question. The enthusiastic person took up the dress and delivered an apostrophe to it, "Were you the dress," said he, "that this lady once young and blooming wore in the time of Washington? No doubt when you came home from the dressmaker she kissed you as I do now!" At this the relic hunter took the dress and kissed it heartily. The practical old lady rather resented such foolishness over an old piece of wearing apparel and

[20] Wilson and Davis, *Herndon's Informants*, p. 174.
[21] Ibid., p. 396.

she said: "stranger if you want to kiss something old you had better kiss my ass. It is sixteen years older than that dress."[22]

3. Lincoln was a notorious prankster from an early age. As a boy, he loved to play pranks on his companions.[23]

Early in his political career he frequently appeared together with a local Democrat, Col. Dick Taylor, who was "a showy, bombastic man with a weakness for fine clothes and other personal adornments."[24] Taylor frequently attacked the Whigs for their "lordly ways and aristocratic pretensions."[25] Once while listening to Taylor speak in this way, Lincoln decided, "as he expressed it, 'to take the wind out of his sails.'" He moved to the speaker's side

and catching his vest by the lower edge gave it a sharp pull. The latter instantly opened and revealed to his astonished hearers a ruffled shirt front glittering with watch-chain, seals and other golden jewels. The effect was startling. The speaker stood confused and dumbfounded, while the audience roared with laughter. When it came Lincoln's turn to answer he covered the gallant colonel over in this style. "While the Colonel was making these charges against the Whigs over the country, riding in fine carriages, wearing ruffled shirts, kid gloves, massive gold watch-chains, with large gold seals, and flourishing a heavy gold-headed cane, I was a poor boy, hired on a flat boat for eight dollars a month, and had only one pair of breeches to my back and they were buckskin.... If you call this aristocracy I plead guilty to the charge."[26]

Lincoln once played a prank within a prank inspired by Robert Burns's comic poem, "Tam o'shanter."[27]

---

[22] Burlingame, *Abraham Lincoln: A Life*, I, p. 55.
[23] Wilson and Davis, *Herndon's Informants*, p. 102.
[24] Wilson and Davis, *Herndon's Lincoln*, p. 128.
[25] Ibid.
[26] Ibid., pp. 128–9.
[27] Wilson, *Honor's Voice: The Transformation of Abraham Lincoln*, p. 74.

[uncorrected letter from J. Rowan Herndon to William Herndon]
There was a man that use to come to salem and get tight and stay
untell dark he was fraid of Gosts and some one had to goe home
with him well Lincoln Perswaded a fellow to take a Sheet and
goe in the Rod and perfrom Gost he then Sent an other gost and
the man and Lincoln started home The Gost made his appeerence
and the man Became much fritend But the Second gost made his
appear[ance] and frightened the first Gost half to Deth that Broke
the fellow from staying untell Dark anymore![28]

Lincoln's pranks often took the form of writing anonymous pieces that ridiculed his political opponents and others
he knew. His two most well-known pranks were of this sort.
The first took place in Indiana where he staged an elaborate
prank at the expense of the prominent local family of Reuben
Grigsby. His sister, Sarah, had married one of Grigsby's sons,
Aaron, and died in childbirth. Lincoln was greatly offended
by the Grigsby family's treatment of his sister and thought
that they looked down on her because she had been "hired
help" for the family before her marriage to Aaron.[29] He was
also offended that he was not invited to the wedding feast
for Grigsby's sons, Reuben Jr. and Charles, who were married on the same day. With the help of several people who
attended the wedding feast, Lincoln arranged it so that the
Grigsby brothers ended up in beds with the wrong wives
on the night of their weddings. During the wedding feast,
someone acting on Lincoln's instructions slipped upstairs at
the Grigsby house and changed the beds that the mother of
the two sons had arranged in advance.[30] The waiters who
conveyed the two brides upstairs to their beds also acted
on his instructions.[31] Lincoln described this scene in "The

[28] Wilson and Davis, *Herndon's Informants*, p. 70.
[29] Wilson and Davis, *Herndon's Lincoln*, p. 145 and Burlingame, *Abraham Lincoln: A Life*, I, p. 45.
[30] Wilson and Davis, *Herndon's Lincoln*, p. 46.
[31] Ibid., p. 47.

Chronicles of Reuben," a piece of Rabelaisian backwoods humor written in a biblical style:

[W]hen they had made an end of feasting and rejoicing the multitude dispersed . . . The family then took seats with their waiters to converse while preparations were being made in the upper chamber for the brides and grooms to be conveyed to their beds. This being done the waiters took the two brides upstairs, placing one in a bed at the right hand of the stairs and the other on the left. The waiters came down, and Nancy the mother gave directions to the waiters of the bridegrooms, and they took them upstairs but placed them in the wrong beds. The waiters then all came downstairs. But the mother, being fearful of a mistake, made enquiry of the waiters, and learning the true facts took the light and sprang upstairs. It came to pass she ran to one of the beds and exclaimed, "Oh Lord, Reuben, you are in bed with the wrong wife." The young men alarmed, both alarmed at this, sprang up out of bed and ran with such violence against each other that they came near knocking each other down. The tumult gave evidence to those down below that the mistake was certain. . . . So endeth the Chapter.[32]

The wedding fiasco and Lincoln's account of it (which was well known and long remembered locally) greatly angered and embarrassed the Grigsby family. A little later, Lincoln satirized another one of the Grigsby sons, Billy, in a very crude poem about Billy being married to another man.[33] Billy Grigsby challenged him to a duel over this, but Lincoln said he would not fight him because he considered Billy much too small for it to be a fair fight. He had his stepbrother, John Johnston, fight Billy in his place.[34]

His most famous prank was a letter he had published in a local newspaper under the pen name of "Aunt Rebecca," a folksy woman from "Lost Townships." This letter ridiculed James Shields, a rising Democratic politician and Illinois state

[32] Ibid., pp. 46–7.
[33] Ibid., pp. 47–8.
[34] Wilson and Davis, *Herndon's Informants*, p. 120, Wilson and Davis, *Herndon's Lincoln*, p. 48, and Wilson, *Honor's Voice*, p. 295.

auditor. Shields was a vain man who fancied himself irre-
sistible to women. Here is a portion of this letter:

Shields is a fool as well as a liar. With him the truth is out of
the question. . . . There's no mistake about his [Shields's] being a
whig – why his looks shows it – every thing about him shows
it – if I was deaf and blind I could tell him by the smell. . . . He
[Shields] . . . spoke audibly and distinctly – "Dear girls, *it is much
distressing*, but I cannot marry you all. Too well I know how much
you suffer; but do, *do* remember, it is not my fault that I am *so*
handsome and *so* interesting."[35]

Three satirical letters were published under the name
"Aunt Rebecca." Apparently, Lincoln wrote just one of
them.[36] These letters caused Shields great embarrassment and
made him a laughingstock on the streets of Springfield.[37]
Shields was a very hot-tempered man who once threatened
to kill his opponent for the U.S. Senate in 1849. On another
occasion, while in court, he hit another attorney over the
head with a heavy law book, saying, "If you have no law
in your head I'll bate some into it."[38] After some questioning, Lincoln admitted to being the author of one of the letters.
Shields demanded a retraction and apology in terms so insulting that Lincoln refused.[39] Then Shields challenged him to a
duel. Even though he opposed dueling, Lincoln felt that he
would be greatly dishonored if he refused the challenge.[40]
Because Shields had challenged him, it was Lincoln's prerogative to choose the weapons, and he chose broad swords. He
also set very specific terms for the positioning of the combatants, which maximized the advantage he enjoyed because

35 Abraham Lincoln, *Speeches and Writings*, I, pp. 99–100.
36 Wilson, *Honor's Voice*, pp. 266–271.
37 Burlingame, *Abraham Lincoln: A Life*, I, p. 190.
38 Ibid.
39 Ibid., pp. 190–1 and Wilson, *Honor's Voice*, p. 271.
40 Wilson, *Honor's Voice*, pp. 281, 277, and 282.

of his much greater height and reach.[41] He expected to be able to easily disarm the much smaller Shields and intended not to harm him.[42] Preparations were made for the duel and the parties set off to fight it on an island in the Mississippi River. However, before it could take place, Lincoln wrote a conciliatory note that persuaded Shields's friends that Shields no longer had cause to fight and they prevailed on him to call off the duel.[43]

This abortive duel had a farcical aftermath. Shields became very angry with one of Lincoln's friends who accompanied Lincoln and challenged *him* to a duel. The friend, William Butler, accepted Shields's challenge. They agreed to fire rifles at each other from one hundred yards. Then one of Shields's friends who had accompanied him, Dr. John Whitesides, helped stop that duel. After that, Whitesides became very angry with another friend of Lincoln, Dr. Merryman, and sent him a harsh note that caused Merryman to write back asking if it was a challenge to a duel.[44]

Lincoln, who was greatly embarrassed by this episode, said that it was "the meanest thing he ever did in his life."[45] Near the end of his life, when questioned about it, he replied, "If you desire my friendship you will never mention the circumstances again."[46]

4. As a young man Lincoln was an extremely partisan politician and given to great flights of rhetorical overstatement; he was often very biting and cruel in ridiculing his political opponents.

---

[41] Ibid., pp. 280–1.
[42] Burlingame, *Abraham Lincoln: A Life*, I, pp. 191–2.
[43] Wilson, *Honor's Voice*, p. 282.
[44] Ibid., p. 286.
[45] Burlingame, *Abraham Lincoln: A Life*, I, p. 190.
[46] Ibid., p. 194.

He wrote a number of coarse and insulting anonymous articles and letters ridiculing prominent local Democrats for a local Whig newspaper, the *Sangomo Journal*.[47] In 1837, Lincoln called a local Democratic candidate, James Adams, a forger, whiner, fool, and liar.[48] Burlingame thinks it likely that Lincoln was the author of anonymous letters in the *Sangomo Journal* attacking Adams.[49] In 1836 "Lincoln called an anonymous critic 'a *liar* and *scoundrel*' and threatened 'to give his proboscis a good wringing.'"[50] In another case, the Democratic judge Jesse Thomas was accused of writing anonymous letters in the press, letters that, in fact, were probably written by Lincoln and other Whigs.[51] Burlingame describes what followed:

[As a consequence of this] Thomas attacked them [the Whigs] in a speech. After this, Lincoln rose to answer.... Lincoln was "terrific in his denunciation" and "had no mercy" as he mimicked Thomas's gestures and accent.... "Lincoln's effort was absolutely overwhelming and withering. He had not proceeded far, indeed, before Judge Thomas began to blubber like a baby, and left the assembly." ... The next day Lincoln apologized.[52]

According to Burlingame, Lincoln learned a lesson from the Shields fiasco and never again wrote anonymous letters, but he "continued to pour sarcasm and ridicule over opponents."[53] Burlingame thinks that Lincoln the statesman, who was respectful of and fair to his political opponents, emerged later – roughly from about 1849 to 1854.[54] Douglas Wilson's book *Honor's Voice: The Transformation of*

---

47 Ibid., p. 107.
48 Burlingame, *The Inner World of Abraham Lincoln*, p. 151.
49 Ibid.
50 Ibid.
51 Ibid., p. 152.
52 Ibid.
53 Ibid., p. 153.
54 Ibid., p. xiv.

Abraham Lincoln discusses the youthful Lincoln's transformation in great detail. Wilson seems to date the time of his transformation somewhat earlier than Burlingame; his book ends with Lincoln's marriage in 1842.

Another example of Lincoln's partisanship is his bombastic 1839 speech attacking the Democratic administration in Washington. Here is a part of that speech:

> I know that the great volcano at Washington, aroused and directed by the evil spirit that reigns there, is belching forth the lava of political corruption in a current broad and deep, which is sweeping with frightening velocity over the whole length and breadth of the land, bidding fair to leave unscathed no green spot or living thing, while on its bosom are riding like demons on the waves of Hell, the imps of that evil spirit, and fiendishly taunting all those who dare resist its destroying course, with the hopelessness of their effort.[55]

Clearly, when he delivered this speech he was not yet a statesman, nor was he yet close to being the writer who penned the Gettysburg Address, the Second Inaugural Address, and his other great speeches. His development as a statesman and writer was a long and slow process.

5. Lincoln was rather indifferent to money. Despite his very great abilities and energy, he devoted very little effort to acquiring wealth.

This characteristic augmented other virtues he possessed. He never used his political position to gain wealth: "thus he could not be bought or bribed."[56] He was also indifferent to physical luxuries and comforts. He never complained about the very crude accommodations and horrible food at small inns while traveling on the circuit court.[57]

---

[55] Abraham Lincoln, *Speeches and Writings*, Volume I, p. 64. Cited in Miller, *Lincoln's Virtues*, p. 144 and Burlingame, *Abraham Lincoln: A Life*, I, p. 151.
[56] Wilson, *Honor's Voice*, p. 315.
[57] Donald, *Lincoln*, pp. 106 and 147 and Burlingame, *Abraham Lincoln: A Life*, I, pp. 326–7.

6. There is a great deal of controversy about Lincoln's religious views. Ascertaining his actual religious beliefs is very important for my purposes in this book because it is relevant to assessing his honesty and understanding his moral views.

If he was not a religious believer, then he was extremely dishonest and deceptive in his frequent references to God in his speeches and public pronouncements. If he did not believe in a God who is a person and has a will, this also calls into question the sincerity of his numerous statements to the effect that we should seek to discern and follow God's will (see Chapter 2.II.6). And even if he believed in a God who has a will and is concerned with human affairs, some question the sincerity of his frequent appeals to biblical precepts, such as "in the sweat of thy face shalt thou eat bread" (Genesis 3:19), which he took to be a prohibition against slavery, and to Christian beliefs (such as calling Christ "the savior").[58] His law partner William Herndon claimed that "Mr. Lincoln was simply a Theist – an unbeliever in Christianity."[59]

I argue here that, during his time as president and probably long before, Lincoln believed in the existence of a God who is a person and has a will. His frequent allusions to God and the need to follow God's will were perfectly sincere. It is much less clear whether he believed in the authority of the Bible and whether he should be called a Christian. But at least by the end of his life, his religious views were similar to those of people we now call "liberal Christians," and he seemed to regard at least some significant parts of the Bible as being divinely inspired. So I conclude that his appeals to biblical

---

[58] Miller, *Lincoln's Virtues*, p. 83.

[59] This is from Herndon's lecture on Lincoln's religion delivered in Springfield in December 1873, included in McMurttrie, *Lincoln's Religion: The Texts of Addresses Delivered by William H. Herndon and Rev. James A. Reed, and a Letter by C. F.B.*, p. 16.

precepts and Christian beliefs while president were *probably* sincere.

Let us first consider the evidence for thinking that Lincoln was irreligious. Bible-based evangelical Christianity dominated the frontier where he grew up. His father and step-mother were members of a Calvinist Baptist Church. Unlike his sister, he did not join his parents' church in Pigeon Creek, Indiana, and he never became a member of any other church.[60] In New Salem, he read and greatly admired Thomas Paine's *Age of Reason*. Paine was a deist who bitterly attacked biblical religion on moral grounds and wrote, "What is it that the Bible teaches us? Rapine, cruelty and murder."[61] He was also a great admirer of Robert Burns's poem "Holy Willie's Prayer," which ridicules religious hypocrisy and belief in a God who "Sends ane [one] to heaven and ten to hell." His friend James Matheny said that this poem was Lincoln's religion.[62] Lincoln particularly objected to the belief in eternal damnation, which he regarded as incompatible with the justice and goodness of God.[63] He liked to repeat the following jingle:

> Here lies poor Johnny Kongapod,
> Have mercy on him, gracious God,
> As he would do if he was God
> And you were Johnny Kongapod.[64]

He was repelled by the emotionalism of evangelical religious revivalists and the fierce doctrinal disagreements between competing religious sects.[65]

---

[60] Miller, *Lincoln's Virtues*, p. 42.

[61] Ibid., p. 85.

[62] Wilson and Davis, *Herndon's Lincoln*, p. 251; also see Wilson, *Honor's Voice*, p. 75.

[63] Miller, *Lincoln's Virtues*, p. 87; Wilson, *Honor's Voice*, pp. 80–1; Wolf, *The Almost Chosen People*, pp. 48, 50, and 193.

[64] Wolf, *The Almost Chosen People*, p. 48.

[65] Trueblood, *Abraham Lincoln: Theologian of America's Anguish*, p. 14.

As a young man in 1834, he wrote a short tract attacking Christianity (or at least certain forms of Christianity). His friend Sam Hill burned it to prevent it from harming Lincoln's reputation.[66] During this period, Lincoln apparently denied the divinity of Christ, the infallibility of the Bible, and belief in an afterlife.[67] His friend and law partner John Stuart said, "Lincoln went further against Christian beliefs – & doctrines & principles than any man I ever heard: he shocked me."[68] Herndon said that Lincoln told him "a thousand times that he did not believe that the Bible, etc., were revelations of God, as the Christian world contends."[69]

However, there is no credible evidence that Lincoln was ever an atheist. There were very few atheists in his time and place, in large measure because the "argument from design" for the existence of God enjoyed very wide support, even among those who rejected traditional Christianity. He himself endorsed the argument from design for the existence of God (see the later discussion). Thomas Paine, whose criticisms of Christianity strongly influenced Lincoln, was a deist, not an atheist.

During his later years in Illinois, Lincoln became much more discreet about discussing his religious views. David Davis, who later became his friend and spent a great deal of time traveling with him on the circuit court, said that Lincoln never talked about religion and that he had no idea what his religious views were.[70]

In 1866, Mary Lincoln gave the following account of her husband's religious views:

Mr. Lincoln had no hope & no faith in the usual acceptation of those words: he never joined a Church: he was a religious man

---

[66] Wilson, *Honor's Voice*, pp. 81–3.
[67] Ibid., pp. 80–3 and 186–7 (especially p. 187); also see Burlingame, *Abraham Lincoln: A Life*, I, p. 239.
[68] Wilson and Davis, *Herndon's Informants*, p. 576.
[69] Burlingame, *Abraham Lincoln: A Life*, I, p. 239.
[70] Wilson and Davis, *Herndon's Informants*, p. 348.

always, as I think: he first thought – to say think – about this subject when Willie died – never before. he felt religious More than Ever about the time he went to Gettysburg: he was not a technical Christian: he read the bible a good deal about 1864.[71]

When he ran successfully for election to Congress against the evangelist Peter Cartwright in 1846, Lincoln's religious "infidelity" was an issue in the campaign. He issued a hand-bill answering the charge that he was "an open scoffer at Christianity."[72] This handbill is a very curious and evasive document in which Lincoln said that he had never been a member of any Christian Church.[73] Yet he "carefully insists not only that *he* does not do any more scoffing, but that he could not himself support for office anyone whom he knew to be 'an open enemy of and scoffer at, religion.'"[74] In the handbill, he also said, "I have never denied the truth of the Scriptures."[75]

There is a prima facie case for thinking that this last state-ment was a lie. If Herndon is correct that Lincoln told him "a thousand times that he did not believe that the Bible, etc., were revelations of God," then this last statement was cer-tainly false. And because it strains belief to think that he could have forgotten his frequent denials of the truth of the Scriptures, there is a case for saying that this statement was a lie. It apparently satisfies the conditions of all standard def-initions of lying: it is a false statement, he knew that it was false, he intended to deceive others by making the statement, and he made the statement in a context in which he was giv-ing a guarantee or assurance of its truth.[76] Herndon might

---

[71] Ibid., p. 360.

[72] Miller, *Lincoln's Virtues*, p. 86.

[73] "Handbill Replying to Charges of Infidelity," in Abraham Lincoln, *Speeches and Writings*, I, p. 139.

[74] Miller, *Lincoln's Virtues*, p. 86.

[75] "Handbill Replying to Charges of Infidelity," in Abraham Lincoln, *Speeches and Writings*, I, p. 139.

[76] For a detailed discussion of the definition of lying and a survey of prominent definitions, see my *Lying and Deception: Theory and Practice*, chapter 1.

have correctly remembered that Lincoln denied the truth of
many parts of the Bible, such as those passages that seem
to say that some people are eternally damned. But that is
compatible with Lincoln having always thought that other
parts of the Bible were true, and in that case, he might have
believed that his statement in the handbill was true (he might
have believed that he never said that the Bible was completely
untrue) in which case it cannot be a lie. In any case, his statement on the handbill is still deceptive, and we can acquit him
of lying only if we suppose that he carefully parsed the meaning of his statement, "I have never denied the truth of the
scriptures," to mean roughly, "I have never denied that *some*
of the things in the scriptures are true," which is something
that most atheists could say.[77]

It is possible some of Lincoln's early friends in Springfield misremembered or misunderstood his religious views.
He belonged to a debating society in Springfield, and it is
possible that some of his strongly antireligious statements
recalled by friends many years later when they communicated with Herndon were made in debates for purposes of
argument and did not reflect his actual views at the time.[78]

There is evidence that Lincoln believed in the existence
of a personal God possessed of a will at least as early as
July 1842. In a confidential letter to Joshua Speed, his most
intimate personal friend, a letter that should be presumed to
be truthful, he wrote as follows:

I believe that God made me one of the instruments of bringing
your Fanny [Speed's wife] and you together, which union, I have
no doubt He had fore-ordained. Whatever he designs he will do

---

[77] Here, I follow Douglas Wilson who says that Lincoln's handbill (and his claim
that he "never denied the truth of the Scriptures") "was misleading at best,
and only the narrowest construction would save it from being an outright
misrepresentation;" Wilson, *Honor's Voice*, p. 311.

[78] Trueblood, *Abraham Lincoln: Theologian of American's Anguish*, p. 14.

for *me* yet. "Stand *still* and see the salvation of the Lord" is my text just now.[79]

Speed himself was not a conventional believer (see the later discussion), so there is no reason to think that Lincoln was writing this to impress Speed with his piety. Isaac Cogdal, Lincoln's friend from New Salem, reportedly talked with Lincoln about religion as early as 1834 and as late as 1859. Cogdal claimed that Lincoln believed in God, but that "he did not believe in Hell – Eternal punishment as the Christians say – his idea was punishment as Educational."[80] But Cogdal did say that Lincoln "believed that nations like individuals were punished for their sins."[81]

James Keyes, who knew Lincoln in Springfield, reported that Lincoln accepted a version of the argument from design for the existence of God:

A reason he gave for his belief was, that in view of the Order and harmony of all nature which all beheld, it would have been More miraculouis [sic] to have Come about by chance, than to have been created and arranged by some great thinking power.[82]

There is very strong evidence that Lincoln believed in the existence of God during his time as president. Late in his life, he made numerous private statements to his friends to the effect that he prayed and believed in God. He told his friend Noah Brooks that he prayed every day.[83] He also told Brooks that many times he was driven to his knees to pray "by the overwhelming conviction that" he "had nowhere else to

---

[79] Abraham Lincoln, *Speeches and Writings*, I, p. 95.
[80] Wilson and Davis, *Herndon's Informants*, p. 441.
[81] Ibid. Fehrenbacher and Fehrenbacher regard Cogdal as unreliable; see their *Recollected Words of Abraham Lincoln*, pp. 110–11. This passage is cited in Carwardine, *Lincoln: A Life of Purpose and Power*, p. 330.
[82] Wilson and Davis, *Herndon's Informants*, p. 464; this passage is cited in Carwardine, *Lincoln: A Life of Purpose and Power*, pp. 38–9.
[83] Wolf, *The Almost Chosen People*, p. 124.

go."[84] His secretary John Nicolay reports that Lincoln prayed and asked others to pray for him.[85]

Lincoln prayed not to get God to do his bidding, but to better see God's will. In a well-known case during the Civil War, a clergyman told him that he hoped "the Lord was on our side." Lincoln replied, "I am not at all concerned about that, for I know that the Lord is *always* on the side of the *right*. But it is my constant anxiety and prayer that *I* and *this nation* should be on the Lord's *side*."[86]

Lincoln's private notes and reflections to himself, which were not written for public consumption, are particularly important pieces of evidence for the proposition that he was a theist. In his "Meditation on the Divine Will," composed in September 1862, he wrote,

In the present civil war it is quite possible that God's purpose is something different from the purpose of either party – and yet human instrumentalities, working just as they do, are of the best adaptation to effect His purpose. I am almost ready to say this is probably true – that God wills this contest, and that it not end yet. . . . He could have either *saved* or *destroyed* the Union without a human contest. . . . Yet the contest proceeds.[87]

In his reflection "On Pro-Slavery Theology," from 1858, he discussed the views of Frederick Ross who defended slavery and claimed that American slavery was in accordance with God's will. He endorsed the idea that we should follow God's will, but said that there is difficulty in ascertaining it: "Certainly there is no contending against the will of God; but still there is some difficulty in ascertaining, and applying it, to particular cases."[88]

[84] Ibid., p.125.
[85] Ibid., p. 124.
[86] Carpenter, *The Inner Life of Abraham Lincoln: Six Months in the White House*, p. 282; cited in Wolf, *The Almost Chosen People*, p. 128.
[87] Abraham Lincoln, *Speeches and Writings*, II, p. 339.
[88] Abraham Lincoln, *Speeches and Writings*, I, p. 685.

At the end of his life, he believed in the existence of a God who has a will. So there is every reason to think that his endorsements of a divine will moral theory were sincere. But were his frequent appeals to biblical precepts and Christian beliefs sincere? He read the Bible a great deal and had a remarkable knowledge of it. He is reported to have said, "I decided a long time ago that it was less difficult to believe that the Bible was what it claimed to be than to disbelieve it."[89] But he was not a fundamentalist or biblical literalist. He said that he could not without mental reservations assent to any long creeds or Articles of Belief [of any established church].[90] But he was probably a believer in biblical religion and probably was what is now called a "liberal Christian" at the end of his life.[91] This interpretation fits well with Mary Lincoln's description of her husband as "a religious man always" but "not a technical Christian." When the word "Christian" is used today to include "liberal Christians," it is used more broadly than it generally was during his lifetime.

One final important piece of evidence of Lincoln's changing religious views is Joshua Speed's report of a conversation he had with Lincoln in 1864:

He [Lincoln] was sitting near a window intently reading his Bible. Approaching him, I said, "I am glad to see you so profitably engaged." "Yes," said he, "I am profitably engaged." "Well," said I, "if you have recovered from your skepticism, I am sorry to say that I have not," Looking me earnestly in the face, and placing his hand on my shoulder, he said, "You are wrong, Speed; take all of this book upon reason that you can, and the balance on faith, and you will live and die a happier man."[92]

---

[89] Wolf, *The Almost Chosen People*, p. 136.
[90] Trueblood, *Abraham Lincoln: Theologian of American's Anguish*, p. 110.
[91] Wolf, *The Almost Chosen People*, pp. 40, 87, and 193.
[92] Trueblood, *Abraham Lincoln: Theologian of American's Anguish*, p. 59.

This passage needs to be carefully parsed. It is unclear what Speed meant when he said that his friend had "recovered from his skepticism." He might be referring to Lincoln's skepticism about the existence of God or his skepticism about the truth of Christianity or the truth of the Bible. Although Lincoln does not explicitly say that he has recovered from his skepticism, the clear implication of his reply is that he *has* recovered from it and thinks that Speed's skepticism is mistaken. Because both men refer to the Bible, it seems that the skepticism that they are referring to has something to do with the Bible.

In this passage Lincoln tells Speed that he [Speed] is "mistaken" in his skepticism and recommends that Speed "take" (accept) the Bible. He says that if Speed takes (accepts) the Bible partly on reason and partly on faith he will be a happier person. It is reasonable to think that he based this recommendation on his own experience and that he was implying that he had become a happier person as a result of "taking" or accepting (much of) the Bible.

Speed was Lincoln's most intimate friend, and because Speed was very discreet and a religious skeptic himself, there is no reason to think that Lincoln was attempting to mislead Speed about his religious views. Lincoln's statements were probably sincere. Herndon interviewed Speed shortly after Lincoln's death, and his notes include the following statement: [uncorrected] "Speed is satisfied that Lincoln was a growing man in religion though no so as to Christianit."[93] This assessment seems somewhat at odds with Speed's account of his discussion with Lincoln about the Bible. But it is also possible that both accounts are fully accurate and that, in speaking with Herndon, Speed was using the term "Christianity" narrowly so as to exclude those we now call "liberal Christians."

[93] Wilson and Davis, *Herndon's Informants*, p. 476.

We should not attach too much significance to the fact that Lincoln never formally joined a church. In his time and place, most Christians were not church members. In 1860 only 23 percent of Americans were church members, but surely most Americans were Christians at the time.[94]

Everything I have said in defense of the view that Lincoln was a religious believer and liberal Christian by the end of his life is compatible with his having serious doubts and reservations about the truth of his religious beliefs. Henry Rankin reports that Lincoln had such doubts during the middle of his life and attributes the following statement to Lincoln during this period:

It is to be my lot to go on . . . questioning and doubting as Thomas did. . . . I go on a seeking spirit of desire for a faith that was with him of olden time, who, in his need, as I in mine, exclaimed, 'Help thou my unbelief.'"[95]

> 7. Lincoln loved children and loved to play with them and take part in their games.[96] Children, in turn, loved him.[97]

He was very fond of his neighbor Stephen Smith's infant son and loved to carry him around over his shoulder.[98] Burlingame describes this as follows:

A minister who lived across the street from the Lincolns' home in Springfield called Lincoln "a great lover of children" and noted that he "loved his neighbors['] children too. Many a time we have seen troops of children, living on the same street, run out to meet

---

94 Trueblood, *Abraham Lincoln: Theologian of America's Anguish*, p. 96.

95 Ibid., p. 22. Lincoln might have had greater confidence in his religious beliefs later in his life. Fehrenbacher and Fehrenbacher say that most scholars think that Rankin is an unreliable source; Fehrenbacher and Fehrenbacher, *Recollected Words of Abraham Lincoln*, p. 374.

96 Wilson and Davis, *Herndon's Informants*, pp. 7, 91, 92, 108, 453, and 512.

97 Burlingame, *The Inner World of Abraham Lincoln*, pp. 57–8.

98 Ibid., p. 59.

him, when he was coming to his meals, and would gambol by his side, and as many as could get hold of him, would swing from his hands."[99]

Lincoln was a very playful man. A grandchild of cabinet member Francis Blair recalled that the president would "join ardently" into children's games and said, "He entered into the spirit of the play as completely as any of us, and we invariably hailed his coming with delight."[100] He engaged in pillow fights with his friends while traveling on the circuit court. His friend Leonard Swett first met Lincoln while Lincoln and David Davis, a future justice of the U.S. Supreme Court, were having a pillow fight in a hotel room.[101]

8. Lincoln was a very indulgent and permissive parent in an era in which harsh discipline and corporal punishment were the norm and most people endorsed the maxim "spare the rod and spoil the child."

Herndon said that "he was the most indulgent parent I have ever known."[102] Herndon continues:

He was in the habit, when home on Sunday, of bringing his two boys ... down to the office to remain while his wife attended church. ... The boys were absolutely unrestrained in their amusement. If they pulled down all the books from the shelves, bent the points of all the pens, overturned inkstands, scattered law-papers over the floor, or threw pencils into the spittoon, it never disturbed the serenity of their father's good nature ... he virtually encouraged their repetition [of the boys' "mischievous and destructive pranks"] by declining to show any substantial evidence of parental disapproval.[103]

---

[99] Ibid., p. 58.
[100] Quoted in ibid., p. 59.
[101] Wilson and Davis, *Herndon's Informants*, p. 732.
[102] Wilson and Davis, *Herndon's Lincoln*, p. 257.
[103] Ibid., pp. 257–8.

But Mary Lincoln frequently beat her boys and her husband rarely interfered. In general, he gave her complete control over all things domestic.[104]

9. Lincoln was passionately interested in acquiring an education and knowledge.

His own remarkable self-education – learning proper English style and grammar, geometry, trigonometry, surveying, the law, and military science, almost entirely on his own – is evidence of his extremely strong desire to become educated. He was also strongly committed to providing educational opportunities for others. He helped pass the Land Grant College Act of 1862 (also called the Morrill Act), which allocated funds from the sale of federal land to states for the purposes of endowing colleges. This act greatly expanded the availability of college education to ordinary people and has continued to benefit millions of people in the twentieth and twenty-first centuries.

10. Lincoln's remarkably successful self-education demonstrates that he possessed extraordinary intelligence and ability.

He was able to master English style and grammar with less than one year of formal education and after growing up with few, if any, models of good style or grammar. He did this almost entirely on his own using a dry and difficult grammar book.[105] He also mastered geometry, trigonometry, the law, and military science on his own. In addition, he invented and patented a device for lifting boats out of shoals.[106] He had very great confidence in his own intellectual abilities. His personal secretary John Hay said, "It is absurd to call

---

[104] Burlingame, *The Inner World of Abraham Lincoln*, p. 63.
[105] Wilson, *Honor's Voice*, pp. 62–6.
[106] Wilson and Davis, *Herndon's Lincoln*, p. 189.

him a modest man. . . . It was his intellectual arrogance and unconscious assumption of superiority that men like Chase and Sumner could never forgive."[107]

11. Lincoln was an exceptionally strong man.

Several of his contemporaries report that he was able to hoist more than one thousand pounds.[108] His physical strength was a very important asset when he was a young man. It helped him gain the respect and esteem of his fellows in the rough world of the frontier where men did very heavy physical labor and often fought and wrestled with each other. At six feet, four inches, he was exceptionally tall for a man of his time.

12. Lincoln was very careless of his dress and appearance.

His clothes seldom fit and were almost always rumpled; his thick coarse hair seldom saw a comb. Once, when posing for a photograph in 1858, he was asked if he wanted a mirror to "fix up" before the photo was taken. He did not want a mirror and said that "it would not be much of a likeness if I fixed up any."[109] He was also very messy and disorganized. He frequently misplaced papers in his law office[110] and it was said that seeds sprouted on the floor of his office.[111]

13. His voice was high-pitched, reedy, and thin, but it carried very well in a large crowd. He had a Southern accent of the kind one can still hear in parts of central and southern Illinois, Indiana, and Ohio. He probably had a bit more of a Southern accent than he is portrayed as having in the Spielberg film *Lincoln*.[112]

---

[107] Ibid., p. 309.
[108] Wilson and Davis, *Herndon's Informants*, pp. 7, 13, and 528.
[109] Ronald White, *A. Lincoln*, p. 256.
[110] Wilson and Davis, *Herndon's Lincoln*, p. 197.
[111] Ibid., p. 198; also see p. 196.
[112] James McPherson, Interview on the Film *Lincoln*.

Conclusion

Lincoln was an extremely complex and interesting human being. He was deeply scarred by the deaths of many loved ones during his youth. This contributed to his melancholy disposition and preoccupation with death and mortality. His disinterest in wealth and luxury, although perhaps not a moral virtue in itself, enhanced his honesty and incorruptibility. His sense of humor, playfulness, and love of children help explain why he was so very well liked by most people who knew him. But, early in his political career, his sense of humor often went too far and was frequently enlisted in the service of underhanded and unfair political partisanship. We need to qualify the claim that he was a kind person in light of some of the very biting things he said and wrote as a young politician. He was immature and had many rough edges, but he outgrew these failings and became a better person before emerging as an important national political figure.

9

Lincoln's Marriage and Family Life, and What They Reveal about His Character

I. Lincoln's Marriage and What It Reveals about His Character

Lincoln married a very troubled and temperamental woman. It is important to ask what his marriage reveals about him as a person.

    1. Mary Lincoln's Faults
        A. *Her Violent Temper.* A number of people who knew her reported that Mary Todd Lincoln committed acts of physical violence against her husband and others.

Michael Burlingame recounts an example of her violent temper that was reported by Mrs. Jacob Early:

Lincoln got a taste of her temper shortly after their wedding. One morning at the Globe Tavern [where they lived after becoming married] she arrived late from breakfast, as usual, inconveniencing the other guests. Boardinghouse etiquette dictated that, in the morning, no one could eat until all guests were seated at the table. Lincoln, evidently irritated and embarrassed, gently chided her as she entered the room. She instantly sprang up, threw a cup of hot coffee at him and fled in hysterics.[1]

---

[1] Burlingame, *Abraham Lincoln: A Life*, I, p. 202.

A similar event took place at dinner one night in December 1860. Thurlow Weed witnessed her outburst when Lincoln "cracked a joke which displeased Mrs. Lincoln because she erroneously imagined it to be at her expense. Quicker than a flash she picked up a cup of hot tea and flung it clear across the table at Mr. Lincoln's head."[2]

Herndon interviewed several people who gave similar reports about Mary Lincoln's temper. Margaret Ryan, who worked as a maid in the Lincoln home, said that Mary hit her husband on the head with a piece of wood while he was reading in the parlor and cut his nose. The lawyers in court noticed his face the next day, but no one asked any questions.[3] Springfield resident Stephen Whitehurst said that he saw Mary chase her husband with a knife in the Lincolns' garden.[4] Lincoln's friend James Matheny reported that a servant girl who worked for the Lincolns was insulted and slapped by Mary Lincoln, who then threw the girl's trunk and clothing outside of the house. The girl complained to her uncle, a man named Tiger. The uncle went to the Lincoln home, where Mary struck him with a broom three times. He then went to Lincoln to demand an apology, and Lincoln said, "*Friend* Tiger, can't you endure this one wrong done you by a mad woman without much complaint for old friendship's sake while I have had to bear it without complaint and without a murmur for lo these last fifteen years."[5]

The former slave Elizabeth Keckley, who was Mary's friend, dressmaker, and most intimate companion while Mary lived in the White House, corroborated the view that Mary had a very bad temper:

---

[2] Ibid.
[3] Wilson and Davis, *Herndon's Informants*, p. 597.
[4] Ibid., p. 722.
[5] Ibid., pp. 713–14.

He [Lincoln] asked nothing but affection from her, but did not always receive it. When in one of her wayward impulsive moods, she was apt to say and do things that wounded him deeply.[6]

> B. *Her Jealousy.* Near the end of her time in the White House, Mary Todd Lincoln exhibited extreme irrational hostility and jealousy toward other women who had any dealings with her husband.[7]

She did so on public occasions in ways that were deeply embarrassing to the president. In March 1865, Mary and her husband were with the Union Army near Richmond. They were supposed to review General Ord's troops, riding past them on horseback. Mary was delayed in coming to the review, and because the troops had been waiting for a long time,[8] Lincoln ordered that it begin. He was joined by General Ord's young and strikingly beautiful wife who rode beside him on a horse. When she arrived, Mary exploded with anger at Mrs. Ord. Here is David Donald's account of what happened next:

When Mrs. Ord rode up to pay her respects, Mary, now hysterical, "positively insulted her, called her vile names ... and asked what she meant following the President."

That night before the guests at dinner aboard the *River Queen*, Mary repeatedly attacked her husband for flirting with Mrs. Ord and demanded that General Ord be removed from command. Deeply mortified, the President tried to ignore his wife's remarks, but she continued her tirade of abuse until late at night.[9]

---

[6] Keckley, *Behind the Scenes*, p. 65.
[7] Ibid., p. 55.
[8] Burlingame, *Abraham Lincoln: A Life*, II, p. 761.
[9] Donald, *Lincoln*, p. 573; for more details about this incident see Burlingame, *The Inner World of Abraham Lincoln*, pp. 289–90.

It is also reported that around this time, while on a river boat near Richmond, Mary struck her husband hard on the face, cursed, and damned him.[10]

Mary was particularly jealous of the beautiful Kate Chase Sprague, the daughter of Salmon P. Chase and wife of a U.S. senator. Mary became furious when Lincoln wanted to invite Kate to a White House dinner.[11] Mary refused to attend Kate's wedding and wanted her husband to refuse to attend also, even though it was the social event of the season in Washington.[12] When Lincoln dressed for the wedding, Mary exploded. When he tried to calm her, she responded by pulling out part of his beard.[13]

Mary caused other embarrassing scenes by verbally abusing people whom she thought did not sufficiently defer to her position as the president's wife. On March 24, 1865, Grant and his wife called on the Lincolns. Mary was offended that Julia Grant sat down next to her without her (Mary's) permission and said to her, "How dare you be seated until I invite you?"[14] She subjected Stanton's wife to similar treatment. Both women became very averse to being in Mary's presence.[15] Indeed, Julia Grant's deep dislike of Mary was the reason that she and her husband were not seated together with the Lincolns at Ford Theatre the night Lincoln was assassinated.[16]

C. *Her Excessive Spending.* When Mary became the First Lady, the White House and its contents were dilapidated; the house was dirty and infested with rats and

---

[10] Wilson and Davis, *Herndon's Informants*, p. 467.

[11] Burlingame, *The Inner World of Abraham Lincoln*, p. 286.

[12] Ibid.

[13] Ibid., p. 287.

[14] Sandburg, *Abraham Lincoln: The War Years*, IV, p. 153.

[15] Burlingame, *Abraham Lincoln: A Life*, II, p. 779 and Donald, *Lincoln*, p. 594.

[16] Burlingame, *Abraham Lincoln: A Life*, II, pp. 806–7; Donald, *Lincoln*, p. 594; also see Burlingame, *The Inner World of Abraham Lincoln*, p. 290.

insects.[17] Congress appropriated $25,000 to redeco-
rate the White House.[18] Mary eagerly took charge of
this project, but she greatly overspent her budget – the
total bill was about $70,000.[19] Congress appropriated
$14,000 more, but Mary and her husband were respon-
sible for paying the difference and thus were saddled
with a very large debt.[20] This caused Mary and the president great distress and embarrassment, and Mary was
widely criticized for her extravagance in this matter.[21]

Some think that the president and the public were too critical
of her and did not adequately appreciate her fine work on
this renovation project. But Mary also spent money lavishly
on clothing and jewelry for herself. Shortly after Lincoln's
death, the New York firm of Ball, Black & Company presented his estate with bills totaling $64,000 – a very large
sum of money at the time (equivalent to roughly $900,000
in 2014 dollars) – for jewelry that Mary purchased without
her husband's knowledge.[22] Mary kept the full extent of her
debts secret from Lincoln and worried about him finding out;
she even remarked to her friend Elizabeth Keckley that she
was relieved that he was reelected, in part, because that meant
she could continue to keep her debts secret from him. Mary
told her that "if he is re-elected, I can keep him in ignorance
of my affairs; but if he is defeated, then the bills will be sent
in and he will know all."[23]

   D. *Her Alleged Corruption.* Some claim that Mary Lincoln
      solicited and accepted bribes from people who wanted

[17] Burlingame, *Abraham Lincoln: A Life*, II, pp. 249 and 251.
[18] Ibid., p. 280.
[19] Ibid.
[20] Ibid., p. 281.
[21] Ibid., pp. 280–3 and 700.
[22] Burlingame, *The Inner World of Abraham Lincoln*, p. 312.
[23] Keckley, *Behind the Scenes*, p. 67.

her to influence her husband to appoint them to government positions and that she also threw temper tantrums to influence his appointments.[24]

Mary's friend Senator Charles Sumner said that she "meddled in nearly all patronage affairs early in her husband's administration."[25] It is also alleged that she solicited and accepted kickbacks from merchants while using government money to redecorate the White House.[26] It is further alleged that when she returned to Springfield after the assassination, she *stole* many trunk loads of silver and linen from the White House.[27] These accusations were current at the time and deeply distressing to the Lincolns. At one point, Congress briefly inquired into possible corruption on her part.[28] I offer no view about the credibility of these charges against Mary. In any case, they added considerably to her husband's burdens.

E. *Assessing the Evidence.* Some historians question the truth of many of these stories about Mary Lincoln, particularly those found in reports made to William Herndon. They claim that because of his great dislike for Mary, Herndon asked people leading questions calculated to elicit negative responses and put her in a bad light.[29] Ruth Painter Randall and James Randall argue that Herndon's biases unfairly tarnished Mary Lincoln's reputation.[30]

---

[24] Burlingame, *Abraham Lincoln: A Life*, II, pp. 265–6.
[25] Burlingame, *The Inner World of Abraham Lincoln*, p. 284.
[26] Burlingame, *Abraham Lincoln: A Life*, II, pp. 278 and 280; also see Burlingame, *The Inner World of Abraham Lincoln*, p. 282.
[27] Burlingame, *Abraham Lincoln: A Life*, II, p. 827.
[28] Donald, *Lincoln*, pp. 324–5.
[29] Wilson and Davis, *Herndon's Lincoln*, pp. xvi–xvii.
[30] See Ruth Painter Randall, *Mary Lincoln: Biography of a Marriage* and James G. Randall, *Lincoln the President.*

But independent of the accounts of Herndon and of those who reported to him, there is considerable evidence that Mary Todd Lincoln had a very bad temper, which partly corroborates what Herndon's sources reported. For example, the two incidents in which Mary was alleged to have thrown hot coffee and hot tea at her husband's face were not reported to Herndon. The testimony of Elizabeth Keckley and Charles Sumner is particularly relevant, because they were Mary's friends and, if anything, were biased in her favor. It is undeniable that Mary greatly overspent on jewelry for herself and decorations for the White House and that this caused the president great distress and embarrassment. During her time in the White House, she caused many people to deeply dislike her, among them Julia Grant and Ellen Stanton. Lincoln's private secretaries in the White House, John Hay and John Nicolay, referred to Mary as "Her Satanic Majesty" and "the Hell-Cat."[31] On the most charitable interpretation of the evidence, Mary Todd Lincoln was a difficult and ill-tempered woman throughout her entire marriage. It is also clear that her temperament deteriorated while she was in the White House, largely because of tragic events beyond her control: her son Willie's death in 1862 and a serious head injury she suffered in July 1863 as a result of being thrown from a carriage in an accident and hitting her head on the ground; she suffered violent headaches after sustaining that injury.[32]

Despite all of this, Mary Lincoln loved her husband. She was very proud of him and strongly supported him in his political ambitions. After his marriage, Lincoln was much more emotionally stable and had no further recurrence of debilitating depression or serious thoughts of suicide. For all the problems that she caused him, his emotional health was considerably better after their marriage than before. Contrary

[31] Burlingame, *Abraham Lincoln: A Life*, I, p. 201.
[32] Donald, *Lincoln*, pp. 448 and 572.

to many contemporary rumors (fueled by the fact that many members of her family sided with the Confederacy and some fought and died for the Confederacy), Mary was completely loyal to the Union cause and fully supported her husband's efforts to end slavery.[33]

> 2. *Lincoln the Husband.* By almost all accounts, including Mary's, Lincoln was a loving, kind, and patient husband. Mary said that "he was the kindest most tender and loving husband and father in all the world."[34]

Harriet Chapman, the granddaughter of Lincoln's stepmother who lived with the Lincolns in the mid-1840s, said that Mr. Lincoln was kind, affectionate, and never uttered an unkind word.[35] Elizabeth Keckley said that he was tolerant and generally good humored in the face of his wife's rages. By every account, he was a faithful husband, despite being very strongly attracted to women and spending a great deal of time away from home, which gave him many opportunities to stray from his marriage vows. His friend Judge David Davis who traveled with him on the circuit court said, "Lincoln was a man of strong passion for women – his Conscience kept him from seduction – this saved many – many a woman."[36] Davis also said,

Lincoln had a terribly strong passions [sic] for women, could hardly keep his hands off of them. And yet he had honor and a strong will, and these enabled him to put out the fires of his terrible

---

[33] On this point see Keckley, *Behind the Scenes*, p. 60; Winkle, *Abraham and Mary Lincoln*, p. 110; and the statement by Frederick Douglass in Blasingame and McKivigon, *The Frederick Douglass Papers Series One: Speeches, Debates, and Interviews*, Vol. 5, pp. 343–4.

[34] Wilson and Davis, *Herndon's Informants*, p. 357.

[35] Ibid., p. 407.

[36] Ibid., p. 350; also see Donald, *Lincoln*, p. 108.

passions.... I have seen Lincoln tempted, and I have seen him
reject the approach of woman.[37]

Lincoln deserves credit for his marital fidelity, and he deserves
special credit for his magnanimity and forbearance as a
husband.

But he was not an ideal husband. He was moody, emotionally distant, and often distracted and absent-minded. He
was not demonstrative and did not give his wife the affection that she needed, nor did he talk with her as much as
she would have liked.[38] He also stayed away from home too
much. Mary said she could have loved him better if he had
been at home more.[39] During most of his marriage, Lincoln
spent roughly three months of the year away from home on
the judicial circuit,[40] traveling with a judge and other lawyers
from town to town to hear local court cases in county seats.
(He and other lawyers needed to travel on the judicial circuit to earn a good living.) He enjoyed life on the circuit –
its camaraderie and storytelling with other members of the
court. Unlike most of his contemporaries on the circuit court,
he seldom returned home on weekends, even after railroads
made that travel possible.[41] In the late 1850s, he spent even
more time away from home because of his frequent political travels. In 1858, he wrote that he was away from home
"perhaps more than half of" his time.[42] Even when he was
in Springfield, he put in very long hours at his office. According to Herndon, "he frequently left home between seven and
eight A. M. and returned at midnight or even later."[43]

---

[37] Miller, *Lincoln's Virtues*, p. 77.
[38] Burlingame, *The Inner World of Abraham Lincoln*, p. 318 and Donald, *Lincoln*, p. 108.
[39] Burlingame, *The Inner World of Abraham Lincoln*, p. 321.
[40] Burlingame, *Abraham Lincoln: A Life*, I, p. 322.
[41] Wilson and Davis, *Herndon's Informants*, pp. 194 and 349.
[42] Burlingame, *Abraham Lincoln: A Life*, I, p. 223.
[43] Ibid., p. 224.

He undoubtedly stayed away from home more than he should have for the good of his marriage and children, but that said, Mary drove him away by making his home life very unpleasant. Their marriage was marked by a pattern of Mary's anger and Abe's withdrawal; it became a vicious cycle.[44] Some of his friends, including Speed, thought that if his marriage and home life had been happier, he might have been a happy domestic man without great political ambitions.[45]

It might be objected that the primary cause of Mary's irritability was Lincoln's frequent absence rather than the other way around. Clearly, the causation went in both directions. The testimony of Speed and others about Lincoln's capacity for domestic happiness noted earlier lends some support to the view that Mary's irritability was more the cause of his frequent absence than the other way around. But this is far from conclusive. It should be noted that Lincoln had to be away from home much of the time traveling on the circuit court to earn the kind of income that Mary expected him to make,[46] and in the 1850s she shared and supported the political ambitions that kept him away from home so much. Although his absences and distractions might have warranted considerable irritation and anger, they did not justify or excuse Mary's violence against him and others.

We can speculate that Mary's life and character might have turned out much better if the times she lived in had not confined her to the domestic role for which she was ill suited

---

[44] Burlingame, *The Inner World of Abraham Lincoln*, p. 319.

[45] Wilson and Davis, *Herndon's Informants*, pp. 63 and 729. Burlingame writes, "The Lincoln's marriage was . . . a fountain of misery, yet from it flowed incalculable good for the nation" (Burlingame, *The Inner World of Abraham Lincoln*, p. 326). Mary strongly pushed and supported her husband's political ambitions – in this they were of one accord.

[46] That said, he seldom came home from the circuit court on weekends, even after railroads made that possible.

and she could have been able to pursue a career in which she could have made use of her considerable talent and ambition. The severely limited opportunities for women and the strong stigma against divorce at the time they lived trapped the Lincolns in a very unhappy marriage. This was a personal tragedy for both of them.

> 3. *Lincoln's Decision to Wed Mary*. What about his decision to marry her? Why did he marry her? Did he know what he was getting into? Did he know how very bad her temper was?

Herndon and Burlingame think that Mary kept her violent temper under wraps before their marriage and that it was not fully revealed to him until after their marriage.[47] As a young woman, Mary Todd was very charming, very intelligent, proud, very witty, passionate, vivacious, quick-tempered, an excellent conversationalist, a graceful dancer, and very ambitious. She was considered to be very attractive to men. She was clearly a woman of very great ability, charm, and appeal.

Herndon also thinks that Lincoln was drawn to Mary because of his ambition; he wanted to marry a woman from a prominent family to help him gain increased access to polite society. He was acutely conscious of his lack of social graces and thought that marriage to the right woman would help him in that respect.[48] According to Douglas Wilson, when Herndon tried to get Lincoln's friend and former law partner, John Stuart, to speak about the Lincoln marriage,

all he [Stuart] would say was that he thought "that the marriage of Lincoln to Miss Todd was a policy Match all around." By "policy" he apparently meant that, on both sides, it was a course of action

---

[47] Burlingame, *The Inner World of Abraham Lincoln*, p. 323.
[48] Wilson and Davis, *Herndon's Lincoln*, p. 132.

considered "expedient, prudent, or advantageous." Love, Stuart seemed to be saying, had very little to do with it.[49]

Lincoln was very strongly attracted to Mary, but despite this, he was also very ambivalent about marrying her. After they became engaged, he fell in love with another woman, Matilda Edwards. According to his friend Orville Browning, Lincoln fell in love with Matilda Edwards and proposed marriage to her, but she turned him down. All the while Mary continued to flirt with other men, including Stephen Douglas, to make Lincoln jealous.[50] To further complicate matters, Lincoln's closest friend, Joshua Speed, also fell in love with Matilda Edwards and proposed marriage to her at roughly the same time.[51] After he fell in love with Matilda Edwards, Lincoln told John Hardin he did not love Mary Todd and that it would be a great wrong if he married her.[52] He resolved to tell Mary that he did not love her and end their engagement. When he told her that he did not love her, Mary became very unhappy. Unable to bear seeing her so unhappy, he wept and hugged and kissed her. This she took to be a renewal of the engagement.[53] Herndon continues the story as told to him by Joshua Speed:

"And that's how you broke the engagement," sneered Speed. "You not only acted the fool, but your conduct was tantamount to a renewal of the engagement, and in decency you cannot back down now."

"Well," drawled Lincoln, "if I am in again, so be it. It's done, and I shall abide by it."

---

[49] Wilson, *Honor's Voice*, p. 292.
[50] Wilson, *Honor's Voice*, p. 222. Matilda Edwards was a beautiful eighteen-year-old who captivated many young men; she received twenty-two offers of marriage; Burlingame, *Abraham Lincoln: A Life*, I, p. 181.
[51] Wilson, *Honor's Voice*, pp. 230, 246, and 319.
[52] Burlingame, *The Inner World of Abraham Lincoln*, p. 315.
[53] Wilson and Davis, *Herndon's Lincoln*, p. 136.

Convinced now that Miss Todd regarded the engagement ratified – instead of broken as her suitor had first intended – Lincoln
continued the visits.[54]

None of this resolved his ambivalence, and he later ended
their engagement. According to Mary's sister Elizabeth
Edwards, he jilted Mary and failed to show up for their
wedding.[55] Herndon accepts this account and says that the
wedding was scheduled to take place on January 1, 1841. He
places the aborted wedding on this date, because a very candid and personal letter from Lincoln to Joshua Speed talks
about his breakup with Mary and refers to the "the fatal
first of Jany. '41."[56] However, Douglas Wilson and Rodney
Davis think that the story of the jilting is almost certainly
false. Other members of Mary's family strongly claimed that
no aborted wedding ever took place.[57] "No wedding license
having been registered, and no other confirming evidence
having been brought to light, it seems likely that Elizabeth
Todd Edwards was confused about the occasion at which
AL failed to have appeared, which may have been a dinner
to announce an engagement."[58] Wilson also discounts Elizabeth Edwards' story about the jilting because "no one else
remembered this abortive wedding ceremony, and it now
seems reasonably certain that she [Elizabeth Edwards] was
mistaken."[59] According to Wilson, Lincoln's reference to the
"fatal first of Jany" probably refers to something that happened to Speed on that day, not the aborted wedding. Wilson
also thinks that Mary Todd may have been out of town that
day.[60] Davis and Wilson's view that Lincoln failed to show

[54] Ibid., pp. 136–7.
[55] Wilson, *Honor's Voice*, p. 226.
[56] Abraham Lincoln, *Speeches and Writings*, I, p. 93.
[57] Wilson and Davis, *Herndon's Lincoln*, p. 335.
[58] Ibid., p. 434 n11.
[59] Wilson, *Honor's Voice*, p. 226.
[60] Ibid., pp. 227 and 233.

up for an announcement of their wedding, in a way that humiliated Mary, is the most likely account of how he ended his first engagement with Mary.

Many things are uncertain, but we know that Lincoln was very ambivalent about marrying Mary Todd and broke off their first engagement in a way that hurt Mary a great deal. He felt very badly for hurting Mary in this way. In a letter to Joshua Speed, he wrote that it "kills his soul" to have made Mary so unhappy.[61]

Some time between the end of his first engagement to Mary (around January 1841) and his marriage to her in November 1842, he may have proposed marriage to a woman roughly half his age, Sarah Rickard, then aged sixteen. This is reported by two separate sources including Rickard herself.[62]

Later, Lincoln and Mary renewed their engagement. But, even after doing so, he was apparently still very ambivalent about their marriage. He told his friend Orville Browning that he had made a mistake in having become engaged to Mary again, but that he felt honor bound to marry her. Browning "always doubted whether, had circumstances left him entirely free to act on his own impulses, he would have voluntarily made proposals of marriage to Miss Todd."[63]

The Lincolns were married on very short notice; their wedding guests learned about the wedding only a few hours beforehand.[64] Several people think that his ambivalence continued right up to the time of his wedding. As he dressed for the wedding, Burlingame recounts that "he was asked where he was going. 'I guess I am going to hell,' he replied."[65] Burlingame continues, "His best man, James Matheny,

---

[61] Abraham Lincoln, *Speeches and Writings*, I, p. 93; Wilson, *Honor's Voice*, pp. 257–8.

[62] Wilson, *Honor's Voice*, pp. 254 and 284.

[63] Burlingame, *The Inner World of Abraham Lincoln*, p. 316.

[64] Wilson, *Honor's Voice*, p. 291.

[65] Burlingame, *The Inner World of Abraham Lincoln*, p. 317.

thought, 'Lincoln looked and acted as if he were going to the slaughter' and 'more like one going to his grave than one going to his wedding.'"[66] However, Mary's sister Francis Wallace said that Lincoln was "cheerful as he ever had been, for all we could see."[67] It is possible that they married on short notice as a precaution against his indecision. This could have been a way of ensuring that he would keep his new resolution to go through with the marriage.

Yet it is puzzling that he married Mary, given his strong reservations about their marriage. His friends Matheny and Speed thought that he felt compelled by honor to marry her. Speed said, "Lincoln married her for honor – feeling his honor bound to her."[68] Matheny said that Lincoln told him that he was driven into the marriage by Mary and her family and that Mary told Lincoln that he was duty bound to marry her.[69] Herndon said that, by marrying Mary, Lincoln saved his honor, but sacrificed his domestic peace.[70]

Why did Lincoln feel honor bound to wed Mary? He might have felt bound to honor his earlier promise to marry her (this is Herndon's view[71]), but this is a very poor reason for entering into a marriage. Wedding engagements are intended to allow the parties time to think about what they are doing and to give them the option to change their minds. The promise to marry someone that is given when getting engaged is understood to not be binding if one later has a change of heart. If Lincoln married Mary merely to keep an earlier promise that he regretted having made at the time of his marriage, his decision seems quite unreasonable and indefensible.

---

[66] Ibid.
[67] Wilson, *Honor's Voice*, p. 291. Kenneth Winkle thinks that Lincoln was entirely comfortable at his wedding; see Winkle, *Abraham and Mary Lincoln*, p. 46.
[68] Wilson, *Honor's Voice*, p. 289.
[69] Ibid.
[70] Wilson and Davis, *Herndon's Lincoln*, p. 145.
[71] Ibid.

Burlingame proposes an alternative explanation for why Lincoln felt honor bound to wed Marry on very short notice: they had had sexual relations prior to being married, and she demanded that he marry her.[72] Burlingame thinks that this is a plausible theory, but is not provable. I agree. This theory makes good sense of certain facts. Mary gave birth to Robert Todd Lincoln a few days short of nine months after their wedding. Burlingame's theory also explains why Lincoln felt honor bound to wed Mary on very short notice.

An alternative explanation of his decision to wed Mary is that his attraction to Mary, his desire to enter more fully into polite society, his desire to end the unhappiness he caused her by breaking off their engagement, and his desire to honor his earlier promise combined to trump his reservations about the marriage.

Clearly this entire episode was extremely fraught and messy. Lincoln is to be criticized for hurting Mary with his indecision. He should also be strongly criticized for continuing his relationship with her. And discounting Burlingame's theory that he had sexual relations with Mary that obligated him to marry her, he should be strongly criticized for going through with the marriage despite his grave doubts and reservations. He was much too concerned with keeping his promises and commitments, come what may. He said apropos of engagements, "My old Father used to have a saying that 'If you make a bad bargain, *hug* it the tighter.'"[73]

---

[72] Burlingame, *Abraham Lincoln: A Life*, I, pp. 197–8. Given the sexual mores of the time, Mary's not being a virgin and possibly being pregnant would have meant that she was considered unsuitable for marriage in "polite society." Men in Lincoln's position were expected to marry women (women of polite society) with whom they had sex. Failure to do so was perceived to be, and likely was, very harmful to the women in question. Also, at the time of her marriage, Mary was twenty-three years old and was already considered something of an "old maid."

[73] Abraham Lincoln, *Speeches and Writings*, I, p. 91.

4. *Lincoln's Earlier Engagement or Near-Engagement to Mary Owens.* This earlier engagement sheds light on his ambivalence and indecision in his courtship with Mary Todd. He exhibited the same ambivalence about marriage and the same determination to keep his word in his earlier engagement (or near-engagement) with Mary Owens.

Mary Owens was a well-to-do and well-educated woman from Kentucky. Lincoln met her when she visited her sister in New Salem in 1833. He liked her and found her "intelligent" and "agreeable."[74] Three years later Mary Owens's sister suggested to Lincoln that "she bring her sister Mary back from Kentucky for him to wed."[75] He accepted this suggestion, and Mary Owens returned to New Salem to be courted by him. He said that he found her far less attractive than he had remembered – he commented unfavorably about her weight and lack of teeth in a letter to his friend Eliza Browning and said that "she now appeared to be a fair match for Falstaff."[76] Burlingame describes what happened next:

Despite his reservations, Lincoln felt honor-bound to follow through on his pledge: "I had told her sister that I would take her for better or worse; and I made a point of honor and conscience in all things to stick to my word, especially if others had been induced to act on it...." He "really dreaded" the prospect of wedding Mary Owens.[77]

[Burlingame then quotes from Lincoln's letter to Eliza Browning cited earlier.]

After this, in August 1837 Lincoln wrote Mary Owens a very strange letter in which he proposed marriage while also

[74] Burlingame, *Abraham Lincoln: A Life*, I, p. 169.
[75] Ibid.
[76] Abraham Lincoln, *Speeches and Writings*, I, pp. 37–9.
[77] Burlingame, *Abraham Lincoln: A Life*, I, p. 169.

expressing his willingness that she end their relationship if that was her wish:

I want... more than anything else to do right with you, and if I *knew* it would be doing right, as I suspect it would, to let you alone, I would do it... you can now drop the subject, dismiss your thoughts (if you ever had any) from me forever, and leave this letter unanswered, without calling forth one accusing murmur from me.... What I do wish is, that our further acquaintance shall depend upon yourself. If such further acquaintance would contribute nothing to your happiness, I am sure that it would not to mine. If you feel yourself in any degree bound to me, I am now willing to release you, provided you wish it; while, on the other hand, I am willing, and even anxious to bind you faster, if I can be convinced that it will, in any considerable degree, add to your happiness.[78]

He was surprised and mortified that she turned him down and ended their relationship shortly after this ham-handed, half-hearted proposal of marriage. Later he wrote about this episode in a very candid letter to Eliza Browning, dated April 1, 1838:

My vanity was deeply wounded by the reflection, that I had so long been too stupid to discover her intentions... that she whom I had taught myself to believe no body else would have, had actually rejected me with all my supposed greatness; and to cap the whole, I then for the first time, began to suspect that I was really a little in love with her.... Others have been made fools of by the girls; but this can never be with truth said of me. I most emphatically, in this instance, made a fool of myself. I have now come to the conclusion never to think of marrying; and for this reason; I can never be satisfied with anyone who would be block head enough to have me.[79]

---

[78] Abraham Lincoln, *Speeches and Writings*, I, p. 20. Quoted in Burlingame, *Abraham Lincoln: A Life*, I, pp. 171–2.
[79] Abraham Lincoln, *Speeches and Writings*, I, p. 39.

Burlingame questions whether Lincoln cooled immediately toward Mary Owens after her return to Springfield because of her physical appearance. He thinks that Lincoln's account of his relationship with Mary Owens in his earlier letter to Eliza Browning is inaccurate and motivated by an attempt to ease his wounded vanity. According to Burlingame, the correspondence between Lincoln and Mary Owens after her return to Springfield shows that he was very fond of her, but was stung by her frequent criticisms of his ungentlemanly ways and lack of social graces. He says that Lincoln began to back away from his engagement to her only after she wounded him repeatedly on account of his oafishness and poor manners.[80] Burlingame's interpretation puts Lincoln in a considerably better light than Lincoln's own account of things in his letter to Eliza Browning, which suggests that he cooled toward Mary mainly on account of her looks.

Mary Owens *was* very put off by Lincoln's poor manners and lack of social graces. She wrote,

Mr Lincoln was deficient in those little links which make up the great chain of woman[']s happiness, at least it was so in my case; not that I believed it proceeded from a lack of goodness of heart, but his training had been different from mine, hence there was not that congeniality which would have otherwise existed.[81]

This supports Burlingame's interpretation. His interpretation is quite possible, but I think it more likely that Lincoln's letter to Eliza Browning should be taken at face value and that we conclude that his dissatisfaction with Mary's appearance caused him to cool toward her.

5. *What Do Lincoln's Romantic Relationships and Marriage Reveal about His Character?* Although he had

---

[80] Burlingame, *Abraham Lincoln: A Life*, I, p. 169–170.
[81] Wilson and Davis, *Herndon's Informants*, p. 256.

great self-confidence about most matters, the young Lincoln was very unsure of himself around eligible women (especially eligible women who were part of the polite society he wanted to join) because of his looks and complete lack of social graces.

As a young man, he was awkward, bumbling, and extremely insecure in his relationships with eligible young women. His insecurity was no doubt increased by the fact that Springfield was a very difficult place for a young man to find a wife: men of marriageable age outnumbered women of marriageable age by a ratio of 2.6 to 1 in the 1840s.[82] So he knew that he could not afford to be too choosy. He desperately wanted love and marriage, but was quite inept in pursuing them.

His courtship of Mary Todd and of Mary Owens and his indecision about marrying them reflected considerable ambivalence about marriage and his lack of confidence in his dealings with women. His relationship with these two women also seemed to reflect an overcommitment to keeping his promises and resolutions come what may, even to the extent of marrying badly.[83]

But his conduct during his marriage also strongly confirmed the image of him as kind, magnanimous, forbearing, and forgiving. More than anything else, his unhappy marriage showed his strength and force of will in accomplishing the things he did as president under extremely difficult circumstances. His achievements as president are all the more impressive when one contemplates the extreme difficulty of his personal life and the crushing workload he bore. His wife was a serious hindrance to him during his time as president, particularly after Willie's tragic death and her carriage accident.

---

[82] Winkle, *Abraham and Mary Lincoln*, p. 37.
[83] See Burlingame, *The Inner World of Abraham Lincoln*, p. 135.

But, on the understanding of Lincoln's marriage that we get from Herndon and Burlingame, we might also say that enduring such horrible treatment from his wife showed that he was lacking in proper dignity and self-respect. (Some might say that he showed a similar lack of dignity and self-respect by enduring so much disrespect from General McClellan [see Chapter 7.I.2, note 23].)

Lincoln's marriage suggests two other possible criticisms of his character. The first criticism is that he entered into a relatively loveless marriage that was likely to bring unhappiness to himself and Mary because of his ambition and desire to advance in society. The second criticism is that he neglected his family and sacrificed the welfare of his sons to his career and political ambitions by spending so much time away from home. He gave Mary complete authority over domestic matters.[84] I believe that he should not have left his boys alone under Mary's control so much or allowed her so much authority over them. A servant who worked in the Lincoln home, Margaret Ryan, reported that Mary whipped her son Robert a good deal.[85] There are also reports of Mary abusing her youngest son Tad. She "held a private-strapping party" with her youngest son Tad, after he fell into a mud puddle.[86] Tad's White House playmate Mary Pinkerton recalled that Mary "had a terrible temper" and that she punished Tad severely.[87]

It is not clear what we should say about the first criticism, because we do not adequately know Lincoln's motives for marrying Mary, nor do we know the extent of his knowledge of her temper and other faults before they married. The

[84] Ibid., pp. 318–23.
[85] Wilson and Davis, *Herndon's Informants*, p. 597; also see Burlingame, *Abraham Lincoln: A Life*, I, p. 203.
[86] Burlingame, *Abraham Lincoln: A Life*, I, p. 203.
[87] Ibid., I, p. 204.

second criticism is more serious. Lincoln's career and political activity kept him away from home a great deal of time, particularly during the late 1850s. Normally that kind of ambition is contrary to virtue and the demands of morality. But Lincoln needed to be away from home and to travel on the circuit court to earn a good living for his family. Mary said that his frequent absences troubled her and that she could have loved him more if he had been at home more, but she also pressured him to earn a good living. His extensive political travels during the late 1850s were justified by the great good he did as president. After the senate race in 1858 made him a national figure, and after his extremely successful speaking tour in the East in early 1860, it was likely that he could do great good for the world. As president, Lincoln spent almost all of his time living with his family. During this period, he was an extremely loving and attentive father to his two youngest sons, Willie and Tad, and spent a great deal of time with them. His oldest son, Robert, was away at college during most of this time, and their relationship was more distant and less affectionate. Robert did not know his father as well as he would have liked.[88]

Lincoln can be justly criticized for frequently staying away from home on weekends while traveling on the judicial circuit after the expansion of railroads made it possible for him to return home on weekends, as did most of the other members of the court. No doubt, Mary's temper drove him away, but he should have returned home more frequently for the sake of his children. It is understandable that Lincoln would try to keep peace within his marriage by ceding Mary control over their home and their children, but he went too far and should have done more to protect his sons from their mother's temper.

---

[88] Burlingame, *The Inner World of Abraham Lincoln*, pp. 60–1.

II. Was Lincoln a Bad Son?

Lincoln had a very strained relationship with his father, Thomas Lincoln. He never introduced his father to his family during the eight years that Thomas Lincoln lived after Lincoln's marriage. He never brought his family to visit his parents or invited his father and stepmother to visit him in Springfield. Thomas Lincoln lived near Charleston, Illinois, less than one hundred miles from Springfield, but never met Lincoln's children, who were his only biological grandchildren. However, Lincoln himself regularly visited his father and stepmother, although he did not stay with them when he did so.[89] He also did much to help them financially (see Chapter 7.III).

The letter Lincoln wrote to his father while Thomas Lincoln was on his deathbed has been the subject of much comment and criticism by his biographers. It was a reply to letters from his stepbrother, John Johnston, reporting that Thomas Lincoln was near death and wanted to see his son before he died. Lincoln wrote back saying that his business[90] prevented him from leaving home and added that, in addition to concerns about his business, he needed to stay with his wife because she was sick in bed after having given birth to Willie Lincoln three weeks earlier. His letter continues:

I sincerely hope that Father may yet recover his health. . . . Say to him that if we could meet now, it is doubtful whether it would not be more painful than pleasant; but that if it be his lot to go now; he will soon have a joyous meeting with loved ones gone before; and where the rest of us, through the help of God, hope ere-long to join them.[91]

---

[89] Ibid., p. 41.

[90] Had he gone to see his father, Lincoln would have been absent from cases being heard by the Illinois Supreme Court and the U.S. Circuit Court. "But if he had truly wanted to go, he could have entrusted his cases to his partner or asked for postponements," Donald, *Lincoln*, p. 153.

[91] Abraham Lincoln, *Speeches and Writings*, I, p. 256.

His statement that "it is doubtful whether it [a final visit from Lincoln to see his father] would not be more painful than pleasant," seems cold and hurtful, because it implies that, on balance, he had an unfavorable view about their relationship.

However, the background to this letter puts it in a better light. In 1849, Lincoln received several letters (one from his stepbrother John Johnston) saying that Thomas Lincoln was dying and desperately wanted to see his son again. These letters sounded a false alarm: Thomas Lincoln was not near death. At great inconvenience to himself, Lincoln visited his father and put off a planned trip to Washington, D.C. This visit to his father might have cost him the appointment as commissioner of the General Land Office, something he badly wanted at the time. So his initial reaction to the letter he received from Johnston in the winter of 1850–1 was to think that "his stepbrother was crying wolf again."[92]

Lincoln's treatment of his father does not give us reason to lower substantially our overall assessment of his character. He had many reasons to dislike his father. A. H. Chapman, who married into the Hanks family (Lincoln's relatives on his mother's side), said that Thomas was unkind to his son and preferred his stepson, John Johnston, to Abe. Chapman did add that later, when Abe became a prominent person in the world, "the old man appeared to be very proud of him."[93] According to Chapman, "Thomas Lincoln could treat his son with 'great barbarity.'"[94] Lincoln's cousin Dennis Hanks, who grew up with Lincoln, reported "that Thomas Lincoln would sometimes 'slash' his boy for reading instead of doing chores."[95] Hanks also said, "When strangers

[92] Donald, *Lincoln*, p. 153.
[93] Wilson and Davis, *Herndon's Informants*, p. 134; also see Donald, *Lincoln*, p. 33.
[94] Burlingame, *The Inner World of Abraham Lincoln*, p. 38.
[95] Ibid.

would ride along and up to his father's fence, Abe always, through pride and to tease his father, would be sure to ask the stranger the first question, for which his father would sometimes knock him with a rod."[96] Thomas Lincoln insisted on his prerogative to be the first person in his family to talk to strangers who passed by the farm. According to David Donald, "when Abraham as a little boy thrust himself into adult conversations, Thomas sometimes struck him."[97] Lincoln and his father clashed over religion, and Thomas was offended by the way his son often mimicked and parodied sermons that he heard in church.[98]

Thomas Lincoln also actively thwarted his son's attempts to get an education and regarded reading and education as a complete waste of time. Thomas sometimes hid Abe's books or threw them away.[99] He wanted to forbid Abe from doing any reading at all and only permitted him to continue reading after his wife, Sarah Bush Johnston Lincoln, intervened and changed his mind.[100] In addition, Lincoln greatly resented the fact that his father hired him out to work, often very heavy backbreaking work, for neighbors and then took all the money that he earned. He was legally required to surrender his earnings to his father until he was twenty-one. Later, he said that he used to be a slave, and in his writings and speeches about slavery he repeatedly emphasized how slavery deprived people of the fruits of their labor, just as his father had deprived him.[101] Although he was an extremely forgiving and magnanimous person, his father had hurt him too deeply in too many ways for Abe to be fully reconciled with him.

---

[96] Ibid.
[97] Donald, *Lincoln*, p. 32.
[98] Ibid., p. 33.
[99] Burlingame, *The Inner World of Abraham Lincoln*, p. 39.
[100] Wilson and Davis, *Herndon's Lincoln*, p. 35; Burlingame, *The Inner World of Abraham Lincoln*, p. 39; Burlingame, *Abraham Lincoln: A Life*, I, p. 28.
[101] Burlingame, *The Inner World of Abraham Lincoln*, Chapter 2.

Lincoln's treatment of his stepmother, Sarah Bush John-ston Lincoln, provides stronger grounds for criticism. She was, by all accounts, including his, a wonderful person to whom he was deeply indebted. In his own way, he loved her very much and was very grateful to her. One of the last things he did before he left Illinois for Washington in 1861 was to pay her a very emotional visit. But why did he never introduce her to his family during the eighteen years of his marriage that he lived in Illinois? Why did he never invite her to his home? If the principal reason for this is that he was ashamed of his poor and uneducated stepmother, that would speak very poorly of him.[102] But this seems not to have been the case. There is evidence that Mary was adamantly opposed to having her sons meet Sarah Bush Johnston Lincoln and that her husband acquiesced to this demand to keep the peace at home. Burlingame recounts this as follows:

When Eleanore Gridley interviewed neighbors and friends of Lin-coln, she "found verified evidence that Mrs. Lincoln would neither permit her children to see the old stepmother, of whom Lincoln was fond, nor allow her to visit them at her home...." According to Herndon, "Mrs. Lincoln held the Hanks tribe in contempt and the Lincoln family generally – Thomas Lincoln & his good old wife.... Thomas Lincoln and his good old wife were never in this city [Springfield]."[103]

Similarly, when Lincoln promised his stepbrother, John John-ston, that Johnston's adolescent son, Abraham, could stay with him in Springfield in order to go to school there and

---

[102] If this were true, it would mean that he was very much like the character Pip in Dickens' *Great Expectations*. Pip was an orphan under the care of his cruel sister and her very kind and loving husband Joe. Pip was greatly indebted to Joe, but once he came into his fortune and started to associate with "gentlemen," he was ashamed of Joe and his humble background. Pip snubbed Joe when Joe came to visit and later repented bitterly of this and begged Joe's forgiveness.

[103] Burlingame, *Abraham Lincoln: A Life*, I, p. 207.

"get a fair start in the world,"[104] Mary Lincoln "refused furiously."[105]

It is still arguable that Lincoln should have insisted on having his boys meet his stepmother, but we should not fault him greatly for trying to keep peace in his very difficult and unhappy marriage. People often do morally questionable things to keep peace with their spouses, and there are very serious moral questions about what it is permissible for people to do in such circumstances. I leave this question open in the present case. It seems to me to be something about which reasonable people can disagree.

Conclusion and Transition to Chapter 10

Lincoln had a very troubled marriage. He had a cold and distant relationship with his father, and he was frequently absent as a father. There are thus grounds to criticize him as a husband, father, and son. But none of these criticisms reveals deep flaws of character. He was a very loving father, despite his frequent absences from home, and his achievements as a public figure are all the more impressive because of the great difficulties of his personal life.

Lincoln was an extraordinarily good human being in many important respects. However, some claim that he was a racist. I turn now to this criticism.

---

[104] Ibid., p. 812, n321; Lincoln, *Speeches and Writings*, I, p. 258.
[105] Burlingame, *Abraham Lincoln: A Life*, I, p. 207.

10

Was Lincoln a Racist?

Lincoln was an extremely good human being in many important respects. However, some claim that he was a racist. I turn now to this criticism of his character. Because my conclusions are complex and cannot be stated simply, it will be helpful to begin by summarizing them.

Was Lincoln a racist? The short answer is that it depends on what we mean by racism and what times in his life we are talking about.

Racism is a contested concept that is defined differently by different people. The most salient definition for understanding Lincoln's time and place is that racism is the belief that certain races of people are inferior to others and that it is permissible for members of superior races to exploit and enslave members of inferior races. Most defenders of American slavery in the nineteenth century held this belief.[1]

---

[1] In the antebellum South, people discussed whether "slavery in the abstract" was a defensible view. This view justified slavery not on the grounds of the alleged inferiority of slaves, but on the grounds that it benefited the slaves themselves. Few, if any, people endorsed making slaves of whites, but many common arguments in defense of slavery claimed or implied that many white workers in the North would have been better off and better treated if they had been slaves on Southern plantations. See Fox-Genovese and Genovese, *Slavery in Black and White*, pp. 1–4 and 289–93.

Two other important definitions are the following: "racism is racially motivated ill will toward members of a certain race of people," and "racism is racially motivated indifference to the welfare of members of a certain race of people." Being a racist in any of these three senses is a serious moral failing. It is clear that Lincoln was never a racist according to any of these three definitions. He never thought that certain races were justified in exploiting or enslaving other races of people, and he was never hostile to or indifferent to the welfare or interests of blacks or other races. There is considerable evidence to the contrary.

Racism is also sometimes defined as the belief that certain races are morally or intellectually superior to other races. Being a racist in this fourth sense is a matter of having certain beliefs. It is debatable whether mere beliefs can constitute traits of character, and it is also unclear whether or not Lincoln was a racist in this fourth sense.

For the purposes of assessing Lincoln's character, we need to pay particular attention to yet another (fifth) definition of racism that I take from J. L. A. Garcia: to be a racist is to be *disrespectful of (or inadequately respectful of)* a certain race of people on account of their race, or to be *inadequately concerned with the welfare of* a certain race of people on account of their race. There is strong evidence that Lincoln was a racist in this sense during most of his political career, but we need to make an important qualification. In certain respects, he had a very great concern for the welfare of black people – he was very concerned for their happiness, their freedom, and their right to enjoy the fruits of their labor. His racism (in Garcia's sense) was combined with very significant elements of virtuous benevolence and concern for the welfare of the people who were the objects of his racist attitudes. Lincoln's racial attitudes also changed during his time as president. It is unclear that he was a racist according to Garcia's definition at the end of his life.

Lincoln was very clearly not a racist in any senses of the term in which racism is a grave moral failing. Even on the least charitable interpretation of his racism that is at all defensible, this vice was too mixed with very virtuous benevolence for the same people who were the objects of his racist attitudes to detract *greatly* from the goodness of his other virtues. He was, on balance, a very good and morally virtuous person, even if he had some limited racist vices. But now we need to consider the details.

I. The Concept of Racism

The word "racism" did not exist prior to the twentieth century and was not commonly used before the 1930s.[2] Because "racism" was not a word or concept employed by Lincoln or any of his contemporaries, some object that it is a case of "presentism" to apply present-day moral concepts to people in the past who did not think in those terms. But many of our present-day moral concepts clearly *do apply* to people in the past, even if they did not wield those concepts or think in terms of them. Genghis Khan and his near descendants did not have the concept of a moral right, but nonetheless, they surely violated the moral rights of the millions of people they killed. But an important truth still underlies the objection about presentism. When we apply moral concepts to people who did not themselves possess or understand those concepts, we must be cautious about the conclusions we draw. The people in question lacked knowledge of relevant moral considerations and moral arguments that those concepts enable *us* to understand. The concept of a moral right is a product of the Western philosophical tradition and did not emerge clearly before the work of John Locke. Genghis Khan and the other Mongolian conquerors who followed him did not

---

[2] Frederickson, *Racism*, pp. 156 and 158.

possess this concept. They did not take themselves to be violating people's moral rights (and they *could not* have taken themselves to be violating people's moral rights).

Racism is what philosophers call a "thick normative concept" – it is a concept with both descriptive meaning and evaluative meaning. The descriptive meaning of "racism" consists in the fact that it applies or does not apply to someone on the basis of her having certain non-normative properties (e.g., being someone who thinks that certain races are inherently more intelligent than others). "Racism" also has evaluative meaning, in that most people understand it to be a term of disapprobation or even great disapprobation. Our ordinary concepts of virtues and vices are clear examples of thick normative concepts. The words "generous" and "honest" express favorable evaluations of the persons and actions to which they are applied. There are also clear descriptive criteria for using such terms. It is a mistake to apply them to things that do not satisfy those criteria. For example, I am clearly mistaken if I call someone generous who never willingly gives anything of value (including time or effort) to anyone else, even though that person has an abundance of wealth and free time and many clear opportunities to help people in need.

1. *The Definition of Racism.* Racism is defined in many different ways and the differences between these definitions are very important for our purposes. The following nine definitions of racism draw on important work in contemporary philosophy.

1. Racism is the belief that some races of people are morally or intellectually superior to others and that this superiority is due to inherited biological differences. (I dub this "belief-racism.")[3]

---

[3] This is similar to the first definition in *The New Shorter Oxford English Dictionary* – "Belief in, adherence to, advocacy of, the theory that all members of each race possess characteristics, abilities, qualities, etc. specific to that race,

2. Racism is the belief that some races of people are morally or intellectually superior to others, that this superiority is due to inherited biological differences, and that discrimination against the "inferior" groups is justified for that reason. (I call this "belief-discrimination racism.")[4]

3. Racism is the belief that some races of people are morally or intellectually superior to others, that this superiority is due to inherited biological differences, and that members of "superior" groups are justified in exploiting or using members of the "inferior" groups for the benefit of the superior groups. (I call this "belief-exploitation racism.")[5]

4. Racism is the combination of (A) the belief that some races of people are morally or intellectually superior to others and that this superiority is due to inherited biological differences and (B) hatred and/or ill will for those races of people one believes to be inferior. (I call this "belief-malevolent racism.")[6]

esp. distinguishing it as inferior or superior to another race or races" – and to Boxill's definition in his "Racism and Related Issues," p. 1056: "Racism involves several assumptions. Prominent among these assumptions are that human beings are divided into races; that some of these races are morally, intellectually or physically superior to others; and that this superiority is due to inherited biological differences." Contrast 1 with the following much wider definition of racism (racism 1'):

1'. Racism is the belief that some races of people are morally, intellectually, athletically, musically, or artistically superior to other races (or that some races are superior to others in physical beauty) and that this superiority is due to inherited biological differences.

4 Compare this to the second definition in *The New Shorter Oxford English Dictionary*: "prejudice discrimination or antagonism based on this" (based on the belief mentioned in the first definition).

5 This closely follows Albert Mosley's definition in "Racism [Addendum]," p. 227. Mosley's definition is as follows: "Racism is the view that (1) the human species is composed of different racial groups, (2) these groups are arranged from least to most superior, and (3) superior groups have the right to use inferior groups for the benefit of the superior group."

6 *A Digressive Note on the Meaning of the Word "Superior" in Definitions 1–4.* Arguably, believing that one race of people has *slightly* greater moral

5. Racism is hatred or ill will for certain races of people on account of their race. (I call this "malevolent racism.")

6. Racism is indifference to the welfare of certain races of people on account of their race. (I call this "cold-hearted racism.")

or intellectual genetic endowments than another race is not tantamount to believing that it is *superior to* the other race. In order to be a racist in senses 1, 2, 3, or 4, it is arguable that one must believe that some races of people have *substantially greater* biologically inherited intelligence/moral virtue than other races.

Also, what should we say about people who believe that one race is genetically inferior to other races in some respects and genetically superior to other races in other respects? Is this racism? Is one a racist if one believes that all races, on balance, have equal (but different) genetic endowments?

Harriet Beecher Stowe wrote,

The Negro race is confessedly more simple, docile, child-like and affectionate, than other races; and hence the divine graces of love and faith, when in-breathed by the Holy Spirt, find their natural temperament a more congenial atmosphere (*A Key to Uncle Tom's Cabin*, p. 26).

(This suggests that Stowe thought that Negroes were in some respects inferior to and in other respects superior to and morally better than members of other races.)

Horace Mann said,

The blacks as a race, I believe to be less aggressive and predatory than the whites, more forgiving, and *generally* not capable of the white man's tenacity and terribleness of revenge. In fine, I suppose the almost universal opinion to be, that in intellect the blacks are inferior to the whites (Burlingame, *Abraham Lincoln: A Life*, I, p. 525).

Mann seemed to think that blacks were (in some important ways) morally superior to whites, but also intellectually inferior to whites.

In "Notes on the State of Virginia," Thomas Jefferson said things along these lines, though he seemed to think that whites were quite superior to blacks, on balance. He said that both blacks and whites find white women and women of mixed race to be more beautiful than black women (Jefferson, *Writings*, pp. 264–5). He said that "in music they [blacks] are more generally gifted than whites with accurate ears for tune and time," and "it appears to me, that in memory they [blacks] are equal to the whites; in reason much inferior" (p. 266). He also said that he believed blacks to be equal to whites in matters "of the heart" (p. 269). Jefferson stressed that these last two judgments were conjectures in need of further evidence: "Whether further observation will or will not verify the conjecture, that nature has been less bountiful to them in the endowments of the head, I believe that in those of the heart she will be found to have done them justice" (pp. 268–9).

7. Racism is inadequate concern for the welfare of certain races of people (short of ill will or indifference to their welfare) on account of their race. (I call this "inadequate-benevolence racism.")[7]

8. Racism is disrespect for certain races of people on account of their race. (I call this "disrespect racism.")

9. Racism is inadequate respect (short of disrespect) for certain races of people on account of their race. (I call this "inadequate-respect racism.")[8]

Racists of types 5–9 may or may not be aware of their racism, and they may or may not reflectively endorse their racist attitudes and think them justified. Some racists of types 5–9 think that their attitudes are unjustified and consciously try to alter them.

Being a racist in senses 1–4 requires that one have certain factual beliefs, but being a racist in senses 5–9 does not.[9]

---

[7] I take definitions 5, 6, and 7 from J. L. A. Garcia's paper "The Heart of Racism," though he does not state them as separate definitions, as I do. Garcia writes,

> My proposal is that we conceive of racism as fundamentally a vicious kind of racially based disregard for the welfare of certain people. In its most vicious form, it is a hatred, ill will, directed against a person or persons on account of their assigned race. In its derivative form, one is a racist when one does not care at all or does not care enough (i.e., as much as morality requires) or does not care in the right ways about people assigned to a certain racial group, where this disregard is based on racial classification (p. 6).

[8] I take definitions 7, 8, and 9 from Garcia's paper, "Three Sites for Racism: Social Structures, Valuings, and Vice" (pp. 43–4).

[9] *Scholarly Digression.* This difference parallels Appiah's distinction between intrinsic and extrinsic racism. Roughly, Appiah would classify people who are racists in my senses 2, 3, or 4 as extrinsic racists. He would classify people who are racists in senses 5–9 and who *do not* base their racism on factual beliefs about the characteristics of racial groups, as intrinsic racists. Appiah writes,

> Extrinsic racists make moral distinctions between different races because they believe that the racial essence entails certain morally relevant qualities. The basis for the extrinsic racists' discrimination between people is their belief that members of different races differ in respects that *warrant* the differential treatment – respects, like honesty and courage or intelligence, that are uncontroversially

Definition 5 ("malevolent racism") underscores the fact that one could be very hostile or antagonistic to members of certain racial groups without believing they are biologically inferior to other people and that one could have racist hostility toward racial groups one regards as in some ways superior to or more successful than others.[10]

Some people hold that certain races have more desirable characteristics than other groups, but think that those differences are rooted in cultural or environmental factors rather than inherited biological differences. These kinds of attitudes and beliefs do not count as "racist" according to any of the forgoing definitions. However, such beliefs are often characterized as racist. For example, in the 1960s Daniel Patrick Moynihan was widely denounced and called a racist for his description of the breakdown of black families, even though he did not attribute it to heritable biological characteristics of black people.

There is a large and growing philosophical literature that debates the merits of alternative definitions of racism. Garcia thinks that the word "racism" refers to a single concept with a nature or essence that we should endeavor to discover and elucidate. Lawrence Blum, in contrast, claims that "racism" is a looser term that has several different meanings.[11] I do not enter into these debates here, but instead examine different

---

held ... to be acceptable as a basis for treating people differently. Evidence that there are no such differences in morally relevant characteristics ... should thus lead people out of their racism if it is purely extrinsic (Appiah, *In My Father's House*, pp. 13–14).

[I]*ntrinsic racists* ... are people who discriminate morally between members of different races, because they believe that each race has a different moral status, quite independent of the moral characteristics entailed by its racial essence. ... For an intrinsic racist, no amount of evidence that a member of another race is capable of great moral, intellectual, or cultural achievements, or has characteristics that, in members of one's own race, would make them admirable or attractive, offers any ground for treating that person as she would treat similarly endowed members of her own race (Ibid., pp. 14–15).

[10] See Blum, *I'm not a Racist, But...*, pp. 10–11.

[11] Blum, "What Do Accounts of 'Racism' Do?," p. 75.

senses of racism corresponding to these nine definitions and ask whether Lincoln was a racist in any or all of these different senses of the term.

We can ask whether he was a racist according to a particular definition of racism without assuming that the definition in question is or is not the correct definition of racism and without assuming that there is or is not a single preferred definition of racism. This approach is helpful and illuminating for discussing his character because, as I argue, several of these definitions are morally salient. My list of definitions is sufficiently long and representative of the literature that all or most of what is morally objectionable about racism is mentioned in at least one of these definitions.[12]

2. *The Moral Salience of These Definitions.* Some definitions of racism are more morally salient than others, and some definitions are more morally salient for thinking about Lincoln's life and character than others.

Beliefs about racial differences often cause people to have morally objectionable attitudes and perform morally wrong actions. In addition, people can often be faulted morally for coming to hold such beliefs. But such beliefs themselves, independently of their origins or consequences, cannot contribute much, if at all, to the goodness or badness of one's character.

Is being a belief-discrimination racist (2) or a belief-exploitation racist (3) tantamount to possessing a trait of character or a moral vice? If we count any belief or attitude that strongly influences one's motivations and actions as a

---

[12] But unavoidably, I have been selective in choosing to focus on certain definitions and not others. I have chosen definitions that are prominent in the philosophical literature. Some of these definitions reflect common popular understandings of racism, and some are important in that they help explain why racism is a term of condemnation or disapprobation. Because I am primarily concerned with assessing Lincoln's character and criticisms of his character, I do not speak to the literature on "institutional racism," which does not shed much light on his personal character.

trait of character, then racism in senses 2 or 3 counts (or at least can count) as a trait of character and moral vice. However, Aristotle's theory of virtues and vices ties virtues and vices to emotions and affects. Aristotle defines moral virtue as a mean in both actions and emotions:

Our discussion has established 1. that moral virtue is a mean and in what sense it is a mean, 2. that it is a mean between two vices, one of which is marked by excess and the other by deficiency.... 3. that it is a mean in that it aims at the medium in emotions and action (*Nicomachean Ethics*, Ostwald translation, 1109a).

According to Aristotle, having a moral virtue involves hitting the mean in both actions and emotions. Racism in senses 2 and 3 is simply a matter of having certain beliefs, albeit false and very harmful moral beliefs, and racism of these kinds alone cannot be considered moral vices on Aristotle's view. Clearly, racism in sense 4, 5, 6, 7, 8, or 9 is a moral vice on any reasonable understanding of the nature of character and vices.[13]

Other things being equal, belief-discrimination racism is a greater moral failing than belief racism alone. Other things being equal, belief-exploitation racism is morally worse than belief-discrimination racism, because it justifies worse injustices. Making slaves of a certain race of people is much more unjust than excluding them from certain activities/opportunities. This difference (the difference between 2

---

[13] For our present purposes, we need to try to imagine being a racist in senses 2 or 3 without also being a racist in sense 4, 5, 6, 7, 8 or 9. This is very difficult. It is especially difficult to imagine a belief-exploitation racist who is not very disrespectful of or very inadequately concerned with the welfare of those he claims to be justified in exploiting. A defender of an Aristotelian account of character can (and should) say that the racism of the great majority of people who are racists in senses 2 and 3 is a moral vice and that the reason why the racism of those people is a moral vice is that they are also racists in senses 4, 5, 6, 7, 8, or 9.

and 3) may be a matter of degree, but it is morally significant nonetheless. I should also add that belief-discrimination
racism (2) is an *extremely broad* category that could involve
endorsing moderately unjust types of racial discrimination,
or alternatively, it could involve endorsing extremely unjust
kinds of discrimination that fall short of racially based slavery. Being a racist in senses 4, 5, or 6, counts much more
against the goodness of one's character than being a racist in
sense 7 or 9. Ill will or indifference to the welfare of others
on account of their race (5 or 6) is more at odds with the
demands of morality than insufficient benevolence or insufficient respect for others on account of their race (7 or 9).
Other things being equal, it is much worse and much more
vicious to despise or disrespect someone on account of her
race than to inadequately respect her for that reason. Other
things being equal, it is much worse and much more contrary to virtue to have ill will for someone or be indifferent
to her welfare on account of her race than to be inadequately
concerned to promote her welfare on account of her race.
But it is open to debate whether malice or indifference to the
welfare of others is worse than being positively disrespectful
of them (see 10.VI). Still I am inclined to think that racism
of types 4 and 5 (belief-malevolent racism and malevolent
racism) are the worst kinds of racism, because racists of these
kinds are malevolent and aim directly at the bad of many
people (Garcia agrees; see the later discussion).

My overall conclusions are these. Lincoln was very clearly
not a racist in those senses of the term in which racism is a
grave moral failing. Lincoln was *clearly* not a racist according
to definitions 3–6; he never thought that whites were justified
in exploiting or enslaving members of other races, and he
was never hostile or indifferent to the welfare of any race
of people. However, there is a case for thinking that he was
a racist of types 1 (belief-racism), 2 (belief-discrimination
racism), 7 (inadequate benevolence), 8 (disrespect), and/or

9 (inadequate respect) during certain periods of his life. So I focus mostly on these definitions. The case for thinking that Lincoln was a racist of type 7, 8, and/or 9 is stronger than the case for thinking that he was a racist of type 1 or 2. Therefore, definitions 7, 8, and 9 are particularly important for assessing his character.

> 3. *Garcia's Definition and His View that Racism is a Moral Vice.* Because I take definitions 7–9 from Garcia, his views merit further discussion here. In this section I explain his reasons for thinking that racism is a moral vice and why his account does not commit him to the controversial view that biologically distinct races of people actually exist. I also argue that applying Garcia's definition (and my definitions 7 and 9) is often very difficult and that in some cases doing so requires answering difficult and controversial issues in ethical theory.

Garcia defines racism as follows:

Racism, at its core, then, consists in racial disregard, including disrespect, or most gravely, ill will. Racially based or racially informed disregard (or ill will) is an indifference (or opposition) to another's welfare on account of the racial group to which she is assigned. Since, so conceived, racism is primarily a matter of what a person does or does not wish, will, and want for others in light of their race – the contents of her will, broadly conceived – I call it a volitional concept of racism.[14]

According to Garcia, racial disregard includes insufficient concern or "insufficient good will" for other people on account of their race.[15] This account explains why racism can be conscious or unconscious and also why the term "racism"

---

[14] J.L.A. Garcia, "Three Sites for Racism: Social Structures, Valuings, and Vice," pp. 43–4. Garcia's most recent definition encompasses my definitions 5–9. If one is racist in any of these senses, then one is a racist according to Garcia's most recent definition.

[15] Ibid., n6, pp. 43–4.

is properly pejorative.[16] Garcia's account is "volitional" in that it holds that racism is "a matter of what a person does or does not wish, will, and want for others in light of their race."[17] It makes perfect sense of the idea that racism is a moral vice that is directly opposed to the cardinal virtues of benevolence and justice: "The ill will or disregard that constitutes racism is inherently contrary to the moral virtues of benevolence and justice, and often to others as well."[18]

Many question whether the concept of race and different races of people is consistent with our best understanding of human biology. If races do not exist, then it seems that we cannot define racism in terms of beliefs or attitudes about different races of people. Garcia addresses this issue and says that we can still define racism in terms of *racial classifications*:

Racists are *against* those assigned to a certain race. Notice that I do not say simply those *of* a certain race: I leave open the vexed question of whether race is real. What matters is that racial assignments are real.[19]

If races are not real, then my definitions of racism can be revised along similar lines in terms of people's racial classifications.

Now we come to a difficult but important point. Given knowledge of relevant facts, it is generally a straightforward matter to determine whether or not someone is racist in senses 1, 2, 3, or 4, although there can be borderline cases for each of these definitions. The same holds for definitions 5 and 6. Welfare is a normative concept and philosophers debate its nature, but given relevant factual information, it is often a straightforward matter to determine whether someone is

[16] Ibid.
[17] Ibid., p. 44.
[18] Ibid.
[19] Ibid.

malevolent toward another person or indifferent to her welfare. If I go to great lengths to kill someone or inflict great
bodily injury and suffering on her and do not do so as a means
to anything else, then I have ill will for her (i.e., I desire that
she be harmed). If I refuse to make the slightest sacrifice to
prevent you from dying or suffering grave bodily injury, and
do not refuse to do so as a means to anything else, then I am
either indifferent to your welfare or else have ill will for you.
If, other things being equal, I have no preference between (1)
things that would greatly harm your happiness and welfare,
(2) things that would greatly enhance your happiness and
welfare, and (3) things that would not affect your happiness
or welfare, then I am indifferent to your welfare.

But applying definition 7 (inadequate benevolence) to cases
is not a simple straightforward matter, and in some instances,
we cannot know how to apply it without having answers to
difficult and controversial questions in ethical theory. How
much benevolence do we owe others? Surely we owe everyone (or almost everyone) some measure of benevolence so
that indifference to the welfare of others on account of their
race or racial classification is clearly a serious moral vice.
But the notion of "adequate concern" is very much open to
debate: there are deep questions in ethical theory about this
concept. Some people, including utilitarians and many Christians who take seriously Christ's command to "love your
neighbor as yourself" and his many admonitions to care for
the poor, think that we owe others, even strangers, a great
deal of benevolence. Others, including many libertarians, do
not think that we have much of an obligation to help others. Libertarians and utilitarians often disagree about what
counts as "adequate concern" for other people's welfare, and
those disagreements are sometimes relevant to questions of
whether someone counts as a racist according to definition 7.

The concepts of respect and adequate respect used in definitions 8 and 9 need much more unpacking and explanation

than I can give them here. What is respect? Why do we owe it to others? What counts as having/showing adequate respect for others? What kind of moral failing is involved in not respecting someone or not respecting someone adequately? Why is failing to respect others (or respect them adequately) on account of their race a moral vice?

These questions notwithstanding, there are still some clear cases of disrespect for people on account of their race. Lincoln's use of the word "nigger" and his strongly stated aversion to interracial marriage (he said that he was "horrified" at the thought of it) were clearly disrespectful of blacks and people of mixed race.

These questions about the nature of respect and what counts as adequate concern for the welfare of members of a race of people are not objections to definitions 7–9 or Garcia's definition of racism. For better or worse,[20] our concept of racism implies that fully explaining the concept and fully explaining when it does and does not apply are difficult, complicated matters that sometimes compel us to address fundamental questions in ethical theory.

4. *The Implications of Some Recent Work in Psychology for the Concept of Racism*. Recent work in moral psychology suggests that actual virtues and vices possessed

---

[20] *Digressive Footnote for Philosophers*. Perhaps it *is* for the worse. It seems likely that there are cases in which whether or not someone is a racist in senses 7 or 9, inadequate benevolence/respect, depends on the answers to controversial questions in ethical theory. But, because there will be at least some cases in which there are no clear descriptive criteria for applying definitions 7 and 9, racism in those senses is a concept that will often be difficult to apply and is likely to be misused and misapplied. Another problem with our existing concept(s) of racism is this. Racism is a term of strong disapprobation, but many take it to be obviously true, or even analytically true, that anyone who believes that one race is inherently more intelligent than another race (or morally superior to another race) is a racist. But it is debatable whether all people who believe that one race is more intelligent or morally better than another race (regardless of their reasons for believing this) are worthy of strong moral disapproval.

by real people are generally narrow or modular; rarely do broad virtue terms such as "honest" and "courageous" describe people without qualification.

Instead many people have narrower modules of these virtues (e.g., being honest in business, being honest in making change from the cash register, being courageous in the face of artillery fire, and being courageous in the face of danger while sailing). These findings are summarized and defended in John Doris's *Lack of Character* and Robert Adams's *A Theory of Virtue*. Here is an important piece of evidence they cite. In a famous study from the 1920s, Hartshorne and May sought to test honesty in schoolchildren. They measured the frequency of lying, cheating, and stealing and correlated them with other variables. Adams writes,

The experimenters found that individual children were fairly consistent, or stable, over time in repeated tests of their honesty or dishonesty, in the *same* type of situation. But they also found, to their surprise, that individual results in *different* types of situations showed low correlations, and thus little cross-situational consistency.[21]

As Adams notes, the English word "honesty" has a very broad meaning. Being honest involves possessing (1) the disposition not to lie or deceive others, (2) the disposition not to cheat in rule-governed activities, and (3) the disposition not to steal from others. These are very disparate dispositions, and there is no reason to think that they are strongly correlated. The Hartshorne-May study would seem to show that it is very rare for people to be consistently honest in all these respects in a wide range of different circumstances. But their study also supports the view that narrower modules of these virtues (e.g., not cheating in sports, not cheating in one's academic work, not lying to one's spouse, not lying

---

[21] Adams, *A Theory of Virtue*, p. 116; also see Doris, *Lack of Character*.

to one's clients, and not stealing from one's employer) are common and reasonably robust in determining our behavior.

Given the evidence for Doris and Adams's views about the narrow modular nature of virtue, it should not be surprising if the vice of racism often turned out to be narrow or modular in the same way. Racism in senses 5, 6, 7, 8, or 9 could be modular in that it involves attitudes directed toward some but not all members of a particular racial group. For example, a person might dislike, disrespect, and have ill will for black men (or young black men), but not other black people.[22] (This kind of modularity might conceivably describe Lincoln late in his life; he seemed to have had considerable respect for black soldiers in the Union Army and educated blacks, though possibly not for other blacks; see 10.V and 10.VI).

The vice of racism in senses 8 or 9 (disrespect or insufficient respect) could be modular in the sense that it could be mixed with virtuous attitudes about the same group of people one disrespects or inadequately respects. For example, someone might disrespect members of a certain race, but also be benevolent toward them. One might even disrespect a certain race of people and yet have virtuous supererogatory concern for the welfare of its members. Alternatively, one might adequately respect a race of people, but not be adequately concerned with their welfare. The distinction between 7, 8, and 9 is important for our purposes, because it is possible that Lincoln was a racist in sense 8 or 9, but not sense 7. There is a case for saying that he was adequately (or more than

---

[22] I take this example from Blum, *I'm not a Racist, But...*, pp. 30–1. He says that this kind of case involves "selective racism." Here is another example of modular racism or selective racism. A person is benevolent to and respectful of most whites, but not poor whites with Southern accents who live in trailer parks. He disdains and dislikes them and calls them "trailer trash," "hillbillies," and "poor white trash." Yet he does not have similar disdain for people of other races who are otherwise similar to these people. (This kind of attitude is freely expressed in many sectors of "polite society.")

adequately) benevolent toward blacks, but that his benevolence was condescending and disrespectful. (This kind of attitude is what Garcia calls "Kiplingesque racism."[23]) If that is correct, Lincoln's attitudes about blacks were a mixture of virtue and vice.

The German theologian and physician Albert Schweitzer is a very interesting person to think about in connection with the distinction between definitions 7, 8, and 9. Clearly, he was an unusually kind and benevolent man who devoted most of his life to helping Africans, and he gave up many great personal goods in order to do this. His benevolence for Africans was supererogatory and extremely virtuous. However, although he was a strong critic of European colonialism, he was paternalistic and condescending to Africans and, in that sense, was quite disrespectful of them. Although Schweitzer said that there should be "a real feeling of brotherliness" between black and white people, he also said,

The Negro is a child, and with children nothing can be done without the use of authority. We must, therefore, so arrange the circumstances of daily life that my natural authority can find expression. With regard to the Negroes, then, I have a formula: I am your brother it is true, but your elder brother.[24]

Schweitzer, it seems, was a racist in senses 2 and 8, but not in sense 7.

II. Some Senses of "Racism" in which Lincoln Was Clearly *Not* a Racist

Very clearly Lincoln was *not* a racist in senses 3, 4, 5, or 6. He was not a belief-exploitation racist; he was not a

[23] Garcia, "The Heart of Racism," pp. 18–19.
[24] Bentley, *Albert Schweitzer: The Enigma*, pp. 192–3.

belief-malevolent racist; he was not a malevolent racist; and he was not a cold-hearted racist.

Definition 3 (belief-exploitation racism) is the definition of racism that is most salient for thinking about American slavery. Those who justified American slavery on the grounds of the alleged inferiority of Africans were racists in this sense. Lincoln was never this kind of racist; he did not think that there were any differences between blacks and whites that made it permissible for whites to enslave and exploit them. He always thought that slavery was very wrong and unjust. He said,

Certainly the Negro is not our equal in color – perhaps not in other respects.... In pointing out that more has been given to you [whites], you cannot be justified in taking away what little has been given him [the Negro]. All I ask for the negro is that if you do not like him, let him alone. If God gave him but little, that little let him enjoy.[25]

Suppose it is true that the Negro is inferior to the white in the gifts of nature; is it not the exact reverse [of] justice that the white should, for that reason, take from the Negro, any part of the little which has been given him? 'Give to him that is needy' is the christian rule of charity; but 'Take from him that is needy' is the rule of slavery.[26]

In all these cases it is your sense of justice and human sympathy, continually telling you, that the poor negro has some natural right to himself – that those who deny it, and make mere merchandise of him, deserve kickings, contempt, and death.[27]

Lincoln said that if a white person endorses enslaving blacks and justifies this because he claims that they are less intelligent than he is, then he commits himself to saying that

[25] Speech at Springfield, Illinois, July 15, 1858, in Abraham Lincoln, *Speeches and Writings*, I, p. 478.
[26] Ibid., p. 685.
[27] Speech at Peoria, Illinois, October 16, 1854, in ibid., p. 327.

it would be permissible for someone who is more intelligent than he is to enslave him. He wrote,

> If A. can prove, however conclusively, that he may, of right, enslave B. – why may not B. snatch the same argument, and prove equally, that he may enslave A? –
>
> You say A. is white, and B. is black. It is color, then; the lighter, having the right to enslave the darker? Take care. By this rule, you are to be slave to the first man you meet, with a fairer skin than your own.
>
> You do not mean color exactly? – You mean the whites are intellectually the superiors of the blacks, and, therefore have the right to enslave them? Take care again. By this rule, you are to be slave to the first man you meet, with an intellect superior to your own.
>
> But, say you, it is a question of interest; and, if you can make it your interest, you have the right to enslave another. Very well. And if he can make it his interest, he has the right to enslave you.[28]

This argument is very sophisticated and provides strong reasons for thinking that American slavery was morally wrong, even on the assumption that blacks are intellectually inferior to whites (an assumption that most of Lincoln's contemporaries would have endorsed).

Lincoln abhorred the exploitation inherent in slavery that deprived enslaved people of the fruits of their labor. He had a very personal and visceral hatred for this aspect of slavery. His own personal experiences as a young man, who was frequently hired out by his father to do heavy backbreaking work on neighboring farms and forced to hand over all of his wages to his father until he reached the age of twenty-one, gave him great sympathy for American slaves. He said that he himself used to be a slave; however, he recognized that, though white men like himself could make themselves free, black people could not.[29] In his writings and speeches about

---

[28] "Fragment on Slavery," in ibid., p. 303.
[29] Burlingame, *The Inner World of Abraham Lincoln*, p. 36.

slavery he repeatedly emphasized how slavery deprived people of the fruits of their labor, just as his father had deprived him of the fruits of his labor.[30] He often referred to the biblical command that we should eat our bread "in the sweat of" our faces (Genesis 3:19). He thought that slavery was a clear violation of that command, because it involves "wringing . . . bread from the sweat of other men's faces."[31] His empathy for the plight of slaves was largely a result of this personal identification with their situation.

Additional evidence of Lincoln's deep concern for the welfare of African American slaves can be found in his 1857 speech on the Dred Scott decision. He spoke then of the position of Negroes in American society:

In those days our Declaration of Independence was held to be sacred by all, and thought to include all; but now, to aid in making the bondage of the negro universal and eternal, it is assailed, and sneered at, and construed, and hawked at and torn, till, if its framers could rise from their graves, they could not at all recognize it. All the powers of earth seem rapidly combining against him. Mammon is after him; ambition follows, and philosophy follows, and the Theology of the day is fast joining the cry. They have him in the prison house. . . . One after another they have closed the heavy iron doors upon him, and now they have him, as it were, bolted in with a lock of a hundred keys, which can never be unlocked without the concurrence of every key; the keys in the hands of a hundred different men, and they scattered to a hundred different and distant places.[32]

The Republicans inculcate, with whatever of ability – they can, that the negro is a man; that his bondage is cruelly wrong, and that the field of his oppression ought not to be enlarged. The Democrats deny his manhood; deny, or dwarf to insignificance, the wrong of his bondage; so far as possible, crush all sympathy for him, and cultivate and excite hatred and disgust against him; compliment

---

[30] Ibid., Chapter 2.
[31] Second Inaugural Address, Abraham Lincoln, *Speeches and Writings*, II, p. 687.
[32] Abraham Lincoln, *Speeches and Writings*, I, pp. 396–7.

themselves as Union-savers for doing so; and call the indefinite outspreading of his bondage "a sacred right of self-government."[33]

Racism in senses 4 and 5 involves ill will toward a certain race of people; racism in sense 6 is indifference to the welfare of a certain race of people on account of their race. Very clearly, Lincoln was never a racist in any of these senses. He never had ill will for blacks, nor was he ever indifferent to their welfare. He desired the liberty and welfare of all human beings and was greatly concerned to promote the welfare of blacks, as he understood it. This concern was morally virtuous.

III. Understanding Lincoln in His Historical Context

As we saw in Chapter 3, extreme racial prejudice and extreme aversion to the very presence of blacks were the norm in Illinois during Lincoln's lifetime: black codes and black exclusion laws were supported by a large majority of the electorate. In fact, some historians think that racial prejudice and aversion to African Americans were stronger in the central and southern parts of Illinois and Indiana than anywhere else in the United States[34] (see Chapter 3.III). Lincoln lived roughly half of his life in central Illinois and spent most of his childhood in southern Indiana; his racial attitudes must be understood in that light. It was his very bad moral luck to grow up and live in a region of the country where extreme racial prejudice and animus were so prevalent.

Because the case for calling Lincoln a racist depends largely on statements he made in his debates with Stephen Douglas, I need to provide a historical context for those debates. Slavery

---

[33] Ibid., pp. 402–3.
[34] Miller, *Lincoln's Virtues*, p. 358. Alexis de Tocqueville thought that white racial prejudice was stronger in states that did not have slavery than in slaveholding states, White, *A. Lincoln*, p. 276.

was the main issue in both the 1858 Illinois senate race and in the 1860 presidential election when Lincoln and Douglas ran against each other. Lincoln and the Republicans opposed the territorial expansion of slavery and held that slavery should be prohibited in federal territories. He expressed the hope that this would make it unlikely that any new slave states would be admitted to the Union. (His reasoning was that, because few slave owners would settle in territories where slavery was prohibited, it was very unlikely that voters in those territories would later vote to make them slave states.) Douglas supported what he called "popular sovereignty," which called for the voters in each new state to decide whether that state would be free or slave. He wanted to permit people to practice slavery in federal territories, which would make it more likely that the territories would be settled by slave owners who would later vote to allow slavery in those newly created states. Douglas said that he did not care whether or not new states voted to have slavery. Lincoln very pointedly noted this sentiment in the Galesburg debate where he quoted Douglas as saying that he [Douglas] "don't care whether Slavery is voted up or down."[35]

During the debates, Douglas shamelessly appealed to the racial prejudices of the voters and repeatedly claimed that Lincoln wanted to bring about the social and political equality of blacks and whites. Here are some of the things Douglas said at the first debate in Ottawa:

We are told by Lincoln that he is utterly opposed to the Dred Scott decision . . . for the reason that he says it deprives the negro of the rights and privileges of citizenship. (Laughter and applause [by members of the audience]). . . . I ask you, are you in favor of conferring upon the negro the rights and privileges of citizenship ("No, no " [said by members of the audience]). . . . If you desire negro citizenship, if you desire to allow them to come into the

[35] Abraham Lincoln, *Speeches and Writings*, I, p. 708.

State and settle with the white man, if you desire them to vote on an equality with yourselves, and to make them eligible to office, to serve on juries, and to adjudge your rights, then support Lincoln and the Black Republican party.... ("Never, never.")....I am in favor of conferring citizenship to white men...instead of conferring it upon Negroes, Indians and other inferior races ("Good for you." "Douglas forever.")[36]

I do not regard the negro as my equal, and positively deny that he is my brother or any kin to me whatever. ("Never.")....For thousands of years the negro has been a race upon the earth, and during all that time, in all latitudes and climates, wherever he has wandered or been taken, he has been inferior to the race which he has there met. He belongs to an inferior race, and must always occupy an inferior position. ("Good," "that's so.")[37]

At the second debate in Freeport, Douglas supporters displayed a large banner saying "No Nigger equality."[38] At the Charleston debate, Douglas supporters displayed a large banner that pictured a white man, a black woman, and a mixed race boy with the words, "Negro Equality" – this was not intended as an endorsement.[39]

It is important to note that many prominent abolitionists and radical Republicans had deeply racist views and attitudes: it would be a mistake to assume that all, or even most of them, held enlightened views about questions of racial equality. The radical Republican Senator from Ohio, Ben Wade, said that Washington, D.C., was "nigger ridden" and that he was repelled by the smell of "niggers."[40] Wade also said that he favored colonization of blacks and wanted "to hear no more about negro equality or anything of that kind....we shall be...glad to rid ourselves of these people."[41] In 1859,

[36] Ibid., p. 504.
[37] Ibid., p. 505.
[38] White, *A. Lincoln: A Biography*, p. 269.
[39] Ibid., p. 275.
[40] Burlingame, *Abraham Lincoln: A Life*, I, p. 259.
[41] Ibid., p. 366.

Lincoln's friend, Congressman Joshua Giddings, who earlier had been the most radical antislavery member of Congress, said on the floor of the House, "We do not say the black man is, or shall be, the equal of the white man; or that he shall vote or hold office."[42] In 1860, the strongly antislavery Massachusetts senator Henry Wilson said, "I do not believe in the equality of the African with the white race, mentally or physically, and I do not think morally.... So far as mental or physical equality is concerned...I believe the African race inferior to the white race."[43] Similar sentiments were expressed by Owen Lovejoy, William Seward, Lyman Trumbull, and Cassius Clay.[44] In late 1860, Frank Blair, a leader of the antislavery forces in Missouri, said that the "Republican party is the white man's party, and [that, by keeping slavery out of federal territories, it] will keep the Territories for white men."[45] Lincoln, himself, gave similar arguments in his debates with Stephen Douglas – arguments to the effect that excluding slavery from the territories would reserve them as homes for free white men.[46]

IV. Was Lincoln a Belief-Racist and a Belief-Discrimination Racist?

The short answer to this question is that we do not know. It is possible that he was a racist in these senses and possible that he was not. Although he endorsed unjust racial discrimination against blacks during most, if not all, of his political career, it is not clear that he was a racist in sense 2. To be a belief-discrimination racist (2), one must be a belief-racist (1). Contrary to what many scholars confidently claim and

[42] Ibid., p. 525.
[43] Ibid., p. 526.
[44] Ibid. pp. 525–6.
[45] Ibid., p. 526.
[46] Abraham Lincoln, *Speeches and Writings*, I, p. 379.

assume, there is no clear evidence that he was a belief-racist after the time he became an important national politician and antislavery spokesman in the mid-1850s.

The case for thinking that he was a belief-racist is inconclusive. Nowhere in any of his writings or speeches does he say that whites are inherently morally or intellectually superior to blacks – but nowhere does he say that blacks are morally and intellectually the equal of whites either. So we do not know whether or not Lincoln was a racist in senses 1 and 2. There are reasons to think that he did not have clear and fully determinate beliefs about these matters. Questions of racial equality were not salient issues for him, because he thought that it was possible to show that slavery was wrong independently of any issues about the inherent biological equality of the races. His very explicitly and repeatedly expressed doubts about the widely presumed moral and intellectual inferiority of blacks are also evidence that he had no clear or firm convictions about such issues. Therefore, on the worst possible construal of his racial beliefs (on the assumption that he was a belief-racist and belief-discrimination racist), his racism was hedged by skeptical doubts, and he was only weakly or marginally a racist in these senses (at least after the mid-1850s).

But let us look at the details. Here is why the evidence for thinking that Lincoln was a belief-racist or a belief-discrimination racist is insufficient.

1. *Lincoln's Endorsement of Racial Discrimination.* During the 1858 senatorial campaign and earlier, he defended unjust and discriminatory laws that denied free African Americans full social and political rights.

His most well-known statement about this came in his debate with Douglas in Charleston, Illinois. Here is part of that statement:

I will say then that I am not, nor ever have been in favor of bringing about in any way the social and political equality of the white and black races, [applause] – that I am not nor ever have been in favor of making voters or jurors of negroes, nor of qualifying them to hold office, nor to intermarry with white people; and I will say in addition to this that there is a physical difference between the white and black races which I believe will ever forbid the two races living together on terms of social and political equality. And inasmuch as they cannot so live, while they do remain together there must be the position of the superior and inferior, and I as much as any other man am in favor of having the superior position assigned to the white race.[47]

This passage appears as the frontispiece in Lerone Bennett's book *Forced into Glory: Abraham Lincoln's White Dream*, which, together with Bennett's earlier article in *Ebony Magazine*,[48] is probably the harshest and most well-known statement of the claim that Lincoln was a racist. Bennett apparently regards this statement as his single most damning piece of evidence against Lincoln. In the first debate in Ottawa, Lincoln made a similar statement in his reply to Douglas's criticisms. He rejected full equality for blacks and whites but he went on to add,

But...notwithstanding all this, there is no reason in the world why the negro is not entitled to all the natural rights enumerated in the Declaration of Independence, the right to life, liberty, and the pursuit of happiness. [Loud cheers.] I hold that he is as much entitled to these as the white man. I agree with Judge Douglas he is not my equal in many respects – certainly not in color, perhaps not in moral or intellectual endowment. But in the right to eat the bread, without leave of anybody else, which his own hand earns, *he is my equal and the equal of judge Douglas, and the equal of every living man.* [Great applause.][49]

---

47 Ibid., p. 636. In his rejoinder to Douglas at the end of the Charleston debate, Lincoln reiterated that he was against citizenship for Negroes.
48 "Was Abraham Lincoln a White Supremacist?" February 1968, reprinted in Holzer, ed., *The Lincoln Anthology*, pp. 737–52.
49 Abraham Lincoln, *Speeches and Writings*, I, p. 512.

In a similar vein, he said that if human beings were created in the image of God, then "the justice of the creator" must be extended equally "to *all* His creatures, to the whole great family of man." He also said that "nothing stamped with the Divine image was sent into the world to be trodden on, and degraded, and imbruted by its fellows."[50]

Lincoln also rejected giving full social political rights to blacks on other occasions. In his Peoria speech on the Kansas-Nebraska Act, given in October 1854, he said that his feelings would not admit of making blacks socially or politically the equals of whites:

My own feelings will not admit of this; and if mine would, we well know that those of the great mass of white people will not.[51]

Then he questioned whether these feelings were justified:

Whether this feeling accords with justice and sound judgment, is not the sole question, if indeed, it is any part of it. A universal feeling, whether well or ill-founded, cannot be safely disregarded.[52]

He repeated this view in a speech in Springfield from 1858.[53] Shortly after his Springfield speech in the first senatorial debate with Stephen Douglas, Lincoln quoted from and endorsed this passage from his Peoria speech in which he said that his feelings were against making blacks socially or politically the equals of whites.[54] In his fourth debate with Douglas, he said that he was against making citizens of Negroes (and giving them all the rights of citizens):

Now my opinion is that the different states have the power to make a negro a citizen under the constitution of the United States if they choose. The Dred Scott decision decides that they have not that

---

[50] Carwardine, *Lincoln: A Life of Purpose and Power*, p. 40.
[51] Abraham Lincoln, *Speeches and Writings*, I, p. 316.
[52] Ibid.
[53] Ibid., pp. 477–8.
[54] Ibid., p. 511.

power. If the state of Illinois had that power I should be opposed to the exercise of it.[55]

He reiterated this opposition to giving citizenship to blacks in his final debate with Douglas.[56]

So during his debates with Stephen Douglas, Lincoln clearly endorsed unjust racial discrimination. He was also willing to appeal opportunistically to the racial prejudices of Illinois voters. In three well-known speeches from 1854, 1856, and 1858 he said that he wanted the western territories of the United States to be homes for free white people.[57] He hoped to gain votes by convincing people that they should side with him in trying to stop the spread of slavery, which would, in turn, make it impossible for many black people to settle in the new territories.

It is undeniable that Lincoln endorsed unjust racial discrimination throughout most of his political career (and arguably throughout his entire career), but this alone is not evidence for calling him a racist in sense 2. To be a racist in sense 2, one must believe in the inherent moral, intellectual, or physical inferiority of a certain race of people. Although it is widely assumed that he believed that blacks were inherently intellectually inferior to whites,[58] there is very little firm evidence for this view.

[55] Ibid., p. 675.
[56] Ibid., p. 791.
[57] Ibid., pp. 331, 346, 379, and 454.
[58] See Lind, *What Lincoln Believed*, p. 112. Lind says, "During the Lincoln Douglas debates he [Lincoln] suggested that God gave the blacks 'but little...'" But, in its entirety, the passage from Lincoln reads as follows:

Certainly the Negro is not our equal in color – perhaps not in other respects.... In pointing out that more has been given to you [whites], you cannot be justified in taking away what little has been given him [the Negro]. All I ask for the negro is that if you do not like him, let him alone. If God gave him but little, that little let him enjoy (Abraham Lincoln, *Speeches and Writings*, I, p. 478).

Lind fails to acknowledge that Lincoln was speaking conditionally: "Perhaps" the Negro is not the equal of whites, "in other respects," "If God gave

2. *Did Lincoln Believe that Blacks Were Morally or Intellectually Inferior to Whites?* Lincoln *never* said that blacks were morally or intellectually inferior to whites in any of his public statements, and in several public statements, he expressed doubts about the alleged moral and intellectual inferiority of blacks.

Recall his statement from the debate in Ottawa: "he is not my equal in many respects – certainly not in color, *perhaps* [my emphasis] not in moral or intellectual endowment."[59] On another occasion, when speaking with respect to white racial prejudice, he said, "A Universal feeling, whether well or *ill-founded* [my emphasis], cannot be safely disregarded."[60] He registered these doubts on other occasions.[61] He was not confident about the truth of commonly held beliefs about the inferiority of blacks. He freely expressed these doubts, but was not willing to make a major issue about this.

Nowhere, in any of his writings or speeches, did Lincoln flatly say that blacks are intellectually inferior to whites.[62]

---

him little . . . " The passage Lind quotes from Lincoln's July 17, 1858, speech is an argument against slavery. Lincoln claimed that slavery is wrong, even *if* God gave blacks but little. He never stated that whites were superior to blacks in any respect other than color. He said that "perhaps" blacks were unequal to whites [in intellect]. Lind to the contrary, there are many reasons to doubt that Lincoln had a "low opinion" of the intellectual abilities of blacks. Also note the following passage from Lincoln's notes, "On Pro-Slavery Theology" (this was quoted earlier in 10.II):

Suppose [my emphasis] it is true that the Negro is inferior to the white in the gifts of nature; is it not the exact reverse [of] justice that the white should, for that reason, take from the Negro, any part of the little which has been given him? (Abraham Lincoln, *Speeches and Writings*, I, p. 685).

Lind also cites a passage from an article that Gideon Welles wrote for *Galaxy Magazine* in 1877, which I discuss later.

[59] Abraham Lincoln, *Speeches and Writings*, I, p. 512.
[60] Speech at Peoria, Illinois, October 16, 1854, in ibid., p. 316.
[61] Recall his guarded statement quoted earlier: "*If* [my emphasis] God gave him [the Negro] but little . . . " Speech at Springfield, Illinois, July 15, 1858, in ibid., p. 478.
[62] In a letter to Henry Raymond from December 1860, Lincoln wrote that he "does not hold the black man to be equal to the white, unqualifiedly"

Nowhere did he flatly say that blacks are morally inferior to whites. (But nowhere did he flatly say that blacks are morally and intellectually equal to whites either.) The writings in question include private notes to himself about such matters as slavery. It is noteworthy that none of those speeches or writings endorsed racist beliefs about the native abilities of blacks.

This raises the question of whether he ever endorsed such beliefs in private conversations. The strongest evidence that he did comes from his Secretary of the Navy, Gideon Welles. In an article in *Galaxy Magazine* from 1877, Welles reported that Lincoln believed that blacks were intellectually inferior to whites. He said that Lincoln

opposed the whole system of enslavement, but believing the Africans were mentally an inferior race, he believed that any attempt to make them and the whites one people would tend to the degradation of the whites without materially improving the blacks, but that separation would promote the happiness and welfare of each.[63]

This passage is part of a long discussion of Lincoln's colonization policy.[64] Welles said that although Lincoln was disappointed by the failure of the colonization schemes – in particular, the failure of the colony created on Cow Island off the coast of Haiti – he "by no means abandoned his policy of colonization and emancipation, for the two were in his mind indispensably and indissolubly connected."[65]

Welles also wrote,

The President doubted if Africans as a race were themselves capable of organizing as a community and successfully maintaining a government without supervision, or individually susceptible of

(Abraham Lincoln, *Speeches and Writings*, II, p. 193). But he did not explain in what respects he thought that blacks and whites were not unqualifiedly equal.

[63] Welles, "Administration of Abraham Lincoln," p. 438.
[64] Ibid., pp. 438–41 and 444.
[65] Ibid., p. 439.

high intellectual cultivation. There might be and were exceptional cases, but they were by nature dull, inert, dependent and of little foresight – an ignorant and inferior race, who needed to be governed, were not as a class able or qualified to participate intelligently in self-government. If they were to exercise the high privilege of suffrage . . . it must be at some distant day in the future after several generations of education and nurture.[66]

These passages are very important for our purposes here. They are arguably the strongest pieces of evidence for thinking that, during his time as president, Lincoln believed that blacks were intellectually inferior to whites. Welles is generally considered to be one of the best sources of inside information about the Lincoln administration. It is very possible, and, in my view more likely than not, that Welles correctly and accurately reported views that President Lincoln expressed to him. *But* there is also reason to think that Lincoln did not say these things late in his life.

Welles reported that Lincoln *believed* that the inferiority of blacks made colonization imperative. However, as we saw in Chapter 3.II, Lincoln abandoned the idea of colonization (on any large scale) long before the end of his life. Further, he went on record as favoring giving many blacks the right to vote before the end of his life and thinking that justice required doing so (see Chapter 3.V). So it is very unlikely that he told Welles that blacks were an "ignorant and inferior race," and that for that reason "if they were to exercise the high privilege of suffrage . . . it must be at some distant day in the future after several generations of education and nurture," at any time near the end of his presidency. This statement, if he actually made it, does not represent his final views. Welles's statement that Lincoln did not abandon his policy of colonization is mistaken or at least very misleading. Lincoln never publicly mentioned colonization after

[66] Ibid., p. 440.

December 1862[67] and never pushed it on a large scale after that time (see 3.II). He abandoned colonization as a policy that he actively pushed for, though it is possible that he still privately continued to wish for colonization.

There is further evidence from Welles. In his diary entry from September 26, 1862, just four days after the preliminary version of the Emancipation Proclamation was issued, Welles reported several recent cabinet meetings that discussed "deporting the colored race."[68] Welles wrote that Lincoln "thought it essential to provide an asylum for a race which we had emancipated, but which could never be recognized or admitted to be our equals."[69] But this passage is ambiguous regarding the issue of racism. Was Lincoln saying that blacks *are not* equal to whites or was he saying that, because of popular prejudice, whites will never *recognize* blacks as their equals? This passage does not specify the sense in which blacks and whites are (or are thought to be) unequal and calls to mind Lincoln's statement that the black man "is not my equal in many respects – certainly not in color, perhaps not in moral or intellectual endowment." I think that his talk of being unequal in color was blather to pander to the prejudices of the voters. Welles's diary was written at nearly the same time as the events it records; it is more reliable than his recollections in the *Galaxy* article written twelve to sixteen years after the events it describes. Welles himself had grave doubts about the intellectual capacities of blacks,[70] and he may have been incorrectly attributing his own views to Lincoln. It is also possible that Welles and others on the cabinet had expressed such doubts or beliefs and took the president to be concurring with their views, even though Lincoln did not explicitly state or express those views himself.

[67] Oakes, *Freedom National*, p. 280.
[68] Welles, *The Diary of Gideon Welles*, I, p. 150.
[69] Ibid., p. 152.
[70] See Niven, *Gideon Welles*, p. 222.

So Lincoln gave at least one of his colleagues reason to believe that he thought that whites were intellectually superior to blacks. But he never said this *on the record* publicly, nor did he write anything to this effect in any of his many private notes and ruminations on slavery that survive. Therefore there is no reason to think that his beliefs about the inferiority of blacks, if he actually had them, were strongly or confidently held. Even if he said or assented to roughly what Welles reported that he said about the intellectual capacities of blacks, this is not good evidence of his beliefs at the end of his life.

In the longest of the three passages from the *Galaxy* article quoted earlier, Welles reported that the president believed that blacks could "some distant day in the future after several generations of education and nurture" be given the right to vote (this implies that Lincoln thought that in the future the intellects of blacks could improve to the extent that it was appropriate for them to be given the right to vote). This is evidence that Lincoln accepted the Lamarckian theory of the inheritance of acquired characteristics, according to which abilities and talents developed by people during their lifetimes could be passed on biologically to their descendants. (Mendelian genetics had not yet been developed, and many people during Lincoln's lifetime endorsed Lamarckian views.) So it was possible to believe that education and acculturation, as opposed to eugenic practices, could raise the inherited intelligence and abilities of a racial or ethnic group over time. (Nietzsche, for one, endorsed this view. He thought it very important that Europe became civilized much later than the "Orient."[71])

Here is my conjecture about these passages from Welles. Lincoln was a very moody man given to doubts and worries. He *feared*, perhaps strongly (as did most of his associates),

[71] Nietzsche, *The Anti-Christ*, sections 20–4.

that blacks were inferior to whites in ways that would make it a bad idea for blacks and whites to live together on terms of full equality; he also feared that blacks were intellectually inferior to whites in ways that made it a bad idea for them to be given the right to vote. If he did say the things that Welles reported that he believed, I think that Lincoln was expressing his fears but not any clear firm beliefs.

Other Evidence that Lincoln Was or Might Have Been a Racist in Senses 1 and 2. In the fifth Lincoln-Douglas debate, Lincoln denied that his views committed him to holding that the white and black races should be perfectly equal socially and politically:

I have said that, in their right to "life, liberty, and the pursuit of happiness," as proclaimed in that old declaration [the Declaration of Independence], the inferior races are our equals.[72]

From the context, it is clear that he meant that blacks are one of the inferior races, but he did not explain in what sense(s) he believed blacks to be inferior. His reference to "inferior races" raises serious questions, but it might have been blather to pander to the prejudices of the voters.[73]

Especially in light of his clearly and repeatedly expressed doubts about the moral and intellectual inferiority of African Americans, something that was generally assumed by his contemporaries, there is no reason to think that Lincoln had clear and fully determinate beliefs about these matters. These were

---

[72] Abraham Lincoln, *Speeches and Writings*, I, p. 704.
[73] Here is another piece of evidence. In an 1859 "Lecture on Discoveries and Inventions," Lincoln said,

To be fruitful in invention, it is indispensable to have the *habit* of observation and reflection.... But for the difference in *habit* of observation, why did yankees, almost instantly discover gold in California, which had been trodden upon, and overlooked by indians and Mexican greasers, for centuries? (Abraham Lincoln, *Speeches and Writings*, II, p. 5).

This might be evidence that he thought that Yankees were intellectually superior to American Indians and Mexicans, but it does not bear on the issue of his racist beliefs about blacks.

not salient questions for him, because he thought that they were *irrelevant* to the morality of slavery: he thought that slavery was wrong regardless of whether blacks were inferior to whites (see 10.II). However, these questions are arguably relevant to questions about voting rights, serving on juries, and other rights and duties of citizens. Those issues became salient issues for him only near the end of his life, and he never fully thought them through.

Any racist beliefs he might have held by the time he became an important national political leader (roughly 1854–8) were at most weakly held and hedged by doubts. In his debates with Douglas and in other speeches he gave around this time, Lincoln's standard formulation of his racial views was to say that blacks were unequal to whites in color and that they might or might not be unequal to whites in their intellects and moral capacities. What did he mean when he said that blacks and whites were "unequal in color"? He did not just mean that blacks and whites are *different* in color; he strongly implied that whites are somehow *better* in this respect. Very likely, this was prattle to pander to the voters' prejudices. But it is also possible that this statement was connected with what he said in the Charleston debate about "physical differences" making it impossible for blacks and whites to live together on terms of equality. It is possible that Lincoln was reporting that he and other whites found the physical appearance of blacks to be displeasing. His 1857 speech in which he talked about the "natural disgust in the minds of nearly all white people, to the idea of the indiscriminate amalgamation of the white and black races" suggests this interpretation.[74] The popular pictorial images of blacks in the mass media at the time included many nasty and grotesque caricatures that influenced how most whites in the North, who had very little direct contact with blacks, pictured and imagined them.

[74] Abraham Lincoln, *Speeches and Writings*, I, p. 397.

It is quite possible that Lincoln was not a belief-racist or a belief-discrimination racist, or that he was only minimally a racist in these senses, but that he was willing to pander and appeal to the voters by endorsing (or not contradicting) these views.

Often, politicians who have strong but unconventional moral convictions must compromise their ideas and pander to public opinion (or at least keep silent about their moral convictions) if they hope to win elections. When public opinion is very seriously in error (as in this case), politicians bent on winning elections cannot be very openly critical of it. Lincoln's political campaigns in 1858 and 1860 were not "teachable moments" on the issue of racism. We should not condemn him for pandering in this way in order to be a viable candidate, though we should deplore the climate of opinion that made this pandering politically necessary.

Here is an important question: at the time of his debates with Douglas, did Lincoln really think that racial discrimination against blacks was justified, or was he just appealing to the prejudices of the voters? (In either case, he presumably believed that *his endorsement* of racial discrimination was justified – either on its merits or for reasons of political expediency.) Should we think better or worse of him if he did not really believe that whites were justified in discriminating against blacks? This is an important question, but one that I leave to others.

Both practical politicians and visionary idealists who always speak frankly and never play up to public opinion have honorable and important roles to play in the political arena. I am not arguing that the abolitionists and those who favored equal treatment for members of all races were mistaken. (The term "abolitionist" refers to those who called for the immediate abolition of slavery. Those who, like Henry Clay and Lincoln, wanted to end slavery gradually, were not called abolitionists.) The abolitionists were necessary to push

Lincoln and public opinion toward ending slavery, and they eventually succeeded in doing so. By 1864, they had helped persuade him and many other people in the North to become abolitionists themselves; in 1864 Lincoln ran for reelection on a platform that called for a constitutional amendment to immediately abolish slavery. He modestly said of himself near the end of the Civil War, "I have only been an instrument. The logic and moral power of Garrison, and the anti-slavery people of the country and the army have done all."[75] The abolitionists played a decisive and necessary role in ending slavery, but Lincoln's personal role was also essential. *Given the state of popular opinion in 1860*, America needed its president to do the things he did (see Chapter 2).

So, in sum, we simply do not know whether Lincoln was a belief-racist or a belief-discrimination racist. But we can say this: if he had racist beliefs of the type that are involved in senses 1 or 2, they were not firmly or confidently held – they were hedged by serious doubts, and he never stated them publicly on the record. Yet, he clearly did endorse extremely unjust racial discrimination, and if he was a belief-discrimination racist his racism justified extremely unjust practices.

V. Was Lincoln an Inadequate-Benevolence Racist, a Disrespect-Racist, or an Inadequate-Respect Racist during Most of His Political Career?

These three definitions of racism (7–9) encompass a very wide range of moral vices, ranging from the relatively minor to the very grave. Having slightly less benevolence than morality requires is not a grave moral vice, nor is having slightly deficient benevolence for a race of people because of their race. But being almost completely indifferent to the welfare of an

---

[75] Burlingame, *Abraham Lincoln: A Life*, II, p. 750.

entire race of people falls very far short of the demands of morality and is a very grave moral vice.

1. *During Most of His Political Career, Did Lincoln Disrespect Blacks (or Fail to Respect Them Adequately) on Account of Their Race?* My answer is "yes." There is strong evidence for thinking that he was a racist in sense 8 at the time of his debates with Douglas and probably long before.

Lincoln's strongly expressed opposition to interracial marriage and his disparaging comments about people of mixed race are strong evidence that he was a racist in sense 8. In his debates with Douglas he said that he agreed ("a thousand times agreed") with Douglas in being "*horrified* [my emphasis] at the thought of mixing the blood of the white and black races":

Judge Douglas is especially horrified at the thought of the mixing of the blood by the white and black races: agreed for once – a thousand times agreed. There are white men enough to marry all the white women, and black men enough to marry all the black women; so let them be married.[76]

In light of the forgoing, it seems that he was speaking, or purporting to speak, for himself, as well as "nearly all white people," when earlier in the same speech he said, "There is a natural disgust in the minds of nearly all white people, to the idea of an indiscriminate amalgamation of the white and black races."[77]

After this passage, he went on to pointedly claim that his policy of opposing the spread of slavery would minimize interracial marriage and race mixing: "If the white and black people never get together in Kansas, they will never mix blood

[76] Abraham Lincoln, *Speeches and Writings*, I, p. 400.
[77] Ibid., p. 397.

in Kansas."⁷⁸ This was an attempt to turn Douglas's racist rhetoric and white fears about interracial marriage to his own political advantage. Nowhere in the rest of the debate did Lincoln reject the idea that interracial marriage is disgusting, and he was at pains to stress that his policies would not promote interracial marriage. He protested against "that counterfeit logic which concludes that, because I do not want a black woman for a *slave* I must necessarily want to her for a *wife*."⁷⁹ He also said that Douglas "attempts to fasten the odium of that idea [the idea of interracial marriage] upon his adversaries,"⁸⁰ in a way that implied that he [Lincoln] regarded this as an odious idea.

Interracial marriage continued to be an issue in later debates. Some of Douglas's supporters claimed that Lincoln favored interracial marriage (something that was very unacceptable to most whites). In the fourth debate, Lincoln replied by saying, "I do not understand that because I do not want a negro woman for a slave I must necessarily want her for a wife [Cheers and laughter.]"⁸¹ He then went on to make an offensive and racially disrespectful joke about this at Douglas's expense:

I have never had the least apprehension that I or my friends would marry negroes if there was no law to keep them from it [laughter] but as Judge Douglas and his friends seem to be in great apprehension that they might, if there were no law to prevent them from it, [roars of laughter] I give him my most solemn pledge that I will to the very last stand by the law of this state, which forbids the marrying of white people with negroes. [Continued laughter and applause.]⁸²

This statement opportunistically played up to the racial prejudices of Illinois voters in order to win votes. But it might

⁷⁸ Ibid., p. 401.
⁷⁹ Ibid., pp. 397–8.
⁸⁰ Ibid., p. 397.
⁸¹ Ibid., p. 637.
⁸² Ibid.

have also been expressing, though possibly overstating, Lincoln's personal opposition to interracial marriage. To further complicate things, there is reason to think that his strongly expressed aversion to interracial marriage might have been insincere. David Locke, an Ohio newspaper man, reported that in September 1859 he asked Lincoln why he went on record as favoring the Illinois law forbidding intermarriage of whites and blacks. According to Locke, Lincoln replied, "The law means nothing. I shall never marry a negress, but I have no objection to any one else doing so. If a white man wants to marry a negro woman, let him do it – if the negro woman can stand it."[83] Perhaps it is significant that Locke did not report that Lincoln said anything about marriages between black men and white women.

Michael Lind thinks that Lincoln's opposition to interracial marriage was an important reason why he supported the colonization of blacks abroad and why he opposed the annexation of parts of Latin America.[84]

It is possible that Lincoln's avowed opposition to interracial marriage reflected his aesthetic judgments and preferences, but it is also possible that it reflected his belief in the superiority of whites. In attacking interracial marriage he said what it was in his political interest to say. Politicians strongly tend to say what it is in their political interests to say and believe what it is in their interests to believe. Clearly, he could not have endorsed interracial marriage without making himself unelectable (see Figure 2). Given the extent to which Stephen Douglas stressed this issue, it also would have been damaging to his political prospects for him to have remained silent about it. His statement that he was "horrified" at the thought of blacks intermarrying with whites was clearly disrespectful of blacks and people of mixed race. Whether or not they were sincere, his statements were certainly disrespectful.

[83] Sandburg, *Abraham Lincoln: The Prairie Years*, II, pp. 185–6.
[84] Lind, *What Lincoln Believed*, pp. 198–200.

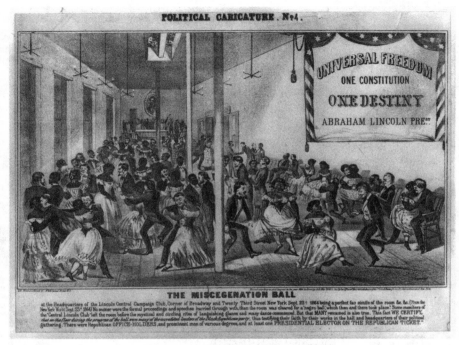

FIGURE 2: American Racial Attitudes, 1864

Lincoln sometimes used the word "nigger" and other racial slur words such as "Sambo" and "Cuffie," although historians disagree about the frequency with which he used them. Bennett claims that he used the word "nigger" "all the time, both in public and private."[85] In contrast, Gates says that he used the word in public until 1862 and that his use of the word was "relatively rare."[86] Henry Samuel claimed that Lincoln used the word "Cuffie" during a meeting at which Samuel was present to discuss the issue of pay for black soldiers in 1864 (before this time black soldiers in the Union Army were paid less than white soldiers). Gates describes this interchange as follows:

[85] Bennett, *Forced into Glory*, p. 5.
[86] Gates, "Abraham Lincoln on Race and Slavery," in *Lincoln on Race & Slavery*, Gates and Yacovone, eds., p. xxi.

Samuel said that Lincoln said in a humorous tone, "Well gentleman, you wish the pay of Cuffie raised," Cuffie being a racist name for slaves widely used in the nineteenth century. Samuel protested Lincoln's use of that term, to which the president responded, "I stand corrected young man, but you know that I am by birth a southerner and in our section that term is applied without any idea of offensive nature. I will, however, at the earliest possible moment, do all in my power to accede to your request."[87]

Lincoln's secretary, Nicolay, claimed that this story is untrustworthy.[88]

Lincoln grew up and lived where use of the word "nigger" was very common, if not the rule, and he did use the word several times during his debates with Stephen Douglas.[89] However, Burlingame claims that when Lincoln used the word, it was usually in a context that suggests he was paraphrasing Douglas and other Democrats[90] who frequently used the word. One instance of Lincoln's use of the word "nigger" is in a passage from his first debate with Douglas in which he paraphrased Douglas sarcastically and ironically:

When...Judge Douglas, came to Chicago...he goes on and...draws out from my speech this tendency of mine to set the states at war with one another, to make all institutions uniform,

---

[87] Ibid., p. lxi.

[88] Ibid., p. lx. Fehrenbacher and Fehrenbacher agree with Nicolay's assessment (*Recollected Words of Abraham Lincoln*, p. 390), but Gates dismisses Nicolay's claims and says that "we have absolutely no reason to doubt" Samuel's story, because "Lincoln's presidential discourse about blacks was certainly peppered with words such as 'Sambo,' 'boy,' 'auntie,' 'nigger,' as well as 'Cuffie,' and occasionally these slippages occurred even after he was president" (p. lxi). For other evidence that Lincoln used the n-word before and after he became president, see Burlingame, *Abraham Lincoln: A Life*, I, p. 109 and II, p. 399. For evidence that he used the word "Sambo," see ibid., p. 369 and *Abraham Lincoln: A Life*, II, p. 399. Also see Chapter 3, note 107 for an anonymous 1836 letter in a local Springfield newspaper written in a style that mocks and exaggerates Negro dialect that Burlingame thinks was in all likelihood written by Lincoln.

[89] Abraham Lincoln, *Speeches and Writings*, I, pp. 517 and 524.

[90] Burlingame, *Abraham Lincoln: A Life*, I, p. 526.

and to set the niggers and white people to be marrying together [laughter] . . . [91]

Burlingame's explanation also seems to hold for the following passage from the same debate, though this is less clear. This passage from his debate with Douglas at Ottawa reads as follows:

I ask the attention of the people assembled and everywhere, to the course that Judge Douglas is pursuing everyday as bearing upon this question of making slavery national. . . . but taking the speeches he makes . . . I ask your attention to them. In the first place what is necessary to make the institution national? Not war. There is no danger that the people of Kentucky will shoulder their muskets with a young nigger stuck on every bayonet march into Illinois and force them upon us.[92]

Another case of his use of the word "nigger" is mentioned by Gates. James Redpath, a journalist and antislavery activist, reported the following: in April 1862 Lincoln was informed that the president of Haiti had offered to send a white man as his ambassador to the United States. According to Redpath, Lincoln responded by saying, "You can tell the President of Haiti that I shan't tear my shirt if he does send a nigger here."[93] Surely he knew that the word "nigger" was hurtful and offensive and that his use of this word was strong evidence of disrespect, at least inadequate respect, for black people on account of their race.

When he met with the underground railroad heroine Sojourner Truth, Lincoln called her "Auntie." He apparently abided by the convention that whites would not address

[91] Abraham Lincoln, *Speeches and Writings*, I, p. 517.
[92] Ibid., p. 524.
[93] Gates, "Abraham Lincoln on Race and Slavery," in *Lincoln on Race & Slavery*, p. xxi. We should not overlook the fact that Lincoln was saying that he would not be bothered if Haiti sent a black person to be its ambassador to the United States.

blacks with the respectful terms "Mr.," "Mrs.," or "Miss" ("Ms." was not then in use). But importantly, he did not just call her "Auntie." He also called her by her name. The evidence for this is a photograph of himself that he signed for Truth's autograph book; he wrote "For Aunty Sojourner Truth A. Lincoln Oct. 19. 1864."[94] In his "Letter from Birmingham Jail," Martin Luther King complained that in the South black women "are never given the respected title 'Mrs'" and that blacks are not addressed properly by their first and last names.[95] Lincoln did not do *that* – he called Sojourner Truth by her full name and, therefore, Lerone Bennett's criticism of him for calling her "Auntie" is overstated. Bennett notes that Sojourner Truth did not object to Lincoln's referring to her in this way, but he neglects to mention her account of her meeting with the president: she said that she was never treated with more kindness and cordiality by anyone (see the later discussion).[96]

Whether or not his frequently stated opposition to making blacks citizens of the United States and permitting them to vote reflected his own views (as opposed to simply being opportunistic, albeit politically necessary, pandering to the prejudices of the voters), it *expressed* clear disrespect for African Americans and their abilities. So clearly he was a racist in sense 8 (disrespect).

However, there is some evidence that Lincoln was very kind and respectful to black people face to face. Frederick Douglass wrote, "In all my interviews with Mr. Lincoln, I was impressed by his entire freedom from popular prejudice against the colored race. He was the first great man I talked with in the United States freely, who in no single instance reminded me of the difference between him and myself, of the

---

[94] Kunhardt et al., *Looking for Lincoln*, pp. 252–3.
[95] King, "Letter from Birmingham Jail," p. 81.
[96] Bennett, *Forced into Glory*, pp. 109–10.

difference in color, and I thought that all the more remarkable because he came from a state where there were black laws."[97] Because Douglass knew almost all of the major white abolitionists, this statement puts Lincoln in a very good light. As we saw earlier, Sojourner Truth said that she was "never treated with more kindness and cordiality than I was by that great and good man."[98] So Lincoln was not an extreme or unqualified example of an inadequate-respect racist: his disrespectful statements about blacks and people of mixed race were combined with other more virtuous and respectful attitudes.[99]

There remains an important question. Would it be morally better or worse if Lincoln's many disrespectful statements about blacks and people of mixed race were insincere? (Is it worse to express unjustified disrespect that one does not actually feel than to express unjustified disrespect that one actually feels?) I leave this as an exercise for the reader.

2. During Most of His Political Career, Did Lincoln Have Inadequate Concern for the Welfare of Blacks? My answer is possibly, even likely, "yes," but it is difficult to say.

In some important ways, Lincoln was very benevolent toward blacks and very concerned to promote their welfare. He was very committed to ensuring their freedom and happiness and

---

[97] Miller, *President Lincoln*, p. 306.

[98] Stauffer, *Giants*, pp. 288–9.

[99] However, Lincoln was dictatorial and condescending in his meeting with black leaders to discuss colonization in August 1862 (for details see Chapter 3.II). As many others have noted, this meeting was a low point for Lincoln. But we should not draw any important conclusions about his character from his conduct in this case, because he was under enormous pressure at the time. Further, he was largely motivated by his very well-founded fears that many people in the North would oppose the Emancipation Proclamation (which he was then planning to issue after a Union victory on the battlefield) on the grounds that it would cause many blacks to move to the North; see Chapter 2.I.5.

their ability to enjoy the fruits of their labor. These concerns were virtuous, and his very active and time-consuming commitment to the antislavery political cause after 1854 (which entailed considerable personal and financial sacrifices for him and his family) arguably went well beyond what morality required. But it is likely that he was inadequately concerned with the welfare of African Americans in other ways (e.g., discounting their desire to remain in their native land and their interest in becoming citizens and fully enjoying the rights of citizens in a democracy). We might say that he was more than adequately concerned with the welfare of blacks in certain respects and inadequately concerned with it in certain other respects. I think that it would be most apt to say that he was adequately (or more than adequately) concerned with the welfare of blacks *as he understood it*, but that his benevolence was paternalistic and condescending (this is what Garcia calls "Kiplingesque racism"[100]). On either description, his attitudes about African Americans were a mixture of virtue and vice.

There is considerable evidence that Lincoln favored the interests of whites over blacks. In a speech from 1859, he discussed Stephen Douglas's racial views and said that Douglas repeatedly "declared that while in all contests between the negro and the white man, he was for the white man, but that in all questions between the negro and the crocodile he was for the negro."[101] Lincoln described his own views as follows:

If there was a necessary conflict between the white man and the negro, I should be for the white man as much as Judge Douglas; but I say that there is no such necessary conflict. There is room enough for us all to be free.[102]

[100] Garcia, "The Heart of Racism," pp. 18–19.
[101] Abraham Lincoln, *Speeches and Writings*, II, p. 67.
[102] Ibid., p. 68.

But this statement might simply be blather to pander to the prejudices of the voters without conceding anything substantive, especially because it says that, in practice, there is no conflict between the interests of the two races.

In the fourth Lincoln-Douglas debate at Charleston Lincoln said,

I will say in addition to this that there is a physical difference between the white and black races which I believe will ever forbid the two races living together on terms of social and political equality. And inasmuch as they cannot so live, while they do remain together there must be the position of the superior and inferior, and I as much as any other man am in favor of having the superior position assigned to the white race.[103]

In this statement, he, in effect, said that if the black and white races remained together (something he did not want to happen at that time) then he wanted the black race to be subordinate to the white. Because he was very aware of the extent of white prejudice and animus against blacks, he had to know that having blacks subordinated to whites would be very harmful to the interests of blacks. If this statement was sincere, it is rather strong evidence that he was not sufficiently concerned with the welfare of blacks. But this characterization has to be hedged. At this time, Lincoln did not want blacks to be subordinated to whites in the United States; instead he wanted the races to be separated and blacks to be colonized in places where they would enjoy full rights. This last statement was perfectly sincere: he was not a proponent of worldwide white supremacy. He supported the ethnically Indian Benito Juarez against the French monarchy in Mexico and was an anti-imperialist. Like Henry Clay, he supported self-determination for nonwhite societies.[104] We also should remember that, politically, it was very inexpedient for him to

---

[103] Abraham Lincoln, *Speeches and Writings*, I, p. 636.
[104] See Lind, *What Lincoln Believed*, pp. 298 and 307–9.

express equal concern for the welfare of blacks to Illinois voters in 1858, because the great majority of them cared much more about the welfare of whites than blacks. It was politically advantageous for him to spin his policies and views so as to *minimize* his concern for the rights and welfare of African Americans.

Lincoln's Letter to Horace Greeley. Lincoln's August 1862 public letter to Horace Greeley is prima facie evidence for the view that he was inadequately concerned with the welfare of African Americans. In this letter, he said that his "paramount object" in fighting the war was to keep the country together. He wrote, "What I do about slavery, and the colored race, I do because it helps to save the Union; and what I forebear, I forebear because I do not believe it would help save the Union."[105] This seems to show that he was morally obtuse in worrying much more about keeping the country together than combating the enormous evil of slavery and in thinking that the abolition of slavery was of only instrumental importance compared to the goal of keeping the nation together. It also seems to show that he was very insufficiently concerned for the rights and welfare of blacks. But these appearances are misleading. First, we need to understand this letter in its proper political context, and second, we should not assume that it was completely candid. Given his legitimate worries about the Supreme Court and his need for support from the border states and many soldiers in the Union army who were not willing to fight to end slavery, it clearly would have been very risky and politically inexpedient for him to say that he was fighting the war primarily to end slavery. (There is reason to think that only 30 percent of Union soldiers supported emancipation as a war aim at the time the Emancipation Proclamation was issued, see Chapter 2.1.3, note 73.)

[105] Abraham Lincoln, *Speeches and Writings*, II, p. 358.

Lincoln cared very much about keeping the country together, arguably too much (see Chapter 4.II.2). But he also cared a great deal about the rights and welfare of the American slaves. He loathed and hated slavery and devoted his entire political career after 1854 to fighting it. Further, his concern to keep the country together cannot be separated from his concerns about slavery. He knew and feared that an independent Confederacy would expand and prolong slavery. After he was elected, he was *not* willing to try to placate the South and preserve the Union by abandoning his opposition to the further extension of slavery.

Lincoln did not think that it was constitutional for the federal government to prohibit slavery in the states, and that *was* the correct interpretation of the Constitution in 1861. But he thought that the Constitution permitted the U.S. government to prohibit slavery in federal territory and to try to keep it out of new states. He repeatedly said that he wanted to stop the spread of slavery into the territories and new states and that doing so would be the "first step in setting slavery on the path of ultimate extinction." He *always* had the long-term aim of ending slavery and always expressed it very clearly – this infuriated people in the South. Early in the war, he did not intend to abolish slavery *by means of fighting the war*, but the reason he did not try to do this was not that he did not care very deeply about slavery and the rights and welfare of its victims. He correctly believed that he would not have enough support from non-abolitionists (who were the overwhelming majority of people in the North and the border states) if he made abolishing slavery an explicit aim of the war.

Near the beginning of the war, he sought to end slavery *by other means* (means other than the war). He wanted the federal government to pay money to states to induce them to abolish slavery and began to push for this early in the war (see Chapter 2.I.3). On July 12, 1862, he met with border state congressmen and again pushed his proposals for compensated emancipation. They again rejected his proposals. *The very next day* he told two members of his cabinet that he had decided to issue the Emancipation Proclamation.[106] The timing of these events is very significant, and it paints a very different picture of his motives and intentions than the one his letter to Greeley (taken alone and out of context) suggests. So, despite strong appearances to the contrary, his letter to Horace Greeley is not evidence for the view that he was inadequately concerned with the freedom and welfare of black slaves.

The Views of Frederick Douglass. In a very well-known passage from his speech in memory of Lincoln at the dedication of the Freedman's Monument to Lincoln in 1876, Frederick Douglass argued that Lincoln was inadequately concerned with the interests of blacks. Because this argument is very well known and widely endorsed, it is worthy of special attention here. The reasons Douglass gave for thinking that Lincoln was inadequately concerned with the welfare of blacks are weak and unconvincing. Further, in the later parts of the speech he greatly qualified this criticism and retracted some of it. It is therefore misleading to quote Douglass's criticisms of Lincoln near the beginning of the speech without attending to the speech as a whole. Later in his speech

---

[106] "On July 12 [1862] (the same day Congress passed the Second Confiscation Act), Lincoln met with twenty-seven border state Congressmen and Senators and urged them again to support a program of compensated emancipation. Their failure to do so profoundly disappointed him. Hard on the heels of his unsuccessful interview with the border state congressmen, Lincoln made his fateful decision to emancipate the slaves by executive order. In a private conversion with Navy Secretary Gideon Welles and Secretary of State Seward on July 13, he told them of his intention" (Grimsley, *The Hard Hand of War*, p. 132).

Douglass called him a "great and good man" and praised his political leadership even more lavishly:

Taking him for all in all, measuring the tremendous magnitude of the work before him, considering the necessary means to ends, and surveying the end from the beginning, infinite wisdom has seldom sent any man into the world better fitted for his mission than Abraham Lincoln.[107]

Later in his life, Douglass praised Lincoln extravagantly. In 1883, Douglass called him "the greatest statesman that ever presided over the destinies of this republic" and the person most responsible for "American liberty."[108] In 1886, he described Lincoln as "a very great man, as great as the greatest."[109] In an 1888 speech, "The Black Man's Debt to Abraham Lincoln," Douglass said,

He was a man so broad in his sympathy, so noble in his character, so just in his action, so free from narrow prejudice.... To have known him as I knew him, I regard as one of the grandest privileges experienced by me.... I knew him. I would not part with that peep into that noble soul for all the wealth... that could be bestowed upon the most successful conqueror.[110]

He added that when he first went to meet the president in the White House he knew that he was "going to see a great man – a *great* man."[111] In his 1893 speech "Abraham Lincoln, The Great Man of Our Century," Douglass said,

---

[107] "Oration in Memory of Lincoln at the Dedication of the Freedman's Monument," in 1876, in Blasingame and McKivigan, *The Frederick Douglass Papers Series One: Speeches, Debates, and Interviews*, Vol. 4, p. 437.

[108] Blasingame and McKivigan, *The Frederick Douglass Papers Series One: Speeches, Debates, and Interviews*, Vol. 5, p 78. Cited in Stauffer, *Giants*, p. 311.

[109] Frederick Douglass, from *Reminiscences of Abraham Lincoln by Distinguished Men of His Time*, in Holzer, ed., *The Lincoln Anthology*, p. 280.

[110] Blasingame and McKivigan, *The Frederick Douglass Papers Series One: Speeches, Debates, and Interviews*, Vol. 5, p. 340.

[111] Ibid., p. 341.

I ... [have] seen many great men.... but I have met with no such man, at home or abroad, who made upon my mind the impression of possessing a more godlike nature than did Abraham Lincoln.[112]

However, in the first part of his 1876 speech at the dedication of the Freedman's Monument, Douglass said that Lincoln was "entirely devoted to the welfare of white men" and that Lincoln's opposition to the extension of slavery had its "motive and mainspring in his patriotic devotion to his own race."[113] Whites were "First midst and last" "the object of his deepest affection and his most earnest solicitude."[114] Douglas also said,

It must be admitted, truth compels me to admit, even here in the presence of the monument we have erected to his memory, Abraham Lincoln was not, in the fullest sense of the word, either our man or our model. In his interests, in his associations, in his habits of thought, and in his prejudices, he was a white man. He was preeminently the white man's President, entirely devoted to the welfare of white men.[115] He was ready and willing at any time during the first years of his administration to deny, postpone, and sacrifice the rights of humanity in the colored people to promote the welfare of the white people of this country.

To protect, defend, and perpetuate slavery in the states where it existed Abraham Lincoln was not less ready than any other President to draw the sword of the nation. He was ready to execute all the supposed guarantees of the United States Constitution in favor

---

[112] Ibid., p. 536; cited in Stauffer, *Giants*, p. 311.

[113] "Oration in Memory of Lincoln at the Dedication of the Freedman's Monument in 1876," in Blasingame and McKivigan, *The Frederick Douglass Papers Series One: Speeches, Debates, and Interviews*, Vol. 4, p. 432.

[114] Ibid.

[115] By contrast, earlier, in his June 1, 1865, eulogy for Lincoln at Cooper Union in Manhattan, Douglass had said that although Lincoln was "unsurpassed in his devotion to the welfare of the white race," nonetheless, he was also "in a sense hitherto without example, emphatically the black man's President: the first to show any respect for their rights as men.... He was the first American President who ... rose above the prejudices of his time and country" (Burlingame, *Abraham Lincoln: A Life*, II, pp. 829–30).

of the slave system anywhere inside the slave states. He was willing to pursue, recapture, and send back the fugitive slave to his master, and to suppress a slave rising for liberty, though his guilty master were already in arms against the Government. The race to which we belong were not the special objects of his consideration.[116]

I concede to you, my white fellow-citizens, a pre-eminence in this worship at once full and supreme. First, midst, and last, you and yours were the objects of his deepest affection and his most earnest solicitude. You are the children of Abraham Lincoln. We are at best only his step-children; children by adoption, children by forces of circumstances and necessity.[117]

The evidence that Douglass cited for thinking that Lincoln was "entirely devoted to the welfare of white men" (and thus attached little, if any, intrinsic importance to the welfare of black people) – his postponement of emancipation and his willingness to enforce the Fugitive Slave Law – is quite unconvincing. Lincoln's postponement of emancipation was morally justified: it promoted rather than harmed the interests of blacks (see Chapter 2.I.5), and it was perfectly compatible with his having equal intrinsic concern for the rights and interests of blacks and whites. He was also justified in being willing to enforce the Fugitive Slave Law and to oppose slavery only by legal means, because any attempt on his part to defy the laws would have been counterproductive (see Chapter 2.I.2). Douglass's statement that the Union was "more dear to" Lincoln than the freedom and future of African Americans[118] is misleading because in preserving the Union Lincoln understood himself to be opposing slavery (opposing its expansion and perpetuation; see Chapter 2.I.3 and 4.II.4). Like many other critics of Lincoln, Douglass in

---

[116] "Oration in Memory of Lincoln at the Dedication of the Freedman's Monument in 1876," in Blasingame and McKivigan, *The Frederick Douglass Papers Series One: Speeches, Debates, and Interviews*, Vol. 4, p. 432.

[117] Ibid.

[118] Ibid. p. 434.

this part of his speech failed to acknowledge that Lincoln's devotion to the Union was perfectly consistent with his opposition to slavery.

Douglass's speech is puzzling because later in it he said things that seemed to retract some of his earlier criticisms. He acknowledged that Lincoln needed the support of a large number of non-abolitionists in the North and border states to win the Civil War (non-abolitionists were a considerable majority of the population of the Union states at the beginning of the Civil War):

His great mission was to accomplish two things: first, to save his country from dismemberment and ruin; and, second, to free his country from the great crime of slavery. To do one or the other, or both, he must have the earnest sympathy and the powerful cooperation of his loyal fellow-countrymen. Without this primary and essential condition to success his efforts must have been vain and utterly fruitless. Had he put the abolition of slavery before the salvation of the Union, he would have inevitably driven from him a powerful class of the American people and rendered resistance to rebellion impossible. Viewed from the genuine abolition ground, Mr. Lincoln seemed tardy, cold, dull, and indifferent; but measuring him by the sentiment of his country, a sentiment he was bound as a statesman to consult, he was swift, zealous, radical, and determined. Though Mr. Lincoln shared the prejudices of his white fellow-countrymen against the Negro, it is hardly necessary to say that in his heart of hearts he loathed and hated slavery.[119]

In effect, this passage said that Lincoln was justified in many of the actions that Douglass had criticized earlier in his speech.[120]

Douglass also discussed the abolitionists' harsh criticisms of Lincoln during the Civil War in two later speeches. In 1888 he said that Lincoln

---

[119] Ibid., pp. 436–7.
[120] Gates also notes this in "Abraham Lincoln on Race and Slavery," in Gates and Yacovone, *Lincoln on Race & Slavery*, pp. li–lii.

had been abused. Oh, good men are apt to be abused.... Some...
blamed him very much that he hadn't brought the war to a close;
another blamed him for not making it an abolition war, and others
blamed him for making it an abolition war, so he was blamed on all
sides, and he answered them all in one single sentence, and such a
sentence I had never heard from the lips of any man in his position
before. He said [Douglass quotes a sentence from Lincoln's Second
Inaugural Address]: "Fondly do we hope, fervently do we pray,
that this mighty scourge of war shall pass away; yet if God wills
it continue till all the wealth piled up by two hundred years of
bondage shall have been paid for by one drawn with the sword, we
must still say, as was said three thousand years ago, the judgments
of the Lord are true and righteous altogether."[121]

In this speech Douglass strongly implied that the criticisms
of Lincoln for not making the Civil War a war of abolition
earlier than he did (criticisms that Douglass himself made
early during the war) were unjustified. He said that these
criticisms "abused" Lincoln and that Lincoln gave a good
answer to them. Douglass repeated this argument in a speech
from 1893.[122]

Douglass's 1876 speech may not be fully consistent rhetor-
ically, but it seems more consistent when we note that he
talked about the ways in which Lincoln had disappointed
blacks and taxed their faith in him: "Our faith in him was
often taxed and strained to the uttermost."[123] But then he
went on to say that "we [blacks] were able to take a comprehensive view of Abraham Lincoln and make reasonable
allowance for the circumstances of his position."[124]

---

[121] "The Black Man's Debt to Abraham Lincoln," February 12, 1888, in
Blasingame and McKivigan, *The Frederick Douglass Papers Series One:
Speeches, Debates, and Interviews*, Vol. 5, p. 343.

[122] Ibid., p. 543.

[123] "Oration in Memory of Lincoln at the Dedication of the Freedman's Monument in 1876," p. 433.

[124] Ibid.

But later in the speech, Douglass repeated his claims that Lincoln had the prejudices typical of white men and that he did not care much about the welfare of blacks. But Douglass suggested that this attitude was essential to Lincoln's eventual success in helping free the slaves:

> I have said that President Lincoln was a white man, and shared the prejudices common to his countrymen towards the colored race. Looking back to his times and to the condition of his country, we are compelled to admit that this unfriendly feeling on his part may be safely set down as one element of his wonderful success in organizing the loyal American people for the tremendous conflict before them, and bringing them safely through that conflict.[125]

It is unclear what Douglass meant by Lincoln's "unfriendly feeling" toward blacks, but it seems to imply that Lincoln cared little about the welfare of blacks. Lincoln did think that ending American slavery would benefit whites. But Douglass's suggestion that Lincoln had little concern for the welfare of blacks is unsupported and contradicted by a large body of evidence, much of which has been presented earlier. To mention just a few matters again here, Lincoln was deeply distressed and pained by the plight of American slaves, and his opposition to slavery stemmed largely from concern for the welfare of blacks (see his letter to his friend Joshua Speed quoted in Chapter 7.I.1). This concern was also evident in his reflections on the morality of slavery in private notes to himself. These candid statements, some in personal letters and notes to himself, clearly expressed *great concern* for the well-being of the victims of slavery.

Douglass also criticized Lincoln because he would not order the execution of Confederate prisoners of war in retaliation for the shooting of black Union prisoners by the Confederates.[126] In July 1863, the president did issue an

---

[125] Ibid. p. 436.
[126] Ibid., p. 433; Stauffer, *Giants*, pp. 282–3.

order that threatened to execute Confederate prisoners of war in retaliation for the killing of black prisoners, but this was apparently a bluff that was never carried out (see Chapter 5.III). Douglass's criticisms of Lincoln's actions are very questionable, because it is doubtful that what he wanted Lincoln to do (order the execution of innocent men) was morally permissible. Lincoln was willing to punish and execute those personally responsible for murdering black prisoners.[127] In addition, despite very strong criticisms, Lincoln halted the exchange of prisoners of war for a very long time until the CSA agreed to exchange black prisoners, see note 131 and Chapter 5.III.

To summarize our findings in this section, at the time of the Lincoln-Douglas debates and well into his presidency, Lincoln was a racist in sense 8 (disrespect).[128] He might also have been inadequately concerned for the welfare of blacks (7) in important respects. But he also had a very great and virtuous concern for the welfare of blacks in other respects. Frederick Douglass did not give adequate evidence for his famous claim that Lincoln was "entirely devoted" to the welfare of white people and that Lincoln had "unfriendly feelings" toward blacks, both of which imply that he cared rather little about the welfare of black people. These two claims are sharply contradicted by a large body of evidence.

We have seen that Lincoln was never a racist in any of the senses of racism in which being a racist is morally awful (3–6). For most of his political career, he was clearly a racist in sense 8 (disrespect) and likely also in sense 7 (inadequate-benevolence). We do not know whether he was a racist in senses 1 or 2 (belief-racism, belief-discrimination racism).

---

[127] Miller, *President Lincoln: The Duty of a Statesman*, p. 308.
[128] Because senses 8 and 9 are mutually exclusive (9 is inadequate respect *short of* disrespect), he was not a racist in sense 9.

VI. Was Lincoln a Racist in the Sense of Inadequate-Benevolence, Disrespect, or Inadequate-Respect at the End of His Life?

My answer is that probably Lincoln was adequately concerned with the welfare of blacks at the end of his life (he was probably not a racist in sense 7 at the end of his life). Although he seems to have ceased being positively disrespectful of blacks by the end of his life, we do not know whether he was still inadequately respectful of them. I think that it is most likely that, at the end of his life, he was a racist in sense 9 (inadequate-respect), but only in sense 9.

His attitudes about black people changed considerably during his time as president. He came to greatly respect and admire black soldiers in the Union Army and went out of his way to acknowledge their valor and vital contribution to the Union cause; see his public letter to James Conkling quoted at length in Chapter 7.I.3. Lincoln also met and grew to greatly admire Frederick Douglass and several other well-educated black leaders such as Martin Delany. He stopped pressing for large-scale colonization of blacks abroad (see Chapter 3.II) and wanted blacks to be citizens of the United States.[129] He endorsed providing education for all blacks[130] and recommended that voting rights be given to some (but not all) blacks, with the understanding that this measure could be expanded later. But because this proposal to give voting rights to some blacks still permitted unjust discrimination against many/most blacks, we might take it to be evidence of condescension and disrespect for blacks, albeit much less than before. However, as we saw in Chapter 3.V, it was right and prudent for him to move cautiously with regard to this issue while the Civil War was still continuing and the Thirteenth

---

[129] See Foner, *The Fiery Trial*, p. 258.
[130] Burlingame, *Abraham Lincoln: A Life*, II, p. 588 and McPherson, *The Battle Cry of Freedom*, p. 709.

Amendment had not yet been ratified. We do not know what kinds of policies he would have endorsed had he lived until the end of his second term of office. So it is possible that he was still a racist in the sense of being inadequately respectful of blacks (9) when he died, but it is also possible that he was not. At the end of his life he was clearly much more respectful of blacks than he had been before.

What about racism in sense 7? Was Lincoln adequately concerned with the welfare of black people at the end of his life? There are two strong pieces of evidence that he was. For a considerable period of time during the war, despite intense public criticism based on concern for the suffering of Union prisoners of war in Andersonville and other horrendously bad and inhumane Confederate POW camps (see the photo plates for a shocking picture of a skeletal Union prisoner from Andersonville),[131] he halted an exchange of prisoners of war with the Confederates until they very reluctantly agreed to exchange black prisoners of war in January 1865.[132] He was thus no more concerned with the fate of white prisoners than that of black prisoners.

President Lincoln's firm insistence that the Emancipation Proclamation be upheld and his later insistence that slavery be completely abolished as a condition for ending the Civil War were policies that attached very great weight to the freedom and welfare of black people. Because it is possible that he could have ended the war much earlier if he had been willing to allow slavery to continue, these policies might have cost the lives of many thousands of soldiers, the great majority of whom were white.

Although this is strong evidence for thinking that Lincoln was greatly concerned with the welfare of blacks, it is

---

[131] The Lincoln administration's willingness to halt prisoner exchanges in order to try to protect black prisoners was denounced by the editors of the *New York Times* and Walt Whitman; see Witt, *Lincoln's Code*, p. 259.

[132] See Chapter 5.III and Burlingame, *Abraham Lincoln: A Life*, II, p. 703; also see Foner, *The Fiery Trial*, p. 255.

compatible with his having been inadequately concerned with their welfare in other respects. The fact that he never supported giving full social and political rights to all blacks might be taken as evidence for his being racist in sense 7 (inadequately benevolent). But this inference is dubious. He was right to move slowly and cautiously on these issues during his lifetime. We do not know what he would have done about them if he had lived longer. The best evidence about whether or not he was inadequately concerned with the welfare of blacks at the end of his life is evidence about what he would have done about the rights and status of the freedmen if he had lived out his term of office. But even if we had that evidence, it would not be fully determinative, because it might be the case that both (1) he would never have supported giving blacks full social/political rights, and (2) he was nonetheless adequately concerned with their welfare. There are other reasons that might have caused him not to support equal rights for African Americans: excessive caution, concern for popular opinion, his fears about a continuation of the Civil War by means of guerrilla war, a commitment to a reading of the Constitution that makes the political and civil rights of citizens the prerogative of individual states rather than the federal government,[133] a misplaced hope that former Confederate states would deal fairly with the newly freed slaves, and his desire to be merciful to the South. The wisdom and justice of his policies about reconstruction are distinct from issues about racism and his character.

We do not know whether or not Lincoln was a racist in sense 1 (belief-racism) or 2 (belief-discrimination racism) at the end of his life. If he was a racist in either of these senses, his racist views were only weakly held and hedged by doubts. The case for thinking that he was a racist in one or both of these senses is much weaker than is generally supposed. Because of this and because we know that he clearly was not

---

[133] Niven, *Gideon Welles*, p. 491; also see Chapter 3.V.1.

a racist in senses 3–6 (he did not endorse the exploitation of blacks or have ill will for them, nor was he indifferent to their welfare), it is particularly important to ask whether he was a racist in senses 7 (inadequate-benevolence), 8 (disrespect), or 9 (inadequate-respect).

The available historical evidence does not give us a clear unambiguous answer whether Lincoln was a racist in sense 7, 8, or 9 at the end of his life. Four interpretations of the available historical evidence are reasonable:

1. At the end of his life, though Lincoln was, in some ways, very benevolent to blacks, he was also inadequately concerned with their welfare in certain important respects. Thus, on balance he still was somewhat of a racist in sense 7 (inadequate-benevolence). He was also still a racist in sense 8 (disrespect), albeit much less of one than he had been before.
2. At the end of his life, he was not a racist in sense 7, but he was a racist in sense 8 (disrespect), although less of one than he had been before.
3. At the end of his life, he was not a racist in sense 7 or 8, but he was a racist in sense 9 (inadequate-respect).
4. At the end of his life, he was not a racist in sense 7, 8, or 9.

On the basis of the evidence presented earlier, I think that 3 is the most reasonable interpretation of the historical evidence and 4 is the least reasonable interpretation.

According to interpretation 4, not only did Lincoln lack the vice of racism by the end of his life but his attitudes about other races of people were also quite virtuous, because they involved great, self-sacrificing benevolence. Given interpretations 1–3, he exhibited one or more vices in his attitudes about black people, but the badness of that vice (those vices) was largely counterbalanced by his modules of great self-sacrificing benevolence for blacks and members of other races.

VII. Racism and Lincoln's Character

Lincoln had very bad moral luck in that *none* of his friends or close associates in his childhood and early manhood transcended the white racism of popular culture.[134] Yet Lincoln was able to adopt more enlightened racial views after becoming president. As Henry Louis Gates writes, "Lincoln grew and evolved, he faced and confronted his own prejudices, and, to a remarkable extent, overcame them."[135] *On balance*, he deserves considerable credit for being much less prejudiced than most people of his own time and place and for very largely overcoming his own prejudices.

Only a very virtuous person would have been patient under the very harsh criticisms of the abolitionists, would have learned from them, and would have become friends with them; for example, with Frederick Douglass. The abolitionists were often unfair and bigoted in their attacks on Lincoln. Senator Ben Wade and William Garrison attributed his racial attitudes to his origins among "poor white trash."[136] Commenting on Lincoln's First Inaugural Address, Frederick Douglass wrote that Lincoln "stands upon the same level with [the slave-holders] and is in no respect better than they."[137]

---

[134] Miller, *Lincoln's Virtues*, pp. 36–7 and 43; also see Donald, *Lincoln*, pp. 21 and 45–6. In this connection, recall Lincoln's statement in the Charleston debate quoted earlier: "I will add to this that I have *never* [my emphasis] seen to my knowledge a man woman or child who was in favor of producing perfect equality, social and political between negroes and white men." This might be overstated, but it is clear that support for full racial equality was extremely unusual among Lincoln's acquaintances.

[135] Gates, "Abraham Lincoln on Race and Slavery," in Gates and Yacovone, *Lincoln on Race & Slavery*, p. lxiii.

[136] Burlingame, *Abraham Lincoln: A Life*, II, pp. 203 and 391.

[137] Guelzo, *Lincoln's Emancipation Proclamation*, p. 27.

Douglass also denounced the "weakness imbecility and absurdity" of his actions in the case of Fremont in Missouri.[138] But, as we saw in Chapter 2.I.4, Lincoln's actions in this case were entirely justified. It would have been very dangerous and unwise if he had done what Douglass wanted him to do, because it would have risked causing the Union to lose the war.

In reference to Lincoln's support for the voluntary colonization of blacks abroad, Douglass spoke of his "contempt for Negroes and his canting hypocrisy."[139] He said that Lincoln was a "genuine representative of American prejudice and Negro hatred."[140] This last criticism was quite unfair – Lincoln was much less prejudiced than typical white Americans and he never hated blacks; to the contrary, he cared deeply about their welfare. As we saw in Chapter 3.II, his proposals for colonization were motivated by his view that white prejudice would prevent blacks from being treated as equals in the United States and his belief that colonization would minimize opposition to the Emancipation Proclamation among many people in the North who were bitterly opposed to permitting newly freed slaves to settle in the North. A normal person would have been greatly offended and angered by this criticism and would have never deigned to meet with Frederick Douglass or been willing to learn from him. However, Douglass's frequently expressed low opinion of Lincoln did not prevent Lincoln from meeting him, learning from him, becoming his friend, and calling him one of the most admirable men in America. Later, by the time of the Second Inaugural Address and after Lincoln's death, Douglass came to hold a much more favorable view of Lincoln (see 10.V.2).

Here, it is relevant to mention that Lincoln grew up in a family that *hated* American Indians. His father, Thomas,

---

[138] Burlingame, *Abraham Lincoln: A Life*, II, pp. 203.
[139] Foner, *The Fiery Trial*, p. 225.
[140] Burlingame, *Abraham Lincoln: A Life*, II, pp. 390–1.

witnessed the death of his father at the hands of Indians as a young boy and narrowly escaped being killed by an Indian on that same occasion. Thomas Lincoln's older brother, Mordecai, also witnessed the killing of their father and shot an Indian to save Thomas's life. Mordecai Lincoln harbored a tremendous hatred for American Indians and murdered several of them. A. H. Chapman reports that Mordecai Lincoln "swore eternal vengeance on all Indians an oath which he faithfully kept afterwards during times of profound peace with the Indians killed several of them in fact he invariably done so when he could do it without it being known that he was the person that done the deed."[141] Lincoln did not share his family's hatred for American Indians. For example, during the Blackhawk War, he risked his life to save an old Indian man who wandered into his camp. Lincoln's men, who were armed, wanted to kill the old man. He interposed himself between his men and the Indian and said that he would fight them if they tried to kill the man. His men backed down, and the old man was spared. This was an extraordinarily virtuous and praiseworthy action that exhibited both courage and a transcending of popular prejudice.[142] We should not diminish the significance of this act just because Lincoln was the commanding officer of his unit. In fact, this was a very ill-trained and ill-disciplined militia, and the men elected their own officers.

His intellectual and moral virtues – his skepticism, independence of mind, and his willingness to accept criticism (and learn from people who were often harsh and unfair in what they said about him) – enabled him to become a more tolerant and less prejudiced person. Frederick Douglass himself recalled that Lincoln was "tolerant toward those who differed from him and patient under reproaches."[143]

---

[141] Wilson and Davis, *Herndon's Informants*, p. 96; also see pp. 220 and 439.
[142] Miller, *Lincoln's Virtues*, p. 256.
[143] "Oration in Memory of Lincoln at the Dedication of the Freedman's Monument," p. 436.

Great self-sacrificing benevolence of the sort that Lincoln displayed in saving the life of the Indian man in the Black-hawk War is a very rare and great virtue. I think that the goodness of this virtue fully counterblances the badness of any racist attitudes he may have continued to have at the end of his life: indeed, I think that it outweighs it. Therefore, I believe that, on balance, Lincoln's racial attitudes toward African Americans at the end of his life were virtuous. But I will not insist on this point because my judgment might reflect my utilitarian leanings. Kantians, who attach greater moral significance to respecting others, might disagree. To the extent that debates between utilitarians and Kantians in ethical theory remain open (I have not addressed those debates here, much less settled them), there is a range of reasonable overall assessments of Lincoln's character. I conjecture that utilitarians will say that inadequate concern for the welfare of others is a serious vice, but that disrespect or inadequate respect for others (so long as it does not involve inadequate concern for their welfare) is not a vice. However, Kantians will say that disrespect or insufficient respect for others (even when it does not involve inadequate concern for their welfare) is a very serious moral vice.[144]

---

[144] Kant holds that duties of respect are perfect duties that we owe to all other persons. "Every human being has a legitimate claim to respect from his fellows human beings and is *in turn* bound to respect every other" (Kant, *The Metaphysics of Morals*, p. 579). He says that duties of beneficence are imperfect duties that one does not owe to every other person. Everyone has a duty "to promote according to one's means the happiness of others in need without hoping for something in return" (p. 572). According to Kant, we have considerable discretion as to how we fulfill this duty: we can choose to help some people and not others. Kant regards the lack of respect for others as a worse moral failing than the lack of benevolence. He writes,

Failure to fulfill mere duties of love [according to Kant, the duties of love are beneficence, gratitude, and sympathy] is *lack of virtue (peccatum)*. But failure to fulfill the duty arising from the *respect* owed to every human being is a vice (*vitium*) (p. 581).

Conclusion of Part II

Lincoln possessed many important moral virtues, some to an extremely high degree. The most serious criticism of his character is that he was a racist. It is widely held that his racism was a very serious moral failing that detracted greatly from the goodness of his character. This view is mistaken. He was clearly not a racist in any sense of the term that would be sufficient to make him a bad person or completely counterbalance the goodness of all his moral virtues (he was clearly not a belief-exploitation racist, a belief-malevolent racist, a malevolent racist, or a cold-hearted racist). Racism of the type(s) he might have exemplified at the end of his life is a much less serious vice. So even on the least charitable interpretation of Lincoln's racism that is at all defensible, this vice was too mixed with very virtuous benevolence for the same people who were the objects of his racist attitudes to *greatly* detract from the goodness of his other virtues. He was, on balance, a very good and morally virtuous person, even if he had racist vices.

I I

Conclusion

Having examined Lincoln's actions and character, in this chapter I review my main conclusions, beginning with his morally controversial actions. In his role as a politician, Lincoln made many morally fraught decisions regarding slavery and the legal rights of African Americans. Some of those decisions have been the subject of considerable criticism. In practice, he was a utilitarian and would have justified his decisions and policies about those issues on utilitarian grounds. This helps explain his willingness to make compromises and pursue policies that reduced rather than ended injustices in cases in which he thought that it was not possible to completely or immediately end the injustices. Indeed, most of his actions and policies in question can be justified on utilitarian grounds. But defending those actions and policies does not require that we accept utilitarianism. Other reasonable moral principles also justify them.

These are some key examples. Despite the horrendous injustice of American slavery, Lincoln was justified in moving slowly and cautiously to end it. He did not have the power or constitutional authority to completely abolish slavery when he took office. It would have been both futile and counterproductive for him to have declared the complete abolition of slavery at the beginning of his presidency.

His August 1862 letter to Horace Greeley might seem to show that he was morally obtuse in thinking that the abolition of slavery was only of instrumental importance compared to the goal of preserving the Union. But appearances can be misleading. We should not assume that this letter was completely candid. Given Lincoln's legitimate worries about the Supreme Court and his need for the support of the border states and of the many soldiers in the Union army who were not willing to fight to end slavery, it would have been very risky and politically inexpedient for him to say that he was fighting the war primarily to end slavery.

Lincoln cared very much about keeping the country together, perhaps too much. But he also cared greatly about the rights and welfare of the American slaves. He loathed and hated slavery and devoted his entire political career after 1854 to opposing it. His concern to keep the country together cannot be separated from his concerns about slavery. He knew and feared that an independent Confederacy would expand and prolong slavery, and after he was elected president, he was not willing to try to placate the South and preserve the Union by abandoning his policy against the further expansion of slavery.

Lincoln's rescinding of Fremont's order for partial emancipation in Missouri seems prima facie very wrong, because it prevented Fremont from freeing people from bondage. But this action was morally justified because allowing Fremont's order to stand would have seriously risked causing the Union to lose the war. Lincoln's slowness in issuing the Emancipation Proclamation was also justified. Those who criticize him for his actions in these cases greatly overestimate his power and discretion. He was constrained by the U.S. Constitution and the protections it provided to the institution of slavery.

He was also constrained by public opinion because he needed the support of the border states and Northern Democrats to fight and win the war. Further, Lincoln and the Union took a number of strong measures against slavery very early in the Civil War. The received view that Lincoln waited until the middle of the war to fight against slavery and then suddenly and radically altered the Union war aims by issuing the Emancipation Proclamation is quite mistaken. In fact, his policies evolved slowly and steadily throughout his entire time as president.

Lincoln is widely criticized for his support for the colonization of freed American slaves to tropical lands outside the United States, but many of these criticisms are unfair. He never endorsed the most objectionable forms of colonization involving involuntary deportation. Because of the deep and widespread opposition in the Northern states to allowing freed slaves to move to the North, it was necessary for Lincoln to use the prospect of colonization to deflect criticisms of the Emancipation Proclamation. He is rightly criticized for his dictatorial and condescending treatment of black leaders when they met to discuss colonization in August 1862. But he learned from this meeting and other evidence of black opposition to colonization, and after 1862 he never again strongly pushed for large-scale colonization. The final version of the Emancipation Proclamation makes no mention of any plans for colonizing freed slaves.

Lincoln is often criticized for suspending habeas corpus. The criticism that he greatly restricted freedom of expression and political freedom in the United States is often overstated and exaggerated.

Lincoln bears great personal responsibility for the beginning of the Civil War. He deliberately risked provoking the Confederates into attacking Fort Sumter, and he chose to fight a civil war rather than permit the Confederate states to secede peacefully. More than anyone else, he caused the secession of the Confederate states to lead to a civil war. The CSA desired a peaceful separation from the United States.

There appears to be a strong case for saying that, when the Civil War began, the Union did not have just cause for fighting the war. It is debatable whether the good of keeping the nation together and not creating a precedent for further instances of secession in the United States and other democratic nations were enough to justify the immense evil of all the death and suffering caused by the war.

But even if we reject Lincoln's arguments about the harm that Confederate independence would have done to the cause of democracy around the world, the Union war effort was morally justified on other grounds. It would have been a moral catastrophe if the CSA had gained its independence. Had it done so, it is very probable that slavery would have continued much longer in the American South; it is also likely that slavery would have persisted longer in Latin America. Further, the legal rights that blacks would have possessed in the CSA after such time as the CSA abolished slavery would probably not have been nearly comparable to the rights they actually possessed in the United States from 1865 until the present.

Questions of *jus in bello* are also important for any moral assessment of Lincoln's actions as commander in chief. The Union military's treatment of Confederate civilians has been widely criticized, and Lincoln personally authorized and approved the Lieber Code, which permitted much harsher treatment of civilians than some important Union leaders thought proper. Many people claim that the Civil War was a "total war," which involved very harsh and ruthless treatment of Southern civilians on a very large scale. Some infamous statements by several Union generals and certain provisions of the Lieber Code lend credence to this view. But this view is quite mistaken. The number of Confederate civilians who died as a result of the actions of the Union army was very small compared with the number of civilian deaths in other wars that are not generally regarded as total wars. Further, the independence of a powerful and militant Confederate States of America, a nation dedicated to the expansion and perpetuation of slavery, would have been a moral catastrophe. At least during the second half of the war, when the Union's "hard war" policies toward civilians began, the Civil War constituted a "supreme moral emergency" in which normally impermissible means were permissible, provided that they were necessary to win the war.

Lincoln enjoyed very good moral luck in that most of his controversial policies and decisions turned out for the best. But he did not enjoy blind moral luck. He was a remarkably farsighted and prescient leader.

In the second part of the book I assessed Lincoln's character. He possessed many important moral virtues and some, such as his kindness and magnanimity, to an extremely high degree. He was an extraordinarily good person in many important respects. Despite his many outstanding moral virtues, there are also grounds to question the goodness of his character. Many fault him as a husband, father, and son. But, on balance, his character cannot be faulted greatly on account of his personal life.

Lincoln had a remarkable sense of humor that endeared him to those who knew him. But as a young man he often took it too far and engaged in pranks and mockery that were hurtful to others.

Probably the most serious criticism of his character is the charge that he was a racist. Many of his statements and actions concerning racial issues look very bad in retrospect. Lincoln supported very unjust racial discrimination, spoke disrespectfully of blacks and people of mixed race, and frequently pandered to the deep racial prejudices of Illinois voters. Despite all of this, he was never a racist in any sense of the term in which being a racist is a grave moral failing. His racist attitudes were mixed with extremely virtuous benevolence for the same people who were the objects of his racist attitudes. In addition, he deserves considerable credit for largely overcoming the racial prejudices of his time and place by the end of his life. He had very bad moral luck in that he lived in a time and place in which extreme racial prejudice was almost universal among whites. His racism did not detract *greatly* from the goodness of his other moral virtues.

He was, on balance, a very good and morally virtuous person. Indeed, he was a morally exemplary human being.[1] Lincoln deserves the great admiration he has received, and in most respects, he is worthy of emulation.

Some of his virtues, such as his kindness and compassion, were prominent very early in his life. But as a young man, he had many rough edges and faults to overcome. An important part of the story of his life is his capacity for self-improvement, learning from his mistakes, and learning from the criticisms of others. Throughout his life, he worked hard at and succeeded in becoming a better person. He evolved from being a partisan politician who mocked and personally attacked his political opponents in speeches and anonymous newspaper articles to become a great statesman who was fair to his opponents and respectful of them. He changed from being a defender of many of Illinois's infamous black laws to being an abolitionist. As president, he adopted more and more enlightened views and policies regarding African Americans and their place in American society.

Lincoln was an extremely ambitious man. His ambition drove his remarkable self-education and rise from extreme

---

[1] See Linda Zagzebski's *Divine Motivation Theory* for a defense of the idea that we should define fundamental moral concepts such as right and wrong and good and bad in terms of morally exemplary people.

poverty to prominence as a lawyer and politician. Ambition is often a vice, but his ambition was honorable and virtuous because he sought to gain fame and the esteem of his fellow humans by doing good and making himself worthy of the esteem of others. In his rise in the world, he overcame a number of great personal tragedies and sorrows. He also overcame several bouts of severe depression.

Lincoln's virtues helped him to be a great political and military leader. His extraordinary magnanimity enabled him to learn and profit from the criticisms of the abolitionists, even though they were often very unfair and bigoted in their criticisms of him. He was an extraordinarily brilliant and prescient politician with a remarkable sense of timing. He preserved the United States and helped abolish slavery despite the fact that only a small minority of Americans were abolitionists at the beginning of the Civil War. He was a superb war leader. He made a great number of difficult and important decisions about the war and slavery under tremendous stress and pressure. The great majority of his important decisions were the correct ones, both morally and strategically. He handled some things exactly right, most notably, the Fort Sumter crisis, the cases of Fremont and Hunter, the Emancipation Proclamation, and transforming public opinion in the North and most of the border states to support the complete abolition of slavery. In the words of Frederick Douglass, "infinite wisdom has seldom sent any man into the world better fitted for his mission than Abraham Lincoln."[2]

The mythical Lincoln described to American elementary schoolchildren was without flaw – at least the flaws were never mentioned. Yet he was not without flaws, and we need to give a full accounting of them. Such a full accounting requires us to acknowledge his support for many aspects

---

[2] "Oration in Memory of Lincoln at the Dedication of the Freedman's Monument," p. 437.

of Illinois's deplorable black codes, his silence about other provisions of those codes, his slowness in becoming an abolitionist, and his failure to ever publicly support equal social-political rights for blacks. A full accounting also requires us to admit his very cold and troubled relationship with his father and his failure to introduce his father and stepmother to his family, his rough and sometimes hurtful sense of humor, his very troubled marriage, and the grounds for criticizing him as a husband and father.

But the Lincoln myth also omits many of the difficulties and moral hazards of his life and his bad moral luck. It leaves out many of the details of his struggle to become a good and honorable man. The myth omits the terrible prejudices of his family, the extreme racial prejudices of Illinois voters, and the prejudices of almost all of his close associates before he became president. The myth does not give the details of the intense stresses of his life, including his crushing workload as president when he was assisted by a tiny White House staff that included only two personal secretaries. His duties as president were made much more difficult by the disloyalty of General McClellan and Treasury Secretary Chase, the extremely harsh and vicious criticisms that assailed him from all sides, the personal tragedy of the death of his beloved son Willie, and the tragedy of his marriage to a very difficult and very troubled woman. Lincoln achieved the things he did under extraordinarily difficult and stressful circumstances.

The real Abraham Lincoln was as good a person as the mythical Lincoln, but also more complex, more interesting, and more human as well. In this conclusion, I follow W. E. B. Du Bois. Du Bois mentions Lincoln's defects and quotes the most objectionable passages of Lincoln's opening statement at the Charleston debate. Nonetheless he calls Lincoln a "great and good man" and stresses his capacity for growth and improvement. Du Bois writes,

[I] love him not because he was perfect but because he was not and triumphed . . . The world is full of folk whose taste was educated in the gutter. The world is full of people born hating and despising their fellows. To them I love to say: See this man. He was one of you yet he became Abraham Lincoln. I personally revere him the more because up out of his contradictions and inconsistencies he fought his way to the pinnacles of earth and the fight was within as well as without.

The scars and foibles and contradictions of the Great do not diminish but enhance the meaning of their upward struggle . . . it was his true history and antecedents that proved Abraham Lincoln a Prince of men.[3]

[3] W. E. B. Du Bois, from *The Crisis*, September 1922, in Holzer, ed., *The Lincoln Anthology*, pp. 436–7.

Bibliography

Adams, Robert. *A Theory of Virtue*. Oxford: Oxford University Press, 2006.

"American Civil War." Wikipedia. Retrieved from http://en .wikipedia.org/wiki/American_Civil_War.

Appiah, Kwame Anthony. *In My Father's House*. Oxford: Oxford University Press, 1992.

Appiah, Kwame Anthony. *The Honor Code*. New York: Norton, 2010.

Aristotle. *Nicomachean Ethics*. Translated by Martin Ostwald. Indianapolis: Bobbs-Merrill, 1962.

Aristotle. *Nicomachean Ethics*. Translated by Christopher Rowe. Oxford: Oxford University Press, 2002.

Basler, Roy et al., eds. *The Collected Works of Abraham Lincoln*. New Brunswick: Rutgers University Press, 1953.

Bennett, Lerone. *Forced into Glory: Abraham Lincoln's White Dream*. Chicago: Johnson Publishing, 2007.

Bentley, James. *Albert Schweitzer: The Enigma*. New York: Harper Collins, 1992.

Berlin, Ira. *Many Thousands Gone*. Cambridge, Mass.: Harvard University Press, 1998.

Blackmon, Douglas. *Slavery by Another Name*. New York: Doubleday, 2008.

Blasingame, John and McKivigan, John. *The Frederick Douglass Papers Series One: Speeches, Debates, and Interviews*, Vol. 4 1864–1880. New Haven: Yale University Press, 1991.

Blasingame, John and McKivigan, John. *The Frederick Douglass Papers Series One: Speeches, Debates, and Interviews*, Vol. 5 1881–1895. New Haven: Yale University Press, 1992.

Blum, Lawrence. *I'm not a Racist, But...: The Moral Quandary of Race*. Ithaca, NY: Cornell University Press, 2002.

Blum, Lawrence. "What Do Accounts of 'Racism' Do?," in Levine and Pataki, eds., *Racism in Mind*, pp. 56–77.

Boxill, Bernard. "Racism and Related Issues," in *Encyclopedia of Ethics*, Lawrence Becker and Charlotte Becker, eds., New York: Garland, 1992, pp. 1056–9.

Brandt, Richard. *Morality, Utilitarianism, and Rights*. Cambridge: Cambridge University Press, 1992.

Burlingame, Michael. *The Inner World of Abraham Lincoln*. Urbana: University of Illinois Press, 1994.

Burlingame, Michael. *Abraham Lincoln: A Life*, 2 vols. Baltimore: Johns Hopkins University Press, 2008.

Burlingame, Michael and Ettlinger, John R. Turner, eds. *Inside Lincoln's White House: The Complete Civil War Diary of John Hay*. Carbondale: Southern Illinois University Press, 1997.

Butler, Benjamin. *Butler's Book*. Boston: A. M. Thayer, 1892.

Carpenter, Francis. *The Inner Life of Abraham Lincoln: Six Months in the White House*. New York: Hurd and Houghton, 1868.

Carson, Thomas. "Strict Compliance and Rawls's Critique of Utilitarianism." *Theoria* 49 (1983): 142–58.

Carson, Thomas. *Value and the Good Life*. Notre Dame, IN: University of Notre Dame Press, 2000.

Carson, Thomas. *Lying and Deception: Theory and Practice*. Oxford: Oxford University Press, 2010.

Carson, Thomas. "Divine Will/Divine Command Moral Theories and the Problem of Arbitrariness." *Religious Studies* 48 (2012): 445–68.

Carwardine, Richard. *Lincoln: A Life of Purpose and Power*. New York: Knopf, 2006.

Catton, Bruce. *The American Heritage Picture History of the Civil War*. New York: American Heritage Publishing, 1960.

"Confiscation Act of 1861." *Wikipedia*. Retrieved from http://en .wikipedia.org/wiki/Confiscation_Act_of_1861.

Cumings, Bruce. *The Origins of the Korean War*, Vol. II. Princeton: Princeton University Press, 1990.

Cumings, Bruce. *The Korean War*. New York: Modern Library, 2010.

Davis, David Brion. *Inhuman Bondage: The Rise and Fall of Slavery in the New World*. Oxford: Oxford University Press, 2008.

Dickens, Charles. *Great Expectations*. Numerous editions.

DiLorenzo, Thomas. *The Real Lincoln*. New York: Three Rivers Press, 2002.

Donald, David Herbert. *Lincoln's Herndon*. New York: Knopf, 1948.

Donald, David Herbert. *Lincoln*. New York: Simon and Schuster, 1995.

Doris, John. *Lack of Character: Personality and Moral Behavior*. Cambridge: Cambridge University Press, 2002.

"Dred Scott v. Sandford." *Wikipedia*. Retrieved from http://en .wikipedia.org/wiki/Dred_Scott_v._Sandford.

Dworkin, Ronald. *Taking Rights Seriously*. Cambridge, MA: Harvard University Press, 1977.

Evans, Richard J. *Altered Pasts: Counterfactuals in History*. Waltham, MA: Brandeis University Press, 2014.

Faust, Drew Gilpin. "Death and Dying – Civil War Era National Cemeteries." *U.S. Park Service*. Retrieved from http://www.nps .gov/nr/travel/national_cemeteries/death.html.

Faust, Drew Gilpin. *This Republic of Suffering*. New York: Knopf, 2008.

Fehrenbacher, Donald, and Fehrenbacher, Virginia, eds. *Recollected Words of Abraham Lincoln*. Stanford, CA: Stanford University Press, 1996.

Fogel, Robert W., and Engerman, Stanley L. *Time on the Cross*. Boston: Brown Little, 1974.

Foner, Eric. *Reconstruction*. New York: Perennial, 2002.

Foner, Eric. *The Fiery Trial*. New York: Norton, 2010.

Fox-Genovese, Elizabeth, and Genovese, Eugene. *Slavery in Black and White*. Cambridge: Cambridge University Press, 2008.

Franklin, John Hope. *From Slavery to Freedom*, third edition. New York: Vintage Books, 1967.

Frederickson, George. *Racism*. Princeton: Princeton University Press, 2002.

Frederickson, George. *Big Enough to be Inconsistent: Abraham Lincoln Confronts Slavery and Race*. Cambridge, MA: Harvard University Press, 2008.

Garcia, J. L. A. "The Heart of Racism." *Journal of Social Philosophy* 27(1996): 5–45.

Garcia, J. L. A. "Three Sites for Racism: Social Structures, Valuings, and Vice," in Levine and Pataki, eds., *Racism in Mind*, pp. 35–55.

Gates, Henry Louis, Jr., and Yacovone, Donald, eds. *Lincoln on Race and Slavery*. Princeton: Princeton University Press, 2009.

Goodwin, Doris Kearns. *A Team of Rivals: The Political Genius of Abraham Lincoln*. New York: Simon and Schuster, 2005.

Greenberg, Amy. *A Wicked War*. New York: Knopf, 2012.

Grimsley, Mark. *The Hard Hand of War*. Cambridge: Cambridge University Press, 1995.

"Guiana." *Encyclopedia Britannica*, Vol. 10, pp. 955–60, 1960.

Guelzo, Allen C. *Abraham Lincoln: Redeemer President*. Grand Rapids, MI: Erdmans, 1999.

Guelzo, Allen C. *Lincoln's Emancipation Proclamation*. New York: Simon and Schuster, 2004.

Guelzo, Allen C. *Abraham Lincoln as a Man of Ideas*. Carbondale: Southern Illinois University Press, 2009.

Guelzo, Allen C. *Fateful Lightning*. Oxford: Oxford University Press, 2012.

Guyatt, Nicholas. "Review of Eric Foner's *The Fiery Trial: Abraham Lincoln and American Slavery*." *London Review of Books*, December 1, 2011, pp. 27–31.

Hacker, J. David. "A Census Based Count of the Civil War Dead." *Civil War History* 57 (2011): 307–48.

Hart, Richard. "Springfield's African-Americans as a Part of the Lincoln Community." *Journal of the Abraham Lincoln Association* 20(1999): 35–54.

Heidler, David, and Heidler, Jeanne. *Henry Clay: The Essential American*. New York: Random House, 2010.

Holley, Donald. *The Second Great Emancipation: The Mechanical Cotton Picker, Black Migration, and How They Shaped the Modern South*. Fayetteville: University of Arkansas Press, 2000.

Holzer, Harold, ed. *The Lincoln Anthology: Great Writers on His Life and Legacy from 1860 to Now*. New York: Library of America, 2009.

Hooker, Brad. *Ideal Code, Real World*. Oxford: Oxford University Press, 2000.

Horne, Gerald. *The Deepest South: The United States, Brazil, and the African Slave Trade*. New York: New York University Press, 2007.

Howe, Daniel Walker. "Lincoln's Worldwide Audience." *Journal of the Abraham Lincoln Association* 33(2012): 47–52.

Jefferson, Thomas. *Writings*. New York: Library of America, 1984.

Kant, Immanuel. *Metaphysics of Morals*. Translated by Mary Gregor. Cambridge: Cambridge University Press, 1996.

Kantor, MacKinlay. *If the South Had Won the Civil War*. New York: Forge Books, 2001.

Keckley, Elizabeth. *Behind the Scenes*. New York: Penguin, 2005.

Keegan, John. *The American Civil War*. New York: Knopf, 2009.

King, Martin Luther, Jr. "Letter from Birmingham Jail." In King, *Why We Can't Wait*. New York: Mentor, 1964, pp. 76–95.

Kunhardt, Philip, Kunhardt, Peter W., and Kunhardt, Peter W. Jr. *Looking for Lincoln*. New York: Knopf, 2008.

Lester, Julius. *Look Out Whitey!: Black Power's Gon' Get Your Mama!*. New York: Dial Press, 1968.

Levine, Bruce. *The Fall of the House of Dixie*. New York: Random House, 2013.

Levine, Michael P., and Pataki, Tamas, eds. *Racism in Mind*. Ithaca, NY: Cornell University Press, 2004.

Levinson, Sandford, and Amar, Akhil Reed. "What Do We Talk about When We Talk about the Constitution?" *Texas Law Review* 91 (2013): 1118–47.

Lieber, Francis, and Halleck, Henry. *General Orders, No. 100* ("The Lieber Code). In Witt, *Lincoln's Code: The Laws of War in American History*, pp. 375–94.

Lind, Michael. *What Lincoln Believed*. New York: Doubleday, 2004.

Lincoln, Abraham. *Speeches and Writings*, 2 vols. New York: Library of America, 1989.

Longley, Robert. "How to Amend the US Constitution." Retrieved from http://usgovinfo.about.com/od/usconstitution/a/amend17.htm.

Malcolm X. *The Last Speeches*. New York: Pathfinder Press, 1989.

McMahan, Jeff. *Killing in War*. Oxford: Oxford University Press, 2009.

McMahan, Jeff. "War Crimes and Immoral Action in War." In *The Constitution of the Criminal Law*, R. A. Duff et al., eds., Oxford: Oxford University Press, 2013, pp. 151–84.

McMahan, Jeff. "Proportionate Defense." Forthcoming in the *Journal of Transnational Law and Policy*.

McMurttie, Douglas. *Lincoln's Religion: The Texts of Addresses Delivered by William H. Herndon and Rev. James A. Reed, and a Letter by C. F. B.* Chicago: Black Cat Press, 1936.

McPherson, James. *Ordeal by Fire*. New York: Knopf, 1982.

McPherson, James. *The Battle Cry of Freedom*. Oxford: Oxford University Press, 1988.

McPherson, James. *Drawn with the Sword*. Oxford: Oxford University Press, 1996.

McPherson, James. *For Cause and Comrades*. Oxford: Oxford University Press, 1997.

McPherson, James. *This Mighty Scourge*. Oxford: Oxford University Press, 2007.

McPherson, James. "Interview on the Film Lincoln." *Chicago Tribune*, November 28, 2012.

McPherson, James. *What They Fought for, 1861–1865*. Baton Rouge: Louisiana State University Press, 1994.

McPherson, James. *Abraham Lincoln and the Second American Revolution*. Oxford: Oxford University Press, 1992.

Mendola, Joseph. *Human Interests: Ethics for Physicalists*. Oxford: Oxford University Press, 2014.

Meyers, Chris. "The Virtue of Cold-Heartedness." *Philosophical Studies* 138 (2008): 233–44.

Mill. J. S. *Utilitarianism*. Indianapolis: Hackett, 2001.

Miller, William Lee. *Arguing about Slavery*. New York: Knopf, 1996.

Miller, William Lee. *Lincoln's Virtues: An Ethical Biography*. New York: Knopf, 2002.

Miller, William Lee. *President Lincoln: The Duty of a Statesman*. New York: Alfred A. Knopf, 2008.

Mitchell, B. R., and Deane, Phyllis. *Abstract of British Historical Statistics*. Cambridge: Cambridge University Press, 1962.

Moore, G. E. *Ethics*, second edition. Oxford: Oxford University Press, 2005.

Morton, Rogers, ed. *Historical Statistics of the United States: Bicentennial Edition*. Washington, DC: U.S. Government Printing Office, 1975.

Mosley, Albert. "Racism [Addendum]." In *Encyclopedia of Philosophy*, second edition, Donald Borchert, ed., Detroit: Macmillan Reference USA, 2005, Vol. 8, pp. 227–9.

Murphy, S. J., James. *War's Ends*. Washington, D.C.: Georgetown University Press, 2014.

Myrdal, Gunner. *An American Dilemma*, ninth edition. New York: Harper & Brothers, 1944.

Nagel, Thomas. *Mortal Questions*. Cambridge: Cambridge University Press, 1979.

Neely, Mark Jr. "Abraham Lincoln and Black Colonization: Benjamin Butler's Spurious Testimony." *Civil War History* 25 (1979): 77–83.

Neely, Mark Jr. *The Fate of Liberty*. Oxford: Oxford University Press, 1991.

Neely, Mark Jr. "Was the Civil War a Total War?" *Civil War History* 50 (2004): 434–58.

Neely, Mark Jr. *The Civil War and the Limits of Destruction*. Cambridge, MA: Harvard University Press, 2007.

The New Shorter Oxford English Dictionary. Oxford: Oxford University Press, 1993.

Nietzsche, Friedrich. "The Anti-Christ," in *Twilight of the Idols and the Anti-Christ*, translated by R. J. Hollingdale, Middlesex: Penguin Books Ltd., 1968.

Niven, John. *Gideon Welles*. Oxford: Oxford University Press, 1973.

Oakes, James. *Freedom National: The Destruction of Slavery in the United States, 1861–1865*. New York: Norton, 2013.

Orend, Brian. *The Morality of War*. Peterborough, Ontario: Broadview, 2006.

Parfit, Derek. *Reasons and Person*. Oxford: Oxford University Press, 1984.

Pratt, Harry E. *The Personal Finances of Abraham Lincoln*. Springfield, IL: Abraham Lincoln Association, 1943.

Randall, James G. *Lincoln the President*. New York: Dodd and Meade, 1945.

Randall, Ruth Painter. *Mary Lincoln: Biography of a Marriage.* Boston: Little Brown, 1953.

Ransom, Roger. *The Confederate States of America: What Might Have Been.* New York: Norton, 2005.

Rawls, John. *A Theory of Justice.* Cambridge, MA: Harvard University Press, 1971.

Rawls, John. *The Law of Peoples.* Cambridge, MA: Harvard University Press, 1999.

Remsburg, John E. *Six Historic Americans.* New York: Truth Seeker Company, 1906.

Roberts, C., and Roberts, D. *A History of England 1688 to the Present,* Vol. 2, second edition. Englewood Cliffs, NJ: Prentice Hall, 1985.

Roberts, Melinda. "The Non-Identity Problem." *Stanford Online Encyclopedia of Philosophy.* Retrieved from http://plato.stanford.edu/entries/nonidentity-problem/.

Rodin, David. "The Moral Inequality of Soldiers," in *Just and Unjust Warriors,* David Rodin and Henry Shue, eds., Oxford: Oxford University Press, 2008, pp. 44–68.

Ross, W. D. *The Right and the Good.* Oxford: Oxford University Press, 2003.

Sandburg, Carl. *Abraham Lincoln: The Prairie Years.* New York: Harcourt, Brace & World, 1926.

Sandburg, Carl. *Abraham Lincoln: The War Years.* New York: Harcourt, Brace & World, 1939.

"Second Confiscation Act." *Wikipedia.* Retrieved from http://en.wikipedia.org/wiki/Second_Confiscation_Act.

Shenk, Joshua Wolf. "The Suicide Poem." *New Yorker,* June 14, 2004.

Shenk, Joshua Wolf. *Lincoln's Melancholy.* Boston: Houghton Mifflin, 2006.

Smith, Jessie Carney, and Horton, Carroll Peterson, eds. *Historical Statistics of Black America.* New York: Gale, 1995.

Stauffer, John. *Giants: The Parallel Lives of Frederick Douglass and Abraham Lincoln.* Boston: Twelve, 2008.

Stegmaier, Mark. "The Imaginary Negro in an Impossible Place? The Issue of New Mexico Statehood in the Secession Crisis, 1860–1861." *New Mexico Historical Review* 84 (2009): 263–90.

Stephens, Alexander, "Cornerstone Speech." *Wikipedia*. Retrieved from http://en.wikipedia.org/wiki/Cornerstone_Speech.

Stevens, Walter Barlow. *Centennial History of Missouri*. Saint Louis: S. J. Clarke, 1921.

Stout, Harry. *Upon the Altar of the Nation*. New York: Viking, 2006.

Stowe, Harriet Beecher. *A Key to Uncle Tom's Cabin*. Boston: John P. Jewett & Co., 1853.

Sutch, Richard, and Carter, Susan, *Historical Statistics of the United States*. Cambridge: Cambridge University Press, 2006.

Thernstrom, Stephan, and Thernstrom, Abigail. *America in Black and White*. New York: Simon and Schuster, 1997.

Thomas, Benjamin. *Abraham Lincoln: A Biography*. New York: Knopf, 1952.

Thomas, Hugh. *The Slave Trade*. New York: Simon and Schuster, 1997.

Trueblood, Elton. *Abraham Lincoln: Theologian of American's Anguish*. New York: Harper, 1973.

United States Census, 1830. Abstract. Retrieved from www2.census.gov/prod2/decennial/documents/1830a-01.pdf.

United States Census, 1840. Compendium. Retrieved from www.census.gov/prod/www/decennial.html.

United States Census, 1850. Compendium. Retrieved from www.census.gov/prod/www/decennial.html.

United States Census, 1860, Introduction. Retrieved from www2.census.gov/prod2/decennial/documents/1860a-02.pdf.

"Universal Suffrage." *Wikipedia*. Retrieved from http://en.wikipedia.org/wiki/Universal_suffrage.

U.S. National Conference of Catholic Bishops. *The Challenge of Peace: God's Promise and Our Response: A Pastoral Letter on War and Peace*. Washington, DC: National Conference of Catholic Bishops, 1983.

Vorenberg, Michael. "Abraham Lincoln and the Politics of Black Colonization." *Journal of the Abraham Lincoln Association* 14 (1993): 23–45.

Vorenberg, Michael. *Final Freedom*. Cambridge: Cambridge University Press, 2001.

Walzer, Michael. *Just and Unjust Wars*. New York: Basic Books, 1977.

Webster's New World Dictionary of American English, third college edition. New York: Webster's New World, 1988.

Welles, Gideon. "Administration of Abraham Lincoln." *The Galaxy* XXIV (1877): 437–50.

Welles, Gideon. *The Diary of Gideon Welles*. Boston: Houghton Mifflin, 1911.

White, Ronald C. *A. Lincoln: A Biography*. New York: Random House, 2009.

Wilson, Douglas. *Honor's Voice: The Transformation of Abraham Lincoln*. New York: Knopf, 1998.

Wilson, Douglas. "Character or Calculation." Presented at conference, "Lincoln: A Question of Character," November 2008, Loyola University Chicago.

Wilson, Douglas L., and Davis, Rodney, eds. *Herndon's Informants*. Urbana: University Illinois Press, 1998.

Wilson, Douglas L., and Davis, Rodney, eds. *Herndon's Lincoln*. Urbana: University Illinois Press, 2006.

Winik, Jay. *April 1865: The Month that Saved America*. New York: Harper Collins, 2001.

Winkle, Kenneth. *The Young Eagle*. Dallas: Taylor, 2001.

Winkle, Kenneth. *Abraham and Mary Lincoln*. Carbondale: Southern Illinois University Press, 2011.

Witt, John Fabian. *Lincoln's Code: The Laws of War in American History*. New York: Free Press, 2012.

Wolf, William J. *The Almost Chosen People*. New York: Doubleday, 1959.

Zagzebski, Linda. *Divine Motivation Theory*. Cambridge: Cambridge University Press, 2004.

Index